Management Information Systems

Management Information Systems

Raymond McLeod, Jr.

Texas A&M University

SCIENCE RESEARCH ASSOCIATES, INC.
Chicago, Palo Alto, Toronto
Henley-on-Thames, Sydney

A Subsidiary of IBM

Acquisition Editor	Stephen D. Mitchell
Project Editor	James C. Budd
Compositor	York Graphic Services
Illustrator	Judi McCarty
Text Designer	Marjorie Spiegelman
Cover Designer	Mike Shenon

Library of Congress Cataloging in Publication Data

McLeod, Raymond.
  Management information systems.

  Bibliography: p.
  Includes index.
  1. Management information systems. I. Title.
HF5548.2.M224   658.4'03   78-14983
ISBN 0-574-21245-0

10 9 8 7 6 5 4

To Martha

Contents

Preface

The computer has become commonplace in our lives. Each day, directly or indirectly, the things we do are influenced in some way by the computer. The alarm clock we turn off in the morning and the television set we turn off at night were produced and distributed by companies with computerized operations. The clothes we wear and the food we eat have been created by processes that are computerized to some extent.

Since the computer affects all of us, we should understand this electronic device. That is the purpose of introductory courses in computer equipment and programming that are offered in college (and even at high school levels). In those courses, students learn the basics of computer operation, the variety of devices that can constitute a computer configuration, and how to prepare programs. In many of these courses, students learn to solve problems by interacting with the computer from terminals located some distance from it.

For many, these introductory courses are sufficient. Only a general understanding is needed, and that is accomplished by the single, general course. For others, however, additional learning is needed. Those students who intend to enter the computer profession as programmers, systems analysts, operators, and computer center managers must take a series of additional courses.

There is another group who needs additional information, and the needs of this group have provided the purpose of this book. This group consists of the future users of information output from the computer—*the managers*. If managers are to use the computer effectively as an information system, they should receive additional material describing such use—material above the introductory level and tailored to their needs.

This textbook is intended for use in a second course for business students at the community college, college, and university level. These students can ultimately be expected to attain management status and use an information system of some type—in many cases a computer-based information system. They should know the potential of the computer as an information system and how such potential can be attained.

The other group of students needing additional information—the future computer professionals—can also benefit from reading this book and enrolling in the accompanying course. It will be the task of these professionals to meet the needs of the manager. To do this, the professionals must understand the manager's responsibilities and needs. This understanding has not always been present in past computer projects and has been a primary cause for project failures. Just as the manager must know something of the computer, the computer people must know something of management use of the computer. This book is intended to help bridge this communication gap.

Basic Organization of the Text

The textbook is organized into five main parts. Part 1 is a one-chapter, general introduction to the subject of management information systems (MIS). Part 2 contains three chapters describing the systems aspect of the subject. Much of this material is theory—of systems and of management and organization. In addition, there are descriptions of how business problems can be solved by applying systems concepts.

Part 3 deals with the computer as an information system. Chapters 5 through 8 describe various components of a computer system and explain how they can be used in an information system. Chapter 9 describes how the computer can support the manager's information needs, from the preparation of repetitive reports to more sophisticated methods such as linear programming and simulation. All students will not need all of the material presented in Part 3—some will have been covered in an earlier course. The instructor can select those portions that need to be covered.

In Part 4, some examples of information-oriented applications are presented. These applications are based on what companies are actually doing, so they are not "blue-sky," idealistic versions of what companies *should* do. This does not necessarily mean, however, that they are representative. The applications represent the more interesting and potentially valuable applications that have been selected from a much larger number. The applications are presented by functional areas of the firm—marketing, manufacturing, and finance—with a chapter devoted to each.

Part 5 describes how an information system can be implemented in an organization. This step-by-step description, covered in Chapters 14, 15, and 16, emphasizes the role of the manager in the process. This is a *normative*, or *prescriptive*, description of the role—how it *should be done*, not necessarily how it has been or is being done. The description is culled from numerous projects, and those elements selected are believed to offer the best chance of success. The description explains the role of the *understanding* and *participating* manager in a computer project. (Such cooperation is not always found within every manager and every firm. But it is hoped that this will eventually be the case, and it is the intent of this book to contribute to this end.) The final chapter describes the important subject of controlling the computer as it is applied to an information system.

Acknowledgments

Certainly no textbook of an introductory nature can be based entirely on the experiences and ideas of a single author. The author merely synthesizes input from a variety of sources to present a well-organized treatment of the subject. That has been the intent with this work.

Much of the theoretical material contained in the first few chapters has been influenced by another business author, Richard J. Hopeman, whose *Systems Analysis and Operations Management* (1969)[1] was years ahead of its time. Professor Hopeman's description of business activities as resource flows provides an effective way to approach the study of information systems. It is a way of tying together many various elements into a logical arrangement. This has not always been accomplished with other, less rigorous, approaches.

Much of the more practical material—that contained in the latter chapters—has been influenced by my experiences as a marketing representative for International Business Machines and Recognition Equipment, Inc., and as a consultant for Lifson, Wilson, Ferguson, and Winick. Literally hundreds of members of those organizations and their customers and clients provided me with a first-hand look at business systems.

The material contained in this textbook has been developed and refined over a number of years in the college classroom. My former colleagues and students at Metropolitan State College in Denver and in the M. J. Neeley School of Business at Texas Christian University have not only served as "guinea pigs" but have contributed many important ideas.

This book represents the collective contributions of hundreds of business people, college faculty, and students. While the author alone is responsible for the shortcomings of the work, these other people are due the credit for the strengths.

1. Richard J. Hopeman, *Systems Analysis and Operations Management*, Charles E. Merrill, Columbus, Ohio, 1969.

Part One

Information Management

Managers always have used information in performing their tasks. So the subject of management information is nothing new. What *is* new is the recent availability of better information. The innovation that makes this possible is the electronic computer.

The computer is a relatively new tool for use in an organization. It became popular only about 20 years ago. When it was first applied to business tasks, the tasks were mainly in accounting. More recently, the value of the computer as a producer of management information has been recognized. The term *management information system* (*MIS*) is a popular one, and it can be assumed that all firms have some type of MIS.

The information systems of some firms are better than those of others. And some firms have computer-based systems, while others use key-driven machines, punched card machines, or manual methods. These two differences do not necessarily relate to each other—the better systems are not always the computer-based ones. The quality of the MIS is determined by the people who design it—the managers and computer professionals—not by the type of equipment.

This control that the MIS designers have over information is called *information management*. The manager can use his or her information just as any other resource. A body of knowledge has been assembled that describes how information can, and should, be managed. The objective of the first part of this text is to introduce the topic of information management.

Chapter 1

Introduction to Management Information Systems

Overview

This book regards information as one of the basic resources available to the manager—just as valuable as those of a human, material, or financial nature. Information is especially valuable in that it *represents* the other, tangible, resources. This representation becomes more important as the scale of business increases.

The manager of a small newsstand in the lobby of a hotel can manage by observing the tangible ingredients—himself or herself, his or her merchandise, the cash register, the room, and the customer flow. As the scale of operation increases to the size of a firm with several hundred or thousand employees and with operations scattered over a wide area, the manager relies less on observation of the physical operation and more on information representing that operation. He or she uses many reports that reflect the firm's condition. It is easy to imagine the almost complete reliance that the chairman of the board for General Motors or IBM or Sears must place on information. These executives probably regard their information as their most valuable resource.

If information is recognized as a resource, then it must also be recognized that information, like other resources, can be managed. The other resources (manpower, money, material, and machines) are acquired and assembled so that they might be available for use when needed. Very often the assembly process is one of converting an essentially raw material into a refined form, such as training an employee or constructing a piece of special machinery. Once these resources are assembled, it becomes the responsibility of the manager to use them in the most efficient way. The manager attempts to minimize the amount of time in which they are idle and to keep them functioning at their highest efficiency. Finally, the manager must replace these resources at a critical time—before inefficiency or unavailability affects the entire organization.

The management of information as a resource follows the same pattern. The manager is responsible for the gathering of raw data and processing it into usable information. He or she must assure that appropriate individuals within the organization receive the information in the proper form at the proper time so that it can assist in the management process. And finally, he or she must discard out-of-date, incomplete, or erroneous information and replace it with a form that is usable.

Importance of the Subject

Interest in information management has increased during recent years—both in the college classroom and in the world of business. Two main reasons account for this—the increased complexity of the management task, and improved decision-making tools.

The increasing complexity of the management task

Management has always been a difficult task, but it is more so today than ever before. One reason is the sheer *size of organizations*. In addition to an increase in number of organizations (especially the very small) in the past decade, the large have become larger. For example, the number of employees for the nation's 500 largest industrial firms increased from 11.3 million in 1965 to 15.5 million in 1973 while assets increased from $252 to $556 billion.[1]

Another factor is the *increasing complexity of technology* that is employed within the organization. Today, if the manager is to keep pace with technology, the effort must be a continuing one. And the computer is not the only example of increasing complexity. Increasing mechanization is taking place in practically every part of the firm; this is evidenced by automated machine tools, automated merchandise storage and movement, electronic inspection and quality control, and even automated vending machines in the lunchroom.

In addition to this increase in scale and complexity of operations, the manager's *time frame* for action is shrinking. The necessity to act quickly is a response to outside pressures from customers, competition, and stockholders. The entire span of business operations is moving more rapidly today than ever before; sales representatives cover their territories by jet, sales orders arrive at headquarters by telephone or satellite transmission, and filled orders are shipped the same day.

---

1. *Statistical Abstract of the United States 1974*, U.S. Department of Commerce, Bureau of the Census, Washington, D.C., 1974, p. 486.

Not all environmental pressure is to produce; some, ironically, is *not* to produce. This is true in the case of products and services that society, or some part of it, finds to be undesirable. Thus, social pressure adds an additional dimension to the task of business decision making. Not only must decisions be based on economic factors, but they must also consider social costs and payoffs. Plant expansion, new products, new sales outlets, and other similar actions affecting the local and national community must all be weighed in terms of short- and long-term impact.

Each of these factors—scale and complexity of operation, social pressure, and the demands of time—influences the management task at all levels.

The availability of decision-making tools

The manager is receptive to any and all techniques or tools that make the decision-making task easier and more effective. Evidence of this receptivity is not difficult to find. Enrollment in graduate-level executive training programs, membership in professional organizations (such as the American Management Association), and the success of seminars and conferences offered by colleges, universities, and consulting firms all indicate the willingness of managers to learn new and better techniques for making decisions.

Many of these management development programs stress mathematical techniques. In fact, these techniques dominate the scene so that this might be termed "the age of quantitative decision making." An infant in the mid-forties, quantitative analysis has enjoyed a continued growth and widespread acceptance.

Aside from the inherent value of these techniques (often called *operations research* or *management science*), this approach has been enhanced by a device that makes their use almost simple—the electronic computer. Both the techniques and the computer may be considered outgrowths of the Second World War; both have had a synergistic, or self-enforcing, effect during the past three decades. The computer has contributed to the popularity of the quantitative techniques, and vice versa.

These quantitative techniques tend to be complex and can involve a laborious process of calculation. In fact, those involving several variables interacting simultaneously could not be performed rapidly enough for management's requirements without a computer. The manager can study the techniques, understand their use and how to interpret the results. The computer and its prewritten instructions can do the rest. Use of these sophisticated techniques becomes so easy that many management scientists fear they will be used indiscriminately. What began as a movement toward a decision-making technique with a small following has been transformed to a concern by management scientists that the technique may be becoming too popular. Courses in information management, data processing, statistics, and accounting all aim at an informed use of the advanced techniques available to the manager.

The Modern Manager

In early business organizations the manager was a generalist, knowledgeable about all the firm's activities. As the size and scope of the firm increased, this general knowledge gave way to specialization. During the 1950s and 60s, the larger organizations became accumulations of specialists, each knowing more about their particular field than any generalist, but not always working together.

This infliction of specialization was not restricted to business. Kenneth Boulding, a prominent economist, called the lack of communication between specialists in the sciences "specialized deafness."[2] This term could well apply to business.

During the era of specialization, the only individual in the organization who had an overall perspective was the person at the top—the chairman of the board or the president. This situation often resulted in lack of communication and cooperation within the firm, and the outcome was a performance that was less than efficient. Figure 1–1 shows the wall-building aspect of specialization. Top management soon became painfully aware of the problems of coordination created by extreme specialization, and the result has been a swing of emphasis back to a more general orientation. An example of a modern manager with a broad scope of responsibility and proficiency is the *project manager*. The project manager may direct activities in several areas of the company relating to his or her project responsibility, such as research, production, marketing, and finance. Another example is a *brand manager* in a consumer products company, such as Procter & Gamble or General Foods, who has overall responsibility for a particular brand.

Richard J. Hopeman, a management educator, has described the skills the modern manager must use. According to Hopeman:

> Many of the skills required in today's manager are needed. . . .
> These include business judgment, ability to assess and take risks, to weigh subjective factors which defy quantification, and to think in a creative and innovative manner. In addition to this, certain skills would have to be augmented. Ability to analyze the interaction of variables and constants in mathematical and statistical terms and the ability to use the computer effectively to assist in management decision making are two cases in point. In addition to this, entirely new skills would be required. These skills would involve the ability to analyze the operation of the firm in terms of flow networks, to develop

---

2. Kenneth E. Boulding, "General Systems Theory—The Skeleton of Science," *Management Science*, April 1956, p. 199.

Figure 1–1   Extreme specialization builds walls in an organization.

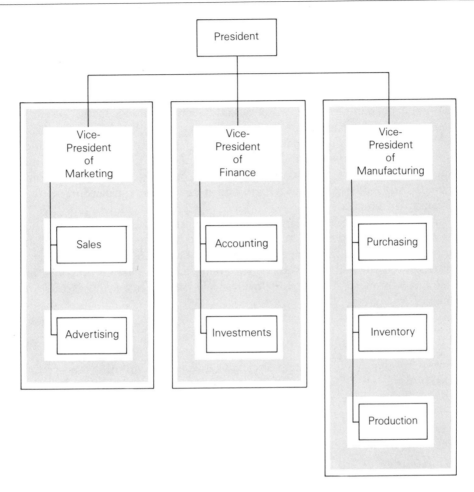

plans with respect to the interaction of these networks, and to utilize system simulation as a laboratory test of planning alternatives.[3]

Hopeman's list recognizes that the modern manager must try to maintain a proficiency in a variety of areas, and must seek to develop a "systems orientation" toward the firm. An important point implied by the list is that

---

3. Richard J. Hopeman, *Systems Analysis and Operations Management* (Columbus: Charles E. Merrill Publishing Co., 1969), p. 141.

decision making will not ultimately be fully computerized or automatic. The human element still will enter into the management process.

The Manager and Systems

Aside from the subjective skills Hopeman identified as being important for the modern manager, other skills have some relationship to systems in one way or another. A popular approach to analysis and decision making is the "systems approach"; the computer is a good example of a system. Thinking of the firm in terms of flow networks is, in effect, regarding the firm as a system; while simulation is a means of subjecting a system to a variety of influences to observe the reaction. Today's manager, and tomorrow's, must understand systems and be able to use more than one system-oriented procedure in the management process.

All of these systems-related topics will be addressed in this book. The systems approach is the subject of Chapter 4. Examples of how it is applied to business problems are given in Chapter 9 and elsewhere. Simulation of system models also is covered in Chapter 9. The computer as a system is described in Chapters 5 through 8. Finally, the flow network concept of a firm is treated in Chapter 3.

What is a system?

Because this book takes a systems approach, a workable definition of a system must be developed. The term has at least two common uses. Students often are heard to say, "I have a *system* for making an A in that course," implying a technique or an approach. This is not the meaning of prime interest to the manager, although all managers would certainly like a *system* for being successful.

The system of primary importance to business and the manager is a structure or arrangement of parts. Thinking in these terms, a *system* can be defined as a group of integrated elements with the common purpose of achieving some objective. This is only one of many definitions supplied by scholars and practitioners. All, however, tend to identify certain key characteristics of a system:

1. *A group of elements.* A system must have more than one elemental part. A rock or a steel ball, for example, is not a system. Both can be part of a system, however. The rock can be an elemental part of a wall that can be regarded as a system. The ball can be an elemental part of a ball bearing assembly that also can be regarded as a system.

2. *Integrated elements.* While not all parts of a system necessarily must work together, there must be some logical relationship. Parts that do not fit the relationship cannot be regarded as part of the system.

Mechanical systems have this logical relationship. Watches, cars, bicycles, tape decks, etc., have been designed to do specific jobs, and all the parts contribute to performing those jobs.

It often is stipulated that the elemental parts of a system must work together in a synchronized manner. While desirable, this is not necessary. A wristwatch that keeps poor time because its parts do not work together still is a system; it is just a poor system. The same is true of a basketball team that cannot play together as a well-coordinated unit. It is a system, but a poor one.

3. *Common purpose to achieve an objective.* The system is designed to achieve one or more objectives. Perhaps one of the objectives is more important than the others, but that is not critical. What is critical is that all elements work toward the achievement of the system goal rather than toward a separate goal for each part.

Purely mechanical systems are designed to achieve this coordinated operation, but those involving human participation often do not. Some systems require interaction of man and machine; the operation of the machine can be so well defined that the human being must perform in a manner to assure coordination. Driving a car is an example. Although automatic and "power" devices have taken much of the work out of driving, the driver must take certain actions. When these actions are ignored or poorly executed, the body shop or the hospital may be the next stop.

Purely human systems, such as workers in an office, lack this built-in requirement for coordination. And it is difficult to attain. The manager or leader of such human systems must motivate participants to coordinate so that system objectives may be reached.

Elements of a system

The elements of a system are integrated in a certain manner as illustrated in Figure 1–2.

Viewed in this manner, the system transforms input into output. A control mechanism constantly monitors the system and regulates its operation so that the transformation process is executed properly.

When this diagram, or model, is used to explain a heating system in a building, the input represents the fuel used—electricity, natural gas, coal, etc. The heating process transforms this fuel into heat—the output. The control mechanism is the thermostat, which can be set at a desired level of performance.

When the model illustrates a business firm, the input consists of basic resources—machinery, materials, money, manpower, and information. The transformation process converts these resources into the output of the firm—products or services. The control is performed by the management. As in the example of the heater, the performance of the firm can be established to achieve a certain level. It is the manager's job to assure this level of performance.

Figure 1–2   Component parts of a system

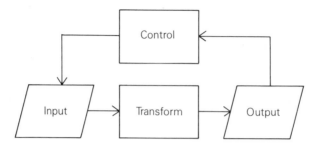

What is a subsystem?

Systems often are comprised of smaller systems, or subsystems. A *subsystem* is simply a system contained within a larger one. Therefore a subsystem is also a system. This means that systems exist on several levels. There are large systems and small systems, and sometimes the smaller ones are part of the larger ones.

An automobile can be regarded as a system. But it is made up of several subsidiary, or lower level, systems—the engine system, the body system, and the frame system. Each in turn may be composed of lower level systems; for example, the engine system is a combination of a carburetor system, a generator system, a fuel system, etc. And these systems may be subdivided further into subsystems or elemental parts. The parts of a system therefore may be either systems (groups of parts) or individual parts. Figure 1–3 illustrates this relationship.

In a business firm, the subsystems—such as marketing, finance, and manufacturing—are the basic functional units. Each of these in turn consists of sub-subsystems and parts. The marketing department, for example, is made up of advertising, sales, and marketing research sub-subsystems.

When a system is a part of a larger system, that larger system often is called a *supersystem*, or *suprasystem*. For example, if the U.S. Postal Service is a system, it is also part of a larger system—the federal government. Here, the federal government is a supersystem, or suprasystem.

The business system

The system that the manager manages is the system of the firm or the organization. The organization may be one of a *nonprofit* nature as well as one with *profit* objectives. Also, it may be *private*, as in the case of a corporation or proprietorship, or it may be *governmental*. In the discussion that follows, the term *firm* is not restricted to profit-seeking business organizations. It applies to any type of organization. This means that the basic fundamentals of information management, described in this book, apply to any type of organization.

Figure 1-3   System composition

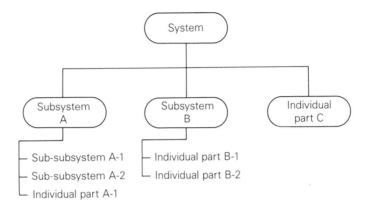

The manager's prime interest is to assure that the firm meets the goals or objectives that have been established. Effort is required to make the various parts of the firm work together as they should. The manager is the control element in the system, keeping it on course toward goal achievement.

Of course, the system of the firm fits into one or more larger systems, or suprasystems. If the firm is a bank, for example, it is a part of the financial community. Also, it is a part of the local community and of the business community. See Figure 1-4.

The system of the firm is likewise composed of smaller systems, or subsystems. The subsystems of the bank may be the savings account department, the demand deposit (checking account) department, the installment loan department, and so on. While each of these subsystems has its own objectives and goals (the installment loan department might have a goal of 50 new accounts per month), these subsidiary objectives support and contribute to the overall objectives of the firm (the bank).

Physical systems and conceptual systems

The business firm is a physical system. A *physical system* is one that physically or actually exists. It is tangible. It can be seen, touched, or kicked. The business firm exists physically; the buildings, trucks, employees, machines, and materials all exist in a physical way. The manager, then, is concerned with the management of this physical system.

What, then, is a conceptual system? A *conceptual system* is one that *represents* a physical one. The conceptual system doesn't physically exist, but corresponds to one that does. The conceptual system commonly resides in someone's mind; or it exists as figures or lines on a sheet of paper, or as magnetized areas of a computer storage medium. Even though the conceptual

Figure 1–4   The firm as a subsystem within larger systems

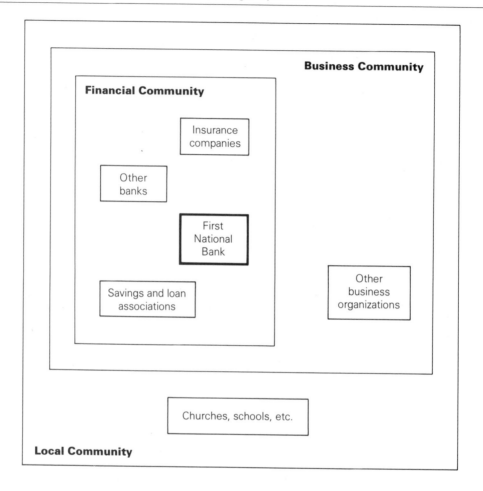

system exists in these forms, it is not the form that is important, but what the system represents. The physical system is important for what it is; the conceptual system is important for its representation of the physical system. The management information system is a conceptual system representing the physical system of the firm.

Perhaps some examples will help. The knowledge and experience of the newsstand proprietor can be viewed as a conceptual system. The proprietor understands his or her physical system and knows its operational details. The proprietor can talk about it, write about it, or even draw pictures of it. All of this knowledge and information represents the physical system—the newsstand with its shelves, magazines, cash register, etc.

Similarly, the board chairman of General Motors receives periodic

*''Miss Dennison, send in some reports, charts, programs, files, data, indices, facts, figures, totals, actuaries, systems analyses, projections, printouts, breakdowns, summaries, rates, records, statements, memorandums, graphs, requisitions . . .''

ⓒ DATAMATION®

reports of his operation. These reports are conceptual descriptions of the physical system. One of the reports, dealing with the manufacturing process, represents the physical manufacturing system. Another report, dealing with the performance of the dealer network, represents that physical dealer network. The board chairman uses these conceptual representations to monitor the corresponding physical systems. The scope of the physical operation simply has become too great to permit management by direct observation.

The Management Information System (MIS)

The conceptual system that the manager uses is an information system. It has been named the *management information system,* or *MIS.*

Although this term has enjoyed increasing use in the past decade, there is no universal agreement on what MIS means. It can be defined to include only systems that *immediately* provide the manager with *any* and *all* needed information. Obviously, such a narrow interpretation would make it practically impossible for such an MIS ever to be realized. The term also can be defined very broadly to include *any* system that provides information to the manager—without specifying the nature of the information. So general a system would be easy to attain; and it could be accepted that every firm or organization has one.

These extreme definitions offer little help to the student of business who is attempting to understand and appreciate the wealth of material generated on the MIS. Obviously, the MIS most frequently described in the literature lies somewhere between these narrow and broad descriptions.

One description that recognizes several important characteristics of the MIS was offered at a meeting of the International Data Processing Conference by Walter J. Kennevan. Mr. Kennevan defined an MIS as:

> . . . an organized method of providing past, present and projection information relating to internal operations and external intelligence. It supports the planning, control, and operational functions of an organization by furnishing uniform information in the proper time-frame to assist the decision-making process.[4]

The depth of Mr. Kennevan's description can be appreciated when each of the component parts is considered:

1. *Organized method.*   The MIS is organized. Since the MIS is a system, the parts should work together in an organized manner to achieve efficient performance.

2. *Past, present and projection information.*   Information is provided to the manager to make it possible to appraise where the firm has been, where it is now, and where it is going. Most systems used by managers before the computer advent were designed to provide only past information. Those systems, using punched card machines, keydriven machines, or manual processes, generated historical reports for the manager. The manager used these reports as a basis for deciding what should be done in the future. The systems were so slow that the manager seldom had a good idea of what was happening presently. By the time present performance was reported, it was past history.

An important characteristic, then, of the modern MIS is the ability to report information about the present and the future—information that was generally nonexistent before the computer era.

3. *Internal and external information.*   Information is provided about what is happening both inside and outside the firm. Compared to previous systems that provided mainly internal information, the MIS places great value on external, or environmental, information. This environmental information is especially important to top-level managers. The president of the J. C. Penney organization, for example, pays more attention to the effect of the U.S. restriction on imports of Japanese color TV sets than to many internal affairs left to competent administrators.

Two earlier comments emphasize the importance of environmental information. First, increasing pressure from the environment increases the complexity of management. Activities of government, competition, customers,

---

4. Walter J. Kennevan, "MIS Universe," *Proceedings 1970 International Data Processing Conference,* June 1970, reported in *Data Management,* September 1970, p. 63.

and society in general, influence the success of the firm. Information describing and explaining these activities must be gathered and reported. Second, the viewing of a business firm as a system recognizes that it exists as a subsystem within a larger system. If this systems approach to management is to be followed, the manager must recognize the important interrelationship between the firm and its environment.

4. *Planning, control, and operational functions.* The MIS is designed to help the manager manage. Students who have completed an introductory study of management will recognize *planning* and *controlling* as two of the manager's basic functions or processes. The third, *operations,* can be viewed as the function of executing the plan. Therefore, the MIS should help the manager plan what to do, execute plans, and control the firm's activity to assure that the plans are carried out. There should be no part of the manager's activity that is not supported by the MIS. The MIS is a broad, comprehensive system, then, in its support of the manager.

5. *Uniform information.* The MIS should be ongoing, providing information on a repetitive basis. This factor separates MIS from other business information-gathering activities. These other activities, such as marketing research or financial research, are directed at solving a particular problem. Data relating to that problem is gathered and converted into information. Management uses that information to solve the problem. Once solved, the data gathering activity is terminated. An example of uniform information is a monthly report prepared for the sales manager showing the return on investment (ROI) for each of the sales offices.

6. *Proper time frame.* The information provided by the MIS must be quickly available. This requirement of responsiveness is especially critical for information describing the current operation. Often the conceptual information system must respond immediately to the needs of the physical system—perhaps in seconds. The term *realtime* describes systems with such fast response ability. When the size of the firm increases, this requirement of responsiveness demands a computer—and often a larger and more expensive computer than if the speed of response were not so great.

Earlier, the shrinking time frame of decision making was recognized. It is not clear whether the shrinking time frame stimulated responsive information systems, or if these systems made possible a faster pace of decision making. Whatever, today's business manager needs a responsive information system.

7. *Assist in decision making.* The MIS is designed to help the manager make decisions. This emphasis reflects the current attitude toward that portion of management responsibility. Many undergraduate and graduate business programs stress the decision-making aspect of management. All quantitative courses, such as statistics and operations research, provide tools and techniques for decision making. The use of a computer to execute these quantitative techniques makes the computer a "decision-making" tool.

If there is a soft spot in the armor of the MIS concept, it is that managers do more than just make decisions. In fact, for some managers, decision making is a minor activity. The people-oriented activity of the manager can be largely free of decision making. This activity deals with motivation of employees, coordination of their efforts, and response to their individual needs. Of course, information should help the manager with these "people" tasks. As an example, a manager can use information to decide which type of compensation is best for a certain group of employees. The information might suggest a plan that is not entirely monetary. It might be one that recognizes the needs of the employees for status, security, and recognition. Thus an MIS can be used in making decisions about the more human and personal part of management. (Such a recognition of the behavioral contributions of the MIS can erase some of the criticism that MIS ignores the human element.)

The requirement for a computer

While much written about MIS implies the use of a computer, nothing makes it an absolute requirement. A firm need not have a computer to have an MIS. The newsstand proprietor could have an MIS—one using his own memory as a data storage area and using his own logical and mathematical ability as the means of processing the data. In fact, such an MIS probably would be more effective than one used by an industrial giant using several large computers. Perhaps the scope of the giant organization is so great that even the modern computer cannot provide all information needed.

The discussion in this book assumes a computerized MIS, and there are real reasons for such an approach. The computerized MIS offers the best description of how a formal information system functions. Also, the computerized version is the type that represents real career opportunities. It should be remembered, however, that the computer is but one part of an MIS, and that part is not required when the scale of operation is small.

The other parts of the MIS

The makeup of the MIS will be studied more thoroughly later. It can be recognized now, however, that the MIS consists of both computerized and noncomputerized data-gathering, transmission, and storage facilities of a firm. In addition, the MIS includes managers, their goals, objectives, and standards of performance, and the means of communicating decisions throughout the firm. MIS is therefore a multifaceted system embracing all activity in the firm concerned with information flow.

Is an MIS attainable?

Very few firms have attained an MIS such as that envisioned when the idea first was conceived. Development of the single total information system has provided a challenge that should keep even the most competent firms busy for years to come. In fact, the "perfect" MIS probably never will be attained.

The rather dismal record of firms achieving such an MIS, however, is not sufficient reason to abandon the concept. On the contrary, only by studying the concept, its potential value, and how to implement it can the state of the art be improved. The achievement of an MIS is extremely costly, both in money and time, but it is a worthwhile goal. Only by recognizing such a goal as the ideal can the flow of information through the firm be planned and achieved in the form of an efficient system. Perhaps many firms will never achieve the goal, but they should be better off than by having no goal at all.

The situation is similar to that of someone who wants to learn to play golf. There are several ways to go about it, but two of the most common involve emulation of successful, professional golfers. The duffer might take lessons from a club pro or buy a book written by one of the big name stars. The duffer realizes he or she probably will never learn to play like the teaching or writing pro, but nevertheless these guides are useful. Striving for the ideal is much better than having no model or overall master plan to follow.

The evolution of the MIS concept

A characteristic of the precomputer period in business was the emphasis on data, rather than information, processing. *Data* consists of facts and figures, and these usually exist in extremely large volume and in no particular order. *Information*, on the other hand, is meaningful data, or processed data. Data is converted into information by an *information processing system*. Data is converted into more data by a *data processing system*. Figure 1–5 illustrates both systems.

The same computer system can be used as both a data and an information processor. In fact, that is the general practice. Computers generate output, such as utility bills, that, to the manager, is data and not information. (These bills are information to respective customers, however.) To the manager, the computer is an information processing system when it produces output that is meaningful and usable.

During the precomputer era, the firms used their machines almost exclusively as data processing systems; they generally ignored the value that could be derived from generating information for managers. The computer changed all of this—but not overnight. It was not until the mid-1950s that manufacturers such as IBM, Univac, Burroughs, and National Cash Register began marketing computer products on a widespread basis. Acceptance of these products was gradual, with application limited to the same areas handled by the keydriven and punched card machines (accounting applications).

Before long, however, users and vendors recognized the inherent power of the computer—its ability to do jobs never before possible. Managers in the manufacturing area realized that the computer could be used for superior production scheduling and more sophisticated inventory control. Engineers saw the potential for design work. News of the power of the computer spread throughout the firm. The computer had been accepted, but as a data processing and computing tool. Its value as a producer of management information still had not been realized.

A few farsighted individuals, however, saw the potential for information

Figure 1–5   Data and information processing systems
                 a. A data processing system
                 b. An information processing system

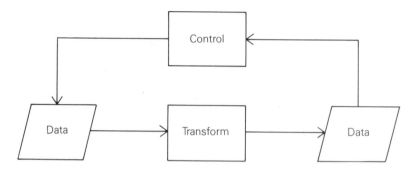

a.   A data processing system

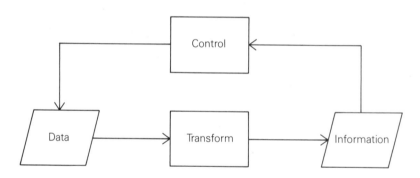

b.   An information processing system

processing. Two were H. P. Luhn and Stephen E. Furth of IBM who developed a use of computers (and also punched card machines) known as *information retrieval*. This development occurred during the late 1950s and early 1960s. If a predecessor of MIS is sought, information retrieval is most likely it. Information retrieval is the storage of particular data files for the subsequent purpose of retrieving selected portions. An example is the storage of abstracts of scientific journals so that scientists may selectively retrieve those that relate to their projects.

While information retrieval and MIS are similar, there are two major distinctions. First, information retrieval is less ambitious. Information retrieval seeks only to store a selected portion of data that exists within an organiza-

Figure 1–6 Information retrieval versus the management information system
    a. Information retrieval
    b. Management information system

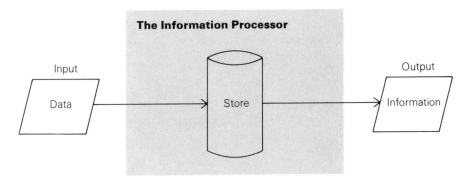

a.   Information retrieval

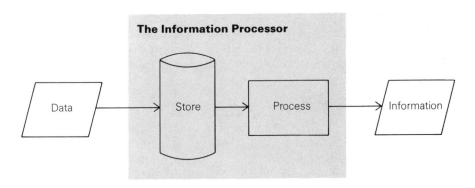

b.   Management information system

tion—data that has a high frequency of use. MIS has no such modest limits but seeks to store a majority of the data that exists within an organization, including that only minimally active. Second, information retrieval simply selects particular data from a large file. MIS not only selects, but also computes, processes, and transforms the data into meaningful information. Information retrieval is a subset of the MIS (Figure 1–6) and remains today an important computer application.

In 1964 something happened that exerted a strong influence on the manner in which the computer was employed. The third generation of computers was developed.[5] This generation offered much greater processing speed and data storage capacity per user's dollar than previous ones. A firm could use a computer with large-capacity storage units and data communication equipment for little additional increase in overall cost. The concept of the MIS was promoted by the computer vendors to justify this additional equipment. The concept was accepted readily by many computer users, since a real need existed for better management information. The time was ripe for the development of this new use of the computer.

The road traveled by these pioneering firms during the past decade has not been easy. As with many new ideas, actual accomplishments seldom have matched those initially envisioned. Many firms still are striving to improve their MIS. A large number, however, have implemented extremely capable information systems.

Some MIS examples

A brief description of several management information systems should afford a better understanding of the concept. The following examples represent a variety of organizations, not just profit-oriented business firms. The primary intent is to offer a cross section of those types of organizations that can benefit from MIS technology. Most of the examples describe the use of mass data storage and data communication terminals. While those devices are not always an absolute necessity, they are extremely useful in meeting the manager's information needs.

Ocean transportation.   The Norsk Pacific Steamship Co. Ltd. transports forest products from the Pacific Northwest to the West Coast, the Caribbean, and Central and South America. Norsk uses a computer, made available by General Electric, to project the profit and loss statement for each voyage before it is made.[6] This information permits the management to isolate and analyze those factors that influence profit and to solve problems before they become serious.

Norsk communicates with the computer by telephone from offices in San Francisco and San Juan, Puerto Rico. In addition to planning, the information enables management to exercise a control over operations never before possible. Future plans call for construction of a mathematical model for ship scheduling, possibly with terminals on board ships linked by satellite with the computer.

---

5. The generations of computers were distinguished by their technology. The first generation employed circuitry of vacuum tubes; the second generation used transistorized circuits. The third generation heralded the development of miniature circuits. The use of "bubble" memory could represent the fourth generation. More information on computer development is provided in Chapter 5.

6. Edith Holmes, "Steamship Company Uses T/S for Financial Control," *Computerworld*, March 12, 1975, p. 9.

Firefighting. In Kansas City, Missouri the city fire department uses a computer to help locate invalids in burning buildings.[7] Approximately 400 invalids live in Kansas City, and data describing their location are stored in the computer. When the dispatcher receives a fire call, the computer file is checked to determine if an invalid lives at that address and if so in what room. The computer also provides a description of the condition of the invalid. With this information, the firemen can take quick action to rescue the invalid with reduced risk of personal injury.

Education. The Educational Testing Service of Princeton, New Jersey has installed computers at four community colleges for use by students in planning their careers.[8] The students "converse" with their computers from type-writer-like terminals and can use any of six programmed subsystems. The *values subsystem* helps the student to identify his or her values; the *locate subsystem* identifies occupations compatible with those values. The *compare subsystem* enables the student to ask questions about the occupation areas identified, including entry requirements, work activities, future outlook, etc. The students then can forecast a likely chance of success in the various occupations by means of a *prediction subsystem*. The two final subsystems enable the student to plan entry into a chosen occupation. The *planning subsystem* outlines the educational program required for entry; the *strategy subsystem* compares the appropriateness of several occupations for the student. The purpose of the computer approach is to augment, rather than replace, counseling and testing services normally available on college campuses. The result is expected to be an improved program of career planning.

These examples illustrate the types of information that can be made available to a variety of users. The availability of this information, when needed, can result in improved performance by managers of a steamship company, fire fighters, and college career counselors. This information could have been acquired in ways other than by computer, but the time and cost would have been too great. The speed and power of the computer make information available that would be impractical to obtain with other techniques.

Achieving an Information System

More and more managers are beginning to realize the importance of information. Some believe it is the key to success. Philip Kotler, a marketing academician at Northwestern University, provides a quote from Marion Harper, Jr., that was made in 1960, several years before the real explosion in information

---

7. Ann Dooley, "File Helps Firemen Locate Invalids," *Computerworld*, May 7, 1975, p. 7.

8. "Minis to Help College Students Make Career Choices," *Computerworld*, July 2, 1975, p. 19.

systems interest. According to Mr. Harper, "To manage a business well is to manage its future; and to manage its future is to manage information."[9]

The manager's task, then, becomes not so much managing the physical resources of the firm, but effectively using the conceptual information resources that represent those physical resources. With this view of management responsibility, it becomes crucial for the manager to have available an information system. Like any other system within the firm, it must be designed and implemented by the manager. If the manager is to have an information system, he or she must build it. A process that a manager can follow in developing an information system is outlined in Part 5 of this book.

Certainly the manager will not build the information system alone; just as he or she does not build a materials handling system or a financial control system alone. The manager must play an active part—in fact, the dominant part—and not turn this role over to a specialist. Rather, the information specialist provides the technical expertise and implements the system specified by the manager.

Identification of information needs

If the information system is to be designed by two individuals—manager and specialist—the two must communicate. The manager must communicate to the specialist what information is required. For various reasons, managers frequently have not taken an active part in the design of information systems, and so the specialists have had to design systems that appeared ideal to *them*. This practice is an open invitation to failure. If the systems are to assist the manager, he or she first must identify what information is needed.

Implementation of an information system

After communicating the information requirements, the manager should remain active in the implementation project that will span several months and possibly several years. Too many managers say, "Well, I've told them what I need; now it is their responsibility to give it to me." This attitude provides a second opportunity for the system to fail. The implementation of an information system is no different from any other project involving similar capital and manpower. Just as the manager would monitor and control construction of a new plant or development of a new product, the same involvement must be made available to the information system project.

---

9. Philip Kotler, *Marketing Management* (Englewood Cliffs, N.J.: Prentice-Hall, 1972), p. 293.

Summary

Information is a valuable resource to be managed and used by the manager. When the manager has available an effective information system, he or she can cope better with increasing managerial demands.

Today's manager must be systems-oriented. The firm must be seen as an integration of parts, all working toward achievement of overall goals. The role of the environment also must be appreciated and understood. The influences of the environment on the firm, and the responsibilities of the firm to its environment, cannot be overlooked or minimized.

Considerable emphasis was placed on the subject of systems in this first chapter. That emphasis will continue throughout the book because of the importance of the subject to the modern manager. A system is an integration of parts, all contributing to achievement of an overall goal. This structural system consists of a transformation process that converts input resources to output and that is controlled in some manner. The manager can see his or her firm as a system of this type. When this systems orientation is followed, the importance of the environment to the system can be appreciated fully; the subdivision of the system into subsystems can also be seen. A subsystem is simply a smaller system contained within a larger one.

The manager must manage this physical system. But this task becomes difficult when the size of the firm increases. The manager of a larger firm must monitor the physical system with the use of another system, a conceptual system that represents the physical one. This conceptual system is an information system—a management information system (MIS).

The MIS provides information to the manager for decision making. The information describes both the internal operation of the firm and its environment. Also, the information describes what has happened in the past, what is happening now, and what is likely to happen in the future.

It is the manager's responsibility to see that an information system is designed and implemented. This responsibility cannot be delegated. Information specialist and manager must work together, but the manager must both initiate and control the effort.

The objective of this book is to afford the student of business management an understanding of the information management task. This task will be critical to the success of the future manager and to his or her organization. According to Shea Smith, III, the Information and Planning Director for Monsanto of St. Louis, Missouri, "How well information is managed and used can mean the difference between success and failure."[10] He

---

10. Shea Smith, III, "V.P. of Information Is in Corporate Future, Job Is Necessary for Survival," *Marketing News*, June 20, 1975, p. 3.

describes how all the information activities of a firm can be centralized within the organization, and then concludes:

> As companies adopt this more efficient approach to managing information, it will become recognized as an opportunity to gain an edge over competition or—vice versa, if you let your competition outdistance you in this area—a threat to survival.[11]

Important Terms

Information Management	Conceptual System
Operations Research	Management Information System (MIS)
Management Science	
Project Manager	Realtime
Brand Manager	Data
System	Information
Subsystem	Data Processing System
Supersystem, Suprasystem	Information Processing System
Physical System	Information Retrieval

Important Concepts

The synergistic effect of the computer and quantitative techniques.

Why the manager should think in systems terms.

The firm as a physical system.

Information management concepts apply to all types of organization.

A manager uses the conceptual information system to manage the physical system.

The manager must play an active role in building an MIS.

11. Ibid.

Important People and Organizations

American Management Association

Kenneth Boulding

Richard J. Hopeman

H. P. Luhn

Stephen E. Furth

Questions

1   Is information more valuable to managers of large firms or small ones? Explain.

2   What caused the increased interest in information management?

3   Why is management more complex today than it was 20 years ago?

4   Are all managers interested in finding better ways to make decisions? Why or why not?

5   Does your college offer any special programs for business people in your community to improve their management skills? What are they?

6   What courses does your college offer to help you sharpen your quantitative skills?

7   A recent ad for a razor, with a replaceable double blade, referred to it as a "shaving system." Is the razor really a system? What are its elements? What is the objective?

8   Is an automobile a system, a subsystem, or a supersystem? Explain.

9   How does a driver of an automobile use past, present, and projection information to build and maintain a good safety record?

10 Must a firm have a computer in order to have an MIS? Why or why not?

11 How could your local police department use a computer as an information system?

Problems

1   You have just been hired as a sales trainee for a small manufacturer of conveyor systems. You remember a magazine from your college days, called *Sales Management*. You discover that your boss, the sales manager, subscribes to the magazine but throws it away without looking at it. You feel that the magazine contains information of value for everyone in the sales department. What should you do?

2   You've almost got it made! The only thing standing between you and a management-training job with a local department store is an interview with its president. You walk into the office, sit down, and the president asks, "Do you consider yourself a specialist or a generalist?" Discuss your response.

3   Draw a diagram showing the basic elements of a system and how they interrelate.

4   Draw a diagram of a data processing system. Draw a diagram of an information processing system.

Part Two

Fundamental Principles

Management information systems are very real. They consist of managers, data, information, communication channels, and often computers for storage and processing. The business student can expect to soon be a part of such a system, either as a provider of information or as a user.

There is a great deal to be learned about management information systems. Actually, the subject is a composite of two complete fields—management and computer science. Much of the MIS material has been developed during the past few years as firms have created their computer-based systems. Other material, however, has evolved over the past century as the subject of business management has become more refined.

To the person first encountering this new subject matter, the volume of material can appear overpowering. It cannot be learned overnight but it can be learned. This process can be expedited and facilitated with an orderly, systematic approach.

The purpose of Part Two is to provide a theoretical foundation—a basic structure—upon which to build an understanding of information systems. This is a general framework, applying to a wide variety of situations. The framework should prove most useful in preparing for any type of business career.

This part addresses three basic topics. The first is *theory*. Theories of both management and organization are presented in systems terms. Second, a *general model* of a firm as a physical system, with a conceptual information system, is described. Third, an approach to business problem-solving, the *systems approach*, is described.

Each topic relates to the idea of a system. This relatively recent way to view business is used in this book so the reader can understand an important part of a business organization—its management information system.

Chapter 2

Theory of Management and Organization

The task of this book is to describe how information can be managed to achieve an efficient use of the other, physical, resources. This description is accomplished through the systems approach. That is, the topic is viewed from a systems perspective.

This chapter lays the theoretical foundation for the material to follow. It describes a systems theory of both management and organization. These are the two large and important bodies of theory in the study of business management. In presenting these systems theories, it is necessary to describe briefly some other theories relating to the same subject matter. These other theories must be included since they provide the basis for much of what is known as *systems theory*. Although no effort is made to describe them entirely, this is not through lack of respect. The other theories are important in their own right and are necessary for a complete description of management. The brief treatment is based simply on the fact that the interest here is in establishing a systems theory of management and business organization.

Theory

Many people don't get too excited about theory. In fact, some dislike it. To some people, theory is something unrealistic. They say, "That's just a bunch of theory," when they feel something is not true.

Actually, those people are not far wrong. Theory does not mean truth; nor does it mean untruth. When something always holds true it is not a theory, but a *law*. A law is something proven to be true. Probably the most widely understood law is that of gravity. It has been proved to exist, and everyone accepts it. It is a law relating to the behavior of physical objects. A number of such laws provide the basis for the physical sciences such as physics and chemistry.

Theory in business

Business is not a physical science. In fact, some doubt it to be a science of any kind. If it is a science, it is a social science—one dealing with people. It is much harder to predict what people will do than what some nonliving object will do. For this reason the social sciences have fewer laws than the physical sciences. In business there are more theories than laws. These theories represent what people believe to be true, but that have not been proved true in all cases. Perhaps nothing is true in all cases where people are concerned. Perhaps there will never be laws of business. Perhaps all that can be hoped for are theories that have been shown to apply in certain instances.

Since business is so complex and covers so many areas, there is no single theory *of* business and probably never will be. There are theories *in* business, however, and these can be expected to increase in importance and in number. They will increase in importance as need arises to learn more about particular business areas. They will increase in number as this higher level of understanding is achieved.

What is theory?

Nearly everyone has heard the term *theory* and has a conception of its meaning. Because it has several different meanings, *theory* probably means one thing to one person and another to somebody else. Any dictionary will show six or eight different definitions.

The definition or meaning of theory that is of interest to the study of management deals with a set of propositions. Theory is a *coherent group* of *general propositions* that are used as *principles* to *explain* some class of *phenomena*. The italicized terms are elaborated on below.

Coherent group. Just as an efficient system is composed of multiple parts that work together, a theory is composed of a coherent group of parts that must fit together in a logical way. A theory can be thought of, then, as a type of system. It is a system of propositions that have a major objective of explanation. The interest here, however, is not in theory *as a system* but a theory *of* systems.

General propositions. A proposition is something offered for acceptance. A general proposition is one offered in a variety of situations, or one used to apply to a variety of situations.

Principles. Principles are generally accepted rules of behavior or action. These are the component parts of a theory. A theory, then, contains more than one principle that fits together in a logical or coherent manner.

Explanation. The purpose of theories in business is to explain and to help understand.

Class of phenomena. The class of phenomena are those that relate to some particular part of business. The phenomena of interest here are those relating to management.

The theory of interest here is that body of generally accepted rules used to explain management. More specifically, this chapter seeks to address those theories that can be offered as explanations of management and organizations in terms of systems. When the firm is viewed as a system and the manager is seen as the control mechanism of that system, the importance of information is clear. An appreciation for that importance is the primary objective of this book.

Why study theory?

Theory by itself has little, if any, value. The real value of theory is its application to a real situation in order to accurately explain that situation. The interest is not in answering the question, *What exists?* Usually *what exists* is very apparent to the observer, in this case the manager. The manager knows what is happening if an adequate information system is available. What the manager usually does not know, however, is *why it exists*. Theory seeks to provide this explanation.

As an example, assume a manager knows that certain employees are motivated better by nonmonetary than by monetary rewards. The manager knows this situation exists but does not know why. If the manager knows why nonmonetary rewards work better for certain employees, that type of reward can be applied intelligently in those situations where its positive effect can be anticipated. The manager can make better decisions because he or she understands why a certain behavior occurs.

Essentially, theory provides the manager with a better understanding of the complex system of business. This understanding helps the manager to do a better job.

Information and theory

Many managers use theories learned in school. Others develop their own from experience. These theories were developed over a period of time. They probably began as crude approximations, then underwent refinement as more was learned about the phenomenon involved (Figure 2–1). The manager's information system, then, has helped the manager develop theories.

The theory warns the manager what to expect. The information system tells what is happening. If real activity is other than what was expected, the theory is refined. Over a period of time, then, theories can be developed that the manager can use to predict behavior of the business system. The information system plays an important role in this development of theory.

What is management theory?

The manager is the person responsible for ensuring that the business system meets its objectives. The manager has certain resources for use in accomplish-

Figure 2–1   Information is used to refine theories.

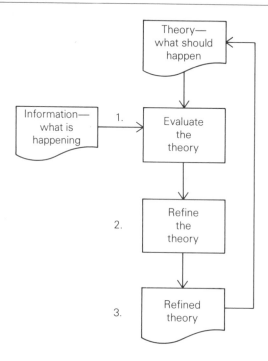

ing these objectives, and these resources should be used as efficiently as possible. Management theory is intended to help the manager perform the management task. Any and all techniques or practices that can be used toward this end are included under management theory.

What is organization theory?

Organization theory deals with how the resources of the firm are arranged or assembled. It deals with a structure. Usually, the structure is thought of as relating only to people, such as that reflected by an organization chart. But this arrangement of people also carries with it an arrangement of other resources—money, machines, and material. For example, the people in the marketing department have available operating funds, any machines required such as company cars, and any needed material such as sales manuals and free samples. When people are segregated into an organizational unit, these other resources go along with them. Figure 2–2 illustrates this principle.

Organization theory therefore is seen as a subset of management theory. Management theory applies to everything relating to the task of management. Organization theory is concerned with only that part dealing with the ar-

Figure 2-2　　Organization of resources

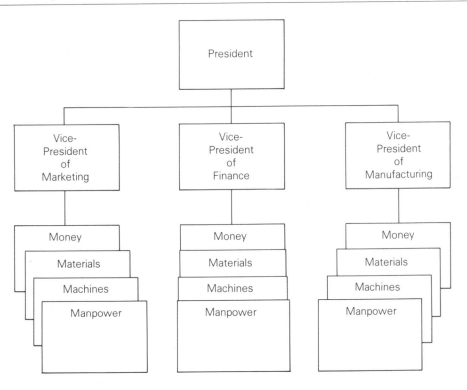

rangement of resources. It has nothing to do with them after they have been arranged.

Importance of management theory to information management

The firm's information system is intended to help the manager manage. If it is to do so, the people designing the MIS must understand management. This requirement is why the manager must be directly involved in the design of the MIS. He or she is more likely to have this understanding than is an information specialist.

The manager should understand theories of management. The MIS then can be designed to help the manager apply these theories in managing available resources. The understanding of management must come first. It is a prerequisite for a good MIS.

Before a firm can consider an MIS, therefore, an adequate management resource must be available. An MIS will help this resource become better. But a poor management resource probably could never develop an MIS. Therefore, an MIS should not be regarded as a perfect cure for poor management. The basic management skill must be present if an effective MIS is to be realized.

The manager's recognition of the psychological impact of an MIS on a firm and its employees is another reason why management theory is important. Since much of management theory is concerned with the psychology of management, this understanding can help in getting the MIS accepted. A new MIS often meets with resistance by employees. Some employees fear that their jobs are in jeopardy or will be changed. Others fear loss of security, power, freedom, and esteem. When the manager understands these fears, why they occur, and how to deal with them, he or she can minimize or overcome them. The MIS relies greatly on the cooperation of all of the firm's employees. Management theory can help the manager achieve this cooperation.

Importance of organization theory to information management

Similarly, the organization structure can affect the MIS. The MIS is based on the concept of an integrated information system supporting the firm as a whole. And the parts of the firm must work together to meet the firm's objectives. If the firm is not an integrated physical system, there can be no hope for an integrated information system. Perhaps all that can be accomplished is a set of separate, fragmented information systems, each supporting its own part of the firm. Therefore, a prerequisite to a good MIS is a good organization structure within the firm, one that enables the different parts to work together. A knowledge of organization theory helps the manager to develop a basic understanding that leads to the attainment of this good organization structure.

MIS also affects the firm's organization. Probably no other project can have such an influence on integrating the parts of the firm. In too many cases this has been a forced integration that fails to consider the psychological factors mentioned above. Such an approach is an open invitation to failure.

The MIS also frequently results in the addition of a new unit to the organization. Because the MIS is supposed to serve the whole organization, it has become rather common practice to set up a separate MIS department or division. In this way, the MIS is not a part of one area, such as finance, to the exclusion of other areas, such as manufacturing or marketing. In some cases the MIS operation is established on the same level as other major functional areas, directed by a vice president of information systems.

The MIS not only affects the organization structure. It also affects the manner in which these organizational units function—what they do and how they do it. MIS has made it possible to connect widely scattered operational units, such as branch sales offices or remote warehouses, to form a single communication network. These units are tied together with a flow of information. The headquarters of the firm is in the center of this network, and information flows from the outlying sites to the headquarters. Decisions are made at the headquarters and flow back to the units (Figure 2–3). The effect of

Figure 2–3   Decentralized operations and centralized decision making

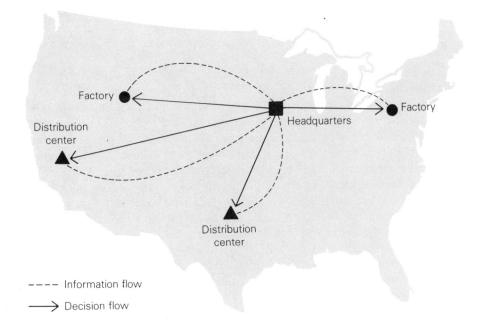

Factory

Distribution
center

Headquarters

Factory

Distribution
center

- - - - Information flow

———> Decision flow

the MIS is greater centralization in decision making. Top managers at the headquarters use the MIS to monitor the firm's sprawling physical system. They can react quickly with decisions that affect the lower level units. Such an effective MIS permits the firm to attempt coverage of a wider geographic area than if such capability did not exist. The result is an impact on organization structure and the activities performed by that structure.

Management Theory

There have been many theories of management. Many have much in common and are grouped into *schools*. Since the purpose here is not to describe the various schools, but to explore a systems theory of management, not all of the schools will be addressed. Two major schools, the classical and the behavioral, will be explained briefly. Also, the quantitative school will be recognized since it relates so closely to the MIS concept. Finally, the characteristics of a systems theory, or school, of management will be presented.

When the foundations of the systems school have been presented, it will be seen that this school is not completely separate from the others. Instead, the systems school is based on integral elements from the other schools.

The classical school

Two men are credited with contributing most to the first body of management theory, the classical school. These men were Henri Fayol, a Frenchman, and Frederick W. Taylor, an American. Both wrote of their ideas early in this century. Many others have contributed, but these two are considered the real founders.

Management functions. Probably Fayol's most significant contribution is his description of *management functions*, or the tasks a manager performs. According to Fayol, all managers plan, organize, staff, direct, and control. Listed in a logical order, these show that the first task is to *plan* what is to be done. Then the proper *organization* structure must be established to permit implementation of the plan. The manager then must *staff* for the planned activity by acquiring the necessary resources. While the term *staff* suggests manpower resources, all types of resources are included. Once these resources have been assembled, the next task is to *direct* their use in the performance of the planned activities. Finally, the manager must *control* the activities so the objectives may be met.

Fayol believed all managers perform these functions, regardless of their level in the organization. This has been called the *universality of management functions*—they apply universally to all managers on all levels.

While this universal applicability is most certainly true, it has been recognized that managers on the top level have different responsibilities and needs than those on the bottom. Names have been given to three management levels in the firm: *strategic* (top), *tactical* (middle), and *operational* (lower). Examples of strategic managers are the chairman of the board, the president, and vice-presidents of major areas such as manufacturing. Tactical managers include managers of plants, regions, and stores. Operational managers consist of supervisors and foremen. Figure 2–4 illustrates how these three levels perform each of the five functions, but how the performance varies from level to level.

All levels *plan*, but managers on the top levels plan further into the future than those on the bottom. Strategic level managers plan the firm's activities 5 or more years into the future. They do not actively engage in solving the day-to-day problems of the firm, or even those of the near future. Those are left to lower level managers. Tactical level managers are involved with what the firm will be doing from 1 to 5 years into the future. The managers who solve current problems are on the operational level.

All levels *organize*, but they organize different parts of the firm. Strategic level managers determine the overall, general organization of the firm. The details of how each part is to be organized are left to lower level managers.

The *staff* function also is performed on all levels, but in a different manner. Strategic management is concerned with acquisition of those resources used on the top management levels. For example, the president will personally select the vice-presidents, but leave selection of lower level employees to lower level managers.

Figure 2–4   Influence of management level on management functions

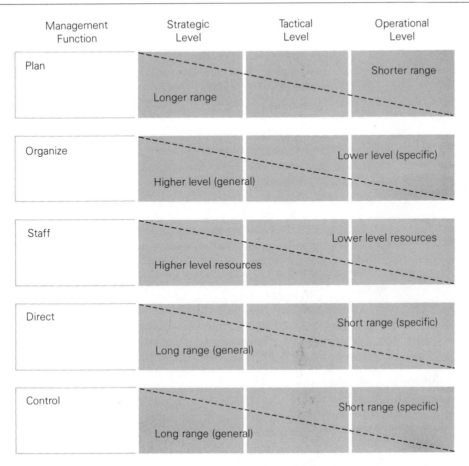

Management Function	Strategic Level	Tactical Level	Operational Level
Plan	Longer range		Shorter range
Organize	Higher level (general)		Lower level (specific)
Staff	Higher level resources		Lower level resources
Direct	Long range (general)		Short range (specific)
Control	Long range (general)		Short range (specific)

All managers *direct* the resources to attainment of objectives. The strategic level is most interested in direction that leads to accomplishment of long-range, general objectives. Lower levels are more interested in immediate, specific objectives.

As the managers direct their resources, they exercise *control* over them. Top levels aim for long-range control, while lower levels have a shorter range of concern.

Since the managers perform these functions in a different manner on each level, they have different information needs. This difference influences the overall design of the MIS in terms of its information support for each management level.

The management levels also have a significant effect on two basic aspects of MIS design. First, they influence the source of data or information; and

Figure 2–5   Influence of management level on MIS design

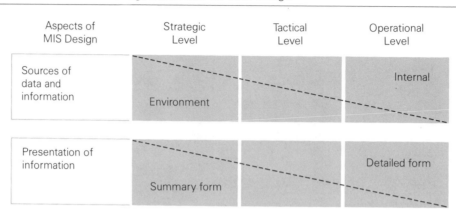

second, they influence how the information is presented. These design aspects are shown in Figure 2–5.

The different levels demand information from different sources. Top level managers have greater need for environmental information than for internal. The opposite is true for the lower level. According to the figure, a manager on the strategic level mostly needs information describing what is happening in the environment, but needs some information on what is happening within the firm.

The management level also influences how the information should be presented to the manager. Operational level managers need detailed descriptions: exactly how many overtime hours were worked last week, the average hourly cost of operating a forklift truck, how many units were produced on machine A, etc. Top level managers are exposed to so much information that it must be summarized into only the most important facts.

While the idea of management levels is quite old, it is of current importance when designing an information system. The different information needs of each level must be recognized and incorporated into the MIS.

Management principles.   Another area of Fayol's work deals with *management principles*. Fayol developed quite a few of these principles, but the ones described below have the greatest significance for a systems theory.

1 Subordination of individual interest. The interests of the employee or the unit should not dominate those of the firm or total system.
2 Centralization of control. There should be some central control mechanism for the overall system.
3 Unity of direction. All elements of the system should work together toward the system goals.

4 Division of work. The work to be done should be divided among employees or subsystems having specialized resources or skills.
5 Order. The system should function in an orderly or efficient way.

These principles have been rephrased to relate to management of a firm as a system.

Standards of performance. The other primary contributor to the classical school, Frederick W. Taylor, can be considered the first "efficiency expert" or industrial engineer. He was mainly concerned with getting the most work out of production workers. His interpretation of management failed to recognize the human needs of the workers, and he has received some criticism because of that. Even so, parts of his theory fit into a systems theory of management.

Most importantly, Taylor believed that *standards of performance* are necessary. In a business firm, these standards are used by managers to evaluate system accomplishments. They tell the manager what the firm *should be* doing. The information system tells the manager what the firm *is* doing. The manager reacts to this information and makes changes in the system that enable it to meet its standards of performance or its objectives.[1]

The reader should understand the difference in the way the manager uses both theory and standards or objectives. Earlier, it was pointed out that the theory tells the manager what to expect when certain decisions are made. The objectives tell the manager what level of performance is acceptable. Usually, objectives are expressed quantitatively such as sales dollars per month. The manager uses both theory and standards of performance to evaluate the activity of the firm.

The exception principle. Taylor also developed the concept of the exception principle. Today this is called *management by exception.* An important concept in the systems approach, it means that the manager doesn't become involved unless performance of the firm varies from preestablished boundaries. For example, if daily sales should range from 500 to 800 units (the boundaries), the manager will take no action unless sales fall outside of those limits. The manager will react to exceptionally good as well as exceptionally bad performance (although he or she will react differently to the two situations). With the severe demands imposed on a manager's time by today's business system, this is an important concept. It permits the manager to apply his or her talent where it can do the most good.

Communication. The importance of *communication* in the firm or system also was recognized by Taylor. In a systems theory, this is seen as an informa-

---

1. In the description of a systems theory of management and organization, the terms *objectives, goals,* and *standards* can be used interchangeably.

tion flow both horizontally (among departments) and vertically (among levels) in the firm. It also is represented in the diagram of a system by the feedback loop. This communication path, as pictured in Figure 1–2, permits management to monitor and control the performance of the system. If this communication network doesn't exist within a firm, its management can have no idea of what is happening.

Systems analysis.   Taylor might also be regarded as the world's first systems analyst. He advocated the *analysis of jobs* to learn the specific details of what people do. When modern information systems are designed, it is the systems analyst who makes this same type of study. In this latter case, the intent is to identify the information needs of the manager.

So, even though classical management theory is quite old, it does provide some of the key elements of a systems theory. This is important. It must be understood that accepting a systems theory does not mean rejecting the other theories. The systems theory might be regarded as a collection of the better parts of the other theories—certainly those parts believed to enable the firm to function as a system.

The behavioral school

In responding to the classical theory, certain psychologists and social-psychologists, known as the *human behavior* group, saw a need to place greater importance on the needs of the employee.[2] Various types of needs were recognized, as were ways in which these needs could be satisfied. A type of "chain reaction" was visualized, as reflected in Figure 2–6.

In step 1 the needs of the employees must be recognized. In step 2 the manager develops motivators that cause the employees to work toward the goals of the firm. The work is performed in step 3, and the firm meets its goals in step 4.

System objectives are very important in a systems theory; the behavioral school provides an approach for meeting them based on the psychology of human behavior.

A group of sociologists, named the *social systems* group, worked along the same lines.[3] They also recognized the importance of the individual if the group, or firm, is to meet its goals. They believed that the goals for both the individual and the group must be compatible. Therefore, when the manager sets a goal for a system, it must be one the employee will regard as compatible with his or her personal goals.

The behavioral school, then, has made some real contributions to a systems theory. The school concentrates on the importance of goals and how

---

2. Psychology deals with the behavior of the individual; social psychology deals with the influence of other people on individual behavior.

3. Sociology deals with the behavior of groups of people.

Figure 2–6 Goals are met by satisfying needs.

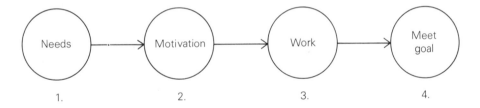

they can be achieved. It would be foolish for a manager of a business system to ignore these suggestions. The business system is not simply a mechanical structure. Its performance level is determined by the people working in it. The behavioral school suggests how these people can be motivated to work together as a system.

The quantitative school

A more modern school of management theory is the quantitative school. It evolved after World War II with the increased use of the computer and advanced mathematical techniques. This school has an important tie with a systems theory in that both recognize the importance of decision making.

Members of the quantitative school believe managers can base decisions on mathematical and statistical analyses of the data relating to the problem. The field of operations research (O.R.) represents this approach, as do the more specialized fields of industrial engineering and management science.[4]

This quantitative consideration is but a single part of a systems theory. Systems theory recognizes the importance of information as a means of managing the system; but it encompasses all types of information, both quantitative and qualitative. It is not necessary that the MIS employ advanced quantitative processes, but they do have a real value when used properly.

A systems theory of management

A systems approach to management can select from these other theories and assemble the applicable parts into a unified theory. It is not necessary to reject the other theories.

Primarily, the manager must regard his or her organization as a system

---

4. *Industrial engineering* (I.E.) applies quantitative analysis to production or manufacturing problems. *Management science* is concerned with solving the problems faced by the manager in all types of situations.

Figure 2–7   The firm is a physical system.

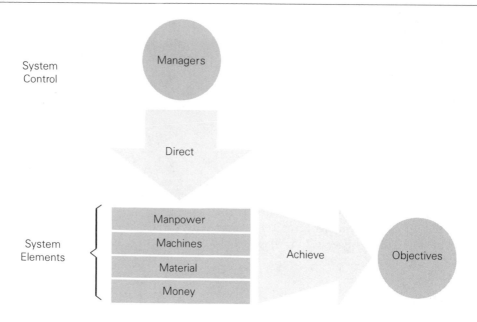

composed of resources. Also, the system must have certain goals. It is up to the manager to use the resources so goals will be met. Psychological and sociological approaches can be used to direct the employees to work toward group goals. This part of the systems theory relates to the *physical system* of the firm (Figure 2–7) that is managed by the manager.

Figure 2–8 illustrates how the manager uses an *information system* to describe the activity of the firm. This information is compared with the objectives, and the manager takes remedial action only when performance varies exceptionally from the objectives. The information provided can originate from the environment or from inside the firm. It can be created by advanced quantitative techniques or be purely subjective. Managers on all levels use the information system in this way, and it provides support for each of the functions or tasks performed. This part of the systems theory relates to the conceptual information system used to manage the physical system.

These are the basic elements of a systems theory of management. They will contribute to the development of a more complete theory in the next two chapters and to an application of that theory in the remainder of the book.

Organization Theory

Management theory encompasses everything relating to management. This is what Fayol implied when he identified the functions of the manager; they

Figure 2–8   Use of information to manage the physical system

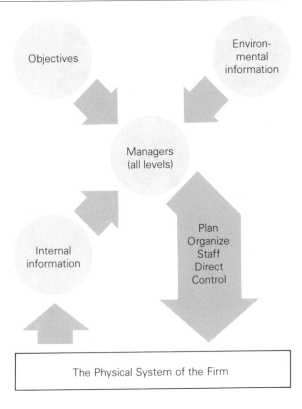

include everything the manager does. One of these functions is to organize; it is so important that a separate body of theory, called *organization theory,* has been developed for it. This theory is concerned only with how the resources will be assembled or interrelated. It has to do with structure or arrangement. As with management theory, several interpretations of organization have been created and they represent separate schools.

The classical school

When Fayol included *organize* as a management function, he also examined some related factors, called tenets. When the manager makes decisions relating to organization, these factors should be considered. Four factors that can be applied to a systems theory of organization are now discussed.

Scalar principle.   This is the chain of command that stretches from the top of an organization to the bottom. Every system must have it. It is represented by an information flow up and down through the organization and a decision

Figure 2–9   Information and decisions flow through the chain of command.

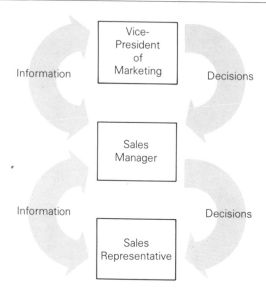

flow down (Figure 2–9). Each level and subsystem within the organization has well-defined areas of responsibility. Information is made available so that decisions relating to the responsibilities can be made.

Unity of command.   According to Fayol, an individual worker should have only one boss. Stated in systems terms, there should be only one control point in a system. This central control point enables all of the subsystems and elements in the system to work together.

Span of control.   A manager can be responsible for only a certain number of manpower resources. The narrower the span, the greater the control. However, the narrower the span, the greater the number of management layers. Figure 2–10 shows the effect of reducing the span of control from four to two employees.

  In both situations, 16 workers are managed. But, in the example on the left, only five managers on two layers do the managing. On the right, 15 managers on four layers are needed.

  Management layers are not the same as management levels. Levels recognize different types of managers based on what they do. Two or more layers can include managers of the same level or type. In Figure 2–10, all of managers could be on the operation level, for example.

  The layers of management influence the responsiveness of the system. The greater the number of layers, the less the responsiveness. It takes longer for

Figure 2–10 Span of control influences management layers.

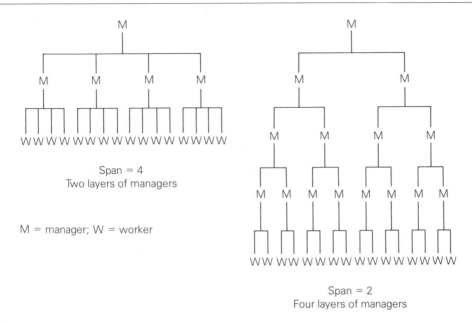

Span = 4
Two layers of managers

M = manager; W = worker

Span = 2
Four layers of managers

information and decisions to travel through the layers. Span of control determines layers, and layers determine responsiveness. The manager should understand these relationships.

Specialization. Resources are grouped according to specialized skills. This grouping has provided the most popular type of organization structure in use today—that based on functional areas.[5] The classical functions are finance, marketing, and manufacturing. Practically all manufacturing firms are organized this way. While nonmanufacturing firms do not have a formal manufacturing function, they do produce products or services. For example, a bank produces money for its customers, a hospital produces medical services, and so on. Viewed this broadly, the three functional areas can be found in practically every type of organization.

Specialization can be carried so far that it prevents the parts from working together. This condition often creates walls within an organization, as described in the first chapter. Systems theory also recognizes the need for specialization, but this is not of a functional type. The systems type of specialization will be discussed toward the end of this chapter.

---

5. *Functional areas* are not to be confused with *management functions*.

Classical organization theory is very formal and rigid. The resources must be arranged along functional lines in an exact manner. There should be no excuse for varying from this structure. The structure should be reflected in an organization chart, and all members of the organization should have specific, well-defined duties.

The neoclassical school

As with classical management theory, some behavioral shortcomings were seen in classical organization theory. To some psychologists and sociologists, the classical approach was too rigid. It did not consider the individual differences of the workers.

The neoclassicists (or "new" classicists) did not reject classical theory. They simply modified the tenets to recognize that variations could be caused by the situation. For example, they said that a particular span of control, such as seven employees, could not be set. The span would depend on the employees being managed and the task being performed. Theirs was simply a more flexible classical theory.

The behavioral school

Some behavioral scientists were not satisfied with the revisions made by the neoclassicists. They wanted a more thorough change. They recognized that the structure reflected in the organization chart seldom told the true story. In addition to the formal relationships represented on the chart, there are also informal groups and connections. These informal units do not appear on the chart. Often the informal communication links, or the "grapevine," are more effective and powerful than the formal ones.

Groups of employees are formed that do not appear on the chart. These informal groups have some need that the formal organization does not provide. They can become very powerful; they can even determine the success or failure of a venture by the firm, such as the development of a new product or the implementation of an information system.

This influence by informal groups and their communication links must be recognized when an MIS is implemented. Failure to recognize such structure can prevent the success of the project. Considerable time must be spent in identifying the needs of the informal groups that are not being met and the reason why the formal communication system is not providing all of the needed information.

A systems theory of organization

A systems theory of organization views the firm as a system with all elements or subsystems working toward the overall goals. This approach is shown in Figure 2–11.

The firm transforms input resources into output and this process is

Figure 2-11   The firm as a system

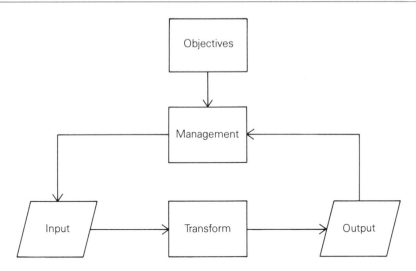

monitored and controlled by management. The management is the feedback loop, as explained in Chapter 1. The management uses the firm's objectives to keep the system on course.

The resources the manager controls do not remain within the firm, but flow through it. The firm can be regarded as a system of flow networks representing physical resources and information, as shown in Figure 2–12. These networks originate outside the firm in its environment, flow through the firm, and finally return to the environment.

Five basic flow networks can be identified. First, there are the "four M's": manpower, material, machines, and money. In this classical breakdown, *manpower* includes both female and male resources. *Material* includes semi-processed units, parts, and subassemblies as well as raw materials. *Machines* include land and buildings, as well as machinery and devices of all kinds. And *money* includes all means of payment such as checks and drafts as well as currency and coins.

The four M's will accommodate all of the physical flows and provide a simple method of classification.

The fifth flow is that of information—the conceptual representation of the physical system. Managers use information to manage the other, physical, resources when direct contact with those resources becomes difficult. This is true in the case of a large firm or of managers on higher levels. While information is valuable to all managers, it is an absolute necessity for managers in large firms and for managers on upper levels.

Most of the flow of physical resources occurs at the lower, or operational, level. The flows of machines and material are at this level as they move

Figure 2–12   The firm as a network of resource flows

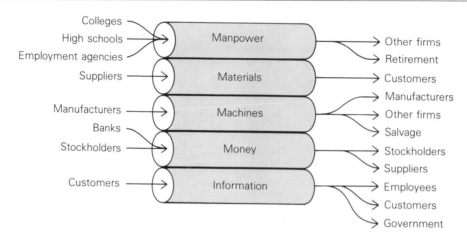

through the manufacturing process. Money also flows at the operational level—between the firm and its customers, vendors, and financial institutions. Management is very interested in these flows, but does not participate in them directly. The managers do not operate the machines or handle the materials. The managers monitor these physical flows, but they do so by the use of the information flow. The only physical flow at upper levels is manpower; management is actively involved in manpower through organizing, staffing, directing, and motivating other employees on those same levels.

Even though the firm may be considered in flow network terms, it seldom is organized along those lines. Instead, firms normally are organized into functional groups such as finance and marketing; or they may be organized by certain geographic areas or by products.

Some firms have approached the flow network structure while maintaining an essentially functional organization. This is usually done by separating the material flow and assigning it to a new function—logistics. This new functional area has responsibility for all material flows from the environment, through the firm, and back to the environment. Other firms have separated out particular parts of the material flow and assigned them to product or brand managers.

If firms have organized or subdivided other than by flow network, just what is the value to be derived from thinking in flow network terms? The main advantage, and perhaps the only one, is that it recognizes the firm as a single system, not a conglomeration of several systems. As an example, it is possible to trace a single flow from the environment, through the firm, and back to the environment without getting caught up in the functional complexities that vary from one type of organization to another.

There probably will be a continued adoption of the flow network concept, but the classical functional approach will probably never be replaced completely. Functional organization is too well established, and this situation is not likely to change. Certainly, it will not change as long as business education remains geared to functional specialties of finance, marketing, accounting, and the like.

Nevertheless, the flow network concept provides a good model for use in designing business systems dealing with both physical and conceptual flows. It permits analysis of those flows in terms of the objectives of the firm as a system. Once understood, those flows can be incorporated into a traditional functional organization without serious loss of efficiency.

This concept is extremely important. It means that the manager can use a systems theory of organization even though the firm is structured functionally. The flow network concept provides a means of studying and understanding the firm as a system. Once this understanding has been achieved, the functional organizations can be created or changed to facilitate the resource flows.

Because functionalism is so widely accepted, and because it can be followed along with the systems approach, it has not been discarded in this book. Instead, a structure for an information system is presented along functional lines in Part 4. Such a structure reflects the direction that functionally organized firms have followed in design of management information systems.

Once the flow network idea is understood, it is easy to regard the manager as a controller of those flows. This concept of management is illustrated in Figure 2–13. The owners of the firm entrust certain resources to the manager and expect certain results. There is usually a limit to the resources within which the manager must work. For example, there may be only a given number of employees with certain skills, only particular machines or equipment, only certain facilities, and a limited budget. This limitation on resources makes the job of management much more difficult than if it did not exist, but it is a situation with which every manager learns to live. Probably no organization in the world is without such a resource limitation on its management.

As shown in Figure 2–13, the manager has a "pool" of available resources. When these resources are committed to an assigned task, they are removed from the pool and allocated to the transformation process. They are returned to the pool when the transformation is completed. Resources that cannot be employed for one reason or another remain in the pool—either they cannot perform the required tasks or there are no tasks to be performed.

When management is viewed in this manner, the efficiency of the management task can be measured to a certain extent by the size of the resource pool. Resources in the pool essentially are wasted; they are costing the firm and are returning nothing.

It might appear that the manager's ultimate objective is to eliminate the pool completely. While desirable, this is not very realistic. If profit is to be maximized, resources will be directed to tasks most profitable, not those

Figure 2–13   The manager strives for optimum use of the firm's resources.

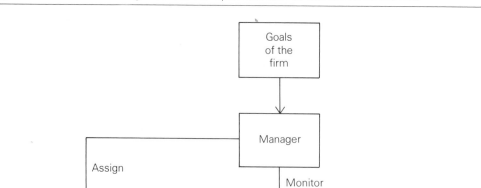

resulting in least cost through reduction of the resource pool. Over the long term the manager seeks to acquire resources that may be employed in the most profitable activities; but in the short term the day-to-day changes in the business prevent a perfect "match" between resources and tasks.

Summary

A systems theory of both management and organization is possible. And it need not be overly complex. It is a theory that can be employed in any type of managerial situation. It is doubtful, however, that a manager will adopt the systems theory exclusively. All of the theories, even the oldest classical one, include some valuable concepts for the modern manager. Perhaps that is why a systems theory has so much potential—it incorporates the best of the other theories.

Systems theory is really a way of thinking about the firm. The manager must think in systems terms. The manager recognizes that the firm is a collection of resources. These resources flow into the firm from the environment and eventually flow back to the same environment. The firm has objectives that should be aimed, primarily, at meeting some environmental need or needs. The manager uses an information flow in the management of the physical resources that comprise the physical system of the firm. While the resources usually are organized functionally, they can be viewed as flow networks. This approach simplifies the analysis of the firm when solving problems and making decisions.

In the next chapter a general model of the firm will be constructed using systems theory. Then, in Chapter 4, a systems approach to decision making will be described. At that point, the reader will be introduced to the important elements of the systems approach to management. The remainder of the book will enable the reader to develop a more complete understanding of this approach, how it is used, and how it can be implemented in an operating business firm.

Important Terms

Theory	Management by Exception
Proposition	Behavioral Management Theory
Principle	Systems Theory of Management
Management Theory	Classical Organization Theory
Organization Theory	Behavioral Organization Theory
Classical Management Theory	Neoclassical Organization Theory
Management Functions	Systems Theory of Organization
Performance Standards	

Important Concepts

Theory helps in understanding a particular subject.

There is a real relationship between information and theory.

Theories of management and of the organization of resources have evolved through various schools over a long period of time.

Systems theories of management and organization build on the older theories, rather than completely replacing them.

Systems theories of management and organization help the manager to better appreciate the role of the computerized information system in the firm.

Important People

Henri Fayol   Frederick W. Taylor

Questions

1 Is organization theory a part of management theory, or vice versa?

2 Organization charts usually contain only persons' names or titles. Why don't these charts also show how the other resources of the firm are distributed?

3 Do all types of organizations have a marketing function? A finance function? A manufacturing function? Does a church have a marketing function? Does a hospital have a manufacturing function? Discuss.

4 Why is management theory important to the study of information management? Why is organization theory important?

5 Has the idea of the computer as an information system served to centralize or decentralize business operations in a firm? Is this situation the same as centralized and decentralized decision making? Explain.

6 Which management function is the most important to the firm's president, the director of personnel, the manager of the accounting department, the foreman of the welding shop?

7 Why are strategic level managers so concerned about the environment? Can a person be a good strategic level manager and ignore the environment? Is this environment orientation greater in some industries than others? Explain.

8 Does a systems theory of management relate to the physical system being managed, the information system used to manage the physical system, or both?

9 Would span of control likely be narrower for the chief surgeon in a large city hospital, or for the supervisor of a group of machine operators in a cabinet factory? Explain. What other factors come into consideration?

10 Which functional area is responsible for the manpower flow in a firm? The money flow? Which function or functions handle(s) the material flow? The machine flow?

11 What is the difference between "optimum" use and "maximum" use of the firm's resources?

12 Why are all resources almost never in use at the same time?

Problems

1 Draw a diagram showing how information is used to refine theory.

2 Your company is considering establishing a separate organizational unit to operate its computer system. This unit would be directed by a vice president of information systems, reporting directly to the president. Your boss, the company controller, has asked you for your opinion since you had computer courses in college. The controller is worried that this action will only fragment the organization by adding another unit. Are these fears well founded? Explain.

3 Draw a pie chart showing how you think the president of Reynolds Aluminum allocates time in terms of management functions. Are all "slices" the same size? If not, why are some larger and some smaller?

4 The president of Watermark Papers International receives a daily computer printout showing yesterday's production to be below the lower limit set by the executive committee. The printout also shows that yesterday's sales exceeded the upper limit set by the same group. The president asks the secretary to get both the plant superintendent and the sales manager on the phone. What will likely be discussed with each person?

Chapter 3

The General Systems Model of the Firm

Models

The model has become a popular device in business. It is used to facilitate understanding and as an aid in decision making. An analysis of business literature during the past 10 years shows an almost geometric increase in the discussion of models in textbooks, professional business journals, and periodicals. If the scope of the analysis were pushed back 30 or 40 years, it would appear that modeling is a recent innovation and, like the computer and management science techniques, came into its own after the Second World War. This conclusion is not completely true. Modeling probably has always been an important decision-making aid, but only recently has it attracted the attention of business writers.

What is a model?

A model is an abstraction of something; it is something that represents something else.

The word *model* usually brings to mind the female variety pictured in fashion ads. This type of model is an abstraction of something, such as the woman viewing the ad and putting herself in the model's place. Fashion models—female and male alike—are employed by advertisers to represent those viewers imagining how they will look wearing the dress or the suit.

The idea of a conceptual system was presented in Chapter 1. A conceptual system also has the function of representing something, in this case a physical system. Therefore, both a model and a conceptual system are used to represent something else. In fact, the two terms can be used interchangeably.

Types of models

Since the model has enjoyed such recent popularity, a number of efforts have been made to classify the various kinds. The classification scheme discussed below consists of four types:

1 Physical models
2 Narrative models

3 Graphical models
4 Mathematical models

The fashion model is a *physical model*, as are childhood toys such as dolls and toy airplanes. Most physical models are three-dimensional representations and, in many cases, are smaller than the object represented. The dolls and toy airplanes are smaller than what they represent, and the fashion models usually are slimmer than the prospective purchasers of the garments. But, reduced size is not a requirement, and some models are the same size as their counterparts. Life-size dolls and styling models used by the automakers are examples.

Regardless of size, the physical models represent something else—babies and automobiles. For one reason or another, the model serves a purpose that cannot be fulfilled practically by the real thing; real babies cannot stand the physical wear suffered by dolls, and the automakers can hardly stand the financial wear of using real automobiles as styling prototypes.

So, the model serves a purpose by providing some characteristic not obtainable through use of the object being modeled. In some cases this characteristic is economy; in others it is availability—the model is more readily available than the real object. In the case of the style of a new automobile, the real object does not yet even exist.

Of the four types, the physical model probably has the least value for the business manager. It usually is not necessary for the manager to see something in a three-dimensional form to facilitate understanding or to assist in making decisions.

A type of model used daily by the manager is one seldom recognized as a model; this is the *narrative model*. Since the narrative can be either written or spoken, the narrative model is used by everyone who can speak or write, thus making it the most popular type.

The narrative model represents some subject or topic, and the representation is accomplished with words. The listener or reader can understand the subject from the narrative. At least, that is the intent. All written communications in business fall into the narrative model category. This includes management reports. Also, all oral communications are narrative models, and these are as old as management itself.

Another type of model in constant use is the *graphical model* (Figure 3–2). This is an abstraction of lines or symbols or shapes, often with a narrative explanation. The organization chart is a popular example. The boxes and lines represent the positions and interrelationships. The position titles appear as narrative explanations inside the boxes.

The fourth type of model, the *mathematical model*, has accounted for most of the recent interest in models for decision making. Any mathematical formula or equation is a model; and most students have had years of experience with mathematics when they become students of business management. The mathematical model, then, is no stranger to most college students.

Many mathematical models used by the business manager are similar to

Figure 3–2 An organization chart is a graphic model. (Courtesy of Lawrence D. White Associates, Inc.)

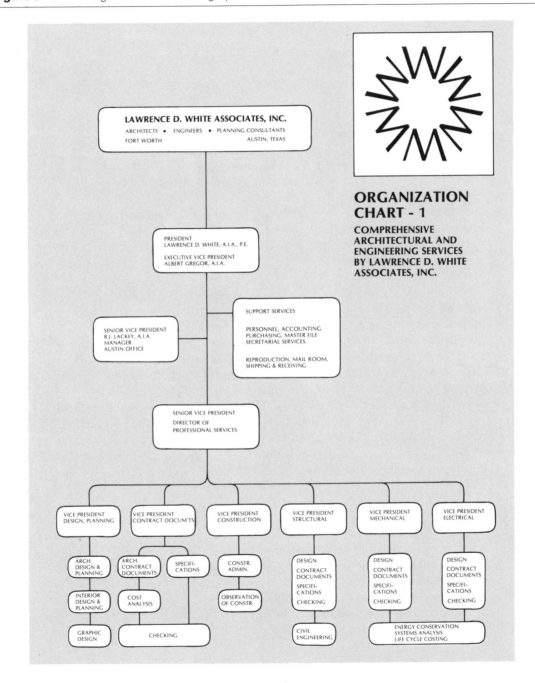

those used in mathematics courses. One such model is no more complex than those studied in high school; this is the formula for calculating the economic order quantity (EOQ) for items in inventory, and a very popular business model.

$$EOQ = \sqrt{\frac{2PS}{M}}$$

where

EOQ = dollar value of an item to order
P = cost to prepare a purchase order
S = annual sales of the item
M = cost of maintaining the item in inventory

Because the language of mathematics is universal, mathematical models know no cultural, political, or geographic boundaries. Anyone who understands the language and knows the meaning of the symbols can understand the model regardless of its origin; this is one of the main advantages of a mathematical model.

Another advantage is precision in describing the interrelationships between the parts of the object. Mathematics can handle relationships expressed in more than the two dimensions of the graphical model or the three of the physical model. To the mathematician, and to the business manager who recognizes the complexity of the many factors affecting the outcome of business decisions, this multidimensional ability of the mathematical model is of great value.

The EOQ model above is but one equation. Many mathematical models used in business employ more than one equation—often hundreds. A financial planning model developed by the Sun Oil Company uses approximately 2,000 equations.[1] The use of multiple equations makes these models more complex, but does not change their status as models. They are still conceptual systems, and their separate equations are subsystems.

Uses of models

It was recognized earlier that the value of the model lies in its ability to depict some characteristic that cannot be depicted by the object of the modeling. Economy and availability are important reasons to use a model rather than the real thing. Another reason is the simplicity that can be achieved in a model. It is common to use a model more simple in construction than the real object. While this leads to benefits in economy—a desirable goal—the primary reason

---

1. George W. Gershefski, "Building a Corporate Financial Model," *Harvard Business Review*, July–August, 1969, p. 39.

for using such simplified models is *understanding*. When the system being modeled is complex, it is easier to understand its interrelationships and workings if these are presented in a simplified way.

Each type of model previously described can be constructed to facilitate understanding. A physical model can represent only features of interest; a narrative can be boiled down to a summary; a diagram can show only the main relationships; and a mathematical equation can contain only primary ingredients. In each, an effort is made to present the model in the most simplified form, frequently the first step in understanding. Once these simple models are understood, they can be increased in complexity for a better understanding of the real object. Models can become complex, but they still represent the system being modeled and *never* match it exactly.

In many cases, it is possible only to approach the complexity of the real system. The business system, for example, is so complex that a model can only approach an accurate description of it. A model is therefore an abstraction of reality, and models exist in various degrees of abstraction. Mathematical models are perhaps the most abstract; and it is difficult for many to understand how a physical system, such as a business firm, can be represented by a series of mathematical equations. If it can be accepted that the equations can represent different parts of the system in an extremely precise way, the value of the mathematical model to the manager can be appreciated.

The recent interest in modeling has not been due so much to the value of the models to aid understanding, however, as to a second important use—*to predict*. Because the manager is concerned about the future impact of decisions on the firm, the ability to look into the future while the decision is being made is of great value. Only the mathematical model offers this predictive power. If the manager is able to predict with the other types of models, it is because of the greater understanding that the model provides. The manager must use this understanding to project what might happen in the future.

One should not get the idea that mathematical models enable the manager to predict the future perfectly. *No* model ever has enjoyed such a batting average. Because the model is only a simplification or approximation of the real system, the result is a device that can be expected to behave similarly but not identically to the real system. This lack of perfect accuracy by the model does not detract from its use by the manager. The model is such an improvement over anything previously available that the manager accepts its shortcomings and takes advantage of its strong points. As long as the manager is aware of the shortcomings, and considers their possible influence on the behavior of the model, this situation is acceptable.

General versus Specific Models

The fact that all models only approximate the system being modeled could mean that all models are general in nature. Figure 3–3 illustrates this point. Efforts can be made, however, to construct the model so that it is very specific

Figure 3–3   All types of models can vary in degree of generality.

Very General		**Very Specific**
An ordinary baby doll	——— Physical ———	A likeness of John F. Kennedy in a wax museum
An article on "Ethics in Business"	——— Narrative ———	The Continental Oil Company policy manual
A "demand curve" (see Figure 11-8)	——— Graphical ———	The Lawrence D. White Associates, Inc. organization chart
The EOQ formula	——— Mathematical ———	The Sun Oil financial planning model

in certain respects. This capability suggests that models can fit on a continuum ranging from the very general to the very specific. The type of model (graphical, mathematical, etc.) has no effect on degree of generality. All types can exist at any point on the continuum.

The examples of very general models shown above have a primary advantage of wide applicability. The baby doll can represent any baby, and the EOQ formula can be used by any type of firm. If this wide applicability is an advantage, it also must be recognized as creating a limitation. The general model, while describing many objects in a rough way, fails to describe any objects specifically.

If one wants to describe a relationship or condition unique to a particular situation, a specific, rather than a general, model must be used. Using organizational relationships as an example, an organization chart can show the exact relationships within the particular firm. The advantage is accuracy, but the gain is made at the price of the other advantage—general applicability. The specific chart probably cannot describe the organizational structure for any firm except that upon which it is based.

Each type of model has its purpose, and the type selected depends entirely on the needs to be fulfilled. If the manager wants to understand a particular situation, the specific model is helpful. If the purpose is to understand a wide variety of situations, the general model is to be preferred.

The value of a general model

Business education at the college level is based on the general approach. Courses are taken that will help the student in a variety of employment situations that may be encountered later. Accounting techniques are learned that can be applied in any type of organization. The same applies to statistical techniques and training in computer programming. Few business courses are aimed at a particular type of organization or profession. Insurance and real estate courses are such exceptions.

This general approach is continued in this book. The principles and fundamentals can be applied to any type of information system in any type of organization. In this chapter a general model of a business firm will be presented. This model is intended for use in a wide variety of situations. The model should provide an effective way to view any type of firm and its information system. As such, it should be of greater value to the future business manager or information specialist than a more specific model. Examples of application of the model to specific situations will be provided later in the chapter.

The simplicity of the general model of the firm facilitates a basic understanding of the firm. This basic understanding will be augmented by additional material later in the book and in later business courses. Subsequent employment opportunities only require that the unique characteristics of the firm be added to the model.

An awkward period in the business student's career is the transition from the classroom to the firm. The first few days on a new job can be confusing. The environment is new and different—new faces, facilities, terminology, etc. When something familiar appears, that something can serve as a reference point for a feeling of stability. Other elements in the environment can be related to it. The general model can provide such a reference point. The student can learn the basic activities performed in any organization and their interrelationships. He or she therefore can be prepared to encounter these activities and the model becomes a useful framework for specific understanding of the new firm.

Besides providing a framework for orientation, the general model can be a yardstick for evaluating the new firm. The new employee expects certain elements and relationships. This use of the general model as a "checklist" of what should be encountered can help identify the parts of the firm that offer opportunities for improvement. The new employee need not always accept the new firm as it is; he or she eventually will be asked for suggestions for improvement. The general model can indicate the need for improvement and the points in the firm where this improvement is needed.

The General Model of the Firm

It has been noted that the firm is a physical system, and that management uses a conceptual system to manage the physical one. The general model to be

Figure 3–4   The physical system of the firm

developed contains both physical and conceptual components. First the physical model will be developed, then the conceptual one.

The physical system

The system model presented in the first chapter can provide the basis for studying the physical system of the firm. As seen in Figure 3–4, input resources are transformed into output resources. Input resources come from the environment, and output resources are returned to the same environment. The physical system of the firm is therefore an *open system*, interacting with its environment by means of the physical resource flows.

Most systems are of the open type. It is practically impossible to identify examples of a *closed system*, or one that is not dependent on its environment. A battery-powered, shockproof, waterproof wristwatch is a closed system, except when new batteries are added. Human beings, puppies, flowers, and business firms are all open systems that exist in a necessary environment.

Figure 3–4 is readily identifiable with a manufacturing operation where raw materials are transformed into finished goods. This is essentially a materials flow and recognizes none of the other flows of physical resources, such as manpower, machines, and money, that enter into the transformation process. There is no doubt that these other flows are involved—manpower and machines to transform the raw materials into finished goods and money to pay for the material, manpower, and machines. Perhaps not readily apparent is the fact that these latter resources also flow through the firm much like the material flow. This is the flow network concept presented in Chapter 2, and a part of a systems theory of organization. Each of the physical flows is described below.

Material flow.   Input materials are received from the vendors or suppliers who provide raw materials, parts, and assembled components. These materials are held in a storage area (raw materials inventory) until required for the transformation process; then they are released to the manufacturing activity (work-in-process inventory). At the conclusion of the transformation, the materials, now in some finished form, are placed in a storage area (finished goods inventory) until they are shipped to customers.

Manpower flow.   Input manpower originates from several points in the environment. Some workers come through organized labor unions, some do not. Some are recruited by the firm and some by private employment agencies. Some are provided by the local community and some result from nationwide search. Some come from college campuses and some do not. A firm obtains manpower from many sources to meet a wide range of personnel requirements.

This input manpower usually is processed through the personnel department of the firm and assigned to separate work areas. While in those areas, the manpower is used in the transformation process, either directly or indirectly. The manpower might be available to the firm briefly or for a long period. Some employees leave the firm shortly after joining it. Others remain for 50 years or more. Whether the duration is short or long, the manpower resource flows through the firm. At some point, the manpower exits. The personnel department processes the termination and the resource is returned to its environment—the local community, competition, organized labor, etc.

Machine flow. Input machines are obtained from specialized vendors and suppliers who manufacture or distribute them. Unlike the other physical resources, the machines invariably remain in the firm for an extended period. Rarely is a machine acquired one day and released the next. Ultimately, however, all the machines must return to the environment. In many cases machines wear out or become obsolete and are scrapped. Some machines can be traded in on newer models or sold to other organizations that have a use for them.

While in the firm, the machines seldom reside in a storage area. They are continually available, either as delivery trucks in the marketing department, desk calculators in the accounting department, or machine tools in the manufacturing department. Because of special supply sources, lack of in-firm storage, and special disposal outlets, the machine flow is the most simple of the physical resources.

Money flow. Money is obtained from many sources. Primary ones are the stockholders or owners who provide investment capital and the firm's customers who provide sales revenue. Other sources include loans from financial institutions, government loans or grants, and interest income from investments.

While many sources provide money, the responsibility for the in-firm flow lies in the financial function—the accounting department. The accounts receivable section collects money owed the firm by its customers, and the accounts payable section pays debts owed by the firm.

The flow of money through the firm is unusual in one respect. Actual money seldom flows through the firm. Rather, there is a flow of something representing money—checks, credit card slips, and so forth. Only on the retail level does cash change hands, and this is continually giving way to credit transactions.

The money flow, therefore, is through the financial institutions used by the firm, and its customers, vendors, stockholders, and employees. In some cases the duration of this flow is long—as for certificates of deposit held by the firm to represent an interest-bearing investment with a bank. In other cases the duration is short—as for sales revenue quickly converted into checks payable to vendors and employees.

The conceptual system

The physical system, as illustrated in Figure 3–4, is an open system in terms of its environmental links. As pictured, it has no feedback loop and control mechanism. Such a system is called an *open-loop system*. There is no feedback from system output to affect changes in system input.

Examples of open-loop systems are not hard to find. A good example is a small gas heater—the kind plugged into outlets to heat older homes. The heater is lighted and it gives off heat. It may give off too much or not enough. It has no self-regulating mechanism to maintain a certain temperature.

There probably are a few business firms of the open-loop type. They set off on a particular course and never change direction. If they get out of control, nothing is done to restore equilibrium. The result is system destruction, or bankruptcy.

Most business firms, however, have a closed feedback loop. The control mechanism built into this loop is the management. A business firm, therefore, can be regarded as a type of *closed-loop system*—one where a control mechanism monitors system output and makes necessary changes to system input.

Figure 3–4 could have included feedback and control elements. Those additions are reflected in Figure 3–5.

The reason management and the feedback loop were not included in the discussion of the physical system is that they are both integral parts of the conceptual information system. It is true that both managers and devices that contribute to the flow of information, such as computers, telephone networks, and the like, are physical resources; but they also are elements in the conceptual information system. Because it is important to recognize that the conceptual information system includes management and data and information communication and processing devices, those elements were held for discussion of the conceptual information system.

With the addition of the feedback loop to the physical system, management can control the system by becoming an integral part of the loop. The control process involves receiving information about the system, evaluating it, and transmitting information back to the system when some type of change must be made. The feedback loop therefore provides a communication channel for the fifth basic resource—information.

Figure 3–5 is a simplified model of the conceptual information system (added to the physical system). However, certain additions and refinements can be made to better describe the conceptual system. First, the manager gathers information other than that relating to the firm's output. It is important to know the status of this output since it represents the contribution of the firm to its environment; but other information is needed as well. The manager must know the status of the firm in terms of internal processes and

Figure 3–5   The physical system of the firm as a controlled system

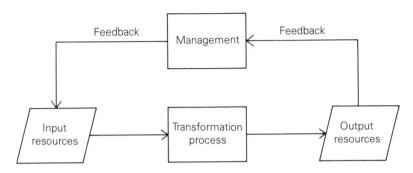

inputs. For example, the manager wants information describing performance of vendors in meeting the firm's needs for input material. Also, the manager wants information describing the production efficiency of the manufacturing operation. Figure 3–6 reflects the addition of information-gathering activity to the input and processing parts of the physical system.

Next, it must be recognized that information does not always travel directly from the physical system to the manager. The manager usually is removed from the physical system and must get information through a communication network. Very often a direct communication path is possible. The manager can receive information directly from the physical system by personal report or by telephone conversation. In many other instances, however, the information must be stored in some intermediate area until the manager needs it. An example is the storage of detailed data during the month for use in preparation of a monthly summary report.

Figure 3–7 includes the addition of an element named the *information*

Figure 3–6   Multiple information sources monitor the physical system.

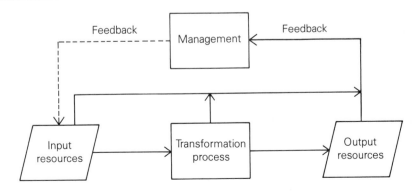

Figure 3–7   Addition of the information processor to the conceptual information system

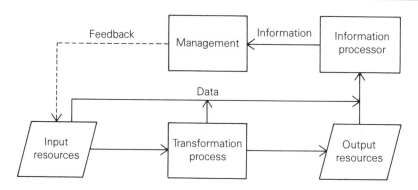

processor. In this discussion it is assumed that the information processor is a computer. There are other ways to process information, however, and that should be remembered in the course of the discussion that follows.

Part Three of this book will provide a description of computing equipment that comprises the information processor. For the time being, this element can be recognized to contain two basic parts—a place to store data, and computer routines that convert these data into information. Figure 3–8 identifies the important parts of an information processor.

This model of an information processor simply is a more detailed version of the information processing system pictured in Figure 1–5.

The distinction between data and information, recognized in Chapter 1, is a very important one. The concept of a data base (or data bank) also is very

Figure 3–8   An information processor

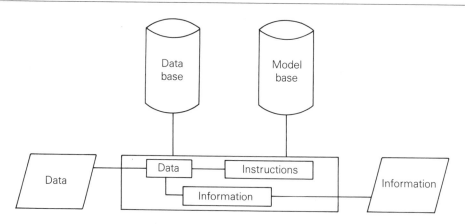

important, and the term is a popular one. A *data base* is a storage area containing data gathered from throughout the firm and from the environment. If the information system is computerized, the data base is housed in a type of computer storage.

It is the role of the information processor to convert data into information. Models are used for this purpose. In this instance, the models are in both mathematical and narrative form. The mathematical models perform calculations; the narrative models make logical decisions and manipulate data.

These narrative and mathematical models are represented in a computerized MIS by the computer programs—the coded instructions that tell the computer what to do. Most firms have hundreds of these programs that have been created over a period of time by the firm's programming staff. Also included are programs acquired from computer manufacturers and other sources. Collectively, these programs (or models) comprise the *model base*. This term has not yet enjoyed such widespread acceptance as has data base.

As the manager identifies information needs, he or she should consider several important characteristics of information:

1. *Quality.* How accurate must the information be? Very often, as in monetary accounting, the information must be very accurate—to the penny. In other situations, such as the forecasting of sales, it is recognized that the

"We're trading you in for another model, Mighty One."

information is only an approximation of what actually exists or can be expected to happen.

2. *Quantity.* How much information is needed? As a rule, information is more highly summarized on top management levels and more detailed on the bottom. The manager can have so much information that it is impossible to select what is most important.

3. *Timing.* How much time can elapse after an action by the physical system until it is reported to the manager? All managers would like an instantaneous signal, but that may not be necessary. Perhaps the manager cannot take immediate action even if the information is made available without delay.

4. *Cost versus Return.* As the manager considers requirements in terms of quality, quantity, and timing, the cost also must be recognized. Most firms simply cannot afford a "perfect" system and must settle for something less. The cost of information should never exceed its value.

5. *Presentation Mode.* How will the information be presented—in the form of numbers, narrative, or graphics? Will the information be printed or displayed on a television-type terminal, or will it be presented in an audible form?

It is the responsibility of the manager to identify the information needs for decision making. Nobody else understands the decision responsibilities of the manager. The manager also knows what information is needed. The information specialist can work with the manager to assure that these specifications are made in a complete and orderly manner. The specialist often will assist the manager in thinking through his or her decision-making responsibilities and information needs so they are specified adequately. The information specialist will take these specifications and create a data base and a model base that will produce the needed information. By these means the contents of the data and model base are determined.

A third change in the evolving model of the conceptual information system is recognition that the manager needs standards for measuring the firm's actual performance. If the manager receives a report indicating that yesterday's sales were $25,000, is that good or bad? Without some standard of performance, it would be impossible to tell. If the firm never before had reached that sales level, the performance would be good; if sales normally averaged $30,000, the performance would be bad. This requirement for performance standards also can be seen in the thermostatically controlled heating system. If the thermostat is to maintain temperature at a certain level, the level must be established by setting the thermostat at a particular temperature. Similarly, if a business firm is to perform at a certain level or rate, some standard of performance must be established. In many cases the managers set the performance level; but in others the level is established by the board of directors or even an element in the environment such as the government or the local community.

The manager controls the system by comparing (1) actual performance, as reflected by information provided by the information processor, to (2) the

Figure 3–9   Addition of system objectives to the conceptual information system

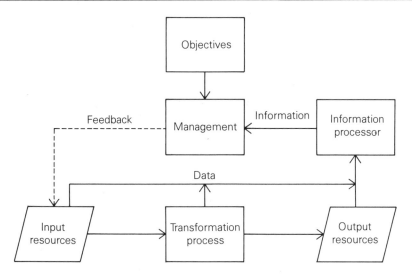

standards of performance, or objectives. Figure 3–9 contains this addition of system objectives.

Most managers have so many responsibilities it is practically impossible to give each the attention it deserves. This is the reason for the long hours worked by most managers. It is not an "eight-to-five" job. Managers learn to direct their attention to matters of greatest importance. Situations of low priority often go unattended.

This practice is called *management by exception*. It means that the manager deals only with exceptional situations. The exceptional situations can be either extremely bad or extremely good performance (Figure 3–10). Students of management often fail to appreciate why exceptionally good performance should be called to the attention of the manager. One is reminded of what Abraham Lincoln is supposed to have said when someone told him that Ulysses Grant, one of his best generals, was an alcoholic. Lincoln is said to have replied "If that is true, I should buy a case of whiskey for all of my other generals." If something is going extremely well in a system, the manager should know about it so that similar success might be achieved in other areas. Lincoln was not recommending alcoholism for his leaders, as he most certainly did not recognize that as the key to military success. Rather, he was making the point that the top executive should know when things are going well so that such superior performance can be realized in a comprehensive manner.

Management by exception requires that standards of performance be established, at both lower and upper levels. As long as performance remains between these levels, there is no need for management attention. The information system can monitor the performance of the physical system and notify

Figure 3-10   Both good and bad performance receive the manager's attention.

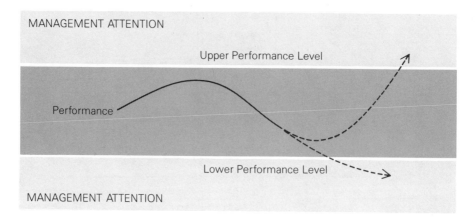

the manager when the levels have been exceeded. For example, if daily shoe sales should range from 125 to 200 pairs, the manager is signaled only when the sales fall below 125 or rise above 200.

Management by exception offers several *advantages*. First, the skills of the manager are utilized to their fullest. And, since fewer decisions must be made, they can receive more thorough attention. Finally, it is a "positive" approach since opportunities as well as problems are identified. These advantages enable the firm to achieve a more efficient use of its scarce management resources.

There are some *limitations*, however, that must be recognized. It is not always easy to measure quantitatively certain types of business performance. An example is customer attitude toward the firm. Management by exception places a high value on quantitative measures of performance. When these measures are difficult, the concept suffers. An effective information system that accurately monitors various types of performance is also needed. And attention must be directed continually to the standards. Are they at the correct level? Have they become obsolete? Finally, the manager must not become passive and simply wait for standards to become exceeded. The manager must supplement the automatic monitoring by the information system with an aggressive search for new opportunities and new problem areas.

A fourth addition to the general model is necessary to reflect the manner in which management decisions can change the physical system. Just as it was recognized that the manager must gather data from all three elements of the physical system—input, processing, and output—it is important to conclude that the manager must also be able to effect changes in the performance of all three elements. As the model is drawn in Figure 3-9, the manager can only communicate feedback instructions or decisions to the input element. Such a limitation would prohibit the manager from responding quickly to changes throughout the entire system. If information from the data base indicates that activity in either the transformation processing or the output area requires adjustment, the manager must be able to effect such change directly, without working solely through the input area. This modification is made in Figure 3–11; the feedback from the manager to the physical system is relabeled "decisions" to reflect the manner in which the manager achieves changes in the system performance.

The basic feedback loop as drawn initially in Figure 3–5 still represents signals from the physical system used for control; but the signals exist in three different forms: data, information, and decisions.

A fifth and final addition to the model reflects the dependence of the firm on its environment. As the discussion of the environment in the next chapter will indicate, its influence on the firm can be very complex. An attempt to show this effect in the general model would complicate it unnecessarily. Therefore, the final form of the general model recognizes only that resources flow into the firm from the environment and from the firm back to the environment. That addition is made in Figure 3–12.

All five types of resources—manpower, machines, material, money, *and information*—enter the firm from the environment. The information is stored in the data base along with data gathered internally. Very often raw data is gathered from the environment for conversion into information. For purposes of simplicity, both environmental information and data are identified as "information" in the model.

Figure 3–11 Changes in the physical system are made through the decision flow.

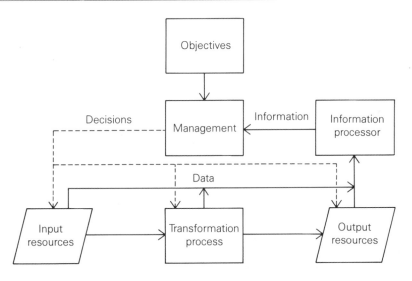

Use of the General Model

During the previous paragraphs, while the general systems model of the firm was being constructed, it should have been rather easy to relate the model to a manufacturing firm. The flow of materials through the physical system and the control exercised by the manager in assuring that production goals are met by the firm are both very apparent. It is not quite so easy to relate the model to other types of organizations, especially those providing services rather than products, and those of a nonprofit nature. In the sections below, two of these more specialized types of organizations are explained in terms of the model. The objective is to show that the model is general in the true sense and can provide a basic structure for the analysis of any type of organization.

A football team

The management control of a football team is exercised by the coaching staff. The coaches must use their resources in the most efficient way. Most teams have objectives or goals they wish to meet during an entire season (such as winning at least eight games) or during a single game (such as limiting the opposition to no more than 10 first downs). Goals employed by coaching staffs are mostly quantitative and there is little question of whether they have been reached. Fans and sportswriters can make this determination very easily.

The most important resource available to the coaches is manpower. Some material is involved, such as uniforms, footballs, adhesive tape, and the like; but it is of much less value to the coaches than the players. Very little machinery is involved. Movie projectors, whirlpool baths, and tackling dummies are about the extent of it. Money may or may not be an important resource, depending on the type of team. Certainly, no professional team could exist without it. As the team becomes more modest in its performance level, money plays a lesser role.

It can be seen that the management of the organization—the coaching staff—has a mixture of resources with which to work, and that the resources have different relative value. Naturally, much of the success of a football team is due to the skill of the coaching staff, but much is determined by the resources available. The coach must do the best he can with what he has.

These resources flow through the organization. In a college team, the players are available for only four years, equipment is used for only a single season, and supplies often last only days. The team begins the season with a budgeted amount of funds, and these probably have been spent by the time the last game rolls around. While the resources are available, the coaches must integrate them into a smoothly functioning team.

All coaches have a conceptual information system of some sort. Those on the sandlot level probably rely entirely on observation from the sidelines. This basic approach to monitoring the performance of the system can be augmented by assistant coaches in the pressbox, by game films, and even by computer

Figure 3–12 The general systems model of the firm

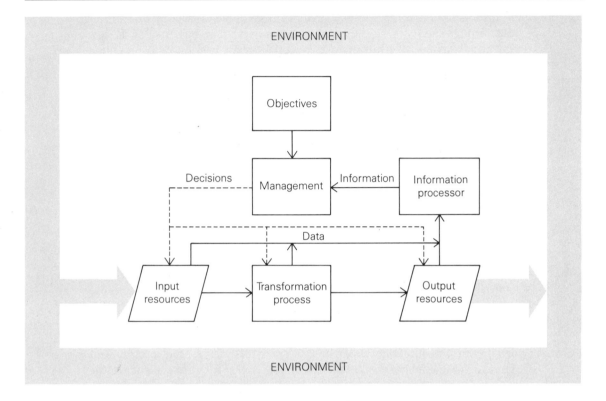

systems. Many professional teams use computers to recruit players and to decipher the strategy of opponents. As a general rule, data does not reside in the data base for a long period of time. During a game, the coaching staff usually can determine by half-time the causes of their team's problems so they can take corrective action. As this information becomes available to the coaches, they make decisions that alter the team's performance. The purpose of such changes is to help the team meet its objectives.

The football team is a service organization. It produces only entertainment for its followers. It employs resources gathered from its environment and returns an output to the environment in the form of entertainment. Although the organization is quite different in many respects from a business firm, there also are many similarities that are brought out in the general model. The model provides a useful framework with which to evaluate the team. A new head coach most certainly will take stock of his resources, evaluate the nature of the goals, and pass judgment on the information system in preparing for the upcoming season. The model serves as a normative, or ideal, model of how the organization should be structured.

A law firm

Several obvious differences exist between a law firm and a football team. The law firm usually is composed of a small number of people who perform their tasks through mental, rather than physical, activity. The objective of the law firm usually is profit, while that of a football team usually is to provide a service.

Even with these differences, a law firm can be described by the same general model used for the football team. Each law firm has some management function that controls the organization. In a large firm this control is exercised by the partners; in a small firm of only a single lawyer, this control is performed on a part-time basis by that person.

The main responsibility of the person or persons managing the law firm is to assure that it meets its objectives. It is doubtful that the goals of the law firm are as specific as those of the football team. A legal firm most likely does not strive to win a certain percentage of court cases or to handle some minimum number of divorce settlements. It can be assumed that a profit objective exists, however, since management must realize that profit is the key to continued operation and service.

The transformation process in the law firm is one of converting the raw materials (clients with legal problems) into finished products (clients whose legal problems have been solved). This transformation is accomplished by the lawyers, who comprise the most important resource available to the firm.

It could be argued that information is the most important resource. That ingredient is absolutely necessary in legal practice. Everyone has seen pictures of legal offices with bookshelves filled with law books; they are evidence of the importance of information in the transformation process. Some legal firms employ computers to provide information on request in a fraction of the time required to obtain it through library research. However, if information were the most important resource, people with legal problems would seek out lawyers with the largest libraries or the fastest computer systems. This is not done. Lawyers most sought are those who can apply professional skills to the solution of the problem; only one of those skills is the ability to identify information requirements and sources.

The performance of a law firm therefore lends itself to the general model. Management of the firm monitors the process by which legal problems are transformed into solutions. Information facilitating this control is provided from the physical system and it is derived from a data base. When the status of the physical system is such that objectives are not being met, decisions are made that alter the physical system. If too few legal problems are being converted into solutions (the firm is losing too many cases), the partners can hire additional lawyers, replace existing lawyers, reassign lawyers to different types of cases, hire legal secretaries, etc.

The general model provides a structure for the basic elements of a legal firm. A new partner can expect to find these elements regardless of whether he or she has ever before served in that particular firm or has any previous knowledge of its structure. The new partner expects to find objectives (for the firm and perhaps for individual lawyers), an information system, and a resource of manpower capable of performing the transformation process in a manner acceptable to the managing partners.

Summary

The main objective of this chapter has been to present a general model of the firm that can be used by the student to better understand the structure of both the physical system of the firm and the conceptual information system and how they interrelate.

The term *model* was introduced, and four types were identified— physical, narrative, graphical, and mathematical. All provide some feature not attainable from the object being modeled. These features, economy and availability, permit the user to better understand the object being modeled and often (for mathematical models) to predict the future to some degree less than perfection.

All four types of models can range from the general to the specific. Each form has its advantages, but the general model provides the best educational basis for a career in business. The latter portion of the chapter includes a general model of the firm and a discussion of how it can be applied to varying types of organizations. It was seen that the model is compatible with the concept of management by exception.

This chapter serves only to introduce the general model to the student. Each part of the model will be analyzed in more detail in the chapters that follow. The student also can apply the general model to the solution of classroom case problems. The general model, along with the systems approach, provides two effective means of solving problems dealing with the management of information as a resource. The systems approach is the subject of the next chapter.

Important Terms

Model	Specific Model
Physical Model	Open System
Narrative Model	Closed System
Graphical Model	Material Flow
Mathematical Model	Manpower Flow
General Model	Machine Flow

Money Flow   Data Base

Open-Loop System   Model Base

Closed-Loop System   Management by Exception

Information Processor

Important Concepts

There are different types of models and each has its own special purpose.

The value of the mathematical model to management is just being realized.

All types of models can exist in a general or specific form and both forms offer special advantages.

A firm can be seen as a network of resource flows (a systems theory of organization).

Management serves as a part of the feedback loop in the firm as a system.

The general systems model provides a good structure for studying the management of any type of activity.

Questions

1 What is a model?

2 What are the four types of models? Give an example of each. What type of model is this textbook?

3 When would a physical model be larger than the item being modeled? When would it be smaller? When would it be the same size? Give examples.

4 Which type of model would be used the most by the vice-president of marketing? By the manager of the accounting department? By the director of purchasing? Which type of model would be used the least by these people?

5 Is the arithmetic expression $X = Y$ a mathematical model? Explain.

6 Why are mathematical models receiving so much attention in the business world?

7 Why are simplified models used?

8 Name two benefits the manager can receive from the use of a mathematical model.

9 What value does a general model have for a college student? A specific model?

10   Give three examples of both an open system and a closed system.

11   Which of the resource flows does the manager want to speed up? To slow down?

12   Of the four resource flows, which takes the most time (on the average) from entry into the firm until exit? Which takes the least time?

13   Does money or something representing money flow through the firm?

14   What are the names of the three areas of a plant where materials can reside?

15   Give three examples of an open-loop system.

16   What are the basic parts of the information processor?

17   Name five characteristics that information should have to be of value to the manager.

18   What are the advantages and disadvantages of management by exception?

19   In what forms does the feedback loop exist in the firm as a system?

20   What contributions did Henri Fayol make to the general systems model? What about Frederick W. Taylor?

21   Trace the flow of information in the model of Figure 3–12. Trace the flow of data. Does data ever leave the firm? Explain.

Problems

1   Draw arrows on the following diagram to show which resources flow into and out of each functional area.

2   Describe how the general model fits your college. Describe each symbol and line on the model.

Chapter 4

The Systems Approach

The Importance of Decision Making

The purpose of the information system is to help the manager make decisions. Certainly managers do other things. In fact, decision making might account for only a small portion of a particular manager's time. However, the importance of decision making is not based on the time a manager spends doing it, but rather on the consequences. A decision might require only a few hours, but could affect the firm's profits to the tune of thousands or even millions of dollars.

The history of a firm, therefore, becomes a series of key decisions that have definite influences on the firm's ability to meet its objectives and to survive. Successful firms can point to a series of correct decisions. Unsuccessful firms can point to a series of incorrect decisions, or perhaps even a single fatal one.

Problem Solving versus Decision Making

Decisions are made to solve problems. A problem exists—say, low sales for a product such as ski boots—that will require multiple decisions to solve. The manager will have to choose among several alternate solutions, such as (1) develop a new product, (2) modify the existing one, (3) change the price, (4) implement a new advertising program, etc. A decision will have to be made about each alternative—whether or not to accept it as the best solution.

Elements of a problem-solving process

Several elements, or ingredients, must exist if a problem-solving process is to be accomplished by the manager. Naturally, there must be a *problem* and a *problem-solver* (the manager). The other ingredients are less obvious; but if any are absent, the end results are likely to be poor. All of these elements are pictured in Figure 4–1.

The solution to the problem must best enable the system to meet its

Figure 4-1   Elements of a problem-solving process

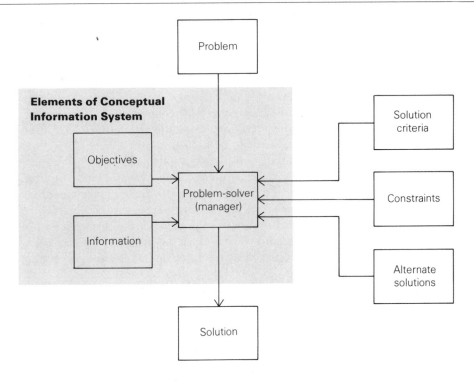

objectives. Therefore, the *objectives* must be specified clearly. These objectives describe the "desired state" the system should achieve. In addition, the manager must have available *information* that describes the "current state" of the system. If the current state and the desired state are the same, no problem exists and the manager takes no action. If the two states are different, some problem is the cause and must be solved. Perhaps there is more than one problem to be solved.

The figure indicates that the problem-solving elements of managers, objectives, and information are also the elements of the conceptual information system from the general model. In fact, these are the elements that achieve the solution. The information system is therefore a problem-solving system.

The information enables the manager to understand the problem existing within the physical system.[1] The difference between the current state of the

---

1. It is assumed that the problem does not exist within the information system. That could well be the situation; but the description here is one of how an effective information system can be used in problem solving and decision making.

system and the desired state represents the solution criterion, or what it will take to bring the current state to the desired state. For example, if the objective is to sell a minimum of 125 pairs of ski boots a day, and sales are averaging 75 pairs, the solution to the problem must be one that can increase sales by at least 50 pairs. This is the solution criterion.

It was recognized above that an important part of problem solving is the consideration of *alternate solutions*. It is the manager's responsibility to identify these alternatives and evaluate each one. Perhaps the information system can identify alternatives, or perhaps the manager uses creativity, ingenuity, and experience. Most certainly, once the alternatives have been identified, the information system can be used to evaluate each.

As the alternate solutions are considered, the manager must be aware of constraints that exist. These can be internal or environmental. *Internal constraints* are in the form of limited resources—men, money, material, machines, or information. Perhaps additional resources can be obtained to solve the problem, but there are limitations and the manager must work within them. Most often, these constraints boil down to limited finances. Some alternate solutions can be eliminated because they demand resources that are unavailable.

Environmental constraints can be just as real. Government laws may prohibit certain solutions. A whole host of laws, most on the federal level, establish constraints on practically every facet of business operation. Also, constraints applied by the other elements of the environment, such as competition, vendors, etc., can prohibit certain alternatives.

When all these elements exist, and the manager understands them, a *solution* to the problem can be realized. All problems have solutions. Some may be difficult to recognize, some may not be easy to achieve, and some might not be optimum, but they do exist.

Types of Problems

Many different kinds of problems are encountered in the day-to-day operation of a business firm. However, they can be classified into broad types, and a number of different schemes have been devised. One, that will be used here, divides problems into two categories—structured and unstructured. A *structured problem* is one that can be formulated or described very specifically. All, or most, of the elements or variables comprising the problem can be identified and their interrelationships specified. An *unstructured problem*, on the other hand, is one that cannot be adequately described in terms of its elements and their relationships.

The main reason that this classification is used here is because it lends itself to the use of an MIS for problem solving. The MIS can solve the structured problems, and can assist the manager in solving those of an unstructured nature.

Structured problems

Some problems are not too difficult to solve. If all of the factors or variables affecting the problem can be specified and quantified, the solution becomes practically automatic. (This assumes that data can be gathered and interrelated for each of the variables to provide the solution.)

Many inventory problems are of this nature. They can be reduced to mathematical expressions, data can be obtained for each of the variables, and the computations can be made. One such problem is determining the reorder point for an item in inventory. The mathematical model for this decision would be:

$$R = L \times U + S$$

> where R = reorder point (in units)
> L = vendor lead time (in days)
> U = usage rate (units per day)
> S = safety stock (in units)

When the value of this expression is computed for an item in inventory, the answer represents a decision of when a purchase order for replenishment merchandise should be prepared. For example, assume that the vendor lead time (L) for an item is 10 days. This means it takes the vendor that long to provide the firm with replacement stock after the purchase order is prepared. The firm uses, on the average, four of these items per day in its manufacturing process. This is the usage rate (U). Therefore, during the lead time period, 40 of the items will be used (4×10). If a purchase order is prepared when the quantity on hand for the item reaches 40, the quantity should reach zero just as the shipment arrives from the vendor. Since most firms don't want to cut the margin of error so thin, an extra amount, or safety stock (S), is added to the balance on hand. Assume in this case it is 10. Then, the reorder point will be 50 ($40 + 10$). When the quantity drops to this point, a purchase order will be triggered.

Figure 4–2 provides a graphical model of the structured reorder point decision. The sawtooth shape indicates how quantity on hand is gradually reduced at a rate of four units per day from the time a replenishment order is received.

A decision such as this becomes automatic, and need not involve a manager every time. Actually, a computer can make the decision. The manager is involved initially, as the problem is studied and a solution approach is selected. Once the variables (lead time, usage rate, and safety stock) are identified and their interaction (lead time $\times$ usage rate $+$ safety stock) specified, the manager need not be involved. The values can be entered into the computer, the formula executed, and the reorder point computed.

Figure 4–2   The reorder point decision

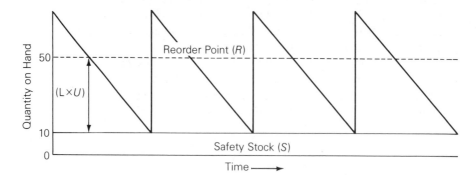

Unstructured problems

When all of the requirements for a structured problem cannot be met, the problem can be regarded as unstructured. Either all of the variables cannot be identified, or their interrelationship cannot be specified exactly. In this case the manager must solve the problem; the information system cannot do it for the manager.

An example of a problem of this type is the selection of a site for a new factory. Many variables must be considered—real estate costs, construction costs, transportation costs for shipping in raw materials, transportation costs for shipping out finished products, labor costs, and many, many more. While these costs can be quantified with assigned values, other costs are likely to be overlooked. And some variables are extremely difficult, if not impossible, to quantify. An example is the attitude of the local community toward the new plant.

While unstructured problems cannot be solved by the computer or any other calculating device, the solutions can be aided by the information system. Information pertinent to a solution can be made available to the decision maker. This information can be weighed and a solution can be reached.

An example of such a use of information is the selection of a vendor or supplier for a replenishment inventory item. Normally a firm has multiple sources for an item. Selection of a vendor involves consideration of performance factors such as item quality, ability to meet quoted delivery dates, ability to provide service, etc. This selection decision usually is not made by the information system, but is made by a person called a *buyer*. The buyer makes an inquiry of the MIS for information on all suppliers of a particular material or type of material, such as janitorial supplies. The MIS prints or displays the information and perhaps makes some quantitative comparisons. Using this information, the buyer selects the vendor for the purchase. Very often, the final selection hinges on a promise of expedited delivery or an attractive price.

The manager solving an unstructured problem does not know whether the solution is a good one until its impact can be measured. He or she does know, however, that the solution was based on the best information available. In such cases a manager can ask for, or deliver, nothing more.

As might be anticipated, the unstructured type of problem causes the manager the most difficulty. This type demands some process the manager can follow to assure that all factors influencing the decision have been considered. Such a process has been developed. It is the systems approach.

The Systems Approach

In recent years much has been written about the systems approach. In many instances there has been no attempt to explain what it is. It has been assumed that the term is self-explanatory. In those instances where definitions have been offered, they have not always agreed. All of this can be very confusing to the manager or student of business looking for a usable technique.

A sequence of steps

Most definitions refer to a sequence of steps to be followed. These steps parallel a process in the physical and behavioral sciences for conducting experiments. This process, called the *scientific method*,[2] involves:

1 Observation
2 Formulation of hypotheses
3 Prediction of what will happen in the future
4 Testing of the hypotheses

These steps have been modified to fit the task of solving business problems, and have been labeled the *systems approach*. They are:

1 Define the problem.
2 Gather data describing the problem.
3 Identify alternative solutions.
4 Evaluate the alternatives.
5 Select the best alternative.
6 Implement the solution and follow up to assure that the solution is effective.

---

2. As an example, assume that psychologists have *observed* that rats physically handled by researchers learn faster than those not handled. A *hypothesis* is formed stating that "Physical handling facilitates learning." It is *predicted* that rats handled physically will learn faster than those not enjoying such treatment. The hypothesis is *tested* by designing an experiment in which some rats receive handling, while others do not, and then evaluating the results.

Some other definitions present the systems approach in terms of analyzing a system. The manager is described as a systems analyst, first addressing the total system and then subdividing it into subsystems. This process of breaking down a problem or a system into its elemental parts is called *analysis*. Then, when the subsystems have been understood and redesigned, they are reassembled by a process known as *synthesis*.

These are the most frequent explanations of the systems approach. Which is correct, or are both correct? Are these the only interpretations, or are there others? These questions should be answered if the technique is to be considered as a means of business problem solving.

The systems approach is a formal means of problem solving. It involves a discipline or a procedure that can be learned and applied to a variety of problems. The approach efficiently uses management resources by incorporating the information processor to help identify and solve problems.

The remainder of this chapter is concerned with development of a workable understanding of the systems approach. It will be seen that the systems approach does not represent a *single* idea or process. Rather, it represents *several* key ingredients. Each of these ingredients is addressed below.

Regard the firm as a system

The manager must be able to see his or her firm as a system (Figure 4–3). This requirement must be met even though the firm is organized some special way, such as geographically, by customer type, by product, by functional area, and so on. The manager must be able to integrate mentally all of the resources so that they form a single system. This is where the general model of the firm described in Chapter 3 is used. The manager must be able to see how the model fits the firm.

Recognize the environmental system

The firm's relationship to its environment also must be seen. The environment represents a larger system, of which the firm is a subsystem. This environment, by requiring certain products and services, provides a reason for the firm's existence. The firm's objectives are geared to meeting certain of these needs.

The environment also furnishes the firm with all of the resources used in producing the products and services. The firm therefore is created from the environment. The management of the firm, performing an entrepreneural function, recognizes environmental needs to be met, acquires the resources to meet those needs, and then manages those resources.

Identify subsystems in the firm

Once the firm can be seen as a single system in a larger environmental system, it is next necessary to identify the major parts of the system. These parts are the subsystems of the firm. It is important that these subsystems work together if the systems goals are to be achieved, or to be achieved efficiently.

Figure 4–3   The manager must see the firm as a system.

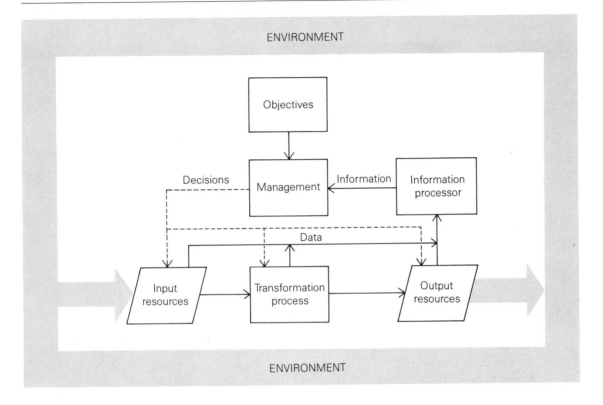

These subsystems can take several forms. Perhaps the easiest for the manager to see are the functional areas of finance, manufacturing, and marketing. Each can be regarded as a separate subsystem. Each subsystem exists on the same level within the firm; one is not superior to the others. This arrangement is shown in Figure 4–4.

The president of the firm must integrate these subsystems into a single system. To do so the president must think in systems terms. So should the vice-presidents in charge of the functional areas.

How are these subsystems integrated or connected? They are connected by the resources that flow through the firm. Here is where a systems theory of organization is used. When the manager can see how the resources must flow from one functional area to another, the necessity for an integrated system can be recognized.

Figure 4–4 is redrawn in Figure 4–5 to show some of the more important resource flows that connect the subsystems. The numbered elements in the figure are explained as follows:

1 The marketing subsystem gets information from the environment that describes needs for products and services.

Figure 4–4   Functional subsystems in the firm

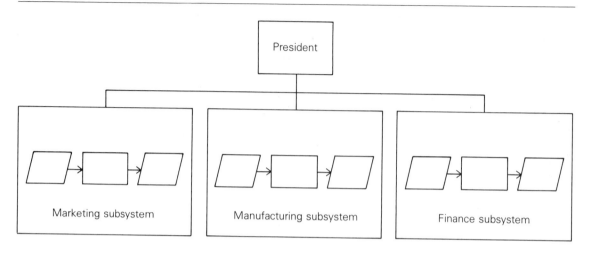

2 This information is transmitted to the other functional subsystems so they can determine what the firm must produce if the needs are to be met.

3 The finance subsystem obtains money from the environment and makes it available to the manufacturing and marketing subsystems so they may perform their functions.

4 The manufacturing subsystem transforms raw material resources into finished goods.

5 These goods then are distributed to customers by the marketing subsystem.

This functional orientation to subsystems also has influenced the design of information systems. Firms have developed financial information systems, manufacturing information systems, and marketing information systems. These are described in Part 4 of the book.

The manager also can regard the levels of management as subsystems. This concept is pictured in Figure 4–6. Here the subsystems have a superior-subordinate relationship and are connected by information flows. The top management, on the strategic level, makes decisions that filter down through the organization. These decisions enable the organization to meet its objectives. Information flows up through the organization from the operational level where the firm creates the products and services for the environment. When the manager sees the firm arranged in this manner, the importance of information flows is emphasized. Without these flows, upper level management is cut off from the physical system of the firm.

While this book does not describe information systems by management level, the practice is not uncommon. The literature of business frequently

Figure 4–5 Interaction of functional subsystems in the firm

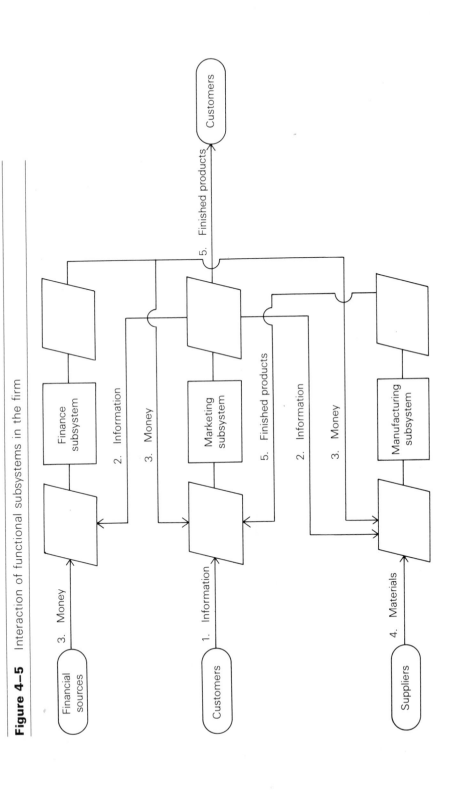

Figure 4–6   Management levels as subsystems

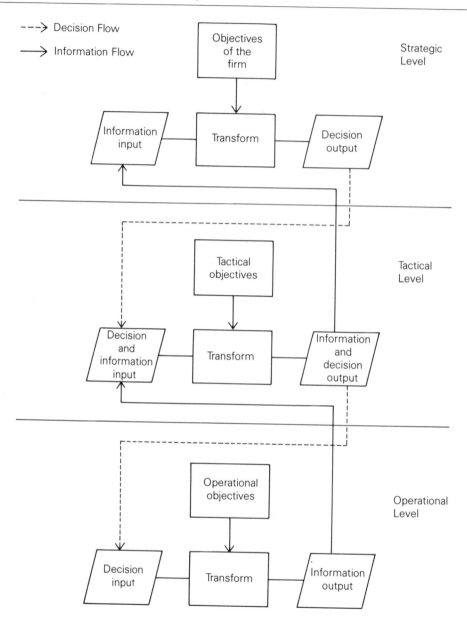

refers to strategic level information systems, tactical level information systems, and so on.

The reader must recognize that Figure 4–6 in its simplified form fails to illustrate two key points about information flow. First, it is not necessary that the information flow up through the tactical level to get to the strategic level.

The strategic level can get information directly from the operational level. Second, only internal information is shown. Management on all three levels must make use of environmental information as well.

Proceed from system to subsystem level

As the manager attempts to understand how the firm is performing, the analysis should begin with the top system, or supersystem, and proceed level by level to the lower ones. The analysis proceeds from the supersystem to the system and then to the subsystem level. The manager conducts this analysis when seeking solutions to either existing or potential problems.

The first level to occupy the manager's attention is the environmental level. The manager must know what elements exist within the environment and how they relate to the firm. Emphasis must be placed on what resources are provided and what constraints or restrictions are imposed by the environment.

There are many ways of looking at the environment. One is to identify eight separate members or elements, as shown in Figure 4–7.[3] Each element is actually a subsystem within a larger system called *society*.

The *vendors* supply the materials used by the firm to produce goods and services for the *customers*. *Labor* provides the manpower resources, and the *financial community* provides the money resources, as do the *stockholders or owners*. *Competition* provides a constraint on what the firm does and often serves as a motivating force to better meet the needs of the environment. The *government*, on the federal, state, and local levels, also provides constraints; it can also assist the firm by buying products and services, providing information, and providing research and development funds. In recent years the *local community* has assumed a bigger role in this environmental system. The firm has responsibilities to this community, such as by using antipollution and safety measures and by contributions to charitable and civic programs.

Just as resource flows connect the internal subsystems of the firm, they also connect the firm with the other environmental elements. All types of resources flow between the firm and the elements, and in both directions. Some flows are more frequent than others. Material flow to customers, money flow to stockholders, machine flow from vendors, and manpower flow from labor are all of a primary nature. Other flows such as money flow from the government (for research, as an example), material flow to vendors (for returned merchandise), and manpower flow to competition (for employees "pirated" by other firms)—all exist, even if on a secondary level.

All resources do not flow between the firm and all elements. For example, machines normally do not flow from the firm to the stockholders; money

---

3. This particular structure for the environmental system is based on that described by Richard J. Hopeman in his book *Systems Analysis and Operations Management*, published by the Charles E. Merrill Publishing Company, Columbus, Ohio, in 1969.

Figure 4–7   Elements in the environment of the firm

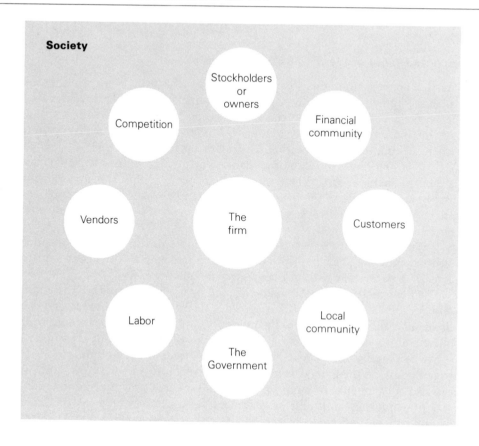

should not flow to competitors, nor should material flow to labor. The only resource that conceivably can connect the firm with all of the elements is information. It doesn't always flow in both directions, however. The firm should not furnish its competition with information. But information can be used by the firm to understand its relationship with each element. As within the firm, the information flow represents physical conditions that exist. It is important that the manager understand these conditions.

An understanding of the resource flows is complicated by the influence that one environmental element can have on another. An element can have an indirect influence on the firm, often as effective as the direct. An example is a strike by organized labor against a vendor, resulting in a lack of needed materials. The firm might have to shut down its manufacturing process. The result is as serious as if the firm's own factory workers went on strike. Similar indirect influences can be identified that involve competition, the government, the financial community, and the local community.

Analyze system parts in a certain sequence

After studying the environment, the manager focuses his or her attention on the firm. Is the firm meeting its responsibilities to the environment? If not, what part is defective? To answer this question, the manager must examine each part. This process can be expedited when the parts are examined in a logical sequence, as shown in Figure 4–8. The following steps correspond to the numbered blocks in the figure.

1 Evaluate objectives. The objectives provide the starting point. First, does the firm have objectives and are they current? If not, work must be performed to develop objectives before proceeding further. The firm must have objectives.

The firm's objectives must possess certain characteristics. They must be *valid*. That is, they must be a good measure of system performance. For example, high sales volume is not a valid objective if the real goal is to maximize profits. Perhaps maximum profits can be achieved at low volumes. The objectives also must be *realistic*. A 20 percent increase in sales is not very realistic if it never before has been achieved and there is nothing to warrant such optimism. In addition, objectives must be *understandable* to those who are expected to meet them. And, finally, the objectives should be *measurable*. If the objective is to "maximize profits," the manager never knows if it has been achieved. "Realize a profit of 10 percent of sales" is the type of objective that leaves no doubt about its degree of attainment.

2 Compare output with objectives. When the manager is satisfied with the objectives, the performance of the firm next is evaluated. First, the output of the firm is compared with the objectives (Figure 4–9).

Figure 4–8   Each part of the system is analyzed in sequence.

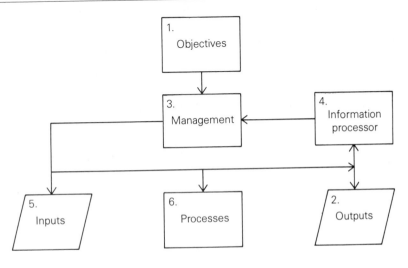

If the firm is meeting its objectives, there is no need to continue with the systems approach to problem solution. There is no problem to solve. The manager can reevaluate the objectives in light of the good current performance. Perhaps this performance level can be increased in the future.

If the firm is not meeting its objectives—in all or in part—the manager must identify the cause or causes. A problem exists that must be solved. The remaining system elements are possible locations of the problem or problems.

3 *Evaluate management.* A critical appraisal is made of the firm's management. Are there adequate numbers of managers in the different areas and on the different levels? The signals that indicate this as a problem include excessively long hours worked by managers, and projects that never get completed.

The quality of the management team also must pass inspection. Do the managers have the skills and experience needed to perform their duties? Errors in judgment, excessive costs, and high employee turnover are signals that management quality might not be satisfactory.

4 *Evaluate the information processor.* It is possible that a good management team is present, but the team simply is not getting the information it needs. If this is the case, the needs must be identified and an adequate information system designed and implemented. This development process is the subject of Part 5 of this book.

5 *Evaluate the firm's resources.* The management resource already has been evaluated. When this level of the system analysis is reached, the adequacy of the management resource is no longer a question. But what about the rest of the employees? Does the firm have the right number of employees, and do they have the right skills? And what about the machine and material resources? Are they adequate? What about money? Is enough money available for the firm to obtain the physical resources it needs to meet its objectives?

Some compromise may be necessary here. Some resources may not exist in the quantities and qualities desired. Even if this is true, these limitations may be overcome through good management. If so, the objectives remain unchanged. If this is unrealistic, the objectives should be modified to match the resources available.[4]

At this point, the organization structure of the firm also can be assessed. Has management assembled the resources in an effective manner? Are the resources functioning as an efficient physical system? A good knowledge of organization theory, as described in Chapter 2, facilitates this portion of the analysis.

---

4. Modification of objectives requires that the analysis revert back to step 2 to compare the system outputs to the revised objectives.

Figure 4–9   Problem identification and system analysis

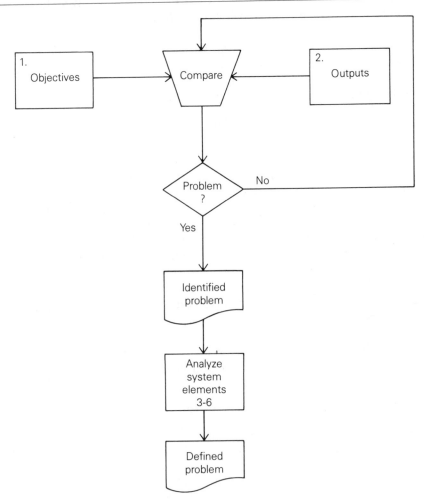

6 *Evaluate the transformation process.* It is possible that the problem lies within the physical system—how the resources are used. Inefficient procedures and practices might be the cause.

Performing the analysis

Step 1 above is conducted when a firm is formed and objectives are established. It also is conducted when there is a question about the adequacy of the objectives. As a minimum, step 1 should be done annually. Ideally, it should be a quarterly activity.

Step 2 can be a day-to-day activity of management. How well is the firm meeting its objectives? This question always should be on the minds of the managers. The information system answers this question easily and quickly. Current and accurate information describing the firm's performance should be at the manager's fingertips.

When the firm is not meeting its objectives, steps 3 through 6 are followed in sequence. When a problem is encountered, it is solved or at least specifically defined before continuing.

If the analysis of the firm as a system indicates problems, they most likely will be solved on the subsystem level. It next is necessary to analyze selected subsystems in the same manner as the firm was studied.

Take, for example, a firm that is having problems with its smaller customers. The information system reports that these customers are not buying as much as expected. Evaluation of the resources of the firm (step 5) indicates a shortage of trained salespersons. The manager then shifts attention to the marketing subsystem of the firm. Steps 1 through 6 are repeated as they apply to that subsystem. This analysis of systems on successively lower levels is followed until the problem is identified and defined completely.

Because the business system is so complex, it is doubtful that any manager will conduct all the analyses alone. He or she probably will lack both the specialized skills and the time required for detailed study. For these reasons specialists frequently are employed to assist the manager. General management consultants can be used at any point in the analysis but are especially effective in evaluating objectives, management, organization, and resources. Information specialists and auditors help in evaluating the MIS; industrial engineers study the efficiency of the transformation processes.

A general model of system evaluation

While it is neither possible nor advisable to present a list of steps to be followed in solving any kind of business problem, there is some value in understanding a general approach. A general model of system evaluation can be built, and one is illustrated in Figure 4–10. It is a logic diagram showing the main decision points (the diamonds) and the problem-solving activity of the manager (the rectangles). The decisions reflect whether or not certain predefined conditions do (Y = yes) or do not (N = no) exist. Once one part of the system has been evaluated and the problem solved (if one exists), the manager directs attention to the next part. This procedure assures that the total system is studied and *all* defective parts are corrected.

The model includes three types of activity that must be performed by the manager: preliminary, monitoring, and problem identification. Before a system can be analyzed, it must have clearly defined objectives. This determination is the preliminary activity. Once these objectives have been established, the manager can monitor how well they are being met. This approach requires an information system that can report the firm's output for comparison with the objectives. When a problem situation is detected, the remaining steps identify the part, or parts, of the system causing the problem.

Figure 4–10   General model of analysis of system elements

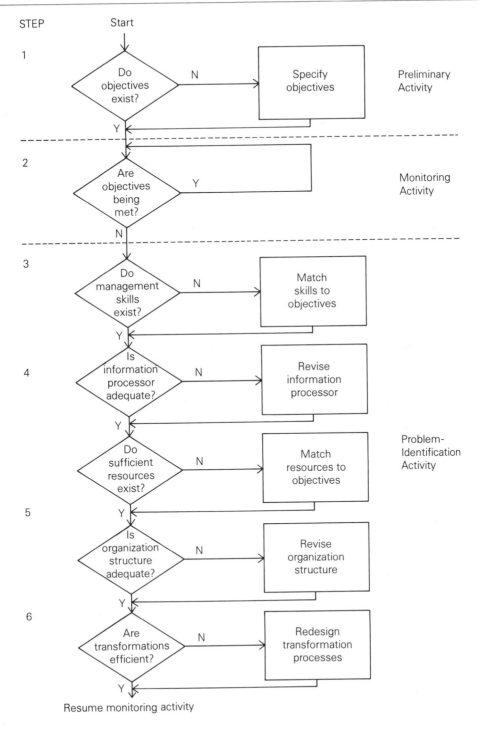

The process of analyzing a system to identify causes of problems is an orderly, sequential one. Each part must check out before proceeding to the next. When a part is found defective, it is analyzed further. This can lead to an analysis of the subsystems of the system.

Evaluate alternative solutions

The diamonds in the general model of the analysis process represent decisions the manager must make in identifying the causes of the problem. The rectangles represent what the manager does to solve the problem once it has been identified and defined. This problem-solving activity also involves decision making. The manager must decide among several possible solutions. This consideration of alternatives is an important part of the systems approach. All feasible alternative solutions first must be identified. They must then be evaluated.

Identification of alternatives is not always easy. This is where experience comes into play. An experienced manager has a good understanding of the alternatives based on the solution of previous similar problems. A new manager must overcome this lack of an adequate experience base by devoting time to a concentrated study of the system.

Certainly, experience is not the only key to alternative identification. Intelligence, creativity, and ingenuity also help. But a good understanding of the system based on experience is valuable.

In some instances the information system can identify the alternatives for the manager. This was seen earlier when the information system identified suppliers to be considered for purchase of replenishment stock.

Once identified, the evaluation process involves subjecting each to tests of some type. The tests measure how well each alternative enables the system to meet its objectives. Cost-benefit analyses are used for this purpose; the alternative that offers the most benefits at the least cost is easily the winner (Figure 4–11). Many times, however, the decision is not so clear-cut. The alternative offering the most benefits may be the most expensive. But, if the objectives of the system have been spelled out with exactness, even these difficult decisions can be made effectively.

As each alternative is evaluated, both the strong and weak points must be identified. The weak points relate to the system objectives. In one way or another they make achievement of the objectives difficult. All alternatives will have certain of these weaknesses. They should be recognized, and no attempt made to cover them up. The best alternative will have the least weaknesses, or the greatest strengths, or some ideal combination.

Once the best solution has been selected, it must be implemented. This, too, is part of the manager's responsibility. The manager must solve the problem, and it is not solved until the system is meeting its objectives. The manager must stick with the problem solution until this is achieved—in other words, until those objectives are being met.

Figure 4–11   Decision making identifies and evaluates alternatives and selects the best.

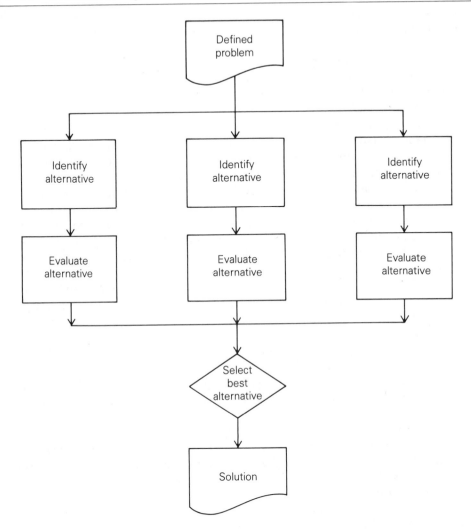

Key ingredients of the systems approach

It was pointed out earlier that there is a great deal of variation in how the systems approach is defined. The discussion just completed reveals that there is more than one key ingredient to the concept.

In most cases, the systems approach has been defined in terms of six steps:

1 Define the problem.
2 Gather data describing the problem.

3 Identify alternative solutions.
4 Evaluate the alternatives.
5 Select the best alternative.
6 Implement the solution and follow up to assure that the solution is effective.

The definition usually does not show how these steps are taken on different system levels, as does this chapter. As each level is studied, a procedure is followed for defining the problem (step 1) by focusing on each of the six system parts.

As soon as the problem is defined, it is necessary to gather data describing the problem (step 2). This data-gathering activity usually requires that lower level systems be studied. These subsystems are studied in the same manner. Each of the six elements is studied in sequence.

As soon as the problem is understood on all system levels, the problem-solving process begins. Problem solution encompasses steps 3 through 6 above.

The first two steps of the systems approach are devoted to *problem understanding*. This is one of the two essential ingredients of the systems approach. The problem must be understood before any work is attempted to solve it.

The last four steps are devoted to problem solution. In solving the problem, it is important to *identify and evaluate alternatives*. This is the second key ingredient.

Systems approach example

An example of the use of the systems approach should help develop an understanding of the concept and an appreciation for the variety of problems it can solve.

Assume that a college has just hired a new baseball coach. He must decide if he has any problems. If he thinks in system terms, he views his baseball squad as a *system*. He recognizes his squad is a part of an *environment*—a college baseball conference with several teams competing for the championship.

With this systems orientation, the coach identifies *subsystems* within the squad. He divides his players into categories based on their skills—pitchers, catchers, infielders, and outfielders. The coach knows that all of these subsystems must work together to win ball games.

The coach then follows a step-by-step procedure for identifying and solving his problems. The team as a system is studied in terms of its six elements. The *system parts are analyzed in sequence*.

1. *Objectives.* The coach understands his objective. It was spelled out to him very clearly when he was hired by the athletic director. The coach's objective, and that of the team, is to "win the championship next year."

2. *System outputs.* The coach then compares the outputs of the system to the objectives. The past performance of the team is studied. Three seasons

ago, the team finished third. For the past two years, the team has finished second. The team is on the right track, but something is keeping it from winning the championship. This is a problem and it must be solved.

3. *Management.* The coach recognizes himself and his staff as the management of the system. He is satisfied that they are capable of doing whatever is necessary to win.

4. *Information processor.* The coach knows that lack of information is not a problem. The team has two student statisticians, and one of the assistant coaches prepares excellent scouting reports on opposing teams. There is no shortage of information.

5. *Input resources.* At this point, the coach realizes a possible cause of the problem. There is a shortage of certain resources. In the past, the team hasn't had an adequate pitching staff (one of the subsystems). He gathers data on the returning pitchers and identifies his needs for next year—a left-handed starting pitcher and a good relief pitcher.

6. *Transformation processes.* The rest of the team possesses the desired skills and experience to play winning baseball. There is no problem with the ability of the players to transform their skills into a first-place team.

At this point, the problem is defined and understood. The coach needs to bolster his pitching staff with a good lefty and a good reliever. The coach has taken the first two of the six systems approach steps: *define the problem* and *gather data*. What remains is a problem solution. He must take the remaining four steps.

He proceeds to *identify the alternative solutions*. There are two. He can recruit pitchers from high schools, or he can recruit them from community colleges.

The next step is to *evaluate the alternatives*. The coach examines the good and bad points of each. If he recruits high school players, he has them for four years, but they might take one or two years to get the seasoning they need. On the other hand, community college transfers are already seasoned, but they have only two years of eligibility.

The coach must now *select the best alternative*. This is the one that best enables the system to meet its objectives. Since the objective is to win as soon as possible, the community college route is followed. It offers the fastest payoff.

The final step is to *implement the solution and follow up*. Community college pitchers are recruited and their performance studied as the team competes for the championship.

Summary

The information system solves structured problems for the manager and assists the manager in solving the unstructured variety. A procedure has been developed for use in solving unstructured problems; it is the systems approach.

From the discussion, it can be seen that the systems approach is not a simple idea. But neither is it overly complex. It is logical and straightforward. In fact, some have said that the systems approach is nothing more than "good management."

The systems approach is more than a series of steps to be followed in an automatic, robot-like manner. First, the systems approach is a way of thinking. It is based on the idea of the firm as a system. The system must be seen as existing in an environment, striving to meet objectives, and consisting of subsystems.

The manager must recognize this hierarchy of system levels. The highest system level is the environment. The manager must understand the environment and how it affects the firm. What does the environment expect from the firm? And, in turn, what does the firm expect from the environment? The manager studies the environment with this purpose of understanding. Since the firm rarely has any control over its environment, problems encountered on this level rarely can be solved here. It is necessary to adapt the firm to work within the environmental limitations and constraints.

A critical, problem-seeking approach is followed on the next lower system level—that of the firm. Here, the six elements of the system are studied in sequence. Comparison of systems output with objectives reveals the existence of any problems. The remaining four elements are studied to determine possible causes of the problems.

When an element is found to be defective, the process shifts from problem definition to problem solution. Alternative solutions are identified and evaluated. The solution best enabling the system to meet its objectives is selected and implemented. Follow-up action evaluates the success or failure of the decision and its implementation.

This is the systems approach. It represents a powerful method for problem solution and decision making. The modern manager skilled in the use of the approach can make decisions in the best interests of the firm. Such decisions permit the firm to continue to meet its responsibilities to its environment in the form of products, services, and profits.

Important Terms

Problem Solving	Unstructured Problem
Decision Making	Systems Approach
Constraint	Analysis
Solution Criteria	Synthesis
Structured Problem	

Important Concepts

Problem solving and decision making are different processes. Decisions are made to solve problems.

The conceptual information system is a problem-solving system.

Some problems are structured in that the elements and their relationships are known and understood. Some problems are unstructured.

A firm can be subdivided into vertical subsystems based on management levels, and subdivided into horizontal subsystems based on units such as functional areas.

The systems approach consists of several integrated problem-solving techniques.

The firm's environment consists of various elements; the firm is connected to the elements by resource flows.

A system can be analyzed most efficiently when the elements are addressed in a particular sequence.

Questions

1 Is the importance of a decision based on the time the manager spends in making it? Why?

2 What determines success or failure of a firm?

3 Do managers solve problems in the process of making decisions or make decisions in the process of solving problems? Explain.

4 Who is the problem solver in a firm? Is amount of compensation (pay) related in any way to problem solving? How?

5 What elements in the general systems model of the firm are used to solve problems?

6 Does a problem exist when the current state of the system is the same as the desired state? Does a problem exist when they are different? How does the concept of management by exception relate to the current and desired state?

7 Who imposes constraints on the problem-solving processes of a firm?

8 What determines whether a problem is structured or unstructured?

9 Can a generalization be made as to whether it is the manager or the computer that solves a problem depending on whether the problem is structured or unstructured? Explain.

10 How can a systems theory of management and organization (from Chapter 2) and the general systems model of the firm (from Chapter 3) be used in the systems approach?

11 In what sequence are the following systems studied when the systems approach is followed?

Subsystems of the firm
The firm as a system
The environment of the firm

12 Does information flow directly from the operational to the strategic level, or does the information flow through the tactical level?

13 Do decisions flow directly from the strategic to the operational level, or do the decisions flow through the tactical level?

14 What is considered to be included in the "local community" as an element in the environment of the firm?

15 What elements of a system are first addressed when the manager seeks to evaluate system performance?

16 Name three characteristics of system objectives.

17 Who can help the manager evaluate (1) system objectives, (2) management, (3) the information processor, and (4) transformation processes?

18 How many alternatives should be evaluated before selecting the best?

19 Is a disadvantage of one alternative always offset with an advantage of another, and vice versa? Explain.

Problems

1 One problem facing college students is how to make good grades. Is this a structured or unstructured problem? Can you identify the key elements in the grading process and describe how they interrelate?

2 Draw a graphical model showing the subsystems of your college arranged horizontally. Now, draw a diagram showing vertically arranged subsystems.

3 Using the names *material, manpower, money, machines,* and *information,* label the arrows connecting the firm to its environment on page 103. *Hint:* Some arrows can have more than one name.

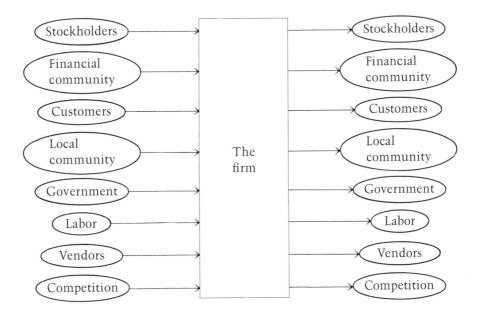

4 You have been working for 3 weeks as assistant to the computer operations manager for a large bank. One day your boss says, "I believe that there are better ways of keeping our managers informed, other than by periodic printed reports. I want you to give me a list of alternatives I might consider." How would you go about making up such a list? Don't be concerned with identifying the alternatives—just determine how to prepare the list in the best way.

Part Three

The Computer

It was stated earlier that a firm need not have a computer to have an information system. Most of the material presented in the first four chapters applies to any kind of information system, whether it be manual, key-driven machine, punched card, or computer. However, the book deals mainly with computer-based management information systems, and the computer plays an important role in the remainder of the chapters. The computer does not play the most important role—that role must be played by the manager. The manager is the most important element in the information system. The manager not only uses the information output, but also participates in the design and implementation of the system.

If the manager is to perform these duties effectively, he or she must have a good understanding of the role played by the computer in the information system. The purpose of this part is to provide that understanding.

The information specialists assisting the manager must likewise have an understanding—an even greater one. These computer professionals must provide the expertise in design and use of computer-based information systems that the manager cannot be expected to possess.

This third part of the book provides an introduction to the computer that will enable both the manager and the specialist to understand what the information system is, what it does, and how it is developed.

Chapter 5 presents some basic information on computers—how they developed, how they relate to other ways of processing data, basic configurations, and so on.

The topic of Part Three is more than simply *the computer*. The topic is the computer system. A large number of devices can be interconnected to form a computer *system*. Chapter 6 describes devices used to get data into the computer and information out of it. Chapter 7 presents methods of storing data and using that data for information processing. Chapter 8 explains how data is communicated from one location to another.

The part is concluded with a presentation of how the computer is used in business problem solving. That discussion, in Chapter 9, combines material presented earlier in Part Three, relating to computing equipment.

Chapter 5

Introduction to the Computer

The electronic computer is a modern invention. It appeared in a rather crude form during the Second World War, and was introduced to business applications in the mid-1950s. Yet its impact on our way of life was so marked, and achieved so rapidly, that the 1960s heralded what many called "the computer age." The computer has assumed such a position of importance that our business system, our government, and our social institutions could not function without it. The computer is a powerful tool that enables a wide variety of jobs to be performed faster, and better, than by any other method. Without the computer, Neil Armstrong would not have walked on the moon; nor could companies offer the wide range of products and services we use every day, or hospitals offer the quality medical services to which we have become accustomed.

It is only fair to point out, however, that there are unsuccessful computer applications. In some cases the computer has been applied to inappropriate tasks. In other cases the efforts of the people implementing the computer have been prone to error.

Even so, it is safe to say that the electronic computer has become a necessity. We could not exist without it. The computer, however, is not the only way to process data—it is only the most powerful and effective way devised by man. Other ways, or methods, are still very important. In fact, more data are processed by these other methods than by the computer. Before the computer becomes the main subject of discussion, the noncomputer methods of processing data will be reviewed briefly.

Noncomputerized Systems

The most sophisticated computer is not the electronic variety; it is the human brain. The brain monitors and controls the most complex of the physical systems—the human body. In monitoring the conditions of the body, the brain functions as an *analog computer*. An analog is something that is similar to something else; it is a conceptual representation of some physical thing. The brain monitors the body by using physical inputs to represent the state of the body. Heart beat, pulse rate, body temperature, and other signals convey the condition of the body to the brain so that changes to the physical system can be made. When the need for changes is recognized by the brain, other physical signals are sent out that result in faster breathing, perspiration, rest, sleep, etc.

Electronic computers also serve as analog control devices. They monitor the condition of electrical power plants, paper mills, and oil refineries. But, even though these computer applications are elaborate, their precision does not match the precision with which the brain monitors and controls the human body.

The brain also functions in another capacity. It solves problems by processing data stored in the brain or captured by the sensory perceptors. When the brain performs in this manner it functions as a type of *digital computer*. Scientists still do not know how data is stored in the brain, but such data is used to solve problems of a digital, or numeric, nature. Algebra problems can be solved, as can problems dealing with household budgets, selection of TV channels, and mixing drinks.

Electronic computers have become most well-known as digital devices. But, only a very narrow range of digital problems has been solved by the electronic computer as compared to the human brain. And electronic computers have made little progress toward solution of nondigital problems—an area where the human brain excels.

Manual systems

The human brain, therefore, is a powerful computer that can be applied to business problems. This application is made every day in every organization. A system employing human processing using only pencil and paper is a *manual system*. There are no labor-saving devices of a mechanical nature. The human does all the work.

In all probability, more data is processed manually than any other way. This is because every person is a functioning manual processor. The jobs performed manually are usually of a low-volume, nontechnical, infrequent nature. When the amount of manual processing becomes significant, mechanical or electronic devices are applied.

Keydriven systems

The first devices applied to reduce the manual processing workload were mechanical and keydriven. Mechanical parts work together, frequently powered by an electrical motor, and they function as a mechanical or an electromechanical system. These systems are controlled by depressing certain keys.

The most well-known of these systems is the *typewriter*. First developed in the late 1800s as a manual device, it has been continually improved with electric power and computer-age components. Its low cost, combined with its

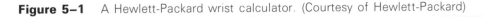

Figure 5–1   A Hewlett-Packard wrist calculator. (Courtesy of Hewlett-Packard)

flexibility and high quality output, makes the typewriter the most popular printing device in business today.

Other keydriven systems have been developed to solve digital problems; *adding machines* add and subtract, while *calculators* also multiply and divide. Data is entered through keyboards, and answers are displayed on dials or rolls of paper. Modern forms of these machines, such as the *pocket calculator*, use computer-age circuitry and display output electronically. The calculator is a good example of how the economies of computer technology have been applied in a wide range of products, including keydriven machines.

The most sophisticated of the electronic calculators is probably the Hewlett-Packard wrist calculator (Figure 5–1). With this device, calculating power always is within fingertip range. Dick Tracy, with his wrist radio, never had it so good.

As the scale of business increased, a need was seen also for an electromechanical system that would combine the printing ability of the typewriter with the arithmetic ability of the calculator. These machines, called *billing*, *posting*, and *accounting machines* (see Figure 5–2), were very popular for a 20 or 30 year period ending about 1960. They are in use today with modern components, but usually handle specialized jobs in smaller organizations.

Figure 5-2   A modern keydriven billing machine. (Courtesy of The Burroughs Corporation)

Punched card systems

A third basic approach to data processing was developed shortly before the turn of the century by Dr. Herman Hollerith, a Buffalo, New York, statistician. Dr. Hollerith invented a group of machines that could process data punched into cards. These machines were used first by the Bureau of the Census in 1890.

In 1912, the rights to Dr. Hollerith's machines were acquired by a company that would later become International Business Machines, or simply IBM. The IBM organization, under the leadership of its founder, Thomas J. Watson, Sr., became a worldwide giant in manufacturing and marketing punched card systems. These systems enjoyed their heyday from the mid-1920s to the mid-1950s, and represented the best way to process large volumes of data.

The basic principle underlying the punched card approach is that data can be punched into cards, and the data from these cards then can be processed over and over by different machines. The data need only be entered a single time, and subsequent processing becomes mechanized. The basic benefits of speed, accuracy, and flexibility have, for the most part, been eclipsed by those of computer systems. However, a number of punched card installations still exist.

Figure 5–3 A punched card used in IBM System/3. (Courtesy of International Business Machines)

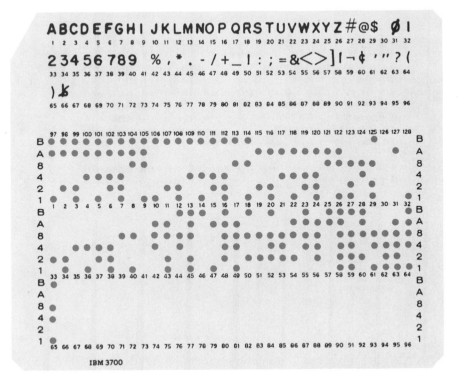

The data is represented in the card by holes punched in certain patterns. Each pattern represents a number, letter, or special symbol. A single card can contain up to 96 characters. A 96-column card used in a punched card system introduced by IBM in 1969, the System/3, is shown in Figure 5–3.

The most common card developed for use in IBM punched card machines is the 80-column card (Figure 5–4). This card is important today, not because of its use with punched card systems, but because it is the most popular way of entering data into a computer.

Processing data punched into cards requires three steps:

1 Record the data.
2 Arrange the data.
3 Process the data.

The data is *recorded* with a keypunch machine (Figure 5–5). The operation of the keypunch is very similar to that of the typewriter. A key is depressed for each character punched in the card.

The cards are then *arranged* with a sorter (Figure 5–6). The cards can be

Figure 5–4   An 80-column punched card. (Courtesy of International Business Machines)

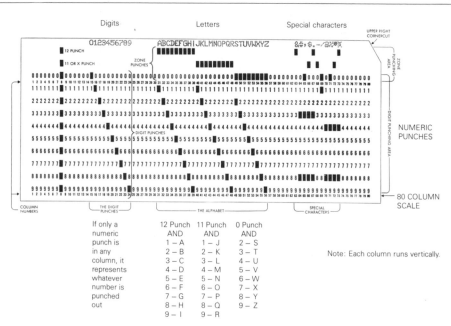

sorted in either alphabetic or numeric sequences at speeds up to 2000 cards per minute.

After the cards have been arranged, they are *processed* by machines that make calculations and print reports. The accounting machine, pictured in Figure 5–7, can add and subtract, and print many different types of documents. A number of other types of machines are used for other, more specialized, processing.

The sorter and the accounting machine have been largely replaced by computer processing. Only the keypunch machine remains widely used as a creator of computer input. Two other punched card machines are also frequently found in a computer installation. The *verifier* confirms the accuracy of cards prepared on the keypunch; the *interpreter* prints characters at the top of cards punched by the computer.

These three noncomputer systems (manual, keydriven, and punched card) have been used more as data processing systems than as information systems. In a data processing system, data is entered into the processor, and more data is generated as output. An example is a billing operation by the telephone company. Customer usage data is used to calculate charges and bills are then prepared. The company prepares thousands of these bills each month. To the telephone company the output is only data. It has no informative content to the management. If the managers want information about the billing operation, they do not get it by sifting through the bills.

Figure 5-5   A keypunch machine. (Courtesy of International Business Machines)

It is not impossible to produce information with these noncomputer systems. They *can* be used as information systems, but that application has not been emphasized. It is much easier to use a computer as an information system, although that has not always been done.

Computerized Systems

For the first few years of its use, the computer simply provided another way of doing the same jobs that had been done previously by the other approaches. Later, it was seen that the computer also could function as an *information processing system*. In an information processing system, data is entered into the processor and information is generated as output.

Figure 5–6   A punched-card sorter. (Courtesy of Sperry Univac)

Brief history

No single person can be given credit for inventing the computer. The origin can be traced back as far as hundreds or thousands of years, and many people made significant contributions.[1]

The first calculating device was probably the *abacus.* This wooden frame with numbers represented by beads originated in the Near East and China about 2000 years ago. It is still being used in many parts of Asia.

---

1. This historical review is based largely on *More About Computers,* IBM publication 505-0020-3, 1974, and *The Computer Age,* IBM publication G-505-0029, 1976.

Figure 5–7   A punched-card accounting machine. (Courtesy of International Business Machines)

In the seventeenth century two developments occurred that can be considered the first efforts to mechanize the processing of data. Blaise Pascal, a French mathematician, built a unit containing rachetlike wheels that could add numbers entered in dials. At the time, 1642, Pascal was only 19 years old. Then, in 1694, Gottfried Wilhelm Leibniz built a machine that could multiply and divide.

During the nineteenth century three additional accomplishments further laid the groundwork for the modern computer. In 1804, Joseph Marie Jacquard built a weaving loom that was controlled by holes punched in long paper rolls. An Englishman, Charles Babbage, applied the idea of punched card control to a machine very similar in architecture to modern computers. This machine, called the *analytical engine*, was to be powered by steam and controlled by instructions punched into cards. Although it never was built, the analytical engine was the first step toward a general-purpose computing system. It was left to Dr. Hollerith to produce devices (his punched card machines) to process large volumes of data mechanically. Although the Hollerith machines had neither the capacity nor logical ability demanded of computing equipment, they marked a milestone in efforts to build devices to solve complex data problems.

During the Second World War, a Harvard professor, Howard H. Aiken, constructed a computing system called Mark I. Mark I consisted of 78 devices weighing 5 tons, and containing 500 miles of wire and 3304 electromechanical relays. Controlled by instructions punched in paper tape, Mark I could multiply two 23-digit numbers in about 6 seconds. Parts of the original machine are on display at the Smithsonian Institution.

Mark I can be regarded as the first program-controlled computer, but it was not electronic. The distinction of developing the first *electronic computer* was to go to J. Presper Eckert and Dr. John W. Mauchly of the University of Pennsylvania. They replaced electromechanical components with vacuum tubes that could be flipped on and off like switches by electronic pulses. Their system, called ENIAC (*Electronic Numerical Integrator and Calculator*), was completed in 1946.

One contribution was needed to prepare the way for what has become the modern computer. A method had to be devised to facilitate the use of extremely large sets of instructions for control. It was left to Dr. John von Neumann to suggest, in 1945, that these instructions be stored inside the computer, along with the data. This was the idea of the *stored program computer*.

It took the manufacturers of data processing machines several years to develop working models of the electronic stored program computer system. By the mid-1950s, IBM, Sperry Rand, National Cash Register, Burroughs, and others were manufacturing and marketing the first commercially available computers. The circuitry of these first systems was composed of electronic vacuum tubes—the approach taken by Eckert and Mauchly. The computers produced until 1958 were of this type and have been labeled the *first generation* of computers.

In 1958 the first transistorized computer appeared—the Univac Solid State 80 and 90 systems. The first transistors were much larger than today, but were only 1/200 the size of a vacuum tube. They permitted faster operations, were more reliable, and generated less heat than the tubes. Computers produced between 1958 and 1965 used transistors and were designated the *second generation*.

In April 1965, IBM announced its line of System/360 computers. They were identified as the beginning of the *third generation*, as they replaced the larger transistors with solid logic technology (SLT). SLT permitted the integration of tiny transistors (28/1000 inch square) on half-inch ceramic modules. These *integrated circuits*, as they were called, could switch on and off in six-billionths of a second and could operate for an average of 33 million hours without failure. Figure 5–8 shows the first three generations of computer circuitry.

Figure 5–8   Three generations of computer circuitry. (Courtesy of International Business Machines)
  a. First generation
  b. Second generation
  c. Third generation

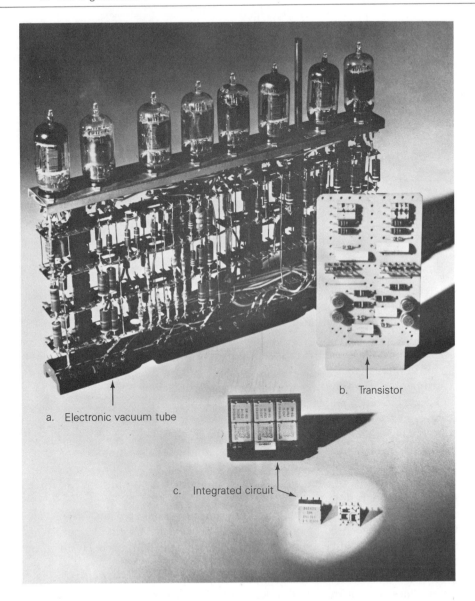

a. Electronic vacuum tube

b. Transistor

c. Integrated circuit

Computer innovations since 1964 have been less dramatic. There is less certainty that present computers comprise the *fourth generation*, although they are significantly improved over those of the late 1960s. Major breakthroughs have been (1) the use of "monolithics" (transistors and circuits integrated onto minute silicon chips) instead of magnetized materials to store

"Of course it's only the basic system."   © DATAMATION®

data, (2) the development of sophisticated control units for input/output devices that assume some of the workload of the central processing unit, and (3) improved input and output devices such as nonimpact printers, point of sale (POS) terminals, and programmable "intelligent" terminals.

Possibly, the most dramatic recent breakthrough in computer technology is the development of a new type of chip storage. In August 1978, Texas Instruments (TI) announced availability of a "bubble" memory. This memory is expected to offer greater capacity at less cost than current main and auxiliary storage media.

Bubble memory, discovered 10 years before the TI announcement by Bell Laboratories, offers more capacity than semiconductor chip memories. Sixteen times as much data can be stored in the same area. As many as 287,000 tiny magnetic domains, or "bubbles," can be contained on a chip that is three-tenths of an inch square.

Since TI has its own line of computers and supplies many of the electronic components used by other computer manufacturers, the impact of this announcement could be dramatic. Only time will tell whether this innovation heralds a new computer generation.

The absence of a clear-cut entrance into a fourth generation of computers does not mean that development has stagnated. The less dramatic nature of the developments means that a high level of sophistication has been achieved in computer design. This is of great value to the computer user. There is no longer the general fear that the firm's computer will be obsoleted before it is installed, as was the case in the early generations. Today's computers are *modular*, in that a firm can increase the size without the need to rewrite all of

Table 5–1   Technological improvements bring increased user benefits[1]

	1955	*1960*	*1965*	*1976*
Technology	Vacuum tubes Magnetic core storage Magnetic tapes	Transistors Faster cores Faster tapes Magnetic disks	Solid logic technology Faster cores Faster tapes Faster disks	Monolithic logic and memory Larger, faster disk files Advanced tapes
Average job cost **(dollars)**	14.54	2.48	0.47	0.20
Average job processing time **(seconds)**	375	47	37	5

1. This table shows how data processing cost and time have declined during the past two decades. It represents a mix of about 1700 computer operations such as payroll and report preparation. Costs are not adjusted for inflation. (From The Computer Age, *IBM publication G-505-0029, 1976, p. 23.)*

the instructions—the program. The computers are also frequently *compatible,* in that programs written for one manufacturer's computer can be used on that of another. In fact, it is even quite common to integrate the equipment from several manufacturers to form a system.

These features mean that today's computer user enjoys improved benefits at a fraction of the cost of just a few years ago. Table 5-1 compares the technology during the past 20 years in terms of two important factors: cost and time.

The computer as a physical system

A distinction was made in Chapter 1 between a physical system and a conceptual system. The computer is a physical system; it is a group of integrated elements with the common purpose of achieving some objective. The elements are the various electronic units connected with wires and cables. The objective is the satisfactory execution of the instructions contained in the storage.

As a physical system the computer can be represented by the model shown in Figure 5–9. This model, called the *computer schematic,* has been around for a long time. Initially it was used to describe the architecture of first generation computers; then it was applied to subsequent generations. It remains useful, since it specifies the component parts that every computer must possess.

Figure 5–9   The computer schematic

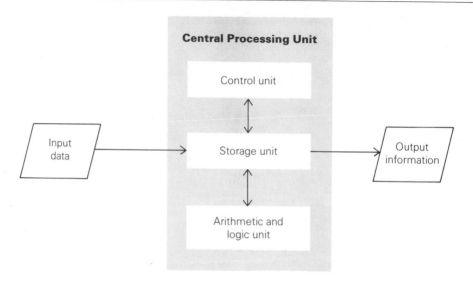

The computer has one or more input devices for entering data into the transformation and control part of the system—called the *central processing unit,* or the *CPU.* The CPU contains a storage unit where the input data is stored. The program also is located in the storage unit (the stored program concept developed by von Neumann). Any calculations or logical decisions are made in the arithmetic and logic unit, and the entire computer system is controlled by the control unit. Processed data and information are transmitted from the storage unit to one or more output devices.

In a small computer (Figure 5–10), all of these devices and units can be packaged in a single cabinet. As a general rule, however, a separate cabinet is used for each unit.

In a large system (Figure 5–11), 20 or 30 or more separate cabinets can be interconnected.

Even though both of the above computer systems are quite different in appearance and performance, they can be represented by the model in Figure 5–9. It is a general model of a computer system.

Computer storage

The storage portion of the CPU is used in four different ways. These uses may be described as the *four conceptual areas* of storage. The areas are not physical, in that the computer storage is not permanently partitioned in that manner.

Figure 5–10   A small computer system. (Courtesy of The Burroughs Corporation)

Output   Input   Central Processing Unit

Nothing physically distinguishes the four areas; the distinction is only in how the areas are used. The four conceptual areas are illustrated in Figure 5–12.

   As data enters the storage from the input device, such as a card reader, it is placed in the *input area*. The program in the *program area* is the list of instructions that guides the computer to the solution of a problem or completion of a task. The program performs the necessary calculations, logical decisions, movements, etc., and places data and information in the *output area*. The data and information are transmitted from this output area to an output device, such as a printer. Most programs require a separate storage area to contain intermediate totals, constants, descriptive characters, and the like. This separate area is the *working area*. The relative size of these areas varies from one program to the next, but the program area usually is the largest.

Multiprogramming

Figure 5–12 illustrates how the storage was used during the first and second computer generations. (A computer only executed a single program at a time.) During the third generation, it was recognized that all of the capacity of a large

Figure 5–11   A large computer system. (Courtesy of Sperry Univac)

computer system usually was not employed for a single program. Some of the input and output units often were idle, and some of the storage often was not needed.

It was learned that a computer could execute more than one program at a time, even though it has only one control unit and one arithmetic and logic unit. While a computer was executing one program, such as a payroll computation, it also could execute another, such as a program to write data from punched cards onto magnetic tape. This use of the computer is pictured in Figure 5–13.

Figure 5–12   Four conceptual areas of storage

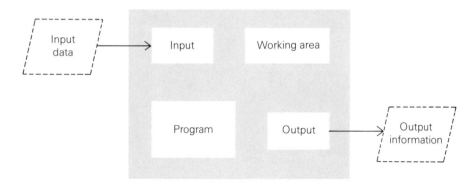

The computer alternates between the two programs. Since the internal speeds of a computer are much faster than those of the input and output units, payroll calculations are made while waiting for the card reader to read a card—or the magnetic tape unit to write a data record. The computer processes the payroll program until the card reader is ready to enter data into storage. The computer halts processing of the payroll program long enough to receive the card input data and move it to the output area used to write the magnetic

Figure 5–13   Executing two programs at a time

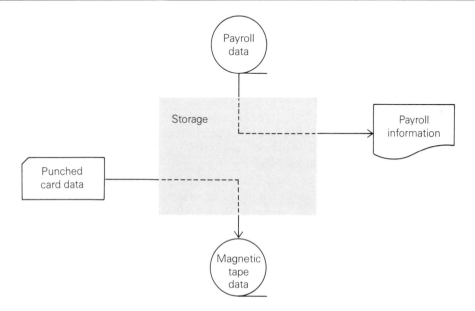

Figure 5–14 Alternation between background and foreground programs

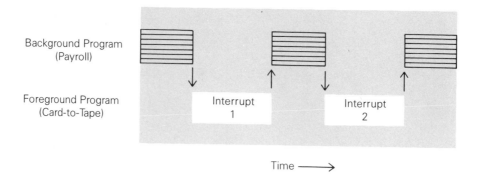

Background Program
(Payroll)

Foreground Program
(Card-to-Tape)

Interrupt 1

Interrupt 2

Time ⟶

tape records. The tape-write operation is initiated, and the control is returned to the payroll program at the point where it was interrupted. While payroll calculations are being made, the card reader is reading the second card, and the data from the first card is written on magnetic tape.

In this example the payroll program is considered the *background program*. It is in the background, waiting to be resumed when the other program does not require CPU time. The card-to-tape program is the *foreground program*. As it requires the CPU, the background program is interrupted. Control is returned to the background program when the foreground program steps have been completed. This alternation between the two programs is shown in Figure 5–14.

This processing of more than one program at a time is called *multiprogramming*. It imposes a control task on the CPU that is much more complex than when only a single program is processed. But this complexity is justified by a more efficient use of the computer.

In order for the CPU to alternate between the multiple programs, it is necessary to have a separate program in the storage—a *control program*. During the second generation, these control programs (also called *monitors* or *executive routines*) were written by the computer users. When IBM announced the System/360 to introduce the third generation, a very elaborate control program was included. This control program was named an *operating system*. From that point on, manufacturers of large computer systems offered operating systems with the computer. In fact, many smaller configurations also now have operating systems. Figure 5–15 shows how the storage of a modern computer is used. In some systems, fixed storage areas, or *partitions*, are available to each program. In other systems, all programs share the same storage area. Each computer model has a maximum number of programs that can be run in a multiprogramming mode.

Figure 5–15 The operating system controls the multiple programs.

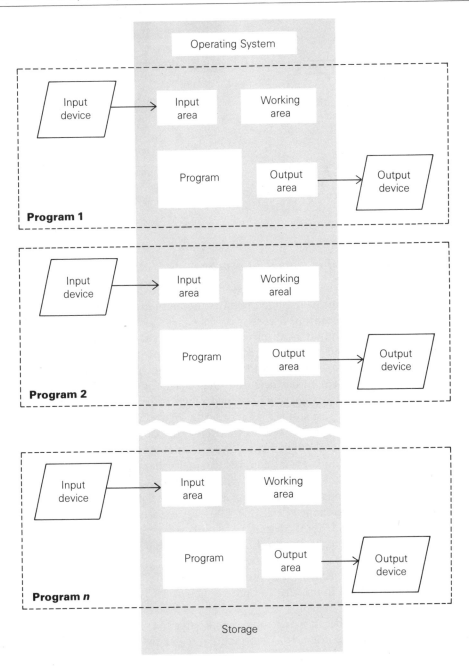

Figure 5–16   Magnetic core storage

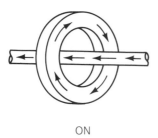

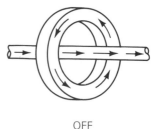

ON

Electrical current sets the
magnetic field of the core in
one direction—the "on" state

OFF

Reversal of the current sets the
magnetic field in the opposite
direction—the "off" state

Representation of material in storage

All of the material (data and instructions) contained in the storage is represented in a coded form. The code permits the computer to operate at maximum speed and at minimum cost.

Since the computer is an electronic device, it is possible to represent numbers, letters, and special characters with groups of tiny electronic elements. Each element can be either *on* or *off*. The most popular form of electronic storage element has been the small magnetic core. These cores can be magnetized in one of two directions by passing an electrical current through the center. This type of storage is pictured in Figure 5–16.

Computers use coding systems that represent all of the characters with combinations of *on* and *off* elements. These elements are called *bits* (derived from *bi*nary dig*it*), and several comprise a single character. Each set of *bits*, representing a character, is called a *byte*.

The most popular coding system is called EBCDIC (Extended Binary-Coded-Decimal Interchange Code). In EBCDIC, each byte consists of 8 data bits. The EBCDIC code for the letters and numbers is shown in Figure 5–17. *On* bits are represented as "1," and *off* bits as "0." If magnetic cores are used for storage, each 1 and 0 represents a separate core.

Another code, ASCII (American Standard Code for Information Interchange), also is used in modern computers such as the NCR Century line, but is not as popular as EBCDIC.

In 1972, IBM began using tiny silicon chips for storage. Four thousand chips can be mounted on a 1/2-inch module, replacing 4000 cores. The chips have the same *on-off* capability as other storage media, and it takes eight of these on-off situations to represent a character. Chip storage is more compact and faster than cores, and costs less to produce. (Some authorities cite this chip storage as an example of fourth-generation technology.)

Figure 5–17 The extended binary-coded-decimal interchange code (EBCDIC)

Character	EBCDIC Bits	Character	EBCDIC Bits
A	1100 0001	T	1110 0011
B	1100 0010	U	1110 0100
C	1100 0011	V	1110 0101
D	1100 0100	W	1110 0110
E	1100 0101	X	1110 0111
F	1100 0110	Y	1110 1000
G	1100 0111	Z	1110 1001
H	1100 1000		
I	1100 1001	0	1111 0000
J	1101 0001	1	1111 0001
K	1101 0010	2	1111 0010
L	1101 0011	3	1111 0011
M	1101 0100	4	1111 0100
N	1101 0101	5	1111 0101
O	1101 0110	6	1111 0110
P	1101 0111	7	1111 0111
Q	1101 1000	8	1111 1000
R	1101 1001	9	1111 1001
S	1110 0010		

EBCDIC code—no special characters shown

The Computer Program

The computer is a general purpose device. It can handle a wide range of data and information processing tasks. It can print payroll checks and then screen customers' credit requests. The program causes the computer to do specialized jobs. A program is written for each job. A small program may require only 8 or 10 instructions. A large one may consist of several thousand. (The way in which these programs are written is discussed in Chapter 16.)

A single instruction is required to cause the computer to take a specific action, such as read a card, multiply one number by another, write a line on the printer, or so on.

The programmer writes the instructions in a special programming language. There are a large number of these languages, with the more popular ones being FORTRAN (*Formula Translator*), BASIC (*Beginner's All-purpose Symbolic Instruction Code*), and COBOL (*COmmon Business Oriented Language*). A programming language consists of a set of different types of instructions— perhaps a hundred. The programmer selects those types needed and arranges them in the correct sequence.

The large number of instruction types available can be grouped into the following five categories:

Category	Function
Input/Output	Causes input units to transmit data to CPU storage, and the CPU to transmit data or information to output units.
Move	Transfers data from one location in storage to another.
Arithmetic	Causes data in storage to be added, subtracted, multiplied, or divided.
Logic	Causes the computer to make logical decisions based on data in storage.
Control	Causes the computer to follow different paths in the program based on the results of logical decisions or predefined conditions.

All of the units of a computer system are interconnected electronically. The program determines when each device or unit is needed and what it will do.

Computer Configurations

Computers have a single CPU, but they differ in the number and types of devices attached.[2] Two general classes of devices are attached to the CPU: input/output and auxiliary storage.

Input/Output Units	Auxiliary Storage Units
Card readers	Magnetic tape units
Card punch units	Magnetic drum units
Line printers	Magnetic disk units
Graph plotters	
Optical character readers	
Magnetic ink character readers	
Typewriterlike terminals	

---

2. Some computers have been built with multiple CPUs. These are called *multiprocessor systems.* They are still rather rare.

Figure 5–18   A card-oriented computer system. (Courtesy of Sperry Univac)

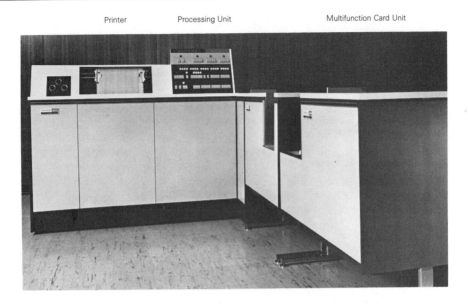

Printer   Processing Unit   Multifunction Card Unit

Most input/output units perform one function or the other—either input *or* output. Card readers are used only for input, and line printers only for output. Some of the units, however, can do both. Typewriterlike terminals can transmit data to the CPU *and* receive information from it. The different kinds of terminals are discussed in Chapter 8.

A card-oriented system

One of the most simple computer configurations is a card-oriented system (Figure 5–18). The only means of data input is with a card reader. Output can either be punched on a card punch unit or printed on a line printer. The input/output units are attached to the CPU. No auxiliary storage units are used.

A card-oriented system can be used by a small firm. This system can process orders, update inventory, print invoices, handle payroll, print management reports, and do other jobs. Such a system leases for about $1200 a month or can be purchased for about $45,000.

A disk-oriented system

As the size of the firm increases, the card-oriented system no longer can handle the volume of transactions. It becomes necessary to add additional units. A common method of increasing the capacity and speed of the system is to add storage in addition to that in the CPU (the *main storage*). This additional

Figure 5–19   A disk-oriented system. (Courtesy of Honeywell, Inc.)

storage is called *auxiliary storage,* and comes in various forms—magnetic disks, magnetic tapes, and magnetic drums.[3] During the first two generations, tapes and drums were the most popular. Recently, the trend has been to disk storage (Figure 5–19). These different types of auxiliary storage are described in Chapter 7.

Disk units are attached to the CPU to provide the storage for inventory files, personnel files, customer files, and the like. The number of units needed depends on the storage needs. Each disk unit contains one or more rotating disks, similar to phonograph records, that can be magnetized to store data. A disk-oriented system leases for $1,000 to $12,000 per month and sells for $100,000 to $600,000.

A disk- and tape-oriented system

Disk storage is best suited for active files where the data records are used every day. As the usage rate becomes less frequent, the cost of maintaining the data on disks cannot be justified. It is less costly to keep relatively inactive data on magnetic tape. A reel of tape costs about $18, while a small stack of disks (a

---

3. Manufacturers have continually searched for more economical forms of auxiliary storage. Magnetic cards and strips of tape have appeared on the market from time to time. These forms generally have not lived up to expectations, however, and most have been withdrawn. The search goes on.

Figure 5–20 A magnetic tape unit. (Courtesy of Honeywell, Inc.)

disk pack) costs about $125. The prices for more advanced disk packs can go as high as $2200.

Tape units (Figure 5–20) can be attached to the system to write data onto reels of tape and also to read data from the tape.

Computer tape units are similar to home tape recorders. A unit can both read data from tape or write data on it. As data is read or written, the tape is wound on a take-up reel. At the completion of processing, the tape is rewound on the source reel.

A computer system with both disk and tape units leases for approximately $10,000 to $20,000, and can be purchased for $500,000 to $1,000,000. Many computer systems are of this configuration. Disk units are used for the more active data, and magnetic tape units for less active, or historical, data.

Figure 5–21   A computer terminal. (Courtesy of Tektronix, Inc.)

A communication-oriented system

The past 10 to 15 years have seen an increased use of the computer as a component of a data communication system. Input/output units located great distances from the computer can be attached by a variety of means. The most common input/output unit is a terminal with a keyboard, and the most popular method of attachment is by telephone lines (Figure 5–21).

Such a communication-oriented system is ideal for firms with operations spread over a wide geographic area. Managers and other employees have the use of the central computer, regardless of their location. The costs of this type of system depend on the number of communication units and the volume of data transmitted.

Minicomputers

A recent hardware development has provided another alternative to computer users. This development is the *minicomputer* (Figure 5–22). As the name implies, the minicomputer is a smaller unit than the traditional processor. It is smaller in size and in cost, but it is not necessarily smaller in terms of

Figure 5–22   A minicomputer. (Courtesy of Wang Laboratories, Inc.)

performance capability. There are some jobs better suited to the minicomputer, or *mini*, than the full-scale computer.

The development of the mini has been rapid since Digital Equipment Corporation announced the first one, the PDP-5, in 1963. By 1975, nearly 40,000 minis were in use, and the number is expected to increase to 86,000 by 1980. Most of these units have been produced and marketed by three firms—Digital Equipment Corporation, Data General Corporation, and Hewlett-Packard. Most of the applications have been in the areas of controlling production processes and solution of mathematical problems. Much less acceptance of the mini has been realized by commercial firms for standard data processing or information processing applications.

As a general rule, the mini has no more than 32,000 positions of main storage and its input/output capability is limited. However, there are exceptions. The main storage of a popular mini, the Digital Equipment PDP 11/45, can be expanded to 262,000 bytes with a cycle time of 300 nanoseconds (billionths of a second). This speed compares favorably with a medium-scale computer such as the IBM 370/135 with a 275 nanosecond cycle time.

The mini doesn't compare as favorably, however, in terms of input/output ability and programming support by the manufacturers. Only a narrow range of input and output units usually is available, and the programming languages tend to favor mathematical, rather than business, problems.

Microcomputers

While the minicomputer has been achieving success in displacing full-size computers for certain jobs, an even smaller unit has emerged. This is the *microcomputer*. The microcomputer is the first real evidence of something that has been in the talking stages for several years—a home computer. It is extremely small, perhaps containing all of the processing circuitry within the keyboard device, and is economically priced. The microcomputer is intended to appeal to individual users in addition to business firms.

It is unlikely that microcomputers will play a key role in the business firm's MIS, at least not in the immediate future. However, they do provide an opportunity for development of more sophisticated personal information systems than ever before.

One microcomputer being marketed as a personal computer is the Radio Shack TRS-80, that was introduced in August 1977. The TRS-80, seen in Figure 5–23, consists of a 53-key input device/microcomputer with connected cassette recorder. The purchase price for this equipment is only $399.95, and is increased to only $599.95 with addition of a video display monitor. Programmed routines are available in cassette form to play games (blackjack and backgammon), compute payroll, perform basic mathematics, handle kitchen calculations such as menu selection, and perform personal finance computations.

Computer Processing

Not only can the computer perform a variety of tasks, it can perform the tasks in different ways. There are five basic approaches to computer processing:

- Batch processing
- Transaction processing
- Realtime processing
- Timesharing
- Distributed processing

Batch processing

Computers first were used to process data in basically the same way as punched card machines—in batches. This approach still is being used in many organizations and in many computerized systems.

Batch processing involves accumulating batches of transactions and performing the processing on the entire batch one step at a time. It is a "mass production" or "assembly line" approach. The main advantage is economy, but it is virtually impossible to maintain the files in an up-to-date condition. The data in the files is current only immediately after the processing. The files then become obsolete as subsequent transactions await the next processing cycle,

Figure 5–23   The Radio Shack TRS-80 microcomputer. (Courtesy of Radio Shack, a Tandy Company)

perhaps the next day. Figure 5–24 shows a batch processing cycle where three files are updated from transaction data.

The files are updated one at a time with the transaction data. The transactions must be sorted into the same sequence as the file before the file is updated. The updating occurs on a cycle basis—once a day, week, month, etc.

Transaction processing

Batch processing initially made efficient use of card- and tape-oriented systems. When disk storage was introduced in the late 1950s, another approach became

Figure 5–24   Batch processing

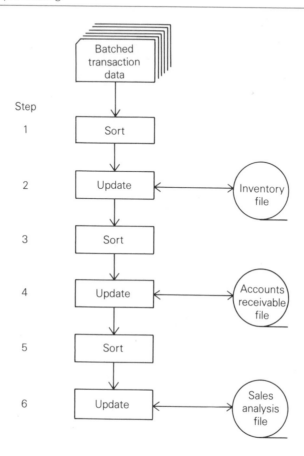

possible. This is *transaction processing* in which the transactions are processed as they occur. Figure 5–25 illustrates how this is done.

Assume that the transaction is a sale by salesperson X to customer Y for a dozen of product Z at a price of $10 each. The single transaction record is entered into main storage and the inventory record for product Z is obtained from the disk file. The CPU can direct a reading mechanism to the area in auxiliary storage where the inventory record is located. This procedure is accomplished in a fraction of a second without the need to scan preceding areas.

The inventory record is updated to reduce the balance on hand by a dozen. In a like manner, the record for customer Y is obtained and updated to show an increase of $120 in accounts receivable. Finally, the record for salesperson X is updated with the $120 sale. This transaction is completed before the next is entered.

Figure 5–25   Transaction processing

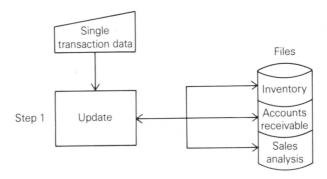

With transaction processing, the data files are current as of the last transaction handled. If a manager wants to know an inventory balance, or the amount of a customer's receivables, or the sales volume of a salesperson, that information is available in a current form. The conceptual information system is an accurate and current representation of the physical system.

This use of direct access auxiliary storage (such as disks) adds greatly to the ability of the computer to function as an information system. With the addition of data communications facilities, the power of the computer as an information system can be extended over a wide geographic area.

Realtime processing

In transaction processing the information system does not control the physical system of the firm. It simply responds to it. This is not true in realtime processing. *Realtime processing* (Figure 5–26) is when the information system monitors the physical system and initiates changes in it. The realtime system is the control element in the feedback loop.

An example of a realtime system is the control of a physical process such as electrical power generation. A power company can use a computer to monitor pressure in a steam boiler. When the pressure reaches a certain level, a signal is transmitted by the computer to open a valve that lowers the pressure.

Another example is the reservation system used by the major airlines and motel chains. When a reservation is entered from a terminal, the computer reserves future space in the physical system. The computer makes changes in the (future) status of the physical system.

If the computer is to initiate changes in the physical system, it must do so without delay. Usually, this means within a few seconds or even a fraction of a second. There is no particular speed that must be achieved by a system to be classified as realtime. A firm may have a realtime system that requires several

Figure 5–26   Realtime processing

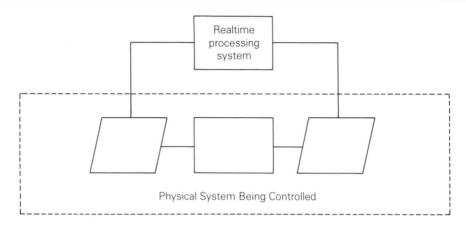

minutes to respond. If this is adequate for the firm, the system can be said to respond in *real*time.

Timesharing

Modern computers operate at such fast speeds that users must work to keep up with them. It takes a lot of jobs to keep the computer busy. Indeed, the more users, the merrier. A particular approach has been created to permit this multiple use; it is known as *timesharing*. All that is needed is a central computer with multiprogramming capability and data communication terminals.

Many terminals can be attached to a central computer. The terminal users can thus *share* the *time* of the computer, i.e., timesharing. As far as each user is concerned, his or her terminal is the computer itself. Data can be entered through a keyboard and transmitted to the central computer. The operating system can allocate the CPU time to the various users by giving each a *time slice.* The processing required by each terminal user is performed, perhaps using central data files, and the output is transmitted back to the appropriate terminal, where it is printed or displayed. All of this can take place in seconds. The user generally is unaware that his or her program is only one of several being processed.

An individual or firm can purchase timesharing services from a computer service center. The center furnishes the computer and, very often, the data files and programs. The user furnishes the data, programs, and terminal, and pays for the communication and computer time used. This can be an attractive alternative to acquisition of a complete computer system. For the same amount of money (or even less), a firm can frequently buy time on another firm's larger and more powerful computer system.

Figure 5–27   A distributed processing network

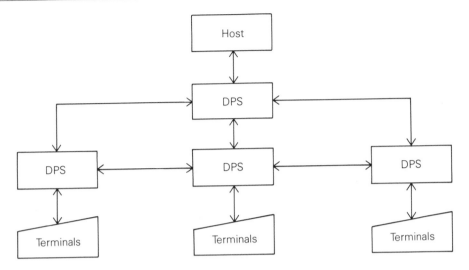

Distributed processing

A recent refinement of the timesharing approach is aimed at further improving the scope of decentralized processing. Called *distributed processing*, this approach involves the interconnection of more than one computer.

Although there can be many variations, a common technique is to use a single centralized computer, referred to as the *host*, and smaller computers at remote sites. These smaller computers, the *distributed processing systems* (*DPS*), can either process data locally for terminal users, or transmit data to the host or other DPS for processing. This network is illustrated in Figure 5–27. Very often, minicomputers serve as the DPS.

Distributed processing offers maximum flexibility to dispersed users of the computer network. Programs can be processed locally or centrally. Development of this approach is only beginning, and it should become more widely adopted in the future.

Summary

The purpose of this chapter has been to introduce the computer and to present several basic principles.

The three noncomputerized approaches to data processing are manual, keydriven machine, and punched card. The popularity of the last two has diminished with the acceptance of the computer. All three approaches have been used primarily as data processing systems.

The evolution of the electronic computer spanned a long period of time with several primary steps beginning as far back as the seventeenth century. (Pascal's mechanical adder, Leibniz's multiplier and divider, and Babbage's analytical engine are examples.) But once manufacturers began producing computers in quantity, the devices evolved through three distinct generations. Present computers closely resemble those of 15 years ago in basic architecture. However, several distinct technological improvements have been made.

The computer is a physical system with input/output and auxiliary storage units connected to the central processing unit (CPU). The CPU contains the control, arithmetic and logic, and storage units. The four basic uses of storage—input, program, working, and output—can be represented as conceptual areas.

A computer can process several programs at the same time; this is known as *multiprogramming*. A control program, the operating system, causes the computer to alternate between the programs for maximum use of the different computer units.

Data is represented in storage in a coded form. Each character is coded with eight data bits, called a *byte*. Until recently, magnetic cores were used almost exclusively to store data. Silicon chips are now being used to achieve improvements in speed and performance.

The program causes the general purpose computer to perform specialized tasks. The programmer selects the appropriate instructions that cause the computer to perform input/output operations, move data, perform arithmetic, and make logical decisions.

Many configurations of computer equipment can be devised. They differ in the assortment of attached input/output and auxiliary storage units. The basic configuration, the card-oriented system, can be expanded with the addition of disk units, magnetic tape units, and terminals.

There are five approaches to the use of the computer. Batch processing is the most economical but is not responsive to changes in the physical system of the firm. Both transaction and realtime processing meet the need of responsiveness, but in different ways. Transaction processing reflects changes in the physical system, while realtime processing initiates such changes. Realtime systems control physical systems, while transaction processing systems do not. The two remaining approaches represent communications-oriented networks. Timesharing makes the power of the computer available to widespread users by means of terminals. Distributed processing links local computers with a central host computer.

The next three chapters will provide additional information on the computer.

Important Terms

Analog Computer

Digital Computer

Manual System

Keydriven System

Billing Machine, Posting Machine, Accounting Machine

Punched Card System

Keypunch Machine

Punched Card Sorter

Punched Card Accounting Machine

Verifier

Interpreter

Electronic Computer

Stored Program Computer

Computer Generation

Modular

Compatible

Computer Schematic

Central Processing Unit (CPU)

Conceptual Storage Area

Multiprogramming

Background Program

Foreground Program

Control Program, Operating System

Partition

Bit

Extended Binary-Coded-Decimal Interchange Code (EBCDIC)

American Standard Code for Information Interchange (ASCII)

FORmula TRANslator (FORTRAN)

Beginner's All-purpose Symbolic Instruction Code (BASIC)

COmmon Business Oriented Language (COBOL)

Computer Configuration

Disk Pack

Minicomputer (Mini)

Microcomputer

Batch Processing

Transaction Processing

Realtime Processing

Timesharing

Distributed Processing

Host Computer

Distributed Processing System (DPS)

Important People and Organizations

Dr. Herman Hollerith

Thomas J. Watson, Sr.

Blaise Pascal

Gottfried Wilhelm Leibniz

Joseph Marie Jacquard

Charles Babbage

Howard H. Aiken

J. Presper Eckert

Dr. John W. Mauchly

Dr. John von Neumann

International Business Machines
   (IBM)

Sperry Rand (now Sperry Univac)

National Cash Register (NCR)

Burroughs

Digital Equipment Corporation
   (DEC)

Data General Corporation

Hewlett-Packard

Radio Shack

Important Concepts

Computers are either analog or digital.

Data can be processed by four basic types of systems—manual, keydriven, punched card, and computer.

The modern computer was developed over a long period of time by many people.

The design of all computers can be represented by the computer schematic.

Four basic uses are made of computer storage, and these can be considered as conceptual areas.

Execution of programs is controlled by an operating system and can be a very complex process.

A variety of programming languages offers special advantages in solving different types of problems.

Computers are of various sizes depending on CPU capacity and speed and on the configuration of attached input/output and auxiliary storage units.

The five basic approaches to computer processing are batch, transaction, realtime, timesharing, and distributed processing.

Questions

1 What are the two basic types of computer?
2 What are three jobs in a company that could be performed by a manual system?

3 Is a typewriter a keydriven system? Is a typewriter a part of a firm's conceptual information system? Explain.

4 What is the difference between a keydriven adding machine and a keydriven calculator?

5 How many characters can be punched into a punched card?

6 What steps are followed in processing data?

7 How is punched card data recorded? arranged? processed?

8 What was the first step toward the development of the modern electronic computer?

9 What is the number of the current computer generation?

10 Can a computer be both "modular" and "compatible"? Explain.

11 Why has the average cost of performing a job on a computer decreased so dramatically during the past 20 years?

12 If computer technology has changed and improved so much, why can the computer schematic still be used to illustrate computer system architecture?

13 Why are the four areas of computer storage called "conceptual areas"?

14 Which of the conceptual areas of storage uses the greatest amount of space? Does this situation ever vary?

15 Are multiprogramming and multiprocessing the same thing? Explain.

16 What determines that a program will be the "background" program or a "foreground" program?

17 What development made multiprogramming possible?

18 How many magnetic cores are necessary to represent an alphabetic letter using EBCDIC?

19 Why would a firm convert from a card-oriented system to a disk-oriented system?

20 Which is smaller: a minicomputer or a microcomputer?

21 Why have business firms been slow to accept the mini as a system for processing commerical data?

22 Which is the most economical: batch processing, transaction processing, or realtime processing? Which is the most expensive?

23 Can a firm process data by batch with a timesharing terminal? Explain.

24 What distinguishes transaction processing from realtime processing, or are they really the same?

25 Can a firm process data by batch with a distributed processing system? Explain.

Chapter 6

Computer Input and Output

In the general model of the firm presented in Chapter 3, the computer is pictured as gathering data from the firm and its environment, and presenting information to management. In the last chapter, the general performance of the computer was discussed. The purpose of this chapter is to describe the different methods of entering data into the computer, and presenting output information to the manager.

There probably have been more improvements during the past decade in this area of computer technology than in any other. Many new companies have entered the peripheral equipment industry, with emphasis on terminals and graphical plotters. These new vendors join the established giants in offering a selection of computer equipment for practically any job needing to be done. The availability of input and output equipment is not holding up attainment of the MIS. The equipment is here. Management only has to learn to use it (and to be able to pay for it).

Computer Channels

A large number and variety of devices can be attached to a modern computer. If these devices (called *peripherals*) were attached directly to the CPU, the CPU could not function efficiently. It would have to halt processing when one of the units was operating. Since the speeds of the input/output units are very slow compared to the speeds of the CPU, much CPU time would be wasted. For this reason, an intermediate unit connects the peripheral units to the CPU. This unit is the *channel*. The channel is a pathway between the units and the CPU. The operation of the channel is illustrated in Figure 6–1.

Transfer of data between the peripheral unit and the channel is *serial*, or one character at a time. As a card reader is reading a punched card, the data is transmitted to the channel one character at a time. While this operation is being performed, the CPU can be processing other data in main storage. When the channel storage area has been filled, the channel signals the CPU that card input data is ready to enter main storage. The CPU halts processing long

Figure 6–1   The operation of the channel

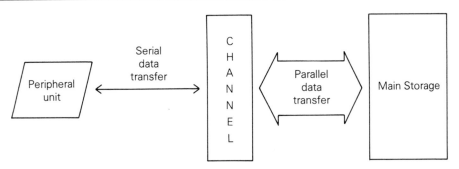

enough to enter the data from the channel. The interruption is very brief since all the characters from the channel are transmitted to main storage at once, or in *parallel*.

Transfer of data from main storage to an output unit works in exactly the reverse sequence. Data is transmitted from the CPU to the channel in parallel and the CPU resumes processing. The channel then transmits the data one character at a time to the output unit.

Most computers have at least one channel. Some have two, three, or more. In the IBM System/370, three types of channels are used. One, the *byte multiplexer channel*, connects slow speed input/output units such as card readers and printers to the CPU. Another, the *block multiplexer* channel, is a sophisticated channel that primarily connects disk units. The third, the *selector channel*, usually connects magnetic tape units. Figure 6–2 shows the different types of units that can comprise a computer system, and how they are connected to the CPU by means of channels.

The remainder of this chapter is devoted to a discussion of the more important and widely used input/output units. Those used in data communications, however, will be covered in Chapter 8. Auxiliary storage units are described in Chapter 7.

Keydriven Input Preparation Devices

Although CPU speeds are measured in millionths and billionths of a second, the most common method of creating input is a keydriven device. This device must be operated in much the same manner as a typewriter. For this reason, people in the computer industry speak of an *input bottleneck*, that is, the problem of getting data into the computer. Many approaches have been developed during the past 20 years to bypass this bottleneck, and they are described in this chapter. But, the primary means of preparing input media remains the operation of a keydriven machine.

Figure 6–2   IBM System/370 schematic. (Courtesy of International Business Machines)

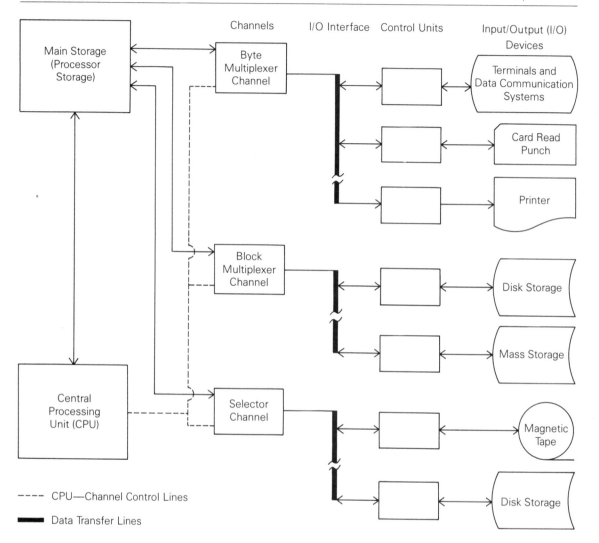

Keypunch and key verifier machines

The only punched card machine to withstand the impact of the computer has been the keypunch. This machine, originating almost a century ago, accounts for the largest volume of input data. A number of refinements have been made over the years; however, it operates in basically the same fashion as when it produced input for punched card systems.

The keyboard is very similar to that of a typewriter. Cards are punched, one character at a time, as the operator reads data from a *source document*

". . . God bless you . . ."

© DATAMATION ®

such as a sales order. The speed of the keypunching operation is measured in keystrokes per hour. An experienced operator can maintain a rate of from 8000 to 12,000. As the character codes are punched into the card, the letters, numbers, and special characters can be printed at the top of the card.

During the era of punched card equipment popularity, the punched card acquired the name *unit record*. It was so called because it included all of the data about a certain activity or transaction (Figure 6–3). As an example, a card punched to represent a sale included the customer number, the identification number of the item bought, the quantity, and the unit price. It also can contain data elements such as customer order number, order date, item description, salesperson number, and total price.

The figure indicates that three basic categories of data are recorded in the card: coded data, descriptive data, and quantitative data. It is the custom to arrange these data elements in the order pictured. The first elements in the record are coded data; the last are quantitative. In a punched card, each data element is known as a *field*.

After the cards have been punched, another machine, similar to the keypunch, is used to check the accuracy. This machine is the key verifier. The punched cards are placed in the verifier and the operator depresses the keys as the source document is read again. The keys depressed must match the holes

Figure 6–3   A punched card is a unit record.

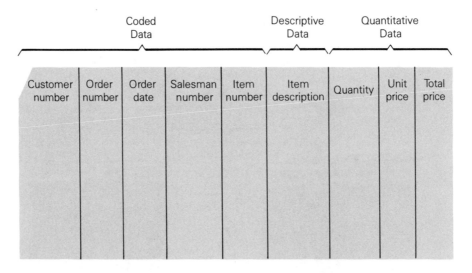

in the card or an error condition is detected. Most cards containing financial data, such as payroll amounts, are key verified prior to entry of the data into the computer.

As late as 1971, approximately one-half million keypunch and key verifier machines were estimated to be in use worldwide. The major manufacturers, IBM and Univac, have continued to improve keypunch technology. In 1968, Univac began production of its 1700 series. Later, IBM announced a combined keypunch and key verifier unit, the Model 129, with a computer-age "memory" (see Figure 6–4).

Key-to-tape and key-to-disk machines

Since magnetic tape and disk data can be read by the computer much faster than data in punched cards, a number of efforts have been aimed at keying data directly to tape or disk.

This movement began in 1964 with the announcement of the Mohawk Data-Recorder. Data was recorded in a buffer storage unit as it was entered in the keyboard. The contents of the buffer were then written on a magnetic tape that was *compatible* with the computer's magnetic tape units. Other manufacturers saw the potential for this approach and developed similar units. In 1968, IBM announced its Model 50 Magnetic Tape Inscriber. The IBM unit recorded the data on a small magnetic tape cartridge that could hold the same amount of data as approximately 275 punched cards. Since the tape cartridge was *incompatible* with the computer's tape units, a special cartridge reader was offered that could enter the data into the System/360 at a speed of 900

Figure 6–4   The IBM 129 card data recorder. (Courtesy of International Business Machines)

characters per second. In addition to cartridges, tape cassettes have also been used. Figure 6–5 shows a key-to-tape cassette unit.

A third approach appeared in mid-1969. Both Logic Corporation and Computer Machinery Corporation announced *multistation keyboard entry* systems with keyboards linked to a small processor. The data from all keyboards is recorded on either magnetic tape or disk. Both the tapes and the disks are compatible with the computer tape and disk units.

By the end of 1969, approximately 30 firms were marketing some type of key-to-tape units, and nearly 50,000 of the devices were in use. Continued improvements have been made and, today, the computer user has a variety of choices. Data can be entered from single or multiple keyboards and recorded on standard computer tapes and disks or on tape cassettes, cartridges, or small plastic ("floppy") disks.

Figure 6-5   A key-to-tape unit. (Courtesy of The National Cash Register Co.)

Figure 6–6 illustrates a tape cassette manufactured by the Maxell Corporation. The cassette consists of 285 feet of polyester on which data can be recorded at a density of 800 bytes per inch. Special cassette readers enter the data into the CPU.

Maxell also produces a floppy disk with a capacity of almost 250,000 bytes

Figure 6-6   A magnetic tape cassette. (Courtesy of Maxell Corporation of America)

Figure 6–7 A floppy disk. (Courtesy of Maxell Corporation of America)

(Figure 6–7). The plastic disk is contained in a 20 centimeter (approximately 7.8 inches) square jacket that permits easy handling. A number of floppy disk drives are available to enter the data into the computer.

Card Reading and Punching Units

Most computer systems include a card reading unit and a card punching unit. These devices often are housed in separate cabinets, but they can be packaged together. Figure 6–8 illustrates a combined card reading and punching unit.

In a card-oriented system, everything is entered through the card reader. Program card decks are read and the program instructions placed in storage.

Figure 6–8   A card read-punch unit. (Courtesy of International Business Machines)

1. Punch hopper

2. Read hopper

3. Card stacker

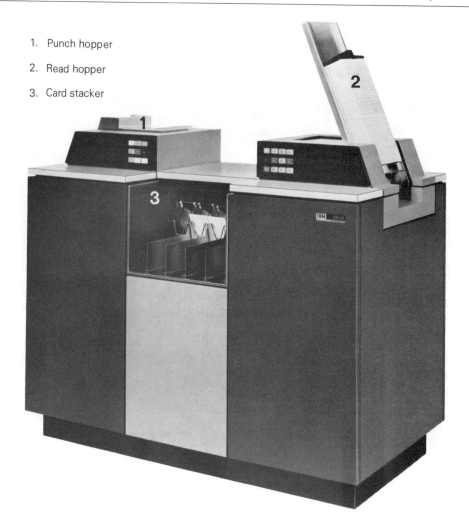

Then data cards representing both master files and transactions are processed. The card punch creates updated master files. An example is the updating of a payroll master file with transaction data representing hours worked for the current period (Figure 6–9). As the file is updated, a printed report, such as a payroll register, can be prepared.

In disk- or magnetic-tape-oriented systems, only the transaction data is entered in cards. The master files and programs are contained on disks or tapes. However, those master files and programs usually are created originally from card data.

Figure 6–9   Updating a master file on a card-oriented system

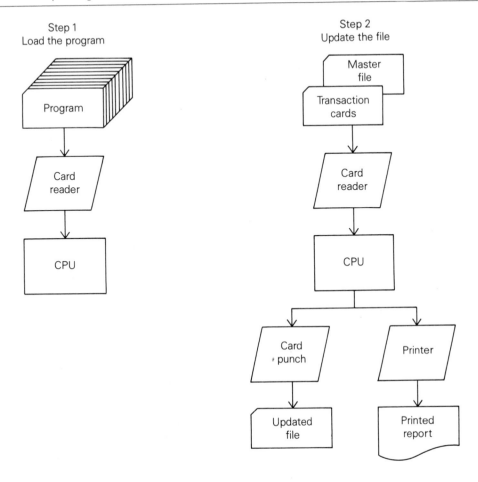

Cards can be read much faster than they can be punched. Card reading speeds of 2000 cards per minute are not uncommon, but punching speeds are in the area of 100 to 250 per minute.

Card reading units

Early card readers used metal brushes to read the holes in the card. The brushes made an electrical contact through the holes. This was the same technology used in punched card equipment. Most readers on the market today use photoelectric cells rather than brushes. The cells detect the presence of the holes when a light passes through them.

Card readers employ either of two basic approaches. They can read the card serially, or in parallel. In a *serial reader* the card is read one character at a time from column 1 to column 80. An increase in speed can be realized in a *parallel reader* that reads all 80 characters at a time. The card is read row by row.

Some readers incorporate checking circuitry to assure the data is read correctly. One approach is to have two reading stations, and compare the impulses read at both stations. The impulses must match exactly before the data is allowed to enter the computer.

Card punching units

Card punching technology has improved little over that of the punched card era. That is the reason computers are used to prepare punched card output only when it is absolutely necessary. Very often cards are punched for later reentry into the system. An example is the punched card often included with a printed bill, such as a telephone bill. When the customer pays the bill, the card is returned. This method eliminates the need to key the payment into a payment card or onto some magnetic media. Cards used in this manner are called *turnaround documents* (Figure 6–10).

Another useful application of punched card output is inventory control. When a firm receives an inventory item from the supplier, a set of cards can be produced by the computer and placed in an envelope attached to the item. As the item moves through the firm from the receiving dock to the warehouse to the sales floor and to the shipping dock, a card can be pulled at each location. These cards can be entered into the computer to "track" the material flow through the firm. Figure 6–11 shows a card used by a manufacturer to track the flow of an air conditioning unit.

Figure 6–10   A turnaround document. (Courtesy of Southwestern Bell Telephone Company)

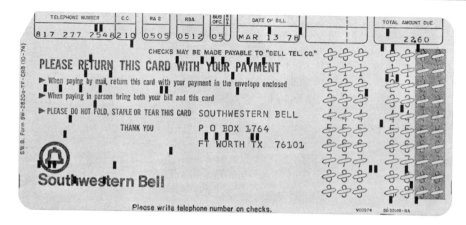

Figure 6-11 An inventory movement card. (Courtesy of Friedrich, A Division of Wylain, Inc.)

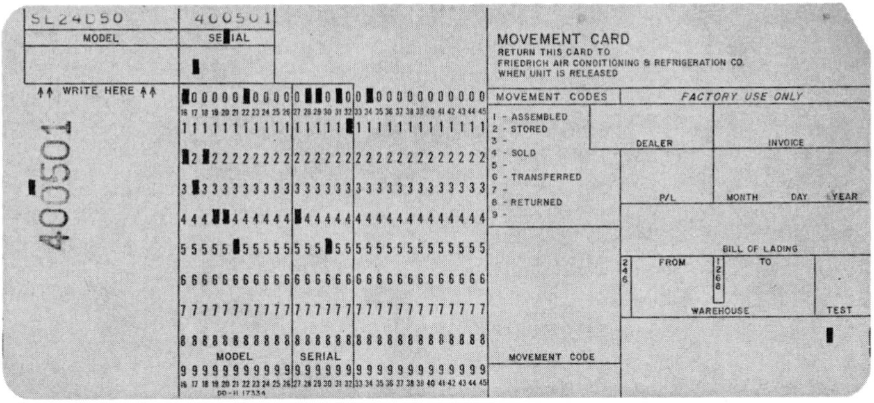

Unique approaches to punched card input

Data can be entered into punched cards other than by keypunch or computer punching units. One method originated with punched card equipment and is named *mark sensing*. Pencil marks can be made with a soft-lead pencil in designated areas on the card. A machine, not attached to the computer, reads these marks electrically, and punches the holes into the same card. The cards then can be read by a card reading unit. A course request card used at the University of Colorado is designed for mark reading. It is shown in Figure 6-12.

Figure 6-12 Mark sensing. (Courtesy of the University of Colorado)

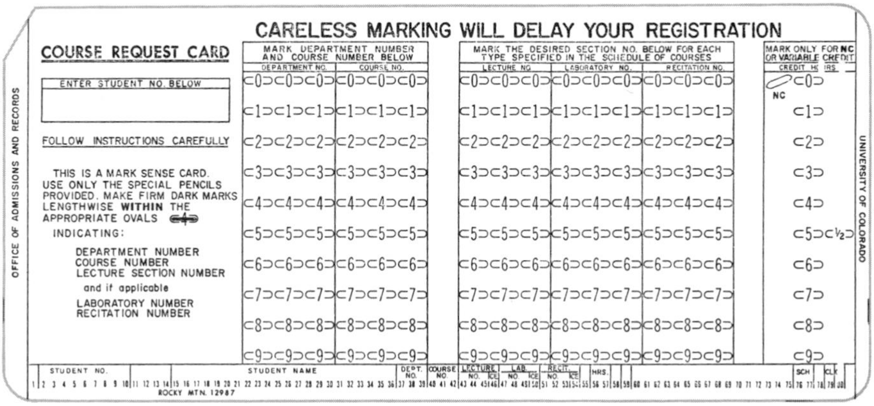

Figure 6–13 Port-a-Punch card. (Courtesy of Don Brotzman)

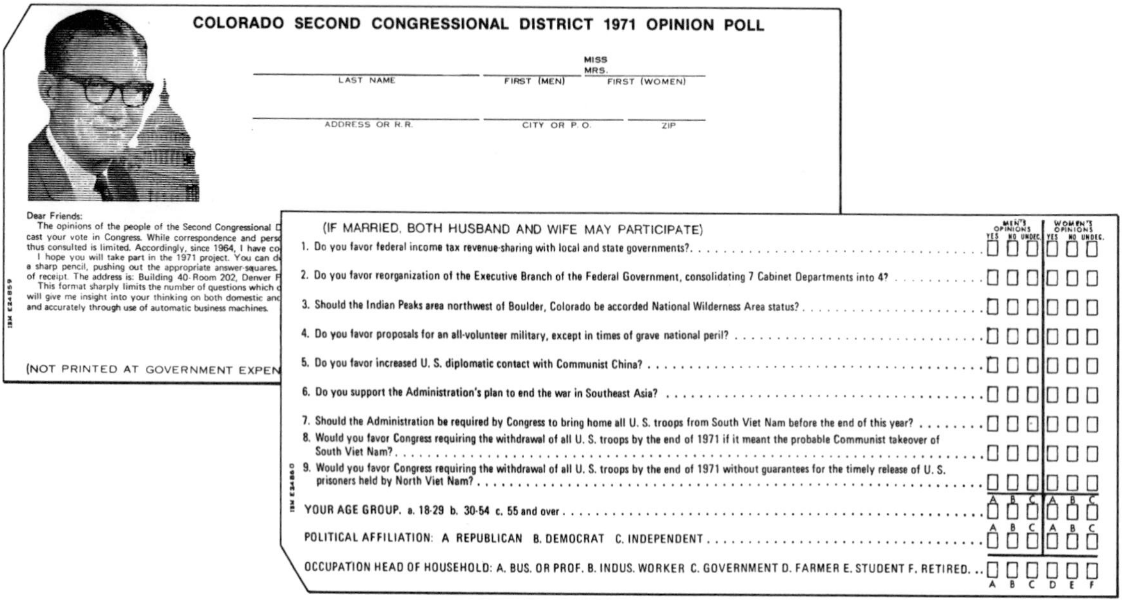
COLORADO SECOND CONGRESSIONAL DISTRICT 1971 OPINION POLL

LAST NAME — FIRST (MEN) — MISS MRS. FIRST (WOMEN)

ADDRESS OR R.R. — CITY OR P.O. — ZIP

Dear Friends:
The opinions of the people of the Second Congressional D… cast your vote in Congress. While correspondence and pers… thus consulted is limited. Accordingly, since 1964, I have co… I hope you will take part in the 1971 project. You can d… a sharp pencil, pushing out the appropriate answer-squares… of receipt. The address is: Building 40-Room 202, Denver F… This format sharply limits the number of questions which c… will give me insight into your thinking on both domestic an… and accurately through use of automatic business machines.

(NOT PRINTED AT GOVERNMENT EXPEN…

(IF MARRIED, BOTH HUSBAND AND WIFE MAY PARTICIPATE) — MEN'S OPINIONS: YES NO UNDEC. — WOMEN'S OPINIONS: YES NO UNDEC.

1. Do you favor federal income tax revenue-sharing with local and state governments?
2. Do you favor reorganization of the Executive Branch of the Federal Government, consolidating 7 Cabinet Departments into 4?
3. Should the Indian Peaks area northwest of Boulder, Colorado be accorded National Wilderness Area status?
4. Do you favor proposals for an all-volunteer military, except in times of grave national peril?
5. Do you favor increased U. S. diplomatic contact with Communist China?
6. Do you support the Administration's plan to end the war in Southeast Asia?
7. Should the Administration be required by Congress to bring home all U. S. troops from South Viet Nam before the end of this year?
8. Would you favor Congress requiring the withdrawal of all U. S. troops by the end of 1971 if it meant the probable Communist takeover of South Viet Nam?
9. Would you favor Congress requiring the withdrawal of all U. S. troops by the end of 1971 without guarantees for the timely release of U. S. prisoners held by North Viet Nam?

YOUR AGE GROUP. a. 18-29 b. 30-54 c. 55 and over

POLITICAL AFFILIATION: A REPUBLICAN B. DEMOCRAT C. INDEPENDENT

OCCUPATION HEAD OF HOUSEHOLD: A. BUS. OR PROF. B. INDUS. WORKER C. GOVERNMENT D. FARMER E. STUDENT F. RETIRED.

Another unique approach allows a person to punch the holes in the card with any type of pointed instrument. This technique, called *port-a-punch,* was developed by IBM in the late 1950s. It since has been used in many interesting ways. It has been used by major league baseball fans to elect players to the All Star Game, and by Congressmen to learn the feelings of their constituents toward key issues. (See Figure 6–13.)

Cards designed for port-a-punch have the punching areas prescored. The holes can be punched by pressing the center with a pencil or stylus.

Both mark reading and port-a-punch were developed as a means of bypassing keyed input. While they have enjoyed wide acceptance, their impact has been less than that of two more advanced techniques. These latter techniques, involving magnetic ink and optical character recognition, will now be discussed.

Magnetic Ink Character Recognition (MICR)

The American banking industry was one of the first to establish a standard approach to the use of the computer. In the mid-1950s, the American Banking Association devised a standard *type font* (or style) to be used in processing checks. The font, named E-13-B, consists of the 10 digits plus 4 special symbols.

Figure 6-14   The E-13-B type font

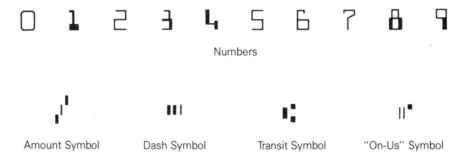

Numbers

Amount Symbol   Dash Symbol   Transit Symbol   "On-Us" Symbol

When blank checks are received from the bank, they are preprinted with numbers identifying both the customer and the bank. These numbers appear at the bottom on the left side. When the check is written, the amount of the check is encoded in the E-13-B font by the first bank processing it. The amount is entered by a keydriven machine called an *encoder*.

After the amount is encoded, the check can be processed on a unit named the *reader sorter*. The reader sorter performs two main activities. First, it reads the MICR encoded data from the checks so that it may be recorded on a computer-compatible storage medium such as tape or disk. Second, it sorts all the checks for each bank into separate stackers. Checks on other banks are

Figure 6-15   A check with MICR encoding

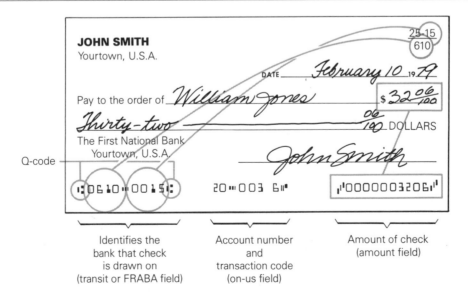

Identifies the   Account number   Amount of check
bank that check   and   (amount field)
is drawn on   transaction code
(transit or FRABA field)   (on-us field)

Figure 6–16   An MICR reader sorter. (Courtesy of The Burroughs Corporation)

forwarded to the clearinghouse, and checks written by the bank's own customers are sorted into customer batches. At the end of the month, the computer prints a statement for each customer using tape or disk data created by the reader sorter. The statement and the checks are mailed to the customer.

The reader sorter can be either a stand-alone or an online unit. A *stand-alone unit* operates independently of the CPU. It creates some computer-readable medium, such as a magnetic tape or disk, for subsequent processing. An *online unit* is attached directly to the CPU. Data is transferred from the unit to the main storage of the CPU. The stored program in the CPU can then direct the data to be recorded on tape or disk.

This reading of magnetically encoded characters, whether by a stand-alone or an online unit, is termed *magnetic ink character recognition* (MICR).

Had it not been for MICR, the banking system could not have handled the large volume of checks during the past 20 years. But, MICR is not a permanent cure. Bankers fear that the future volume of checks will be too great, even for MICR. An alternative is being implemented on a gradual basis to eliminate a large number of the checks. This alternative is the *electronic funds transfer system* (EFTS).

In EFTS, checks are not used to transfer money from one account to another. The transfer is accomplished by computer. An employee does not receive a payroll check, but has the amount deposited in his or her checking account by the employer. Many employers have been doing this for years. Then, instead of writing checks for certain purchases, the money is withdrawn automatically from the account. Repetitive expenses (utilities, auto and house payments, charge accounts) are paid for in this manner. All of the transfers are accomplished by computer. For example, the utility company's computer authorizes a bank to transfer a certain amount from the customer's account to the company's account.

Ultimately, EFTS will incorporate nonrepetitive transactions, such as retail sales. When articles are purchased at a store, a computer record will be created to transfer the payment from the customer's account to the store's account. Special retail terminals, discussed in Chapter 8, will tie into this EFTS network.

Optical Character Recognition (OCR)

Of all the efforts aimed at eliminating the keypunch, none has captured the imagination of computer people to the degree that *optical character recognition (OCR)* has. For the past 25 years, computer equipment manufacturers have been designing machines to read data that is printed on paper with ordinary ink. Many such machines have been built and successfully used, but the general feeling is that the surface has only been scratched.

Styles of characters read

The first OCR units were called *scanners*. A single reading element was employed to scan, or trace, the outline of each character. Units were built to read specific type fonts. After several years, a standard font—OCR-A (Figure 6–17)—was adopted for use in the United States.

Not all OCR equipment manufacturers, however, build units to read only OCR-A. Some, such as Recognition Equipment Incorporated (REI), will provide an OCR unit to read any machine-printed character styles used by a firm.

In addition to reading *machine-printed* characters, OCR units also can read *marks* made with any type of writing instrument; it does not have to be a soft-lead pencil. As long as the mark is dark, it can be read. Many colleges use OCR reading units for scoring true-false and multiple-choice tests. Readers designed to read only marks are much less expensive than those designed to read characters. The units only have to be capable of determining whether a mark is present—not its shape.

The use of OCR that seems to have the most potential is reading hand-

Figure 6–17   The OCR-A type font

printed data. Several manufacturers, such as REI, Compuscan, and Scan-Data, offer models to read *hand-printed numbers*. The numbers must be printed in boxes, and must match a predefined pattern or style, such as:

Print your numerals like this

The Compuscan Model 170 also will read the *hand-printed letters* C, Z, T, S, and X, but not the entire alphabet. Efforts to read the entire alphabet have not met with great success.

There has been even less success in reading *hand-written data*. The irregularities of handwriting continue to defy the designers of OCR equipment.

Sizes of paper handled

OCR units also differ in the sizes of paper documents handled. Some, called *page readers*, read full-sized 8½ by 11 inch pages; others, called *document readers*, read small coupon-sized slips. Some, such as the REI Input 80, can read intermixed documents of varying sizes and paper weights.

Source data automation

The most complete application of OCR has been in the credit card industry. Most of the major oil companies and general credit card firms such as American Express read their credit invoices optically. When a customer makes a credit purchase, an invoice is imprinted with customer number (from the charge card) and the amount. These invoices are read optically at the central processing office and the computer prints the monthly statement.

This is an example of *source data automation;* the source document is designed in such a manner that it can be entered directly into the computer system. Another term, *direct entry*, also is used. The original document is all that is required for data entry. It is not necessary to create an intermediate record that is computer-readable. MICR-encoded checks are another form of source data automation.

The major airlines also employ source data automation in reading tickets. The ticket number and, in some cases, the route code (showing the departing and arriving airports) at the bottom of the ticket are read. This practice permits closer monetary control and interairline accounting.

McDonald's uses source data automation in some of their restaurants. Figure 6–18 shows a form that is marked with the different food items ordered. This form is read optically by a cash registerlike device and the amount of the bill is calculated. Data also is recorded that can be used in inventory control.

Figure 6–18 A McDonald's sales order form. (Courtesy of McDonald's)

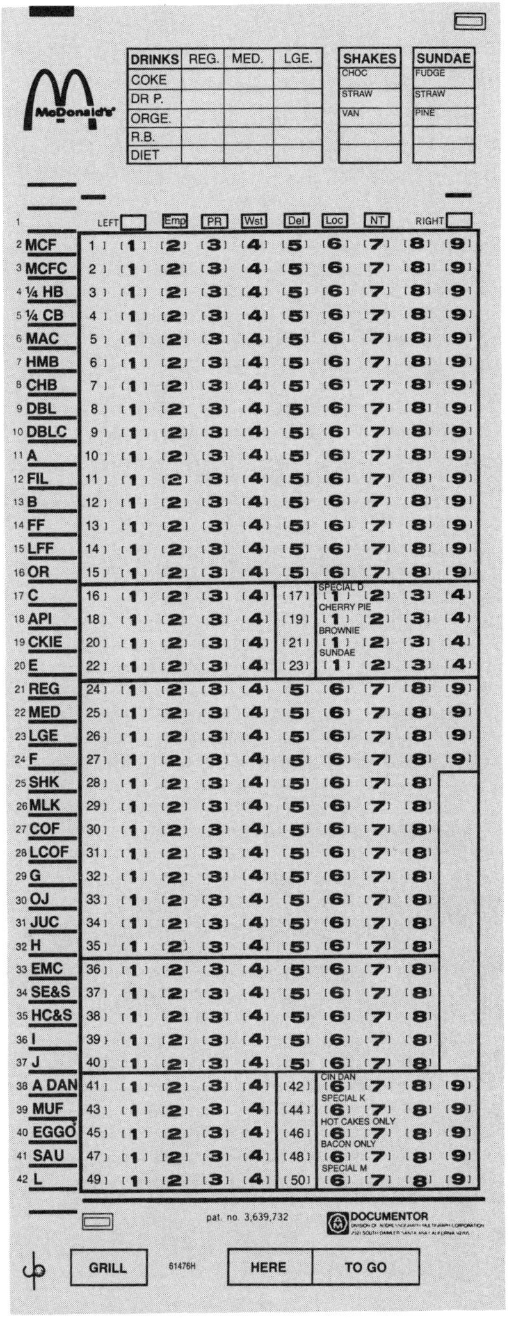

McDonald's

DRINKS	REG.	MED.	LGE.
COKE			
DR P.			
ORGE.			
R.B.			
DIET			

SHAKES
CHOC
STRAW
VAN

SUNDAE
FUDGE
STRAW
PINE

1		LEFT [ ]		Emp	PR	Wst		Del	Loc	NT	RIGHT [ ]
2	MCF	1	1	2	3	4	5	6	7	8	9
3	MCFC	2	1	2	3	4	5	6	7	8	9
4	¼ HB	3	1	2	3	4	5	6	7	8	9
5	¼ CB	4	1	2	3	4	5	6	7	8	9
6	MAC	5	1	2	3	4	5	6	7	8	9
7	HMB	6	1	2	3	4	5	6	7	8	9
8	CHB	7	1	2	3	4	5	6	7	8	9
9	DBL	8	1	2	3	4	5	6	7	8	9
10	DBLC	9	1	2	3	4	5	6	7	8	9
11	A	10	1	2	3	4	5	6	7	8	9
12	FIL	11	1	2	3	4	5	6	7	8	9
13	B	12	1	2	3	4	5	6	7	8	9
14	FF	13	1	2	3	4	5	6	7	8	9
15	LFF	14	1	2	3	4	5	6	7	8	9
16	OR	15	1	2	3	4	5	6	7	8	9
17	C	16	1	2	3	4	17	SPECIAL D 1	2	3	4
18	API	18	1	2	3	4	19	CHERRY PIE 1	2	3	4
19	CKIE	20	1	2	3	4	21	BROWNIE 1	2	3	4
20	E	22	1	2	3	4	23	SUNDAE 1	2	3	4
21	REG	24	1	2	3	4	5	6	7	8	9
22	MED	25	1	2	3	4	5	6	7	8	9
23	LGE	26	1	2	3	4	5	6	7	8	9
24	F	27	1	2	3	4	5	6	7	8	9
25	SHK	28	1	2	3	4	5	6	7	8	
26	MLK	29	1	2	3	4	5	6	7	8	
27	COF	30	1	2	3	4	5	6	7	8	
28	LCOF	31	1	2	3	4	5	6	7	8	
29	G	32	1	2	3	4	5	6	7	8	
30	OJ	33	1	2	3	4	5	6	7	8	
31	JUC	34	1	2	3	4	5	6	7	8	
32	H	35	1	2	3	4	5	6	7	8	
33	EMC	36	1	2	3	4	5	6	7	8	
34	SE&S	37	1	2	3	4	5	6	7	8	
35	HC&S	38	1	2	3	4	5	6	7	8	
36	I	39	1	2	3	4	5	6	7	8	
37	J	40	1	2	3	4	5	6	7	8	
38	A DAN	41	1	2	3	4	42	CIN DAN 6	7	8	9
39	MUF	43	1	2	3	4	44	SPECIAL K 6	7	8	9
40	EGGO	45	1	2	3	4	46	HOT CAKES ONLY 6	7	8	9
41	SAU	47	1	2	3	4	48	BACON ONLY 6	7	8	9
42	L	49	1	2	3	4	50	SPECIAL M 6	7	8	9

pat. no. 3,639,732

DOCUMENTOR

GRILL 61476H HERE TO GO

Printed Output

Up to this point, emphasis has been on means of gathering data and entering it into the computer. To conclude the chapter, the attention turns to output—specifically, printed output.

The final step of an information processing operation is the creation of information in a form facilitating use. Although information can be presented on a televisionlike screen, or spoken audibly, the most common form is printing on paper.

Line printers

Computer printers are called *line printers* since they print an entire line at a time, rather than a character at a time like a typewriter. (See Figure 6-19.)

Printers are designed to print a certain group of characters, called a *character set*. A set consists of the 10 numbers, 26 letters, and a selection of special characters. Most printers only print uppercase letters. The letters usually are printed 10 to the inch, and standard line lengths are 80 and 132 positions.

Until recently, characters were printed by a metal type slug hitting an ink ribbon positioned in front of the paper. A typewriter uses the same method. These printers are called *impact printers*. They are largely mechanical (as

Figure 6-19   A line printer. (Courtesy of International Business Machines)

Figure 6–20   A chain printing mechanism

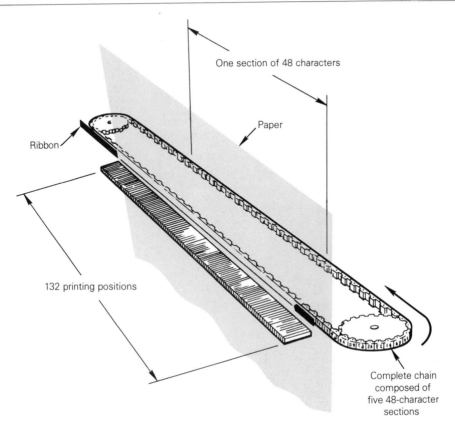

One section of 48 characters

Paper

Ribbon

132 printing positions

Complete chain
composed of
five 48-character
sections

opposed to electronic) devices that have evidenced little improved technology over punched card and keydriven printing devices. The main difference is speed. For example, punched card accounting machines can print 150 lines per minute (lpm), while line printer speeds range from 300 to 2000 lpm.

Where the accounting machines use type bars or wheels, line printers use either print drums or print chains. Most IBM printers use a continuous *type chain* with the type slugs serving as links. (See Figure 6–20.) The chain rotates in a horizontal plane in front of the ribbon and paper. As the appropriate character moves to the correct position, a hammer fires, causing the character to print. The letters are printed "on the fly" and horizontal alignment is very good (letters do not wave up and down on the line). Mohawk, Potter Instruments, and Telex also manufacture chain printers.

Most other manufacturers use a *print drum* (Figure 6–21). Each character appears once around the circumference of the drum for each position to be printed on the line. The shapes of the characters are raised on the metal

Figure 6–21   A print drum

The number of bands corresponds
to the number of printing positions

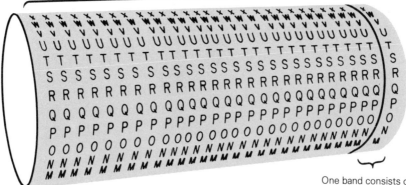

One band consists of all
printing characters used

surface just as they are on the links of the chain and on the type bars of a typewriter. The drum rotates in front of the ink ribbon and paper. When appropriate characters move to the print line area, hammers fire. The horizontal alignment is not as good as the chain printers, but in most cases it is acceptable.

Computer design engineers quickly realized they had pushed the impact technology as far as it would go. They began experimenting with devices that would be less mechanical, and would not require the impact of a hammer on a raised metal character. A new generation of printers, called *nonimpact printers*, was developed. By 1972, approximately nine different models were on the market, produced by six firms. They used ink jet or electrostatic technologies. In an *ink jet printer*, drops of ink are sprayed on the paper forming the characters. In an *electrostatic printer*, powderlike ink clings to electrostatically charged character shapes that are transferred to paper. This latter technology is the same as that used in Xerox copiers. Printing speeds for these early nonimpact printers ranged from 300 to 5000 lpm.

Other manufacturers have since entered the nonimpact printer market. In April 1975, IBM announced the 3800 Printing Subsystem for the System/370 computer (Figure 6–22). The 3800 can print up to 13,360 lpm with three print sizes: 10, 12, or 15 characters per inch. Printing is accomplished with both laser and electrophotographic technology.

A low-power laser forms character images on a light-sensitive photoconductor (PC) covering a rotating drum. The toner, a dry powder, is applied to the photoconductor, adhering only to the character images. The toner is then transferred to the paper. The format of the document (column headings, lines, etc.) can be applied to the paper by means of a forms overlay negative.

Figure 6–22   IBM 3800 Printing Subsystem. (Courtesy of International Business Machines)

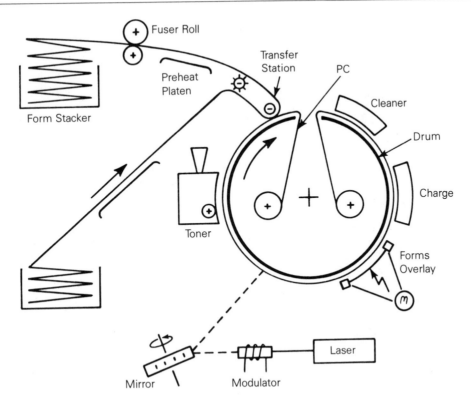

Only single copies can be printed, but the same information can be printed repeatedly—for several managers. Selected information can be deleted from certain copies for security purposes. It also is possible to address each copy of each report individually to speed it to its destination.

At present, nonimpact printers are beginning to find broad acceptance among users. But, these printers have appealed mainly to large firms with heavy printing volumes. As the technology is developed, the devices should find a place with smaller firms as well. Just as copiers such as the Xerox can be found in even the smallest operations, nonimpact printers likely will be found in small computer systems of the future.

Plotters

Very often the manager has a need for graphic information in the form of charts or graphs. A special output device is available to meet this need. The device is called a *plotter*. Some plotters are used online. Others are stand-alone units and operate offline. Some, such as the CalComp Model 960 shown in Figure 6–23, operate either online or offline.

Figure 6–23   The CalComp Model 960 plotter. (Courtesy of California Computer Products, Inc.)

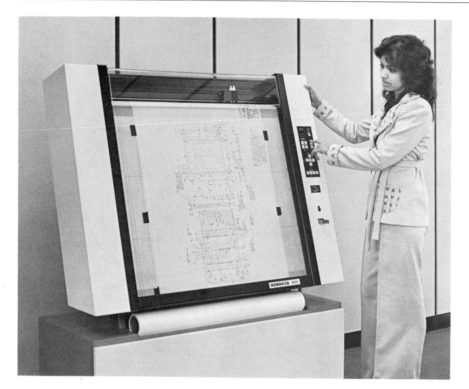

Lines are drawn by a pen that is program controlled either from the computer (when online) or from a controller (when offline). Some plotters employ three or four pens with different ink colors that can be selected by the program. Pens can be either ballpoints or the liquid ink variety.

Figure 6–24 is an example of graphic output, as printed by the Tektronix 4662 using a liquid ink pen.

Another more recent approach to plotting uses the electrostatic process developed for nonimpact printers. The Gould 5005 is such a system; it also features its own programming language, DISPLAY. The Gould system is designed for use with IBM System/360 and 370 computers.

An electrostatic device is much faster than one employing pens. The 5005 operates at speeds up to 3.25 paper inches per second. Pen-type plotters can require 2 or 3 minutes per graphic, depending on the complexity of the drawing.

The availability of a wide selection of plotter models permits the design of an MIS that meets the manager's need for graphic, as well as alphabetic and numeric, information. It will be seen in Chapter 8 that graphics can be displayed on a televisionlike terminal as well. The advantage of the plotter over the terminal is the availability of a permanent copy.

Figure 6-24   Plotter output drawn with an ink pen. (Courtesy of Tektronix, Inc.)

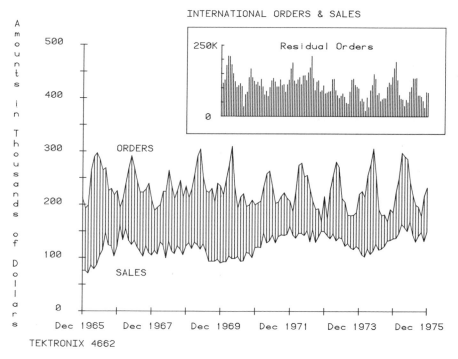

Other Means of Input and Output

There are other means of entering data into a computer and getting data and information out. Those involving the use of data communications equipment are examined in Chapter 8. Two additional input/output media deserve mention. They are punched paper tape and microfilm.

Data can be punched into paper tape, using basically the same coding scheme as that of the IBM System/3 card pictured in Figure 5-3. Ten characters are punched in an inch of the tape. A paper tape reading unit can enter the data into the CPU at a speed of up to 2000 characters per second, whereas a paper tape punch can punch data from the CPU at a speed of 20 to 300 characters per second.

Generally, it is not a practice to use punched paper tape unless it is obtained as a byproduct of some other operation. Punched cards are a more convenient medium. Very often paper tape will be created from a data communication activity (using a Telex or teletype machine) or from a retail sales transaction. In such cases, paper tape serves as an effective and economical means of input to the CPU.

It also is possible to create microfilm from a computer. The microfilm is called *COM* (computer output microfilm). The microfilm can be in roll, strip (microfiche), cartridge, or cassette form. The main advantage of microfilm is its compactness. It is ideal for the storage of data and document images for later retrieval.

Summary

In the general systems model of the firm presented in Chapter 3, an "information processor" converts data into information. As explained in Chapter 5, this conversion can be performed manually, by keydriven devices, by punched card machines, and by computer. All of these approaches include data input and information output.

In a computer system, special devices, called *I/O devices*, are attached to the CPU by means of data channels. These devices read data that has been gathered internally or from the environment, and create either information (for management use) or data (for subsequent processing).

Most data is created for computer input by using some type of keydriven device. The keypunch machine is the most popular single approach; but it is being replaced gradually with key-to-tape and key-to-disk units. The cards created by the keypunch machine are read into the CPU by a card reading unit. The tapes or disks are read by a disk or tape unit. Some of the tapes and disks are compatible with tape and disk units that have been used with computer systems for years. These are the types discussed in the next chapter. Other types are not compatible with these units—they are the cassette tapes, tape cartridges, and floppy disks. These incompatible tapes and disks are entered into the CPU by special reading units. Figure 6–25 illustrates the variations in how data created by keydriven devices is entered into the CPU.

The power and the flexibility of a computer are increased with the addition of input and output devices to the CPU. Many of these devices are general purpose in nature, and can be used by any type of firm. Examples are card readers and line printers. Other devices are special purpose and have been designed to meet the specific needs of a particular industry. Magnetic ink character recognition (MICR) is an example.

Input and output devices (the peripherals) are attached to the CPU by channels. The channels are important in that they permit a computer to overlap processing in the CPU with input and output operations. One type of channel handles the slower speed devices. This is the byte multiplexer channel. The block multiplexer channel and the selector channel handle the higher speed devices.

Many computer systems have only card readers, card punches, and line printers. These are called *card-oriented systems*. Cards can be read much faster than they can be punched. Printing speeds are being increased through nonimpact technology.

Figure 6–25 Keydriven input approaches

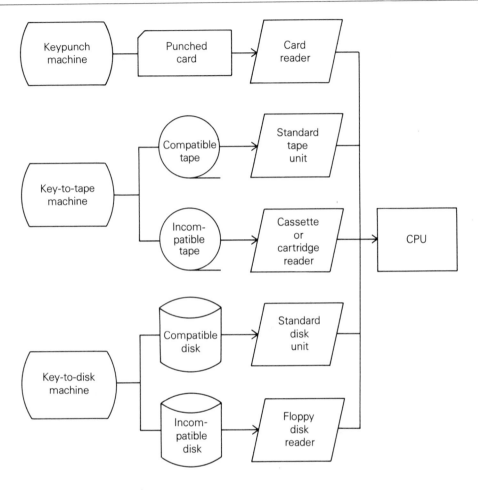

Two successful approaches have permitted direct entry of data from source documents. This technique bypasses a keying operation, and has been named source document automation. One is magnetic ink character recognition (MICR), designed for the banking industry, and the other is optical character recognition (OCR). MICR permits the handling of a large volume of paper checks in our "cashless society." In the future, a "checkless society" will use electronic funds transfer systems (EFTS) to update bank balances with electronically transmitted data. OCR currently is being applied to read credit card slips, airline tickets, restaurant orders, and many other types of paper forms. In some colleges and universities, multiple-choice and true-false tests are read optically for computer grading.

Improvements have been made in all of these devices during recent years. However, none exceed those made in the development of graphical plotters. Today, a wide variety of graphical output devices add a new dimension to information output.

All of these devices permit the computer to better function as an information system.

Important Terms

Peripherals

Channel

Serial

Parallel

Byte Multiplexer Channel

Block Multiplexer Channel

Selector Channel

Source Document

Unit Record

Field

Compatible Tape, Incompatible Tape

Multistation Keyboard Entry

Floppy Disk

Serial Card Reader

Parallel Card Reader

Turnaround Document

Mark Sensing

Port-a-Punch

Type Font

Magnetic Ink Character Recognition (MICR)

Encoder

Reader Sorter

Stand-Alone Unit, Online Unit

Optical Character Recognition (OCR)

Scanner

Page Reader

Document Reader

Source Data Automation, Direct Entry

Line Printer

Character Set

Impact Printer, Nonimpact Printer

Print Chain, Print Drum

Ink Jet Printer

Electrostatic Printer

Plotter

Computer Output Microfilm (COM)

Compatible Disk, Incompatible Disk

Cashless Society

Checkless Society

Electronic Funds Transfer System (EFTS)

Important Concepts

Input/output and auxiliary storage units are attached to the CPU by means of channels.

The keypunch machine is only one of several means of creating input data by depressing keys.

Punched cards can be created in several ways; they offer some unique approaches to data recording.

MICR and OCR ease the input bottleneck by providing direct entry of source data.

A variety of types of line printers are available, with the fastest being the nonimpact type.

Graphical output from the computer is also available with the use of plotters.

Punched paper tape and microfilm are often useful, but are less popular means of input and output respectively.

Important People and Organizations

Mohawk Data Sciences Corporation

American Banking Association

Recognition Equipment Incorporated (REI)

Compuscan

Questions

1   What is the device that attaches input/output and auxiliary storage units to the CPU?

2   What is the difference between serial and parallel data transfer?

3   What are the three types of channels?

4   When is a source document a unit record? When does the source document represent more than one unit record?

5   How do key-to-tape and key-to-disk machines relieve the input bottleneck?

6   What are compatible tapes and disks?

7   Which type of card reader operates at the fastest speeds: serial or parallel? Which would be expected to be the most expensive?

8   How do some card readers detect errors made in reading the holes in the card?

9   What are two examples of turnaround documents, other than utility bills?

10 How does a turnaround document relieve the input bottleneck?

11 What is the main advantage of mark sensing? Of port-a-punch?

12 How is the amount of a check recorded in magnetic ink? Does this process have any relationship to the input bottleneck?

13 Which machine processes a check first: a reader sorter or an encoder?

14 Is a keypunch a stand-alone unit or an online unit? What about a card reader?

15 Why are standard type fonts, such as E-13-B and OCR-A, developed?

16 Does OCR require the characters to be printed in a special ink?

17 Is a typewriter an impact or a nonimpact type of printer? Can a typewriter be considered a line printer?

18 How many copies can the IBM 3800 Printing Subsystem prepare? Is this a disadvantage? If so, how can it be overcome?

19 How can the 3800 contribute to better security of information within the firm?

20 In what forms can the manager receive graphic information?

21 How does the banking industry plan to handle the increasing volume of checks in the future?

Problems

---

1 Draw the layout of a punched card, with fields to contain data from your driver's license.

2 You are a sales representative for IBM. You are calling on the computer center manager for the largest life insurance company in the state, attempting to stimulate interest in the 3800 Printing Subsystem. Before you enter the manager's office you list the advantages the 3800 has over impact printers. What would you list?

3 The systems analyst assigned to your department, financial planning, has asked you how you would like three graphical reports displayed on your television-style terminal. Using the following data, sketch the style of graph that would best convey the information.

Sales

1975	$13,500,000
1976	15,250,000
1977	17,700,000
1978	21,500,000

Personnel by Division

Marketing	63	(17%)
Finance	45	(12%)
Manufacturing	263	(71%)

Men and Women Employees by Year

	Men	Women
1975	198	105
1976	210	126
1977	218	130
1978	232	139

Chapter 7

Computer Storage and the Data Base

The central processing unit (CPU) and the input/output units of the computer system have been described in the two previous chapters. More units can be attached, and they are the subject of this, and the next, chapter. This chapter deals mainly with *auxiliary storage*—storage that augments, or supplements, the main storage of the CPU. The next chapter concludes the description of computing equipment by explaining data communication and terminals.

Main Storage

In Chapter 5 a model of an information processing system was presented (see Figure 5–11). In that model, a part of the CPU is devoted to storage. This storage is used to contain input data, output data, working data, and the program.

This is the *main storage* of the computer—it holds the program being executed and the data being processed. Main storage usually has been constructed of magnetic cores, but now the trend is to silicon chips. Whatever the technology, main storage is very fast, as this determines the computing or processing speed of the computer. The speed of main storage is measured in the length of time required to obtain a piece of data from the storage. This *cycle time* is measured in millionths of a second (microseconds) or billionths of a second (nanoseconds). The cycle time of an IBM System/370 is 2.07 microseconds or less, depending on the model.

The number of digits or characters obtained from storage in a cycle depends on the computer. In some systems, only a single byte is obtained at a time. A *byte* can represent a single character (an alphabetic letter, a special character such as a dollar sign, or a digit) or two digits. When a byte contains two digits, the storage use is called *packed decimal*. In some systems, more than one byte can be obtained in a single cycle. The contents of four bytes is a *word*.

Main storage permits a location containing one or more bytes to be obtained in the cycle time. All locations are available at the same speed—the computer can address any location directly. The computer need not scan locations to reach the one sought, for it has *direct access* to all locations.

Main storage has some specific capacity. The capacity can be rather large,

such as 64K (65,536 bytes) or 512K (524,288 bytes).[1] Although this capacity might seem more than adequate, rarely is it large enough. Large data records and programs tax the capacity of many systems. This effect is especially true when the computer is used in a multiprogramming manner.

Types of Auxiliary Storage

The limitation on the capacity of main storage means that some additional storage area, or areas, must be made available to the CPU. These additional areas are the auxiliary storage. Figure 5–9 can be redrawn, as in Figure 7–1, to show this auxiliary storage.

The two basic types of auxiliary storage are magnetic tape and direct access storage devices (DASD). Both types involve the representation of data in the form of magnetized spots, called *bits*, on some recording medium. The medium can be plastic tape (similar to recording tape) or a metal disk (similar to a phonograph record).

During the brief history of the computer, other technologies have been

Figure 7–1   Addition of auxiliary storage to a computer system

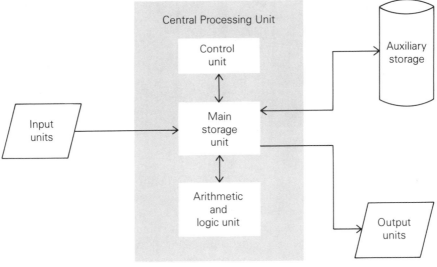

---

1. While K means one thousand, computer storage usually is expressed in increments of 1024 bytes. Therefore, K means 1024, not 1000.

Figure 7–2   The IBM 3850 Mass Storage Facility. (Courtesy of International Business Machines)

employed as auxiliary storage. These have included rotating magnetic drums, magnetic cards, and strips of magnetic tape. Magnetic drums are faster than disks, but the capacity is less. Magnetic cards and tape strips offer huge capacity, but have suffered from mechanical problems.

A new auxiliary storage device offered by IBM might answer the yet unmet need for a relatively inexpensive direct access storage with large capacity. It is the 3850 Mass Storage Facility (Figure 7–2) that is available on the System/370. Data is stored on spools of magnetic tape approximately 3 inches wide and 770 inches long. The spools are contained in plastic cartridges and are mechanically removed when needed. Each cartridge has a capacity of 50 million bytes.

Figure 7–3 A reel of magnetic computer tape. (Courtesy of International Business Machines)

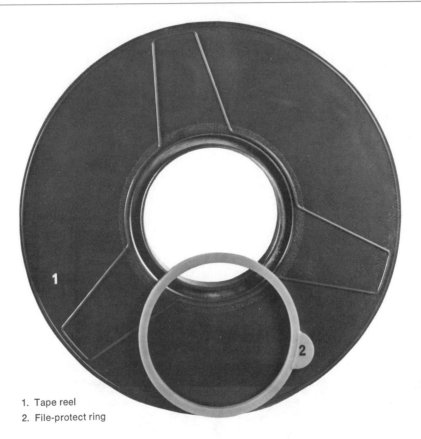

1. Tape reel
2. File-protect ring

Magnetic Tape Storage

Even the earliest computers used magnetic tape (Figure 7–3). It continues to be a popular medium for several reasons. It is very compact: one reel of tape, $\frac{1}{2}$ inch wide and 2400 feet long, can contain over 30 million bytes. Tape is inexpensive.

Computer tape is used in basically the same manner as sound recording tape. Instead of sound being recorded magnetically in frequencies, computer tape contains data recorded magnetically in combinations of bits. The eight data bits comprising a byte are written across the width of the tape (Figure 7–4), along with a check bit. The check bit is used to signal an error caused by adding or losing bits accidentally. A large number of bytes can be recorded in an inch of tape. The standard *recording densities* are 200, 556, 800, and 1600 bytes per inch (bpi).

Figure 7–4 Data bits are recorded across the width of the tape.

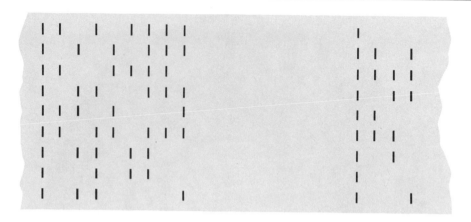

Figure 7–5 A magnetic tape unit. (Courtesy of Sperry Univac)

A reel of tape is placed on a *magnetic tape unit* (Figure 7–5), often called a *tape drive.* The leading portion is threaded through a read/write mechanism, and wrapped around the hub of a takeup reel. As data is written onto the tape or read from it by the *read/write mechanism,* the tape is wound onto the takeup reel. When all the data has been read from the file or written onto it, the reels are rewound and the source reel removed.

How data is recorded on tape

The capacity of a tape reel, in bytes, depends on how the data is recorded on the tape. Figure 7–6 shows how the parts of a tape are used for different purposes.

Part of the tape is used to attach the tape to the two reels. These parts are called *leaders.* Data is not recorded on these areas.

In many systems the first and last records on the tape are used for control purposes. These records are known as *labels.* The one at the beginning of the tape is the *header label.* The one at the end is the *trailer label.* These labels assist in assuring the accuracy of the tape data and their use.

Figure 7–6   A computer tape

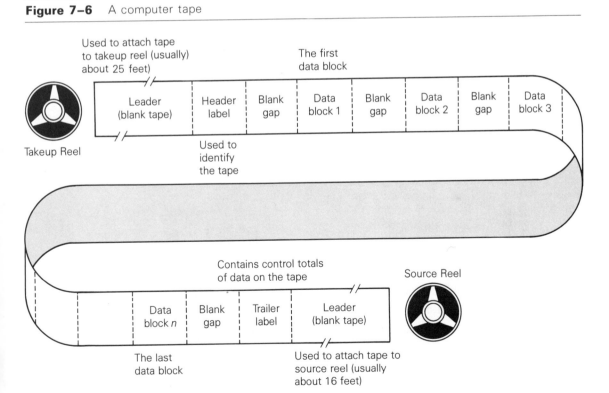

Figure 7–7   A single record written on tape

Blank	Customer number	Order number	Order date	Salesman number	Item number	Item description	Quantity	Unit price	Total price	Blank

Most of the tape is used for recording data. This data is written as *blocks* in the area between the labels. The tape unit writes the blocks and later reads them separately, one at a time. A block can contain a single record, as in Figure 7–7, or multiple records. A *record* is a set of related data. For example, a sales record contains all of the data elements describing the sale. A punched card sales record was shown in the last chapter in Figure 6–3. The same data, recorded on tape, likely would be arranged in the same format.

Figure 7–8 illustrates how single or multiple records can be written in blocks. The number of records in a block is called the *blocking factor.*

It is apparent from the figure that a considerable part of the tape can be used for the blank gaps separating the blocks. More space is used for gaps when multiple records are not blocked than when they are. This is one reason multiple records are blocked, i.e., to use more of the tape for data and less for the gaps.

Figure 7–8   Blocks of data on magnetic tape

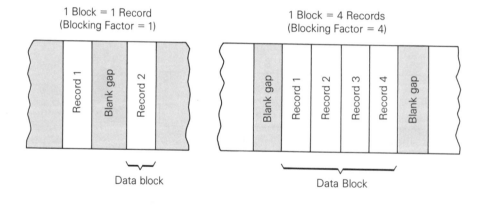

Figure 7–9 Tape data is written and read one block at a time.

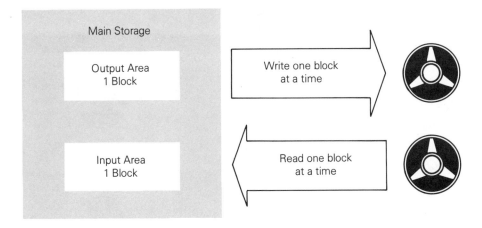

As explained above, one block is read or written at a time (Figure 7–9). Each time the CPU directs the tape unit to write a block, the tape starts to move past the read/write mechanism. Some tape must be passed over before the tape reaches the desired speed so that the first byte can be written. Then, after the last byte is written, some tape must be passed over before the tape comes to a stop. These blank areas become the gaps separating the blocks. They are called *interblock gaps*, and usually occupy 0.5 inch.

The size of the blocking factor depends, in part, on the amount of main storage available. Each block must be "assembled" in main storage before it is written. Then, each block of data read from the tape must enter main storage as a unit. Tape blocks keep the gaps to a minimum and reduce the number of time-consuming tape unit start and stop operations. This is the second main reason for blocking records.

Uses of magnetic tape

A reel of tape usually contains a single file of data. A *file* is a collection of records relating to a particular subject. An example is a payroll file that includes a record for each employee. It is possible to record several files on a single reel; some files are so large as to require several reels. But, it simplifies matters to think of a reel as containing a single file.

One use of magnetic tape is as an *input medium*. For example, payroll data showing employee number and hours worked can be keyed onto a tape using a key-to-tape machine. The tape data can then be read into main storage for a computation of payroll amounts.

In the payroll computation, the employee payroll master record is read for each employee. These records are contained on tape on a payroll master file (Figure 7–10). Thus, a second use is as a *file medium*.

Figure 7–10   Updating the payroll master file

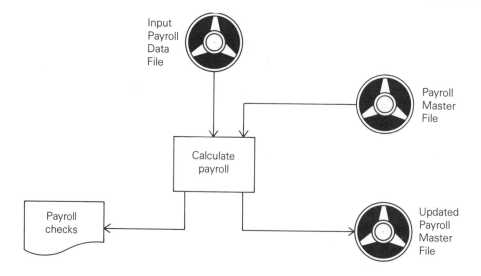

Both the input payroll data file and the payroll master file are in the same sequence, by employee number. This is an example of batch processing. Payroll calculations are made in batches, and all data files must be in a certain sequence. Another name for batch processing is sequential processing.

In Figure 7–10, an input payroll data record is read into main storage, along with the payroll master record. With both records for an employee in main storage, the computer can multiply hourly rate (from the master record) times hours worked (from the payroll data record) to obtain gross pay. Then, deductions can be made, using data from the master record, to calculate net pay. While all this data is in main storage, a payroll check can be printed on the line printer.

Before the next employee's records are read, an updated payroll master record is written. This updated record contains data such as gross pay to date, income tax to date, social security tax to date, etc. These amounts reflect the results of the calculations just completed.

The updated file is never written back onto the input reel. It always is written onto another reel. This is the third use of magnetic tape—as an *output medium*. This new file will provide the master data the next time payroll computations are made. It now contains the current data.

Magnetic tape also can be used as a *historical storage medium*. Since a reel of tape is so inexpensive, and contains so much data in a small area, tape is ideal for historical storage. Accounting procedures require that historical data be retained for a period of time. This data provides the detailed description of what the firm has done. There may be a need to review this data for some reason, but the probability or frequency is too low to keep it in a more expensive form. Such historical files are assumed to have a low activity.

A final use of magnetic tape is as a *communication medium*. A reel can provide the communication from one computer routine to another, such as from the payroll computation described above to a routine that prints a payroll report for management. In addition, tape reels can be mailed or delivered to other computer sites. This use can be less expensive than use of some type of data communication network (described in the next chapter). The U.S. Government, for example, will accept income tax reports on tape, rather than in printed form. These tapes then serve as input to the government computers.

Advantages and disadvantages of magnetic tape

Two advantages of magnetic tape already have been mentioned. It is inexpensive and compact. Additionally, it is fast. Data can be written onto tape or read from it much faster than any of the input and output media presented in the previous chapter. Tape units operate at speeds ranging from about 3000 bps (bytes per second) to over 300,000 bps.

A major disadvantage of magnetic tape is that it must be used in sequential processing. There is no way to directly access a record without starting at the beginning of the file and examining each preceding record. Nonsequential processing of tape data would consume too much CPU time to represent a feasible means of record retrieval.

Direct Access Storage Devices (DASD)

The restricted use of magnetic tape to sequential processing was serious enough to trigger the development of an alternative medium. The saying "necessity is the mother of invention" explains what happened. There was a need for an auxiliary storage featuring direct access. Seeing this need, computer manufacturers developed magnetic drum and disk storage. Since disks are the most popular form, they will be used as the basis of the following discussion.

Early technology

IBM can take credit for pioneering this disk technology that has become so widely accepted. During the 1950s, IBM built a plant at San Jose, California to design and build *direct access storage devices (DASD)*. The first computer system offering DASD was the first-generation IBM 305 RAMAC (Random Access Method of Accounting and Control), pictured in Figure 7–11.

By today's standards, the RAMAC was nothing special. Its input/output units were extremely slow, as was its cycle time. What made it special at the time was a stack of 50 rotating metal disks—a *disk stack*. The stack was permanently housed in its cabinet and could contain 5 million characters. Data was organized in 100-character records, and any of the records could be retrieved in a maximum of $8/10$ of a second. There was no need to scan records sequentially. The *access mechanism* could be directed to any record in the file—direct access. This meant that transactions could be processed as they

occurred; there was no need to batch them. This development marked the beginning of transaction processing.

At the beginning of the chapter, it was explained that the main storage of the computer also has direct access. The term *direct access storage* is not used to describe main storage however. It describes an auxiliary type of storage such as that of the RAMAC.

Record addressing

While RAMAC has been outmoded by greatly improved DASD units, it still serves an educational purpose. It provides a good example of how addresses of the records are determined, and how the access mechanism is directed to those locations.

Just as each location of main storage has an address, each recording location in a DASD unit has one also. The computer program must provide this address to the access mechanism. In effect, the program says "get me the record at location 12345." The access mechanism moves to that part of the disk file and reads the record into main storage. There, the data is processed, and the updated record is written in the *same area* of the disk stack where it was recorded originally.

This is a basic difference between disk and tape updating. Updated tape records never are written back on the same area from which they are read. Disk records usually are.

In the RAMAC, each of the 50 disks had a number—from 00 to 49 (Figure 7–12). Data was recorded on both the top and bottom of each disk in *tracks.* There were 100 tracks on each side, and they were numbered from 00 to 99.

Figure 7–12   Data disks and tracks

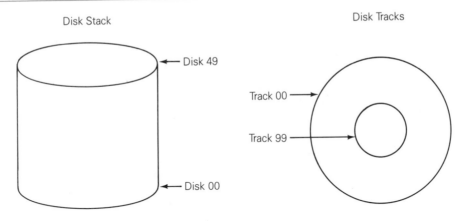

Disk Stack

Disk Tracks

Disk 49

Disk 00

Track 00

Track 99

Each disk also was divided into 10 *sectors*, similar to slices of a pie (Figure 7–13). The top surface of a disk included sectors 0–4, and sectors 5–9 were on the bottom. Each track in each sector had a capacity of 100 characters. (The recording density was greater for the inner tracks.)

The RAMAC had a forklike access arm, shown in Figure 7–14. The fork could move from one disk to another and move in and out of the disk stack. The fork straddled each disk but did not touch the disk surface. Two small read/write heads were attached to the end of the arm, one for the top surface and one for the bottom.

Figure 7–13   Recording sectors

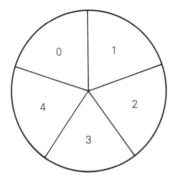

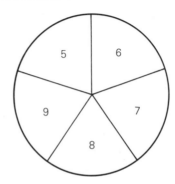

Top Surface

Bottom Surface

Figure 7–14   A single forklike access arm served all 50 disks.

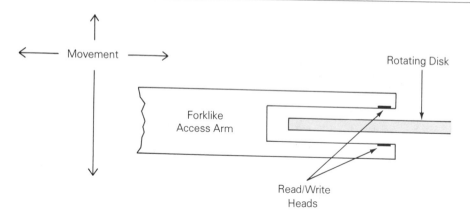

Assume that the program calls for RAMAC record 12345. The positions of the address had special meanings:

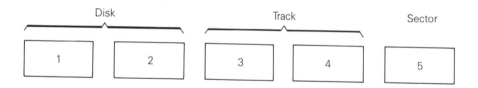

The access arm moved to *disk 12;* then it moved in to *track 34.* As the disk rotated past the arm, the read/write head read the 100-character record from *sector 5.* When the updated record was written back to the file, the read/write head waited until sector 5 was reached before the data was written.

Current DASD units

Current DASD models employ an addressing scheme similar to RAMAC, although a sector is not included. Also, records can be of varying lengths, not just the fixed length of 100 characters. There is still a need to identify the disk surface, the track, and the location on the track where the record is located, and this is accomplished with an address.

Several other major improvements have been made in DASD technology. An important one concerns the access mechanism, or *access arm.* Instead of a single arm that moves up and down and in and out, modern units use a comb-like arrangement of multiple arms (Figure 7–15).

This approach was initiated in the second generation, and is still in use. There is an access arm for each pair of disk surfaces, and the arm fits between

Figure 7–15   A comb-like access mechanism

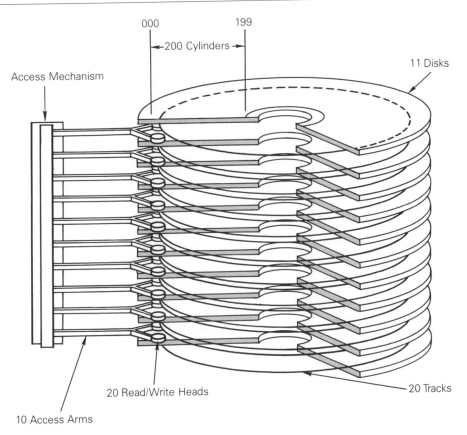

000   199

←200 Cylinders→

11 Disks

Access Mechanism

20 Read/Write Heads

20 Tracks

10 Access Arms

the disks. The disk stack pictured in Figure 7–15 has 11 disks. The top surface of the top disk and the bottom surface of the bottom disk are not used for data recording, thus leaving 20 data surfaces. At the end of each arm are two *read/write heads:* one for the surface above and one for the surface below.

The main improvement made possible by the comb-like mechanism is increased speed. Present-day DASD units offer access times as low as 60, 30, or 12.5 milliseconds (thousandths of a second).

Another improvement made it possible to remove a disk stack, called a *disk pack,* from its cabinet. This feature offers the same interchangeability as tape reels. The disk pack pictured in Figure 7–16 has a capacity of 100 million bytes. A similar pack has a capacity of 200 million bytes.

The disk pack is installed in a disk storage drive (Figure 7–17) to make the data available to the CPU. When not in use, the disk pack is stored with the tape reels in the media library.

Another improvement has added even more speed. This is a fixed-head

Figure 7–16 A removable disk pack. (Courtesy of International Business Machines)

Figure 7–17 A disk storage drive. (Courtesy of Honeywell, Inc.)

Figure 7–18   A data module with built-in read/write heads (Courtesy The National Cash Register Co.)

capability in which each track has its own read/write head. In the *data module* type of disk pack pictured in Figure 7–18, the access mechanism is built into the disk pack. This module has a total capacity of up to 69 million bytes. One-half million bytes are served by fixed heads.

DASD units are available in a wide variety. These are offered by the large computer manufacturers and by smaller firms specializing in peripheral equipment. Most of these are disk units as described above. The large number in use assure that disk storage will be popular for some time. However, the manufacturers are continuing their search for improved technologies. Most likely, the next few years will bring announcements of new developments. These units, whatever their technology, will offer greater capacity and/or speed at less cost than present disks.

How data is recorded on a disk

Although the physical form of disk storage is different from tape, there are several similarities in how both media are used. Disk files also have labels, both header and trailer labels. Moreover, these labels contain the same type of information. The labels are recorded on disk tracks with the header label at the beginning of the file and the trailer at the end.

Also, there are gaps between the records on a track. These gaps are not caused by starting and stopping, since the disk rotates continuously. Rather, the gaps provide time for the CPU to perform some processing between records.

Figure 7–19   Gaps separate data records and addresses on the disk track.

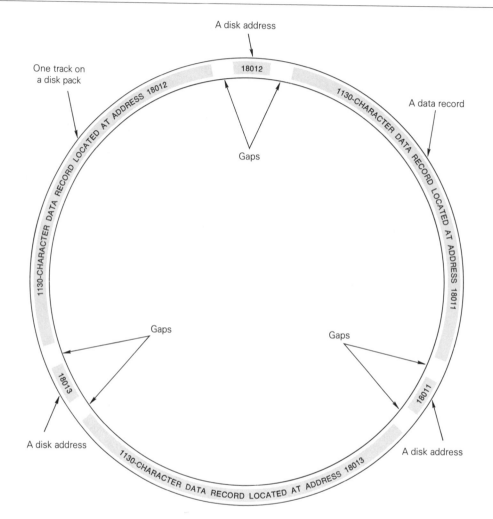

Figure 7–19 shows a track with three data records. There is a gap before and after each record. In addition, each data record is preceded by its address, separated by gaps. These addresses enable the computer to identify a particular record on the track.

As in magnetic tape, data is recorded on a disk in the form of magnetized bits. The same coding structure of eight data bits per byte plus a check bit may be used. The bytes are recorded serially (one after the other) along the track, rather than in the parallel form of the tape (across the width). This arrangement is shown in Figure 7–20.

Figure 7–20   Data bits are recorded serially along the disk track.

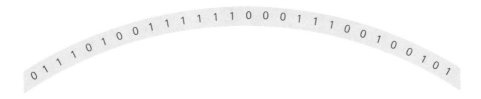

How records are arranged in a DASD file

As seen earlier, magnetic tape records can be blocked, and usually are arranged sequentially. In a payroll file, for example, the record with the smallest employee number is first. The record with the largest number is last.

Records can be recorded on a DASD device in the same way. This *sequential storage* permits the DASD to be used like a magnetic tape (see Figure 7–21). It is not possible to access records directly.

There are three other ways to organize records in a DASD file. One is used for programs and the other two for data. A DASD unit can be *partitioned* into separate areas for each program or subprogram, as shown in Figure 7–22. The access mechanism can be directed to the location of the first instruction in a partition. The entire program or subprogram can then be called into main storage sequentially, one instruction following the next.

A third type of file organization is *indexed sequential*, shown in Figure 7–23. As the name implies, the records are arranged sequentially, as in sequential storage. However, there is something extra—an index. The index

Figure 7–21   Sequential organization of a DASD file

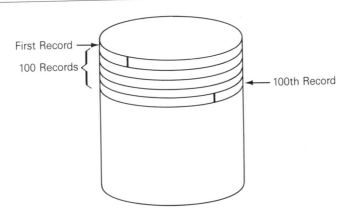

Figure 7–22   Partitioned organization of a DASD file

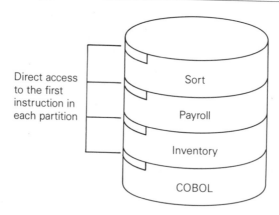

serves as a directory of the records in the file. Although Figure 7–23 shows the index separate from the file, usually it is recorded on the first few tracks.

The index contains a key for each record in the file. The *key* is the identifying code number (employee, part, or customer number). The keys are listed in the index sequentially, and with each key is the DASD address of the record. It is not possible for the key to serve also as the address. The index links the two.

The computer program provides the key for the record needed. The key is compared with each entry in the index until a match is found. The corresponding address is used then to send the access mechanism to the location where the record is stored. The advantage of this approach is direct access. The

Figure 7–23   Indexed sequential organization of a DASD file

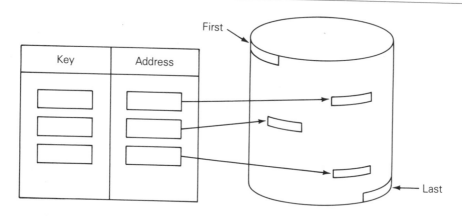

Figure 7–24   Direct organization of a DASD file

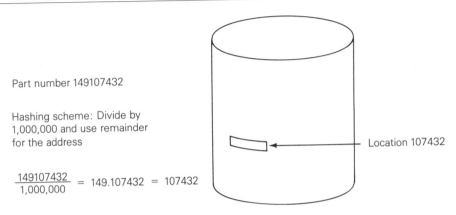

Part number 149107432

Hashing scheme: Divide by
1,000,000 and use remainder
for the address

$$\frac{149107432}{1,000,000} = 149.107432 = 107432$$

Location 107432

disadvantage is the need to search through an index before the address can be determined.

This limitation can be overcome by using the fourth type of file organization—*direct*, as illustrated in Figure 7–24.

With direct organization, the data address can be generated by the program. The address is used to send the access mechanism to the correct location. The easiest approach is to use the key as the address. For example, part number 12345 could identify disk 12, track 34, and the fifth record on the track. The only problem is that few coding schemes match exactly the addressing scheme of the DASD unit. As an example, part numbers contain too many positions, include alphabetic characters, and do not run in continuous sequences.

This means that some type of arithmetic must be performed on the code to convert it into a usable address. Such use of arithmetic is called a *hashing scheme*. In Figure 7–24, part number 149107432 is divided by 1000000 and the remainder, 107432, is used as the address.

The main advantage of direct addressing is that only a single movement of the access mechanism is required. Since access movements are time-consuming (compared with reading, processing, and writing DASD data), more efficient computer use is possible with direct organization than it is with other file organizations. The main disadvantage is the unequal distribution of records that is likely to result in the DASD device. It is possible for the address arithmetic to produce the same address for more than one key. These are called *synonyms*. In this case, all records assigned to a location after the first one must be located elsewhere. The access mechanism is sent to the first location, finds that the record is elsewhere, and looks there next. One or more additional movements of the access mechanism might be required. This is time-consuming and should not occur very often. If it does, a new hashing scheme should be devised, one producing fewer synonyms.

Uses of DASD

DASD units are used for both data and programs with high activity. Customer, inventory, and employee files all have this characteristic. Most of these files are active every day. Certainly not all records within the file are active, but enough are to warrant the expense of DASD. It costs more to maintain data in a DASD form than magnetic tape. A file should not be kept on DASD unless the cost is justified.

Of the five basic approaches to computer processing presented in Chapter 5, three require DASD. These are *transaction processing, realtime processing,* and *timesharing.* In each of these situations, it is impossible to anticipate which program, file, or record will be required next by a user. For this reason, all must be kept in a "ready" state—recorded on a DASD unit available to the CPU. This procedure is shown in Figure 7–25.

In all three approaches, programs are called from the DASD to perform certain computations. Also, data from the DASD is made available to the programs. The data may be updated or it may be used to generate output. In realtime processing, this output changes the status of the physical system (such as reserving a seat on an airplane). In transaction processing and timesharing, the output is that desired by the user (such as the solution to a computation).

In addition to the three approaches to processing, DASD also permits *inquiry.* This ability is especially valuable in an MIS. It enables the manager to inquire into the data files and receive information within seconds. Not all questions demand such immediate response and can be answered with periodic reports. However, immediate response can offer an ability never before available to the manager. Examples of inquiry response will be described in later chapters.

In the above discussion, DASD is used as a *file medium.* It also can be used for *input, output,* and *data communication* in the same manner as magnetic tape. DASD generally is not used for historical storage—it is too expensive.

Advantages and disadvantages of DASD

Magnetic tape and DASD complement each other as reflected in Figure 7–26. The disadvantages of one are the advantages of another. They both offer compactness, but this characteristic is more valuable for magnetic tape since it is used for historical storage. When a firm considers tape or DASD as an auxiliary storage, direct access is the determinant. When direct access is required, such as for timesharing or transaction processing, DASD is selected. Otherwise, magnetic tape will do the job at less cost.

Virtual Storage

Even though main storage can be obtained in large sizes, it can be prohibitively expensive. Since DASD can be obtained in larger sizes at lower costs, users have sought ways of using it as an extension of main storage.

Figure 7-25 DASD makes data and programs immediately available.

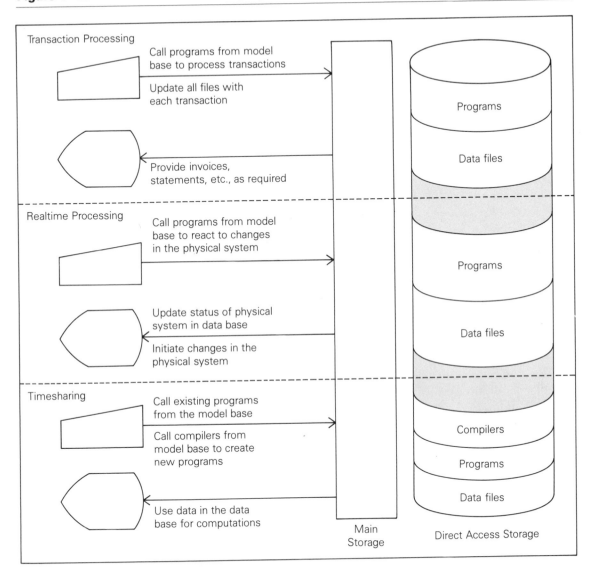

One approach is to divide a large program into *segments* (Figure 7-27). The segment being executed is in main storage, and the others are in DASD. When another segment is needed, it is entered into main storage. The only segment in main storage is the one being executed; the others are in DASD.

With this approach, a program can be larger than the main storage capacity. The only limitation is the maximum address size that the computer can handle. For example, a computer might have a main storage capacity of

Figure 7–26   Comparison of magnetic tape and DASD features

Feature	Magnetic Tape	DASD
Cost	Positive factor: very low price medium	Negative factor: more expensive than magnetic tape
Compactness	Positive factor: very compact medium	Positive factor: very compact medium
Access	Negative factor: direct access not feasible	Positive factor: permits direct access

512,000 positions, but the use of a 24-bit address would permit 16,777,216 addresses. This expanded storage (assuming each address to represent a storage position) is called *address space.* The concept of address space larger than real storage is known as *virtual storage.*[2]

A program for a virtual storage system does not contain actual addresses of the locations it will use in main storage. Rather, it contains *relative* addresses. These addresses are relative to the first location for each segment. For example, a program might have three segments:

Segment	Number of positions	Relative addresses
1	20,000	0–19,999
2	10,000	0–9,999
3	20,000	0–19,999

When the operating system wishes the computer to execute segment 1, it is called from auxiliary storage. It can be entered into any part of main storage

2. A more thorough, yet easily understandable, description of virtual storage can be found in IBM student text GR20-4260-1, *Introduction to Virtual Storage in System/370.*

Figure 7–27   Storage of program segments on a DASD

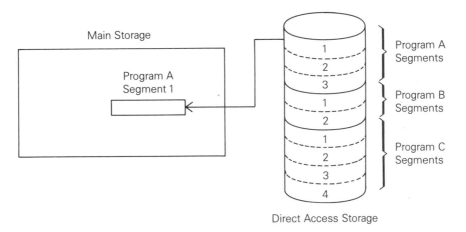

containing 20,000 consecutive locations. The operating system might decide to load the segment beginning at location 80,000. The addresses of the real storage locations for each position of segment 1 can then be determined by adding 80,000 to the relative addresses. Segment 1 resides in locations 80,000–99,999.

Virtual storage is important to the manager. It means that a smaller computer can execute a large program that is divided into segments. Main storage capacity doesn't represent a constraint on the type or size of problem that the computer can handle.

Now that an understanding of computer storage has been achieved, attention can be directed to an important part of the MIS—the data base. In the remainder of this chapter a better understanding will be developed of the data base.

Summary of Computer Storage

Main storage (in the CPU) is very fast and offers direct access to any location. Locations may refer to a single character, called a byte, or to several bytes, called a word. Two digits can be represented by a byte, with the use of packed decimal. Main storage, however, is limited in its capacity, and this has necessitated the use of some type of auxiliary storage.

All but the smallest computers today use some type of magnetic tape or DASD auxiliary storage. Magnetic tape always has been popular because of its low cost. Continuous reductions in the cost of DASD have made it more and more common as a part of the computer configuration. Today, more systems include DASD than magnetic tape.

While it is possible to have a computerized MIS without DASD, the conditions would be very special. That would mean that there was no need for immediate inquiry into the data base. However, the cost of this inquiry capability is so low with DASD that most MIS configurations include it.

While DASD makes the information system responsive, many organizations use magnetic tape for file storage. In these situations, the increased responsiveness of DASD does not justify its added cost.

Some operating systems can maintain the parts of large programs in DASD until a part is needed. Then, the part is entered into main storage. This technique, in effect, expands main storage to a size that virtually has no limits. The use of main storage in this way is called virtual storage.

The Data Base

Auxiliary storage is used to store both programs and data. The data is organized into files that are subdivided into records. Each record is comprised of data elements, often called data fields. The term *model base* has been used to describe the collection of the firm's programs. The term *data base* has been used to describe the collection of data files.

Basic types of files

The three basic types of files are represented in Figure 7–28. The most important are *master files*. They are important in that they represent the status of the firm's resources and certain of the environmental elements. There are master files for the firm's personnel, its inventory, its financial status, and so on. There also are files for the firm's customers, stockholders, vendors, etc.

The firm attempts to keep these master files current. This currency is accomplished by updating them with the results of certain transactions. These transaction records are contained in transaction files—a second basic type. A *transaction file* contains changes of a particular kind to one or more of the master files. Transaction files are prepared for sales orders received from customers, hours worked by employees, inventory receipts from vendors, and other activities.

Finally, there are *intermediate files* that contain semiprocessed data. These files provide the communication link between steps of a multistep procedure. As an example, one step might edit incoming sales orders for completeness, and conduct a credit check. The output of that step is an approved order file that serves as input to the next step of checking the inventory status of the ordered items. The approved order file is an intermediate file as it contains data that has been only partially processed.

What is the data base?

The data base can be defined broadly, to include *all* data within the organization used for any purpose. With that viewpoint, all three types of files are

Figure 7–28   Basic file types

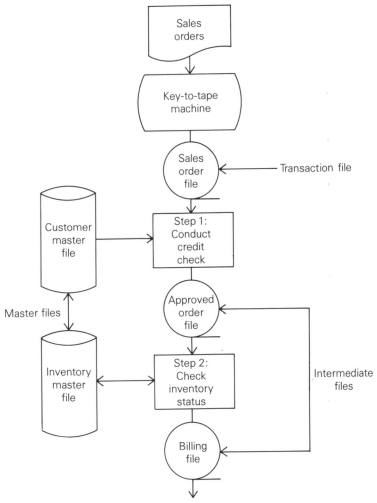

To Step 3: Prepare customer invoices

included. Or, the data base can be defined narrowly, to include only master files used to generate management information. A more moderate stand includes all data files used to generate information for all users of the system. The users include managers, nonmanagement employees of the firm, and members of the firm's environment (customers). This latter view seems to be the most realistic, since it recognizes that others, in addition to the managers, have a need for information about the firm.

Regardless of how broadly or narrowly the data base is defined, the master files are best maintained in some type of DAS device. This custom permits both rapid updating and retrieval of information. The transaction and intermediate files can be recorded in a sequential form, and magnetic tape is fine for this purpose. In fact, punched card files often are used to record transactions in their initial form.

Pre-data base approach

In the early years of the computer, the programmer specified the layout and sequence of the file, or files, used in each assigned program. The programmer performed this task as long as another programmer already had not specified some or all of the files. In this case, the second programmer simply used the file specifications of the first. In file design, it was "first come, first served." Quite possibly, the way a file was designed initially did not meet the needs of subsequent programs.

It didn't take computer users long to see the error of their ways. There had been little or no control over the addition or location of files. New files were added, often duplicates of files already in use. And, files were subdivided and maintained in different locations throughout the company.

Firms launched special studies of their data files, and these produced three main findings. First, it was learned that many files were used by more than one program. For example, the customer file was used to conduct credit checks, to print invoices, to print statements, and to prepare management reports.

Second, it was found that many files contained the same data. This duplication is shown in Figure 7–29.

Third, it was found that files were used separately, i.e., the contents of multiple files seldom were integrated. This result is shown in Figure 7–30.

With this new insight into their file situation, firms began to take steps to improve the value of their data resource. Further abuse was prevented by requiring an *approval* of all new files. New files could be added only when there was a legitimate need. Efficiency and economy in the use of files were achieved by *consolidating* multiple files pertaining to the same subject. As an example, a customer billing file, a customer credit file, and a customer sales statistics file were combined into a customer master file. Also, files that were maintained in different locations were *centralized* into a single file. These central files normally were located at the firm's headquarters. This did not mean that managers of outlying offices could not use the centralized data. Data communication equipment, discussed in the next chapter, made this centralized data available to all potential users.

With the file situation under control, firms looked to their programmers for improved efficiency in the use of the files. Standards were established for the data contents of files. *File specification books* were prepared, with a page for each data element. A sample is shown in Figure 7–31.

Standard sizes and arrangements were established for each data element. For example, all programmers using customer name in their programs used it

Figure 7–29 Commonality of file contents

Data Element	File			
	Customer	Inventory	Salesperson	Vendor
Customer number	X		X	
Customer name	X		X	
Sales territory code	X		X	
Credit code	X		X	
Current period sales	X	X	X	
Accounts receivable	X		X	
Product class		X	X	X
Product number		X	X	X
Product name		X	X	X
Vendor code		X		X
Quantity on hand		X		
Quantity on order		X		X
Warehouse location		X		
Unit cost		X	X	X
Sales price		X	X	

as a 30-position alphanumeric (containing both letters and numbers) field, identified as CUST-NAME. These data standards reduce programming time since file design is performed for the programmer. Communication between programmers is made easier since they all speak the same language; several programmers can subdivide a large program and work on it at the same time; and a part of one program can be incorporated into another.

All of these efforts to improve the quality of data files—approval procedures, consolidation, centralization, and data standards—continue to serve as useful guidelines. They are recognized as good operating procedures, and are followed by progressive computer users.

Creation and maintenance of the data base

As firms worked to maintain the accuracy of their files, the size of the task became apparent—the files had to be built using data from several sources. This data often contained errors generated by systems less exact than the computer. These errors had to be corrected. Then, the files had to be kept

Figure 7–30   Pre-data base use of files

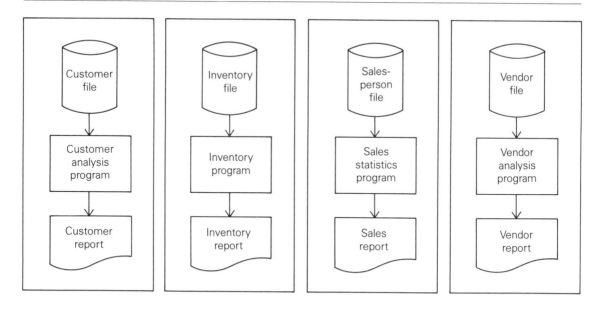

current to reflect additions, deletions, and modifications. Computer users found that this data base effort was as demanding, or more so, than development of the application programs that used the data.

Some firms had the expertise to create and maintain data bases. Many, however, did not have the manpower to devote to this part of the MIS development project. Seeing this need, computer manufacturers and service organizations developed "systems" of programs designed to handle a firm's data base responsibilities. These systems have been labeled the *Data Base Management System* (*DBMS*), *Data Management System* (*DMS*), *Data Base Processing System* (*DBPS*), and *Data Base System* (*DBS*). The term DBPS will be used here.

The Data Base Processing System (DBPS)[3]

The DBPS serves as an interface between application programs and the data base. The application programs are those that perform the different processing routines for the firm: compute payroll amounts, maintain inventory records,

3. Several books have been prepared to explain more fully the activities of the data base processing system. Two examples are David Kroenke, *Database Processing* (Palo Alto: Science Research Associates, Inc., 1977), and James Martin, *Principles of Data-Base Management* (Englewood Cliffs, N.J.: Prentice-Hall, 1976).

Figure 7–31   Data element specifications

Element Name: _____ Customer Name _____

Programming Name: _____ CUST-NAME _____

Description: _____ The name of a customer of the firm _____

_____

Source(s): _____ New Account Application Form _____

_____

Verification: _____ Sight verification by salesperson of new _____

_____ account application form.   Key verification __

_____ of data input cards. _____

Records Appearing In: _____ Customer Master, Credit Master, _____

_____ Accounts Receivable, Sales by Customer _____

_____

Programs Using: _____ Billing, Credit Check, Statements, _____

_____ Sales Analysis by Customer _____

_____

Field Size: _____ 30 _____ Positions

Type of Data: _____ Alphanumeric _____

prepare customer invoices, and so on. As the interface, the DBPS performs three main functions. It *translates* data requests by the application programs into specific data base operations. Then, it *transforms* these requests into commands that specify data needed from the data base. Finally, it *transfers* this data from the data base to main storage as required by the application programs.

Figure 7–32 shows the relationship of the DBPS to the data base and the application programs. This model should be compared with the pre-data base model in Figure 7–30.

Advantages and disadvantages of the DBPS

The use of a DBPS offers several advantages. First, more *rapid response* to management requests for information is possible. Less time must be spent in

Figure 7–32   Role of the data base processing system

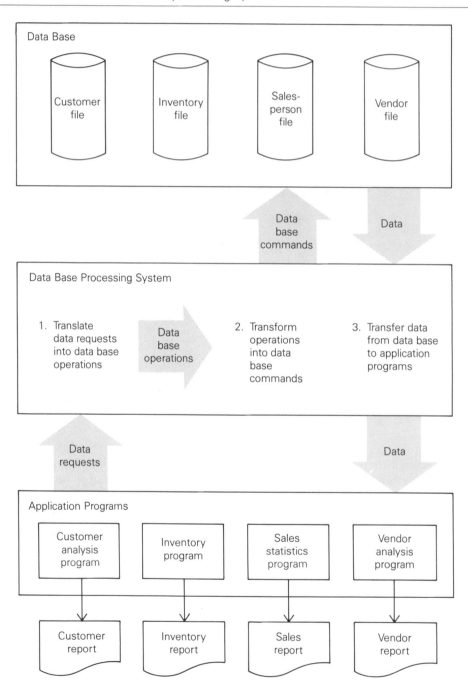

specifying the data sources. Second, *better information* can be provided. Data from several files can be merged and related. For example, a sales report can be prepared that identifies outstanding salespersons (from the salesperson file) and the breakdown of their sales by product line (from the inventory file). Third, it is possible to *conserve file space* by eliminating duplication between files. Data need only be contained within a single file. When that data is needed, it is obtained from that file. And, fourth, *fewer programming changes* are necessary when file changes are made. File changes (adding a new data element, etc.) only require changes to the DBPS, not to the application programs.

However, the DBPS is not without its disadvantages. First, there usually are *high acquisition costs.* If a firm develops its own system, it will require a large number of programmer manhours. If a DBPS is obtained from another organization, the costs still are high. Purchase costs start in the area of $100,000. Second, costs in addition to the DBPS often are incurred. It is quite common for the DBPS to require a *larger computer.* Third, the DBPS is a *more complex* way to use the data base. Both programming and operations are made more difficult. This complexity requires a more sophisticated and expensive computer staff. And, fourth, the information system becomes *more vulnerable* to failure or destruction. The DBPS is the connection between the data base and the application programs. If something happens to the DBPS, the information system is severely crippled.

As a firm considers a DBPS, it must weigh the advantages against the disadvantages. The growing trend toward the DBPS indicates that many firms see the several benefits as outweighing the disadvantages.

The data base administrator (DBA)

The data base is of such importance to a firm's MIS that a new type of information specialist has been created. This is the *data base administrator* (*DBA*). The DBA is given responsibility for the data base or a part of it. Larger firms can have more than one DBA.

The DBA performs several important functions as a part of the information systems staff. First, the DBA serves as the *interface with users* of the data base. The DBA must understand the users' needs so that an adequate data base can be created. Next, the DBA must *select the DBPS* that best meets the needs of the users. Finally, the DBA must make the data base available to the users. This involves both *creation and maintenance.*

Summary of the Data Base

This chapter has described an important part of the MIS—the storage of data for information processing.

Data elements are grouped into records, and the records are grouped into three types of files—master, transaction, and intermediate. Since the master files reflect the current status of the firm, efforts are made to keep them up-to-date. The direct access ability of disk units makes them ideal for master files. This ability is not needed for transaction and intermediate files; rather, magnetic tape or punched cards can be used.

As firms learned more about their data resource, they took steps to eliminate duplicate files by consolidating those with the same or similar contents. They also centralized the location of their files, usually at their headquarters, thus increasing file efficiency. Quality is maintained through the use of data standards, such as file specification books.

As information systems become more complex, a Data Base Processing System (DBPS) becomes necessary. The DBPS performs the work of making data base contents available to the application programs. A firm can create its own DBPS, or a prewritten one can be obtained from a supplier.

The data base is emerging as a separate area of expertise in the computer field. Specialists such as the data base administrator are becoming more knowledgeable of the data base and how to make it available to the manager. This is a big step toward improved information systems.

Important Terms

Auxiliary Storage	Block
Main Storage	Record
Cycle Time	Blocking Factor
Byte	Interblock Gap
Packed Decimal	File
Word	Direct Access Storage Device (DASD)
Direct Access	
Bit	Disk Stack
Recording Density	Access Mechanism, Access Arm
Magnetic Tape Unit, Tape Drive	Track
Read/Write Mechanism, Read/ Write Head	Disk Pack
	Data Module
Leader	Partitioned Organization
Header Label, Trailer Label	Indexed Sequential Organization

Direct Organization

Hashing Scheme

Synonym

Program Segment

Address Space

Virtual Storage

Relative Address

Master File

Transaction File

Intermediate File

File Specification Book

Data Base Processing System (DBPS)

Data Base Administrator (DBA)

Important Concepts

The CPU has very rapid direct access to that storage located in the CPU (main storage).

The limitation on the size of main storage makes additional storage—auxiliary storage—necessary.

Auxiliary storage is of two main types: magnetic tape and direct access storage devices (DASD).

Data is recorded on magnetic tape in much the same fashion as music is recorded on sound tape—in a sequential arrangement offering sequential access.

Magnetic tape is good for certain types of files, and not good for others.

Data is recorded on magnetic disks in much the same fashion as music is recorded on phonograph records—in a circular pattern with the possibility of direct access.

Direct access storage devices are good for certain types of files, and too expensive for others.

Direct access storage devices are required for transaction processing, realtime processing, and time-sharing.

Largely ignored during the early computer years, the data base has evolved into an important part of the information processor.

Data base processing systems have been created to interface the user with the data base.

Questions

1 Why is auxiliary storage necessary?

2 How many alphabetic letters can be stored in a main storage with a capacity of 32,000 bytes? How many digits, using packed decimal?

3 What are the two types of auxiliary storage?

4 What is the most popular type of DASD?

5 What is the difference between tape leaders and tape labels?

6 What is the blocking factor when tape records are not blocked?

7 Why do interblock gaps exist on tape?

8 Define file, record, and data element. Give an example of each.

9 Why is tape good for historical storage?

10 Does each record in a disk file have its own address? What does the address identify?

11 In a modern comb-like access mechanism, how many access arms are there for every two recording surfaces? How many read write heads?

12 In what ways is a disk pack similar to a reel of tape? In what ways are they different?

13 Do disk files have labels? What about gaps? Does the disk stack start and stop as each record is read or written? Explain.

14 What would normally be stored in a partitioned file?

15 Where is the index (for an indexed sequential file) located?

16 What type of DASD file organization produces synonyms? How are they produced?

17 How does a tape-oriented system handle a manager's inquiry?

18 Why is DASD good for inventory master files?

19 How can a program larger than the main storage capacity be handled?

20 What are the three basic types of files?

21 What is the purpose of a file specification book? Have these books always been maintained in computer installations?

22 Explain how a data base processing system translates, transforms, and transfers.

23 Who is the data base administrator?

Problems

1 Assuming a recording density of 800 bpi, how many 100-character records can be recorded on a 2400 foot length of tape with a blocking factor of 8?

2 What portion of a tape will be blank when 80-character records are recorded, unblocked, at 800 bpi? What should the blocking factor be in order for one-half of the tape to be blank? for one-fourth to be blank?

Chapter 8

Data Communication

During recent years, much interest has been shown in communicating data from one location to another. This process has been termed *data communication*, *data transmission*, and *teleprocessing*. Transmission simply implies that something, a *message*, is sent from one source, the *sender*, to a recipient, the *receiver*. Transmission does not imply that the message is received correctly. That is the basic difference between transmission and communication. This accurate receipt is an important part of communication. In the communication model, pictured in Figure 8–1, the message is *coded* by the sender for transmission, using some type of *channel*, and the message is *decoded* by the receiver. It is this coding and decoding that differentiates between transmission and communication. Teleprocessing refers to either the transmission or communication that is a part of a data processing or information processing system.

Data Communication in the General Systems Model

Data communication is an important part of the general systems model of the firm. The data communication network gathers the data describing the activities of the physical system and the environment. This data enters the data base.

Figure 8–1   The data communication model

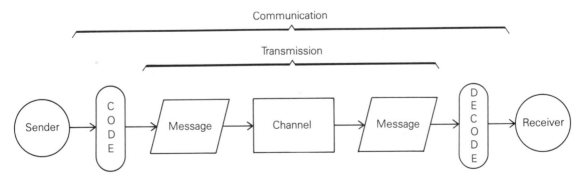

Figure 8–2   Data communication in the general systems model

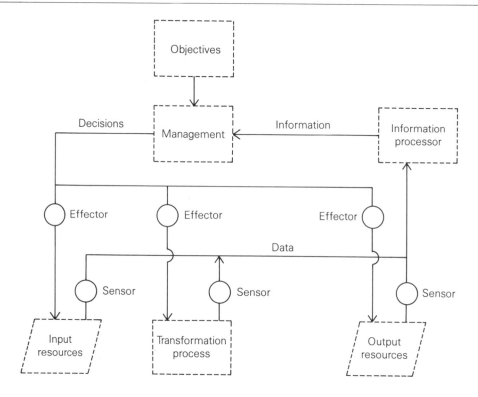

Then, the communication network transmits information to management, and transmits management decisions to the physical system. This role of data communication is illustrated in Figure 8–2.

In a firm with a computerized MIS, *sensors* are located throughout the physical system to gather data. Data terminals usually serve as the sensors. These sensors gather the data that is then transmitted to the data base using some type of channel. Most often, telephone lines serve as the channel. Data terminals also serve as *effectors*. The effectors make the decisions available to the firm, thereby facilitating change. Telephone lines and terminals communicate decisions to the physical system where the desired changes are effected. Figure 8–3 shows how data terminals and communication channels fit into the general model.

A wide variety of terminals have been developed to serve as the sensors and effectors. These are described later in the chapter. As shown in the figure, terminals are used also to provide the manager with information. This use often occurs in response to an inquiry to the information processor. Typewriterlike terminals commonly serve this purpose. They sometimes are equipped with televisionlike screens, called *cathode ray tubes* (CRTs), that display information rapidly and in graphic form.

Figure 8-3   Role of data terminals and communication channels in the general model

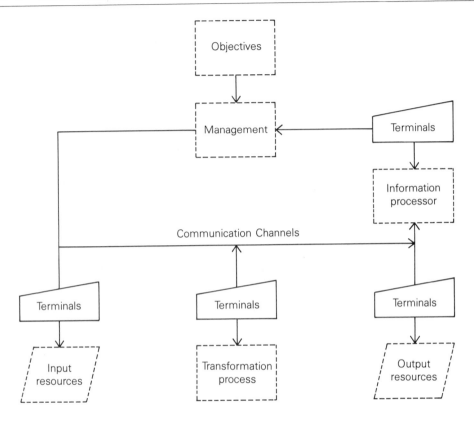

Some Fundamentals of Data Communication

The development of the electronic computer did not mark the beginning of data communication. Data was being communicated long before that. Indian smoke signals and the telegraph were early examples.

Possibly the largest initial user of equipment for transmission of data to be processed by machine was the federal government. This headstart over private business was due to the widespread scale of operations—especially the military branches. These government data processing installations mainly used punched card equipment, and data was communicated *offline*. That is, the data communication equipment was not connected directly to the data processing equipment. A common means of transmission was to read data punched in paper tape at the sending end and punch the data into paper tape at the receiving end. When the paper tape was punched at the receiving end, that data could be converted into punched cards for processing. This transmission method is shown in Figure 8-4.

Figure 8–4   Offline data transmission using punched paper tape

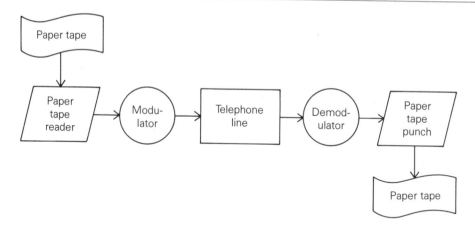

Conversion of communication signals

Two new terms in Figure 8–4 demand attention: modulator and demodulator. The *modulator* is an electronic unit that codes the message for transmission. This coding is necessary because of the difference in the way data is represented, or coded, in data processing and communication equipment. In data processing equipment, data is represented by patterns of short electrical pulses. Each character is represented by a particular pattern of pulses. Data communication equipment, on the other hand, represents data by sound frequencies. Each character is represented by a unique tone. These tone differences can be heard when dialing a Touch-Tone telephone.[1]

After transmission, the *demodulator* converts the signals back to a form compatible with data processing equipment.

This code conversion still is necessary, using more modern data processing and most communication equipment. The communication companies, such as the Bell System, typically provide a single unit that can both code and decode messages. This unit is given a variety of names—*modem* (modulator/demodulator), *data set,* and *Dataphone.*[2]

Types of data transmission

The equipment attached to each end of a communication channel can be designed to function in three different ways. In the most basic configuration,

---

1. "Touch-Tone" is the registered trademark of the Bell System for its telephone with 12 buttons rather than a rotary dial. One is pictured in Figure 8–20.

2. "Dataphone" also is a registered Bell trademark.

Figure 8–5   Simplex transmission

the equipment on one end can only send and the equipment on the other end can only receive. This setup, pictured in Figure 8–5, is named *simplex* transmission, meaning it transmits in one direction only.

It is possible, and quite common, to install equipment on either end of the channel that can send *or* receive. When equipment is attached to the channel in this manner, as shown in Figure 8–6, the transmission is called *duplex*, indicating either direction, but not both at the same time.

It also is possible to both send *and* receive at the same time. This transmission is called *full duplex*. The appropriate type of channel must be available for this to occur.

The most common way to transmit data is by telephone lines. Work on our telephone network began 100 years ago, and it provides extremely thorough coverage of the commercial, government, and private sectors of our society with almost one billion miles of circuits.

The Bell System is the largest provider of telephone service, and its offerings fall in two categories. First, there is *exchange service*, in which public circuits are shared and calls must be dialed. The second type of service is the *private line*, where a user reserves a particular communication channel that is not shared with other users.

Exchange service

Three types of exchange service are offered: ordinary *flat-rate* service, in which long distance calls are charged based on time used for each call; *WATS* (Wide Area Telephone Service) service, in which charges are based strictly on total time used per month; and *foreign exchange* service, in which "local" service to other cities can be purchased for a flat amount per month.

If a firm has only local data communication needs, or only a low-volume, infrequent long distance requirement, ordinary lines will do the job. The term *direct distance dialing* (DDD) is used to describe this type of long distance use.

When the volume of long distance calls increases, a WATS arrangement should be considered. After a 10 hour per month minimum, charges are based on minutes of use. The overall cost can be less, especially when each transmission is of short duration, say 15 seconds. When transmissions are longer, say 15 minutes, WATS may be no more economical than ordinary service. Different WATS arrangements can be obtained—incoming calls only, outgoing only, in state only, and out of state only.

Figure 8–6   Duplex transmission

In certain situations a foreign exchange can reduce long distance charges. If a firm in one city (say, Tulsa) has many offices or customers in another city (such as St. Louis), a local number may be purchased. In this example, all St. Louis customers have the same telephone access to the Tulsa firm, and vice versa, as if the firm were located in St. Louis. The term *direct line* is often used to describe this arrangement.

Private lines

For firms with greater data communication needs, in terms of volume and/or speed, private channels can be leased. These often are called *dedicated lines*, and can be *specially conditioned* to permit faster transmission. While a voice-grade line with no special conditioning (exchange service) can handle only 2400 bits per second, dedicated private lines can handle a maximum of 9600 bits per second. The specially conditioned lines are referred to as being *above voice-grade*.

In addition to transmission by telephone line, there are other, more modern, approaches. Each approach offers greater transmission speed than telephone lines. Telephone companies have laid *coaxial cables* between locations with high call frequencies. These connections are faster than telephone lines, but represent significant installation and maintenance costs for the telephone company. Therefore, their availability does not match that of telephone lines. An improvement in both cost and performance can be achieved by transmitting data by radio signals, or by *microwave*. This type of transmission is by "line of sight," requiring a series of towers to compensate for the curvature of the earth. About 100 towers are needed to transmit data by microwave from coast to coast.

A recent improvement in microwave transmission has been realized by use of communication satellites. In 1974, the first commercial communication satellite, Westar I, was launched by Western Union. It can receive signals for as many as 14,000 telephone calls and bounce them back to earth. Westar I has since been joined by other satellites owned by RCA, AT&T, GTE, and COMSAT.[3]

---

3. Radio Corporation of America, American Telephone & Telegraph, General Telephone and Electronics, and Communications Satellite Corporation.

Figure 8-7   Infrared light beam transmitting and receiving units. (Courtesy of the University of Colorado)

An even greater increase in transmission speed can be achieved by use of *light beams.* All of the telephone conversations for a large city, such as Denver, could be transmitted on a single laser beam. At present, the laser holds the most promise as the transmission mode of the future. Other approaches to light transmission also have been taken. The University of Colorado in Boulder uses an infrared light to transmit data from the engineering building to the computer center across town. Data is transmitted back, using the same type of beam. Figure 8–7 shows both a sending and a receiving unit.

Digital data transmission

The above transmission modes are all *analog* in nature. They require a modem for conversion from and to the *digital* signals of the computer. A new mode that transmits data digitally has been developed by the Bell System for use in more than 150 U.S. cities. DDS (*Dataphone Digital Service*) permits transmission at rates of 2400, 4800, and 9600 bits per second and also at 56,000 bits (56 kilobits) per second. DDS is a real breakthrough in terms of transmission accuracy, yet it also can be extremely economical for the right applications.

All these transmission options offer the possibility of tailoring a data communication system closer to the firm's exact needs. Probably a firm will use some mixture of the above modes. For example, a firm with headquarters in Columbus, Ohio can use digital transmission to and from its 12 regional offices (see Figure 8–8). A regional office, such as Dallas, can be linked with its

Figure 8–8   A multimode communication network

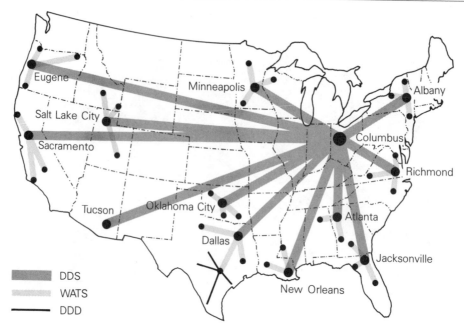

district offices in Houston, San Antonio, and Wichita Falls with a WATS arrangement. Moreover, the district offices can communicate with customers with direct distance dialing.

Communication-Oriented Information Systems

The first computers did not have the speed and capacity of current models. Large firms had to employ several separate computer systems to handle the data volume. Then, improvements in computer technology made possible very attractive cost/performance ratios for large systems. Thus, computer performance could be doubled without doubling the cost.

The larger firms began to recognize the benefit of centralizing their computer operations. One large central computer could do more work at less cost than several smaller ones. Very often, the key to this centralization was data communication. The power of the central computer had to be made available to outlying locations. This trend to centralization influenced the design of information systems of the 1960s and resulted in increased use of telephone facilities for data communication. Telephone company officials announced that the volume of data traffic handled by their system soon would exceed that of voice traffic.

Figure 8–9   Trends toward centralization and decentralization in design of information systems

Period	Direction of Trend	Computing Equipment at Headquarters Location	Computing Equipment at Remote Locations such as Branch Offices and Warehouses
Late 1950s	Decentralization	Several separate computer systems	Small computer systems—one per location
1960s	Centralization	Single large computer systems	Data communication terminals
Early 1970s	Decentralization	Medium-scale computer systems	Minicomputers—no data communication with central computer
Late 1970s	Centralization of data base, decentralization of problem solving (distributed processing)	Large-scale computer systems	Minicomputers—connected to central computer and to other minis by a data communication network

This trend did not continue as expected. The impact of the minicomputer reversed the centralization trend. The low costs of the minis made it more economical to give each outlying location its own computer. This trend influenced the design of information systems in the early 1970s.

It appears that the trend is changing again. Now firms with minis are linking them to centralized host computers. These networks form the distributed processing systems introduced in Chapter 5. Probably the most important single reason for this swing back to centralization is the data base. Firms recognize the value of a centralized data resource. The decentralized terminals and minis enter data into the data base and receive information processed from it. The telephone company officials again are predicting that data traffic will surpass voice traffic. The target date for this event is 1983, and it could well come true.

Data Terminals

A *terminal* is a communication device that accepts keyed or media-recorded data for transmission to a remote computer or another terminal, and/or produces output from data received from a computer or other terminal.[4]

Basic terminal capabilities

According to the above definition, some terminals can only *transmit* data. An example is a data collection terminal (Figure 8–10) used in a factory. Data can be entered from some medium, such as a punched card or a plastic badge, or it can be entered in the keyboard. The data collection terminal can only transmit data to the computer; the computer cannot transmit to the terminal.

There are also terminals that can only receive data. However, they are not as popular as entry-only units. The *receive-only printer (ROP)* (Figure 8–11) usually is located at some remote site where operations are completely controlled by the computer. As an example, in a warehouse the ROP can print a picking ticket for use in filling an order. Here, there is no need for warehouse personnel to communicate to the computer.

Other terminals can both *send and receive* messages. A *typewriter-style terminal* is an example. Data can be transmitted by entering it in the keyboard. Data received is typed on the paper. The speed of data entry depends on the operator. The speed of data receipt depends on the speed of the communication channel or the terminal. Typewriter-style terminals commonly print received data at a speed of 15 characters per second. The Xerox terminal shown in Figure 8–12 prints at speeds up to 45 characters per second. It can print both forward and backward. The Teletype Model 40 ROP prints either 105 or 120 characters per second.

While 105 or 120 characters per second is fast compared with keyed typing, some applications require greater receipt speed. A claims approval operation in an insurance company is an example. A claim is made by a policyholder for some loss covered by the policy for, say, an automobile accident. The claims clerk must display the policyholder record to verify coverage. Some records are quite lengthy, perhaps several hundred characters. It would take a few seconds to type all of the data, and the clerk would have to wait for the typing to be completed. The display could be accomplished more rapidly by a *CRT* (cathode ray tube) terminal (Figure 8–13). Several hundred characters can be displayed on the televisionlike screen in a fraction of a second.

It also is possible to enter data through the CRT screen. A hand-held pointer (see Figure 8–14) can be positioned on a certain part of the screen. The pointer is called a *light pen* or a *selector pen*. The position of the pen can be

---

4. Based on a definition in *IBM Terminals: Student Text*, IBM Manual SR20-4452, September 1975, p. 3.

Figure 8-10   A data collection terminal. (Courtesy of Honeywell, Inc.)

detected electronically by the CRT unit. In this way, the user can delete certain displayed information (in character or graphic form), change it, or trigger additional displays. A publicized use of this ability is the design of automobiles. Engineers at General Motors can change the displayed shape of an automobile by "drawing in" the modifications.

Figure 8–11   A receive-only printer (ROP). (Courtesy of Honeywell, Inc.)

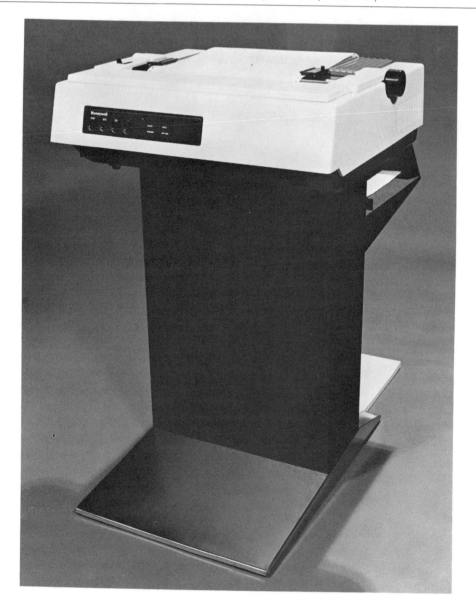

The speed of the CRT display is its greatest asset. Its drawbacks are cost (it is more expensive than a typewriterlike terminal) and lack of a paper copy (called a *hardcopy*) of the displayed information. This second disadvantage can be eliminated by a combined CRT/printer unit. Data can be displayed and typed, but the cost is increased. In the unit pictured in Figure 8–15, data is printed at a speed of almost 300 characters per second on the printer.

Figure 8–12   A typewriter-style terminal. (Courtesy of Xerox Corporation)

Terminal-oriented applications

Three of the basic approaches to information processing described in Chapter 5 require the use of terminals. These include realtime processing, timesharing, and distributed processing.

The terminals can be used with batch and transaction processing even though they are not required. Transactions can be batched and communicated to the CPU with a high speed terminal. Output can be batched by the CPU and transmitted back to the terminal. Such terminals function as small batch processors. They contain all of the input and output devices required of a computer used in a batch environment. The only units missing are the CPU and auxiliary storage devices. A *batch processing terminal* (also called a *remote job entry terminal*), such as the one pictured in Figure 8–16, can enter batched transactions through the card reader. These may be payroll transactions (employee numbers and hours worked) for the current period.

In the IBM 3780 terminal of Figure 8–16, the payroll cards are read at a speed of 400 cards per minute. This data is transmitted to the central computer

Figure 8–13  A cathode ray tube (CRT) terminal. (Courtesy of Tektronix, Inc.)

where the payroll calculations are made. The payroll programs are retrieved from the model base, and the employee payroll records are retrieved from the data base (Figure 8–17).

Output data, such as that used in printing payroll checks, is transmitted back to the remote batch terminal. The terminal operator puts payroll check forms into the line printer and they are printed at speeds up to 300 lines per minute.

In *transaction processing*, transactions such as sales orders can be entered into terminals as they occur. Output documents (invoices, purchase orders, etc.) can be prepared on the terminals to complete the transaction. In *realtime processing*, the status of the physical system is communicated to the CPU from terminals. The instructions from the CPU that change the physical system are then communicated back to the terminals. For example, requests for airline seats are communicated from terminals to the CPU, and acknowledgments of the reservations are returned to those same terminals. In *timesharing*, users write programs and solve problems at their terminals. In *distributed processing*, "intelligent terminals" (often minicomputers) can be used to solve problems at

Figure 8–14   Data input using the CRT screen. (Courtesy of International Business Machines)

remote locations, and to communicate with the host computer and centralized data base.[5]

In addition to the basic computer approaches, other applications lend themselves to terminal use. These applications can be performed on a system

5. An *intelligent terminal* is one that is capable of executing a program in its own storage. It is not simply a communication link with a remote computer.

Figure 8–15   A CRT terminal with printer. (Courtesy of Honeywell, Inc.)

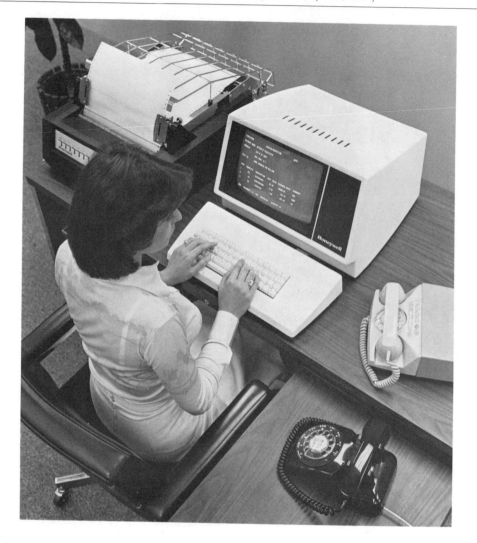

oriented to batch processing as well. These application areas are management inquiries and message switching.

Managers can make *inquiries of the data base* from terminals, as illustrated in Figure 8–18. Perhaps a sales manager wants to know the volume of purchases during the current month for a certain customer. A code is entered into the terminal keyboard indicating that an inquiry into the customer master file is desired. The customer number is then entered. The computer

Figure 8–16   A batch processing terminal. (Courtesy of International Business Machines)

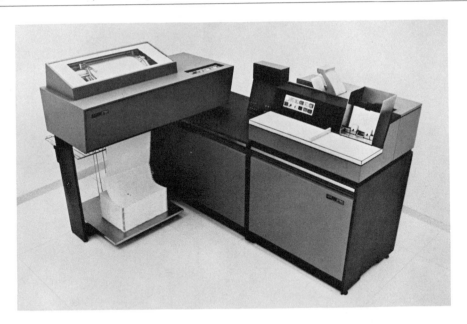

obtains the customer record from the data base and displays its contents on the manager's terminal.

Most firms with widespread geographic operations link the locations with some type of communication network. Telex or teletype machines can be used to transmit printed messages. Computer terminals can also be used in a message switching network. Take, for example, a large bus company headquartered in San Francisco with ticket offices across the country. An office in Salt Lake City can send a message to one in Albuquerque. The message first goes to the central computer in San Francisco. The computer examines the header portion of the message to identify the destination. The message then is sent to Albuquerque where it is typed on the terminal. If the Albuquerque terminal is busy, the computer can store the message in a queue until it can be transmitted. This queuing process is called *store and forward.*

Varieties of terminal equipment

In the mid-1970s period, there probably has been more activity in developing new terminals than any other type of computer equipment. There are two main reasons for this. First, a heavy capital investment is not required for producing terminals. Second, interest in communication-oriented computer applications has stimulated demand. In 1970, approximately 25 percent of the

Figure 8–17 Remote batch processing

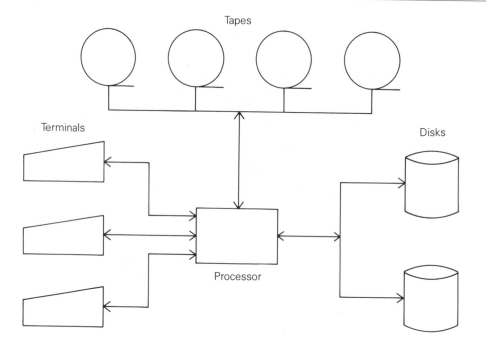

Tapes

Terminals

Disks

Processor

Figure 8–18 Data base inquiry

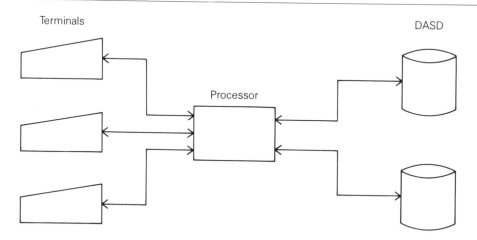

Terminals

DASD

Processor

computer systems had terminals.[6] By 1975, this percentage increased to 54 percent with almost one million terminals in use. The number of terminals projected for 1980 has been set at three million.[7]

The different types of terminals are too many to discuss here. Several types have been presented earlier in the chapter. These include:

- Data Collection Terminal
- Receive-Only Printer
- Typewriter-Style Terminal
- Cathode Ray Tube (CRT) Terminal
- CRT/Printer Terminal
- Batch Processing (or Remote Job Entry) Terminal

Three other types are described below in order to provide an idea of the variety available.

1. *Terminals with audio capability.* One of the easiest ways to enter data and instructions would be to "talk to the computer." Even during the computer's first generation, work toward this end had begun. An IBM engineer, William Dersch, in the late 1950s, assembled a device called "Shoebox" that could respond to his spoken commands. A 10-key adding machine was modified to recognize the spoken digits, plus the instructions add, subtract, total, and subtotal. The engineer could perform basic adding machine operations simply by talking to Shoebox.

While much research has been expended on voice input during the succeeding 20 years, little tangible accomplishment has been realized. The unique voice characteristics of each individual posed a design challenge that has yet to be met to the extent that a general purpose audio input device can be marketed. When such a device is developed, it likely will have a limited vocabulary and the words must be spoken in a particular manner. It will be some time before audio input becomes a feasible alternative in information system design.[8]

Audible output from the computer is something else. The technology long has been present, permitting the computer to output data and information in an audible form. This is accomplished by recording a vocabulary of selected

6. *Systems Auditability & Control: Audit Practices* (Altamonte Springs, Fla.: The Institute of Internal Auditors, Inc., 1977), p. 3.

7. *Systems Auditability & Control: Executive Report* (Altamonte Springs, Fla.: The Institute of Internal Auditors, Inc., 1977), p. 4.

8. The August 20, 1975 issue of *Computerworld*, p. 22, carried a story, "Disabled Enter Data by Voice With SEI Unit," about an operational voice-input system. Scope Electronics, Inc. (SEI) built a terminal that converts spoken utterances to machine-readable code. The terminal enables severely disabled persons, such as quadriplegics, to use a terminal by speaking the instructions.

Figure 8-19   An audio response unit. (Courtesy of International Business Machines)

words on some type of magnetic device such as a drum. In the IBM 7770 Audio Response Unit, shown in Figure 8–19, a basic 16-word vocabulary can be expanded to 128 words. Vocabulary words may be specified by the user.

The computer can be programmed to select the words to form a response. For example, a salesperson might be in a customer's office discussing an order for a certain product. The customer wants to know when shipment can be made. The salesperson asks to use the customer's Touch-Tone telephone (Figure 8–20) and dials the computer's number. The computer responds audibly by prompting the salesperson to enter a code identifying the type of transaction or inquiry to be processed. The computer may say "ENTER A 1 FOR AN INVENTORY REQUEST, A 2 FOR A CUSTOMER REQUEST, OR A 3 FOR A VENDOR REQUEST." The salesperson enters the code (a 1) repre-

senting an inquiry for inventory status. The computer then prompts the salesperson to enter the product number. When the product number is entered, the computer retrieves the inventory record from a DAS device and audibly advises the status—"INVENTORY ITEM 4 3 1 5 BALANCE ON HAND 6 0 0 3." The salesperson then assures the customer that immediate shipment can be made. If the customer agrees to the order, it can be placed by the salesperson, using the Touch-Tone telephone. All input by the salesperson is entered by pressing the buttons on the telephone.

2. *Expanded telephone terminals.* Additions have been made to the Touch-Tone telephone to increase the input and output capability. Data can be entered by punched cards and punched plastic badges. While these approaches likely will not be used by the manager, other employees may use them to update the data base. The manager can then use the up-to-date data base as a source of information describing the status of the firm.

Figure 8–21 A Touch-Tone telephone with CRT display. (Courtesy of Southwestern Bell Telephone Company)

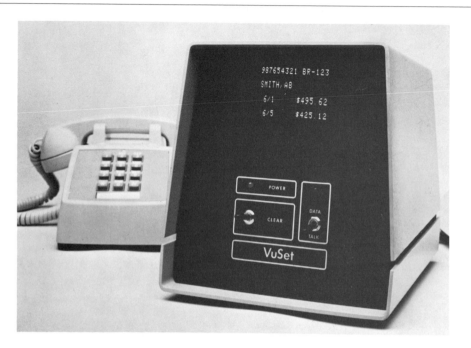

The manager can use a Touch-Tone telephone equipped with a 3-inch CRT to display information (Figure 8–21). A maximum of 132 characters can be displayed.

3. Point of sale terminals. Retailing comprises a large segment of our business system. Retailers long have had a great need for computer processing, but there were barriers to overcome. The retail transaction takes place some distance from the central computer; and it must be performed quickly at no inconvenience to the customer. As a minimum, each item and its price must be identified. Frequently, the credit rating of the customer must be checked. Transactions of this type are known as *point of sale (POS)* activities. Several approaches have been developed to enter this type of data into the computer from the point of the sale.

The most basic approach, and the one requiring the least sophisticated equipment, is a special retail terminal with keyboard entry. This terminal also serves as the cash register. As each transaction is handled, the clerk enters the product number (and perhaps price) into the keyboard. The data is read by the clerk from the price tag.

The terminal can be attached online to the computer, or it can be a stand-alone device. If online, there is no need to enter the price—the computer obtains that from storage. The computer calculates the bill and transmits all of the data back to the terminal where a sales slip is printed. The computer enters a record of each transaction into its auxiliary storage for later use in updating inventory and customer files. Or, these files can be updated as the transaction occurs—transaction processing. As a part of the processing, the computer also can check the customer's credit rating. In this case, the customer's charge card number also is keyed into the terminal.

When the terminal is a stand-alone device, it calculates the bill and records the transaction on punched paper tape, a magnetic tape cassette, or disk for later entry into the computer. The stand-alone terminal does not have the customer data to make a credit check.

The speed of this operation can be increased through the use of optical or magnetic ink reading. In addition to a keyboard, the terminal includes a reading "wand." The clerk merely passes the wand over the printing on the price tag. The wand senses the characters comprising the product number, and they are transmitted to the central computer. The remainder of the processing is the same as the keyboard entry. The wand simply replaces the keyed entry. The POS terminal shown in Figure 8–22 reads the price tag magnetically. The data on the price tag is printed in magnetic ink.

Food retailers have developed a special approach to POS recording. Most items purchased at a food store contain a bar code on the label (Figure 8–23). This *universal product code* (UPC) was adopted in the early 1970s by a trade association of some 1700 food marketing firms.

Part of the bar code identifies the manufacturer, and part identifies the specific item. The price is not included in the code, nor is it printed on the item. While eliminating the expense of price marking, this practice has been the source of consumer resistance. The price is attached to the shelf for the consumer's benefit, and it is stored in an onsite minicomputer for calculating the bill. Labor unions also have resisted UPC. They claim it will eliminate 25 percent to 30 percent of supermarket jobs since there is less need for markers, stockers, and stock counters. The combined resistance by consumers and labor has resulted in several attempts by state legislators to outlaw UPC in their states. This is a good example of environmental influence on MIS design. Figure 8–24 shows the layout of a supermarket using UPC.

Each checkout register contains an OCR unit that reads the bar code when the item is passed over the unit. Items with no code (fruit, candy) require that the code be entered in a keyboard. Items sold by weight (meat, cheese) are weighed on an electronic scale and the price is calculated. As each item is handled, the store mini retrieves the price from storage. A paper tape printed by the checkout register contains a short description of each item along with its price. When all item data has been entered, any tax is calculated and the bill is totaled.

The store computer can record transaction data on cassette or floppy disk, or can communicate with a larger central computer. The store manager can use a terminal to obtain information describing the store's performance.

POS terminals, such as the one shown in Figure 8–25, permit the retailer

Figure 8–22   A retail terminal with a wand. (Courtesy of The National Cash Register Co.)

to offer fast and accurate service at the sales area. Today, retailers are plagued by increasing labor costs. POS terminals offer an effective way of fighting these costs. However, an educational effort is needed to get this point across to customers.

The role of terminals in the MIS

As shown in Figure 8–3, terminals serve two primary functions in the MIS. First, they *permit the flow of data and information* between the data base and

Figure 8-23 The Universal Product Code. (Courtesy of Swift & Company)

Figure 8-24 Layout of a supermarket using UPC

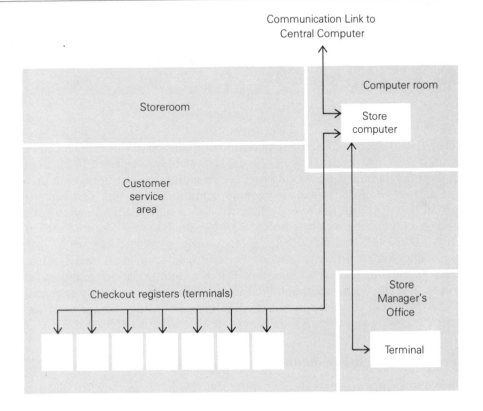

Figure 8–25   A supermarket checkstand equipped to serve as a POS terminal. (Courtesy of The National Cash Register Co.)

the physical system of the firm. All terminals discussed in this chapter can be used in this manner. In Figure 8–26, the terminals are identified in terms of gathering data from the physical system or providing data or information to it.

Most terminals provide a two-way communication link between the physical system and the MIS. In fact, the data collection terminal and the receive-only printer can be combined to provide two-way communications between the MIS and production or other areas.

The second primary function of terminals is to *assist managers in problem solving*. Managers use terminals to obtain information from the data base and to employ the computational power of the computer. However, not all of the terminals discussed in this chapter are used in this manner. Only the typewriter-style and the CRT terminals are suited to this type of use.

Procedure for using management terminals

When managers wish to make an inquiry into the data base, they first obtain a connection between their terminal and the computer by dialing the computer

Figure 8–26   Terminals serving employees in the physical system

Terminal	Gathers Data	Provides Data or Information
Data collection	X	
Receive-only printer		X
Typewriter-style	X	X
Cathode ray tube (CRT)	X	X
CRT/printer	X	X
Batch processing	X	X
Touch-tone telephone	X	X
Point of sale (POS)	X	X
UPC check stand	X	X

number. Then, codes are entered that identify the type of inquiry being made and, perhaps, a record code such as an inventory item number. The manager can receive a response to an inquiry in the same manner as the salesperson using a Touch-Tone telephone described earlier. The manager enters the codes in the terminal keyboard, and the information is typed or displayed.

When managers wish to use the computer in problem solving, a new program can be written, or one can be called from the model base. Some programs require the manager to enter data in a certain form and sequence. The computer can be programmed to tell the manager what to do and when to do it. Computer *prompting* is a valuable technique to the manager. There is no need to memorize sequences of terminal actions. The computer "leads" the manager, step by step, through problem solution.

When the computer and the manager jointly solve a problem in this manner, the computer is said to be in an *interactive mode* (the manager is interacting with the computer) or a *conversational mode* (the manager and computer are talking to each other).

Three dialog techniques have been developed for computer prompting. One is called *menu display*. An example appears in Figure 8–27.

The manager must select from several displayed choices. A choice is made by keying in an appropriate code. This technique is good for managers since they need not memorize all of the choices. It is also fast, since only codes need be entered.

Figure 8–27   The menu display technique

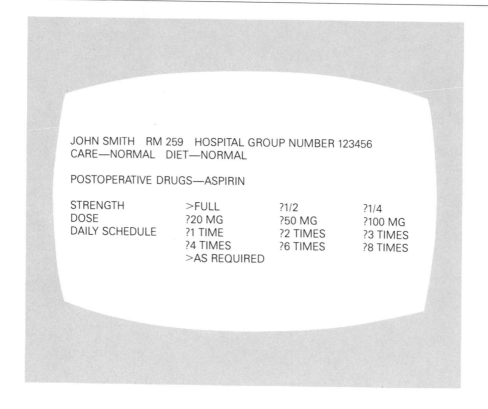

A second dialog technique (Figure 8–28) is called *form filling*. The terminal displays a "form" that must be completed.

The computer prompts the user to enter a particular data element (part number, etc.) with an electronic indicator named a *cursor*. A cursor is a special character, such as an underline mark, that can be positioned anywhere on the CRT. Under program control, the cursor is moved to the next data element requiring entry. The form-filling technique is slow, but is easy to use.

The third technique, called *questions and answers*, is good when the manager must make a series of decisions. The computer can present the manager with a decision in the form of a question (see Figure 8–29). The choices of answers can be displayed (such as YES or NO). Or the questions can be "open ended," such as HOW MANY UNITS WILL BE SOLD AT THIS PRICE? ENTER NUMBER OF UNITS.

Both menu display and form filling are better suited for a CRT than a typewriter-style terminal because of the speed factor. The CRT is faster. The questions and answers technique can be used on both types.

Figure 8-28 The form filling technique

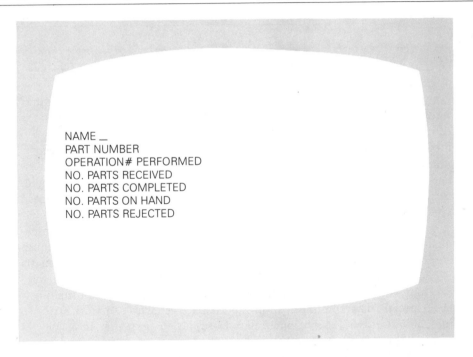

Figure 8-29 The questions and answers technique

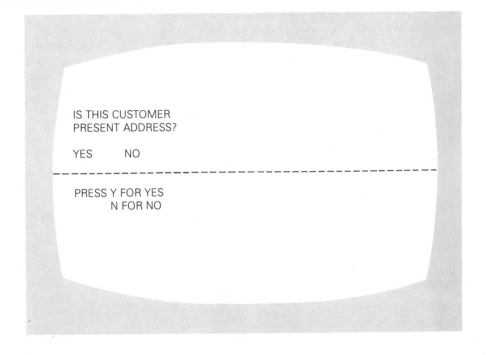

Summary

Data communication plays an important role in the MIS. It is the means of gathering data and information from within the firm and from the environment for entry into the data base. And, it is the means of providing information from the data base to managers and other employees of the firm. It is possible to have an MIS without data communication equipment. Data can be gathered and information presented using other techniques. But, as the size of the firm increases and its operation becomes widespread, data communication equipment becomes necessary. As stated in the chapter, the trend in MIS design is toward communication-oriented systems.

The two basic types of data communication equipment are communication channels and data terminals. The communication channel equipment is obtained from communications companies and very often consists of ordinary telephone facilities. More sophisticated equipment is available for improved performance. Telephone companies in large cities usually have special "data communication representatives" who can work with the computer user. These representatives supply the expertise in a field where knowledge is very specialized.

The data terminal type of communication equipment enables the user to send or receive over the communication channel. There are many types of data terminals, marketed by many firms. Many terminals are general purpose in that they can be used in practically any type of firm. Others are special purpose in that they are designed to meet the needs of certain industries such as banking and hospitals. These special purpose terminals were not discussed in this chapter.

It is important that the manager have a good understanding of terminals. Sooner or later, all managers will most likely be in a position to use a terminal for problem solving. The terminal, with its communication channel, is the link connecting the manager with the computer. The manager and the computer, working together, form a powerful and effective problem-solving team. Data communication serves to bridge the gap between the manager and the computer.

Important Terms

Message	Coding, Decoding
Sender	Channel
Receiver	Sensor, Effector

Cathode Ray Tube (CRT)

Modulator, Demodulator, Modem, Data Set, Dataphone

Simplex

Duplex

Full Duplex

Exchange Service

Private Line

Flat Rate

WATS (Wide Area Telephone Service)

Foreign Exchange

Direct Distance Dialing (DDD)

Direct Line

Dedicated Line

Specially Conditioned Line

Above Voice Grade Line

Coaxial Cable

Microwave

Light Beam

Dataphone Digital Service (DDS)

Terminal

Receive-Only Printer (ROP)

Light Pen

Selector Pen

Hardcopy

Batch Processing Terminal, Remote Job Entry Terminal

Intelligent Terminal

Store and Forward

Point of Sale (POS) Terminal

Universal Product Code (UPC)

Computer Prompting

Interactive Mode

Conversational Mode

Menu Display Technique

Form Filling Technique

Cursor

Questions and Answers Technique

Important Concepts

The data communication model applies in a general way to all communication situations.

Data communication is represented in the general systems model of the firm by the feedback loop.

It is necessary to translate computer signals into communication signals, and vice versa.

The three basic types of data communication are simplex, duplex, and full duplex.

Telephone communication is the most popular technique, and is provided as exchange service or private line.

Developments in computing and data communication equipment have influenced trends to centralized and decentralized computing facilities.

There are various types of terminals.

Terminals may be used with any of the data processing methods (batch, timesharing, etc.), and are required for some. Terminals also facilitate management inquiry.

Important Organizations

The Bell Telephone System   Western Union

Questions

1 What is the difference between transmission and communication?

2 How is data communication used in the general systems model of the firm?

3 Is a terminal a sensor, or an effector, or both? Explain.

4 Why are modems necessary in data communication?

5 Should the communications channel connecting the president's office to the computer be simplex, duplex, or full duplex? Why?

6 What is the difference between WATS, DDD, and DDS?

7 Is the trend toward centralization or decentralization of data and information processing in firms? Has any one development influenced this trend? Which one?

8 Name three types of terminals.

9 When would a typewriter-style terminal best meet a manager's needs? What about a CRT?

10 Is a light pen a cursor?

11 Can terminals be used to process data by batch? Are the same terminals used that are used in timesharing or transaction processing? Explain.

12 Is a batch processing terminal a good example of an "intelligent" terminal?

13 What data would likely be entered into a POS terminal with a wand? What data would be entered through the keyboard?

14 Does UPC have any advantage to supermarket customers? To supermarket owners? To supermarket workers?

15 What two primary purposes are served by terminals in the MIS?

16 Do most terminals gather data, present information, or both?

17 What are three approaches to computer prompting?

Problems

1   Draw the data communication model.

2   You have just been hired as a terminal salesperson by the Aardvark Terminal Corporation, and have completed their 3-day training program. Your boss, the sales manager, has told you to push receive-only printers, CRT terminals, and data collection terminals. As you approach the entrance to your largest customer, the Rattan Furniture Manufacturing Company, you must decide who you should contact! Who would you call upon (give their titles) as the best prospect to use for each of the three types of terminals?

Chapter 9

Computer Support for Problem Solving

Variety of Computer Support

The systems approach provides a good structure for problem solving. Problems are defined and understood before an effort is made to solve them. Several alternative solutions are considered before one is selected. The results of the selection are monitored to assure that the anticipated benefits are realized.

The computer can play a variety of roles throughout this problem-solving process. It can inform the manager that a problem exists or is emerging. It can then provide information enabling the manager to understand the problem. With this accomplished, it can provide information enabling the manager to identify alternative solutions. Admittedly, this is the point in the process where the computer offers the least support. Solution identification is a creative process best performed by an imaginative manager. But an imaginative manager can think of ways the computer can be used for this purpose. Once the alternatives have been identified, they can be easily evaluated by the computer using quantitative data. In some cases, the computer model or program can even identify the best solution. As a final role, after a solution has been implemented, the computer can provide information on how the solution is working out.

The degree to which the computer becomes involved in problem solving depends on the type of problem and the personal characteristics of the manager. Some problems (the structured ones described in Chapter 4) can be solved completely by the computer. Others (unstructured ones) must be solved by the manager with the computer perhaps playing a supporting role. Some managers look to the computer for support where practical, while others prefer to shoulder the entire responsibility.

Because of these variations, few concrete statements can be made about how computers should be used in problem solving. It is possible, however, to provide an idea of what possibilities exist. That is the purpose of this chapter.

Decision Support Systems

Many authorities have used the term *decision support system* to describe the role of the MIS in problem solving.[1] The computer is seen as a support for the manager, rather than a replacement. This concept is illustrated in Figure 9–1.

As a support system, the computer performs two basic types of functions. First, it provides the manager with information describing the performance of the physical system of the firm. This function is accomplished in steps 1, 2, and 6 of Figure 9–1. This information helps the manager detect problems and understand them. As a second function, the computer performs analyses and makes computations as specified by the manager (steps 3, 4, and 5). This computer activity enables the manager to solve the problem, once it has been identified.

The idea of the MIS as a decision support system is a realistic one. It recognizes the inherent difficulty in problem solving and in devising structured solutions. The idea puts the manager in the driver's seat and that is exactly where he or she should be. This is a comfortable viewpoint for both managers and management scientists to take. However, it has not been an easy lesson to learn. Only after considerable failure of computer-centered approaches has the manager-centered one become the currently prescribed route.

Problem Identification Information

The manager may passively sit and wait to be notified of a problem. Or, an active approach can be taken—one of continual search for problems to be solved. In one case, the information system directs information at the manager without requiring specific requests. In the other case, the manager asks for information about different areas of the firm's operations.

Periodic reports

Perhaps the oldest form of information is the *periodic report*. This type of report is prepared on a certain cycle (daily, weekly, monthly, etc.). During the precomputer period and in the early years of computer use, the monthly report was the most popular. The systems were slow, and a monthly cycle was about all that could be handled. Today, it is possible for a manager to receive a daily summary of activity.

---

1. A good discussion of decision support systems can be found in Steven L. Alter, "How Effective Managers Use Information Systems," *Harvard Business Review*, Volume 54, Number 6, November–December 1976, pp. 97–104.

Figure 9–1   Computer support using the systems approach

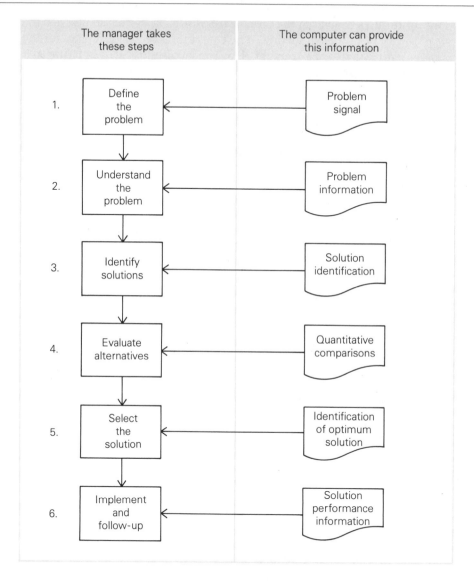

Most accounting systems have been designed to produce a set of these periodic reports. Balance sheets and income statements are examples. Both have companywide interest. Other reports have a narrower following. An aged accounts receivable report is of interest to the credit manager. A sales by salesperson report is prepared for the sales manager. And a report of overtime earnings is used by the plant superintendent.

Figure 9–2   The balance sheet is a snapshot of the firm's financial position. (Courtesy of Aluminum Company of America)

Consolidated balance sheet
Aluminum Company of America and consolidated subsidiaries

(in millions, except share amounts)

December 31	1977	1976
Assets		
Current assets:		
Cash	$ 23.1	$ 28.3
Short-term investments, at cost approximating market	65.6	7.3
Receivables from customers, less allowances: 1977, $2.8; 1976, $2.9	450.6	401.6
Other receivables	41.7	33.4
Inventories (B)	640.0	604.3
Prepaid insurance and taxes	6.4	5.8
Total current assets	1,227.4	1,080.7
Investments (C and D)	446.7	446.5
Other assets and deferred charges:		
Receivables and advances	18.6	21.4
Deferred charges	79.7	67.5
Total other assets and deferred charges	98.3	88.9
Properties, plants and equipment (E)	2,029.6	1,953.4
Total assets	**$3,802.0**	**$3,569.5**
Liabilities		
Current liabilities:		
Accounts payable	$ 286.9	$ 263.5
Accrued expenses	136.2	113.4
Taxes, including taxes on income	120.8	101.5
Long-term debt due within one year	16.4	20.7
Total current liabilities	560.3	499.1
Long-term debt, less amount due within one year (O)	1,166.0	1,158.1
Noncurrent liabilities	26.0	20.5
Deferred income	3.9	2.2
Deferred investment credit	19.4	21.5
Future taxes on income	173.3	179.0
	1,948.9	1,880.4
Shareholders' equity		
Capital stock:		
Serial preferred stock, par value $100, authorized 1,000,000 shares:		
$3.75 cumulative preferred stock, authorized 660,000 shares;		
issued and outstanding, 659,909	66.0	66.0
Common stock, par value $1.00, authorized 50,000,000 shares;		
issued and outstanding: 1977—34,690,583; 1976—34,328,823 (G)	34.7	34.3
Additional capital (F)	132.0	115.1
Retained earnings (G)	1,620.4	1,473.7
Total shareholders' equity	1,853.1	1,689.1
Total liabilities and shareholders' equity	**$3,802.0**	**$3,569.5**

The accompanying notes are an integral part of the financial statements.

Most of these reports perform a valuable service. Balance sheets and income statements are greatly distilled summaries of hundreds or thousands of separate transactions that show, at a glance, the financial position of the firm. Reports such as this are read by strategic and tactical level managers, and are even included in annual reports to stockholders (Figure 9–2).

Other reports are used by operational level managers to monitor performance of their areas. The credit manager uses the aged accounts receivable

Figure 9–3   An aged accounts receivable report

```
                        AGED ACCOUNTS RECEIVABLE REPORT
                                JULY 31, 1978

CUSTOMER      CUSTOMER               INVOICE   -----------AMOUNT DUE-----------
  NO.          NAME                    NO.     OVER 30      OVER 60      OVER 90

  2309      AARDVARK REALTY           30422    120.50
  2412      BARNETT'S HOME SALES      23546                  25.25
  3808      BRUCE'S REPAIR            10089                               10.10
  4104      ELKHORN HOME SALES        31209    119.65
  4110      MIDTOWN REAL ESTATE       36363    212.00
  6290      ROYALTY TITLE COMPANY     12362                              359.00
  7363      SHOFFNER FOUNDATION CO.   28290                  50.90
  7508      SUPERIOR DEVELOPMENT      38904     16.35
  8200      WEST GYPSUM COMPANY       21916                 289.50
  8339      ZANZABAR SAVINGS ASSN.    31242    100.10
  9316      ZEBRA LUMBER COMPANY      31619    219.30

            TOTALS                             787.90       365.65       369.10
```

report (Figure 9–3) to identify poor-paying customers and to direct the firm's collection efforts.

The sales manager uses the sales by salesperson report (Figure 9–4) to identify those representatives performing in an extraordinary manner—either very good or very bad. This objective is accomplished by examining the variance from quota columns shown in the figure.

The plant superintendent uses the overtime earnings report (Figure 9–5) to identify those departments adding the most to production costs by paying extra premiums for labor. This analysis can relate to the current period or the cumulative status for the fiscal year.

All these reports are prepared quite easily by the computer. Accounting data is stored in the data base describing the period's transactions—sales, payments, hours worked, etc. At the end of the period, the appropriate computer programs extract the needed data from the data base, sort them into the necessary groupings, summarize transactions, compute measures of variation, and print the reports. It also is possible to store the report data in the data base for retrieval and display on a manager's CRT terminal when desired.

The operational level reports in Figures 9–3, 9–4, and 9–5 reflect *management by exception*. The computer program has identified the exceptions requiring management attention (e.g., overtime hours in Figure 9–5). It has also made it easy for the manager to identify these exceptions (such as the delinquent customers in Figure 9–3 and the extraordinary salespersons in Figure 9–4).

Figure 9–4 A sales by salesperson report

```
                    SALES BY SALESPERSON REPORT
                         MARCH 31, 1979

   ===SALESPERSON=====    ===CURRENT=MONTH======   ===YEAR=TO=DATE======
    NO.       NAME       QUOTA  ACTUAL  VARIANCE   QUOTA  ACTUAL  VARIANCE

    0120   JOHN NELSON    1200   1083    =117      3600   3505     =95
   10469   LYNN SHERRY    1000   1162    +162      3000   3320    +320
   19261   DARVIN UPSHAW   800   1090    +290      2400   2510    +110
   20234   JANIE EVANS    1500   1305    =195      4500   4110    =390
   61604   TRAVIS BURKE   2000   2333    +333      6000   6712    +712
   62083   CATHY HAGER    1000    990    =10       3000   2319    =681
   63049   STEVE JENNER   1100   1250    +150      3300   2416    =884
   64040   SAM MOSELEY    1050    985    =65       3150   3020    =130

           TOTALS         9650  10198    548      28950  27912   =1038
```

The report in Figure 9–3 is a *detail listing* of all the transactions. This is the aged receivables report, which shows each overdue sales transaction. If 250 sales are overdue, the report will have 250 detail lines. Such a report can become unwieldy because of sheer length. The manager must be very skillful in using a detail listing or will become lost in a sea of data.

Figure 9–5 An overtime earnings report

```
                    OVERTIME EARNINGS REPORT
                        AUGUST 31, 1979

                                            OVERTIME HOURS
   DEPARTMENT NO.   DEPARTMENT NAME    CURRENT MONTH    YEAR=TO=DATE

      16=10         RECEIVING            2305.00          5319.20
      16=11         INSPECTION           1025.60          4386.12
      16=12         MATL'S HANDLING      3392.50         12629.00
      16=13         TOOLING                78.00          1049.00
      16=14         ASSEMBLY                .00            792.80
      16=15         PLATING              3504.90         12635.20
      16=16         SHIPPING             5219.16         18294.16

                    TOTALS              15525.16         55105.48
```

The other reports are *summaries* in which multiple transactions are condensed and represented as a single report line. The higher the manager in the hierarchy, the greater the dependence on summary reports.

One problem with many periodic reports is that they were not designed by the user. The user receives the report and tosses it into the wastebasket. Perhaps the manager doesn't know how to interpret it or how to use its contents. Or, the report may deal with an unimportant aspect of the manager's job.

Graphical information

The modern computer can provide its output in a graphical as well as a *tabular* form. Either plotters or CRT terminals can provide pictures of what has happened, is happening, or is likely to happen in the firm.

Computer graphics provide a second dimension to all types of computer output. When plotters or CRTs are available, graphical output should be considered for all types of reporting.

Manager inquiries

The active manager can look for problems by requesting information on areas of interest. The manager can ask for precomputed information elements or for data analyses. *Precomputed information elements* are pieces of information that have a high frequency of use. These elements are computed from a number of transactions, and the result is stored in the data base. Then, when the manager wants the information, he or she queries the computer (usually from a terminal). The computer obtains the element from its data base and provides it as printed or displayed output.

An example of a precomputed information item is a return on investment (ROI) ratio (Figure 9–6). Such a ratio reveals the return a manager is receiving on an investment. Ratios can be computed and stored for products, salespersons, territories, subsidiary operations, or the entire firm.

A product manager can request an ROI for a product in order to identify possible problems. In Figure 9–6, product 128376 is producing a declining return. The manager might decide it is time for a replacement or a rejuvenating sales campaign.

If a precomputed information element is to be provided in a fraction of a second by the MIS, the need must be anticipated. A program is written to process the data and the data is available in the data base. This anticipation of needs places a real burden on the manager.

In some situations, a need for a new type of information arises. In this case, the data base must be screened and *data analyses* made on the selected data. Again, a program must be available; but perhaps it can be prepared easily using a data base language or a file-manipulating language such as APL (*A Programming Language*). The data must be available, but computations are made *after* the inquiry, not *before*. Figure 9–7 reflects this difference in inquiry response.

Figure 9–6   A precalculated return on investment

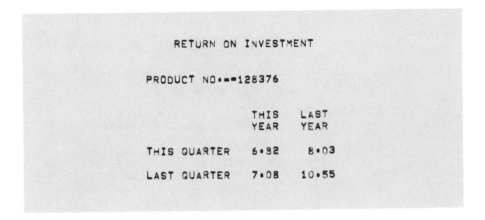

```
                    RETURN ON INVESTMENT

            PRODUCT NO.--128376


                                 THIS    LAST
                                 YEAR    YEAR

            THIS QUARTER         6.82    8.03

            LAST QUARTER         7.08    10.55
```

An example of a data analysis type of inquiry is a request by a plant superintendent for a report of excessive scrap (Figure 9–8). When raw materials cannot be used, they must be scrapped. Production errors—often the cause for excess material—add to costs and must be controlled. An inquiry can be made for information on departments with scrap expenses over some minimum, say $10,000.

Figure 9–7   Response to manager inquiries

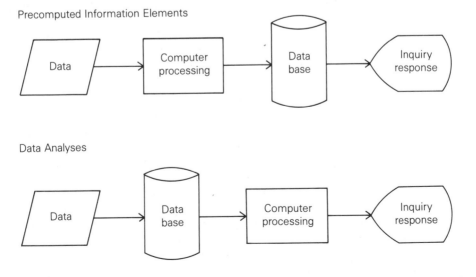

Precomputed Information Elements

Data Analyses

Figure 9–8   Analysis of production scrap

```
                    EXCESSIVE SCRAP REPORT
                        BY DEPARTMENT
                        JUNE 30, 1978

        MINIMUM EXPENSE:     $10,000/MONTH

            DEPARTMENT                SCRAP VALUE
          NO.      NAME        CURRENT MONTH   YEAR-TO-DATE

          16-13   TOOLING         $11,293        $35,162
          16-14   ASSEMBLY        $23,149        $65,089
          16-15   PLATING         $10,029        $24,612
          17-20   PAINTING        $13,323        $36,423
```

A computer program scans the data base for scrap data, summarizes it by department, and selects figures that exceed the minimum. The response can be printed on a terminal or the line printer. Several minutes or hours can pass before the analysis is completed, depending on the priority.

Use of problem identification information

Problem identification occurs on all management levels. This type of activity, however, is more prevalent on the operational level for two reasons. First, problems occur when objectives are not being met. The objectives are jointly set on all levels, but achievement becomes an operational, and often tactical, responsibility. Second, for every single large problem, there are many smaller, or subsidiary, ones. It is the operational level of management that identifies and solves the multitude of subsidiary problems. For these reasons, the big users of the MIS for problem identification are the operational level managers.

Another characteristic of this use of the MIS deserves recognition. This is the reliance on a data base of largely historical data. Actual activities in the firm are compared with standards. Variance calls for problem-solving action. The focus is not on the future, but on the present and the past.

Problem Solution Information

The second basic computer function is to solve the problem once it has been identified, or to help the manager solve it.

Many problems are unstructured the first time they are faced and must be solved almost completely by the manager. But, once solved, the problems become structured and the computer can arrive at the solution.

Use of the computer for solution rather than identification brings about two basic changes. First, users tend to be on strategic and tactical levels. These levels are where policies are set and objectives are agreed upon. The users at these levels are more concerned with planning, and involve themselves with selecting the path the firm will follow. Second, emphasis shifts from a historical data base to quantitative routines that can predict the future. The manager is less interested in what happened in the past, but more interested in what is likely to happen should certain decisions be made.

This is the area of management activity—decision making—where the most glamorous picture has been painted of computer use. The technique receiving the most publicity is the mathematical model.[2]

It is possible for the manager to make a decision and to solve a problem without a mathematical model. In fact, that usually is the case. The manager assembles information from repetitive reports or inquiries, evaluates the information, considers potential results, and decides.

The mathematical model provides support where it is needed—in the consideration of possible results. The model can *simulate* alternate courses of action. Often, those simulations are too complex to be accomplished other than by computer.

The subject of modeling, or simulation, has already been introduced in Chapter 3. This decision-making technique is of such potential value to the manager that the remainder of this chapter will be devoted to its discussion.

Forms of Models

Models can be static or dynamic. A *static* model represents the entity being modeled at a specific point in time. A physical model of a building represents how that building appears at a specific instant. The model doesn't do anything—it just sits there. A physical model of an airplane that flies through the air, however, is a *dynamic* model. It represents the behavior of the entity (the airplane) over a period of time—from takeoff until landing. The types of models presented in Chapter 3 (physical, narrative, graphical, and mathematical) can be either static or dynamic.

Models can also be optimizing or nonoptimizing. An *optimizing* model identifies the single best solution to a problem. An example is a mathematical model that identifies the best selection of merchandise in a warehouse. A *nonoptimizing* model is one that simply projects an outcome of a particular activity—not necessarily the best outcome. A mathematical model can predict sales for a product if the price is set at $79.95. The model doesn't necessarily

2. A good review of the history of computer modeling can be found in Robert H. Hayes and Richard L. Nolan, "What Kind of Corporate Modeling Functions Best?," *Harvard Business Review*, Volume 52, Number 3, May–June 1974, pp. 102–112.

identify that as the best price. It is left to the manager to simulate other pricing strategies and select the one that best achieves the desired results, such as maximum profit. While all model types can be used in a nonoptimizing fashion, the mathematical model is best suited for identifying optimum results.

A final classification of models takes two forms: deterministic and probabilistic. It deals with the degree of certainty with which the elements or parts of the model can be specified. A *deterministic* model is one where all the elements are known to act in a specific way. The EOQ (Economic Order Quantity) model is of such a form.

$$EOQ = \sqrt{\frac{2PS}{M}}$$

The model has only three elements, or variables. P represents the cost to prepare a purchase order, such as $20. S is the annual sales amount for the inventory item. Assume this to be 1000 units. M is the cost of maintaining the item in inventory, say $0.16 per unit per year.

The above numbers are "plugged into" the model, and an economic order quantity of 500 units is computed.

$$EOQ = \sqrt{\frac{2 \times 20 \times 1000}{0.16}} = \sqrt{250,000} = 500$$

There can be no other answer. The variables always interact in the same way.

The other form of model is one where the behavior of the variables cannot be predicted accurately. It is known as a *probabilistic* model. This form uses "probabilities" of things happening. Weather forecasters use this approach when they say there is a "30 percent chance of rain."

Probabilities are expressed in percentages. If one is 100 percent certain something will happen, the probability is 1.00. If one is certain it will not happen, the probability is .00. Probabilities usually lie somewhere between. If one is 60 percent certain he or she will get an A in a particular course, the probability is .60.

Very often, probabilities are multiplied times the values of the outcomes to arrive at "expected" or weighted values. As an example, someone might want to consider the outcome of his fraternity entering into a fund-raising project. One project involves competing with other college organizations in the area in soliciting donors for a blood bank. The organization signing up the most donors receives a $1000 prize. There are no other prizes. The fraternity member could estimate the chances of winning to be 1 in 10, or .10.

The other project is one of selling "mums" during homecoming week. The organization selling the most flowers receives a $200 prize. The fraternity has won four times in the past 5 years, so a probability of .80 is set. In this case, there is some quantitative basis for the probability—the record of past wins. In many cases, the basis is more subjective.

Now the fraternity can evaluate the possibilities offered by the two contests.

Activity	Probability (P)	Outcome (dollars)	Expected outcome
Blood drive	.10	$1000	$100
Sell mums	.80	200	160

The probabilities are multiplied times the outcomes to obtain the expected outcomes. It can be seen that the mum project offers the highest value, so that is the activity selected. Naturally, the expected outcomes are not the sums of money that will be won in either contest, but they do identify the alternative offering the best opportunity.

The elements of deterministic models are usually those under the control of the firm, such as costs and production rates. Elements of probabilistic models are usually those of an external or environmental nature that cannot be controlled. A good example is product demand.

Choosing the Correct Model

Based on the above classification scheme, Table 9–1 identifies eight general categories of models.

Table 9–1   Categories of models

Category	Static	Dynamic	Optimizing	Nonoptimizing	Deterministic	Probabilistic
1	X		X		X	
2	X		X			X
3	X			X	X	
4	X			X		X
5		X	X		X	
6		X	X			X
7		X		X	X	
8		X		X		X

A Linear Programming Model

Linear programming is a good example of a category 1 model. *Linear programming*, or *LP*, is an optimizing technique that identifies the best solution to a static situation. This technique does not require the use of probabilities.

Linear programming terminology

The word *programming* has no special computer-related significance. It does not mean computer programming, but only that a solution can be identified with a certain amount of precision. The word *linear* means that there is a constant ratio between the variables that does not change. For example, if $20,000 in advertising produces $100,000 in sales, then $40,000 in advertising should produce $200,000 in sales.

LP has been a popular computer application since the first generation. One reason for this popularity is that the model focuses on a common management problem—achievement of a particular goal with limited resources. In LP, the limited resources are called *constraints*, and the goal is the *objective function*. The objective can be to maximize something, such as profits, or minimize something, such as costs.

Another reason for the popularity of LP is that the objective and the constraints can be stated quantitatively. Once the numeric values have been stated, the computer can make the many calculations very fast. LP problems can be solved without a computer, but it is a slow process.

Types of problems solved

LP solves two types of problems: (1) determining the best *routing* of resources through an area, and (2) determining the best *mixture* of ingredients, or resources, going into some finished product. Routing problems are determining bus routes in a city or customer delivery sequences in a sales territory. Mix problems are determining the percentage of peanuts in a can of mixed nuts or the portion of cereal in sausage. All of these examples reflect objectives to be met (such as sales or service) with limited resources (such as city buses, sales representatives, or raw materials).

Example of a linear programming solution

A more detailed description of the solution of a real business problem with LP can provide a better appreciation of its value to the manager.[3]

---

3. For other introductory descriptions of linear programming, see Irvine Forkner and Raymond McLeod, Jr., *Computerized Business Systems* (New York: John Wiley & Sons, 1973), pp. 133–137, and Richard I. Levin and Charles A. Kirkpatrick, *Quantitative Approaches to Management* (New York: McGraw-Hill Book Company, 1975), pp. 226–255.

Table 9–2   Floor space for minimum quantities

| | Floor space (sq. ft.) | | |
Item (1)	Each (2)	Minimum quantity (3)	Total (4)
Mattress	9.7	4	38.8
Chair	10.7	50	535.0
Sofa	26	40	1040.0
Dining room suite	32.4	25	810.0
Coffee table	12.2	50	610.0
Bedroom suite	32.9	15	493.5
Bookcase	5.8	25	145.0
Total			3672.3

Assume there is a manager of a retail furniture store in Lexington, Kentucky, who has a problem. The problem is how to allocate space in a warehouse to the most profitable items. The warehouse has 6500 square feet, of which 3672 is to be used for minimum quantities of the seven furniture items carried. The items, the floor space required for each, the minimum quantities, and the total floor space for the minimum quantities are shown in Table 9–2.

The question, then, is how best to use the remaining area of 2828 square feet to maximize profit.

The manager prepares a mathematical expression representing the objective function. To do this, profit figures are assembled for each of the seven furniture items (Table 9–3). A variable name ($X_1 - X_7$) is assigned to each item to represent the quantity of each to be located in the available warehouse area. The LP model will compute the value for each of these variable names.

The manager knows that the total profit from the sale of a certain mixture of items will be the sum of the quantity of each times its profit figure. This is the objective function.

$$\text{Maximum profit} = 20X_1 + 40X_2 + 75X_3 + 170X_4 + 60X_5 + 150X_6 + 65X_7$$

For example, the $20X_1$ means that profit from mattresses will be the product of the profit ($20) times the number of mattresses (X_1). The LP model can assign

Table 9–3   Item profit figures

Item	Variable name	Profit (each)
Mattress	X_1	$ 20
Chair	X_2	40
Sofa	X_3	75
Dining room suite	X_4	170
Coffee table	X_5	60
Bedroom suite	X_6	150
Bookcase	X_7	65

any value to X_1, including zero. Zero means that none of that item is to be included in the solution.

The remaining task for the manager is to identify any constraints that may exist. One constraint is floor space. Only 2828 square feet is available for the seven items. This constraint can be stated mathematically, using the floor space figures for each of the items from Table 9–2.

$$9.7X_1 + 10.7X_2 + 26X_3 + 32.4X_4 + 12.2X_5 + 32.9X_6 + 5.8X_7 \leq 2828$$

The floor space area for each item multiplied by the quantity of each, added together, cannot be greater than 2828.

In a similar fashion, other constraints are expressed mathematically. These constraints are listed below without the accompanying mathematics.

1 Minimum quantities of each item
2 One mattress for every three bedroom suites
3 Twice as many chairs as sofas
4 Maximum investment of $60,000
5 No more than 60 dining room suites
6 No more dining room suites than coffee tables
7 No more than 55 bookcases

The necessary mathematical expressions are entered into the LP model, and the optimum mix is computed. The model determines that only two items should be located in the available area: chairs and sofas. If 113 chairs ($X_2 = 113$) and 57 sofas ($X_3 = 57$) are stocked, the profit from the use of the available area will be $8783. No other mixture of items will produce a profit that large.

An example of the systems approach

The use of LP to solve the problem is an example of the systems approach.

First, the problem is defined. The problem is low profit on the use of limited warehouse space.

Next, data is gathered to aid in understanding the problem. Examples of this data appear in Tables 9–2 and 9–3.

Then, the LP model identifies alternate solutions (different mixtures of furniture items) and evaluates each. This step permits the model to identify the best solution for the manager.

The manager need only implement the solution and follow up on the results.

A Probabilistic Model

Discussion of another type of model will conclude the treatment of problem solving with the computer. This model is an example of category 8 in Table 9–1: it simulates an activity over time (it is dynamic), it doesn't identify the single best answer (it is nonoptimizing), and it deals in probabilities.

Assume, in this case, that the manager of a department store in Chicago doesn't know how many sales clerks to assign to a department since the volume of customer activity varies. Different numbers of customers enter the department at different times throughout the day. The customers make purchases of different values. Data describing these variations in customer activity can be gathered. A model can simulate the effect of assigning different numbers of sales clerks to the department.

The store hours can be divided into 10-minute intervals (9:00–9:10, 9:10–9:20, etc.) and a record kept of the numbers of customers arriving during each interval. The distribution of customers might look like this:

Number of intervals with zero customers	6
Number of intervals with one customer	12
Number of intervals with two customers	20
Number of intervals with three customers	6
Number of intervals with four customers	4
	48

Of the forty-eight 10-minute intervals during the 8-hour day, 6 intervals had no customers, 12 had one customer, and so on.

This distribution of arrivals can be converted into a probability distribution by calculating percentages (or probabilities) for each customer group. All the probabilities must add to 1.00 since they account for 100 percent of the customer activity.

$$
\begin{aligned}
\text{Zero customers} &= {}^{6}\!/_{48} = .12 \\
\text{One customer} &= {}^{12}\!/_{48} = .25 \\
\text{Two customers} &= {}^{20}\!/_{48} = .43 \\
\text{Three customers} &= {}^{6}\!/_{48} = .12 \\
\text{Four customers} &= {}^{4}\!/_{48} = \underline{.08} \\
& \qquad\qquad\quad 1.00
\end{aligned}
$$

The same technique can be used for the dollar values of the customers' purchases. The purchases of the 86 customers are:

No purchase	18
$5 purchase	20
$10 purchase	22
$15 purchase	16
$20 purchase	10
	86

These values can also be converted into probabilities:

$$
\begin{aligned}
\text{No purchase} &= {}^{18}\!/_{86} = .20 \\
\$5 \text{ purchase} &= {}^{20}\!/_{86} = .23 \\
\$10 \text{ purchase} &= {}^{22}\!/_{86} = .26 \\
\$15 \text{ purchase} &= {}^{16}\!/_{86} = .19 \\
\$20 \text{ purchase} &= {}^{10}\!/_{86} = \underline{.12} \\
& \qquad\qquad\qquad 1.00
\end{aligned}
$$

Now the problem is: "how many sales clerks to assign to the department to maximize profit?" If one sales clerk is required to serve one customer during a 10-minute interval, the number of clerks can range from one to four (since a maximum of four customers is in the department at one time). If only one clerk is assigned, there frequently will be customers who cannot be served and sales will be lost. On the other hand, if four clerks are assigned, no sales will be lost. But there will be some idle clerk time and expenses will be higher.

An important assumption of the model is that there is no pattern to either customer arrivals or purchases. They both are strictly random.

Monte Carlo

A technique to simulate such random activity was developed in the Second World War. *Monte Carlo*, the code name assigned to the technique, is based on the selection of random numbers. The numbers range from 00 through 99.

There are 100 numbers and the chance of selecting one at random is 1 percent. It is like putting 100 numbered tags in a hat and selecting one while blindfolded. The chance, or probability, of selecting any particular number is .01.

Series of the hundred numbers can be assigned to each entry in the two probability distributions. For example, the distribution of arrival times looks like this:

Number of Customers	Probability (P)	Number Series
0	.12	00–11
1	.25	12–36
2	.43	37–79
3	.12	80–91
4	.08	92–99

If the computer can randomly generate a number from 00 through 99 (and it can), the chance of generating a number from 00 through 11 is 12 percent, corresponding to the first probability of .12. Similarly, the chance of generating a number from 12 through 36 is 25 percent (since this series represents 25 of the 100 numbers), corresponding to the second probability of .25.

In this manner, the computer can simulate the random arrival pattern of the customers. A number can be generated and it will fall within one of the five number series. The series within which the random number falls determines the number of customers arriving at that particular 10-minute interval.

Other numbers can be assigned to the customer purchases, and that activity can be simulated randomly also.

Value of Purchases	Probability (P)	Number Series
$ 0	.20	00–19
5	.23	20–42
10	.26	43–68
15	.19	69–87
20	.12	88–99

At the beginning of a 10-minute interval, it is not known how many customers will arrive. A random number is generated, say 45, and it is matched with the number series of the arrivals. The number 45 falls within the range 37–79, so it is assumed that two customers arrive. The process works the same way for the customer purchases. A random number is generated for each customer; the number determines the value of the purchase for each. If the computer generates a 12 and a 63, the purchase values are zero (the customer is only "shopping") and $10.

Figure 9–9   Computer printout with one sales clerk

INTERVAL	RANDOM NUMBER-- ARRIVALS	NUMBER OF ARRIVALS	RANDOM NUMBER-- PURCHASES	VALUE OF PURCHASE	CLERK NO. 1 SALES	IDLE TIME	LOST SALES
1	23	1	45	$10	$10	0	
2	64	2	14	$ 0		0	
			59	$10			$10
3	79	2	11	$ 0		0	
			28	$ 5			$ 5
4	49	2	46	$10	$10	0	
			47	$10			$10
5	99	4	60	$10	$10	0	
			25	$ 5			$ 5
			97	$20			$20
			41	$ 5			$ 5
6	50	2	81	$15	$15	0	
			31	$ 5			$ 5
			TOTALS	$105	$45	0	$60

Simulation of the model

A mathematical model is created to simulate the activity of the department, using different numbers of sales clerks. The number of clerks is entered into the model and a printout describes the results. In the example of Figure 9–9, only one clerk is assigned, and the activity of only a single hour is simulated. In actual practice, a much larger number of hours would be simulated.

The computer randomly selects the number 23 to represent the number of customer arrivals for period 1. When matched to the number series of customer arrivals, this number falls within the range 12–36. This means that one customer arrives in period 1. The computer then selects the number 45 to determine the value of that customer's purchase. The number falls within the range 43–68; therefore the customer makes a $10 purchase.

One random number is selected for each time period to represent the number of arrivals. Then, a single random number is selected for each customer arriving in that period to represent the value of each purchase.

Since only one clerk is available, he or she can serve only the first customer arriving in a 10-minute interval. Other customers could have made purchases in the amounts shown, but they leave the store and those sales are lost.

Figure 9–10 Computer printout with three sales clerks

INTERVAL	RANDOM NUMBER-- ARRIVALS	NUMBER OF ARRIVALS	RANDOM NUMBER-- PURCHASES	VALUE OF PURCHASE	CLERK NO. 1 SALES	CLERK NO. 2 SALES	CLERK NO. 3 SALES	IDLE TIME	LOST SALES
1	05	0						30	
2	24	1	00	$ 0				20	
3	81	3	30	$ 5	$ 5			0	
			44	$10		$10			
			62	$10			$10		
4	55	2	48	$10	$10			10	
			02	$ 0					
5	10	0						30	
6	63	2	46	$10	$10			10	
			97	$20		$20			
		TOTALS		$65	$25	$30	$10	100	$ 0

In a similar manner, the other numbers of clerks can be simulated. In the example of Figure 9–10, three clerks are assigned to the department. It can be seen that the pattern of arrivals and purchases differs from the first example. This difference is characteristic of random process simulation.

In this example, sales totaled $65. There were no lost sales, but idle time totaled 100 minutes (out of 180).

The manager now has used the model to evaluate two alternatives. Most likely, simulations would be conducted also of two and four sales clerks. The probabilistic, nonoptimizing model doesn't identify which alternative is the best. The model only prints out the results that can be expected from each.

The selection of the best alternative can be accomplished by comparing costs and benefits, as shown in Table 9–4. Costs are calculated by considering the daily or hourly cost of the clerks. The benefits are the sales produced by the clerks.

According to the example, three clerks produce the most profit. While other factors (idle time, value of lost sales, etc.) might influence the final decision, the model has provided the profit and loss figures. This information will provide the real basis for the decision.

These examples illustrate how models can be used to evaluate several alternative solutions to problems. A single model can simulate different conditions by using values assigned to the variables by the manager. The computer can do the simulation very rapidly, saving much of the manager's valuable time.

Table 9–4   Cost benefit analysis

Number of clerks	Sales	Costs	Profit (loss)
1	$395	$405	$(10)
2	460	435	25
3	515	470	45
4	520	505	15

Summary

The manager follows the systems approach in decision making. The information system can support the manager in each step of the process. This is the idea of the MIS as a decision support system—the manager is supported by the computer, not replaced.

Basically, computer support is of two types. First, the computer helps the manager identify problems. Second, help is provided in solving the problems.

Problems are identified with periodic reports that show actual, historical performance. This performance is compared with standards to identify problems or potential problems. The reports can be detail listings or summaries, and can include graphical information.

Managers also identify problems by making inquiries into the data base. Precomputed information can be retrieved, or special analyses can be performed. Problem-oriented programming languages such as BASIC and APL, along with data base languages, make it relatively easy for the managers to initiate these analyses.

Mathematical routines in the model base enable the MIS to become involved in problem solution. These models can be static or dynamic, optimizing or nonoptimizing, deterministic or probabilistic. Linear programming identifies the single best solution for a static situation, such as the allocation of warehouse space to furniture items. The process of identifying this solution is accomplished without probabilities. A probabilistic model can simulate random situations using the Monte Carlo method. These are situations over which the manager has no real control, such as customer arrival times and purchase amounts.

The computer can function as a powerful decision support system because of its large and accurate data base, and the speed with which the data can be transformed into information. Computations and logical decisions can be made rapidly, following certain processes defined by the manager working with information specialists.

Important Terms

Decision Support System

Periodic Report

Detail Listing

Summary

Static Model, Dynamic Model

Optimizing Model, Nonoptimizing Model

Deterministic Model, Probabilistic Model

Linear Programming (LP)

Constraint

Objective Function

Routing Problem, Mix Problem

Monte Carlo

Important Concepts

The MIS can help the manager solve unstructured problems and can solve those that have been structured.

The MIS can support the manager in each step of the systems approach.

Problems can be identified with periodic reports or with responses to management inquiries.

Mathematical models can be used for problem solution.

Different types of mathematical models are best suited for solving different types of problems.

Questions

1 In what two basic ways can the computer be used to solve business problems?
2 What is a decision support system?
3 In which step of the systems approach has computer support been the least?
4 On which management level are periodic reports the most valuable?
5 How can a periodic report be used with management by exception?

6 On which management level are precomputed information elements the most valuable?

7 The computer can respond to management inquiries in two basic ways. What are they?

8 Which management level uses the MIS the most for problem identification?

9 Which management level uses the MIS the most for problem solution?

10 Give examples of a static and a dynamic narrative model; a physical model; a graphical model.

11 Would it be accurate to say that an optimizing model solves problems that are more structured than those of a nonoptimizing model? If so, in what way are the problems better structured? If not, why can some models identify optimum solutions, and others cannot?

12 Can you comment on the statement that in a deterministic model the probabilities are always either .0 or 1.0?

13 What must a manager keep in mind when considering use of linear programming solutions?

14 How many routing problems can you identify that the administration of your college faces? How about mix problems? Would the situation be the same for a bank?

15 Are probabilistic problems more or less structured than deterministic ones?

16 What is the basis for probability distributions?

Problem

1 Use the following probability distribution and random numbers to simulate the value of purchase for the next 20 customers entering the store.

Probability distribution		Random numbers		
Value	P	02	88	58
$ 0	.05	27	54	12
5	.10	83	70	06
10	.40	81	76	15
15	.35	20	04	54
20	.10	58	79	90
		88	68	

Use the left column of the random numbers first, starting at the top; then use the middle and right columns. Enter your figures below.

Customer	Random Number	Purchase Value
1		
2		
3		
4		
5		
6		
7		
8		
9		
10		
11		
12		
13		
14		
15		
16		
17		
18		
19		
20		

Part Four

Functional Information Systems

It is time to learn more about the MIS. Up until now, the information system has been described in general terms only. More needs to be said about who uses it and how it is used. This is the subject of the next four chapters.

One of the characteristics of the systems approach described earlier is the subdivision of a system into its subsystems. That technique is used to develop a better understanding of the MIS. The MIS is described in terms of its users—the managers. Since managers most commonly are organized by functional area, that is the way the MIS is subdivided. Functional information systems are described that are used by managers of marketing, manufacturing, and finance.

An introductory chapter relates why the functional subdivision is appropriate, and introduces each functional information system. Each system is described as containing two basic types of subsystems: input and output. Input subsystems gather data from within the firm and from its environment. This data is stored in the data base and converted into information by the output subsystems. Each of the three functional information systems is represented by a graphical model and is described in a separate chapter. The intent is to illustrate some of the ways a manager can use an information system.

One precaution must be taken when recognizing the MIS as being composed of subsystems. The reader must not get the idea that these subsystems are separate and isolated. On the contrary, they are integrated into an overall MIS, serving the interests of the entire firm.

Chapter 10

Introduction to Functional Information Systems

Functional Organization Structure

Business firms traditionally have been organized along functional lines. These are not the same management functions that Fayol identified (plan, organize, staff, etc.). Rather, they are the major jobs that the firm performs, such as marketing, finance, and manufacturing.

For years management analysts have criticized this functional structure and pointed to its many shortcomings. To systems theorists, the functional structure makes it extremely difficult to mold the various parts together so that they perform as a single system. Each part tends to operate as a separate system, apart from the others.

There have been partial movements toward other, more modern, structures, but they have barely dented the popularity of functionalism.[1] The functional organization has withstood the criticism and the attempted modifications. It appears that functional organization is here to stay.

A functional organization chart of a manufacturing firm can be seen in Figure 10–1. In this chart, information systems is shown as a fourth major area, on the same level as marketing, manufacturing, and finance. More will be said of the information systems operation in the final part of the book. Information

---

1. Examples of efforts to achieve a modified functional organization include the integration of all materials handling activities into a "physical distribution" department, use of brand managers in firms such as Procter & Gamble, use of project managers in electronics firms, and implementation of a "matrix" form of organization. The first two types of efforts usually are described in introductory marketing texts. The last two are the subject of introductory management texts.

Figure 10–1 A functional organization

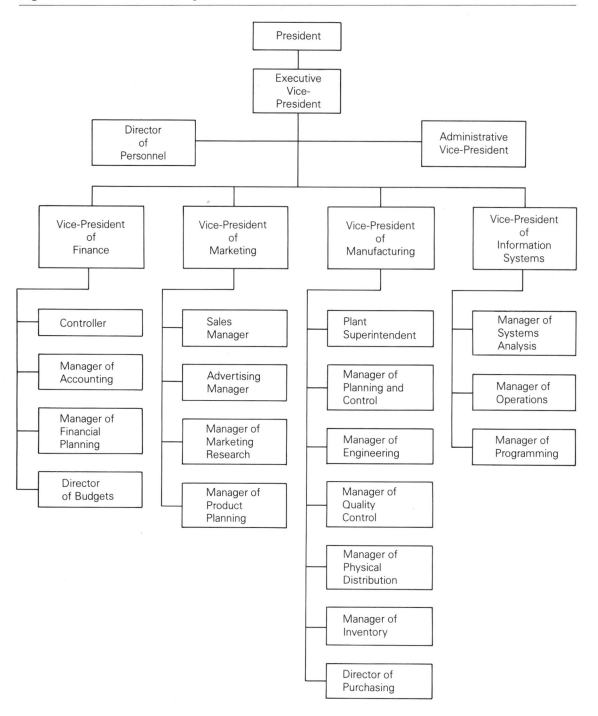

systems is not included as a major functional area in this and the next three chapters.

The two major functions that many firms perform are manufacturing and marketing. The firms make things and then distribute them to their customers. The things made can include either products or services. The manufacturing function has the production responsibility; the marketing function distributes the product or service once it has been created.

This interpretation of production, one that encompasses both products and services, is very broad. It means that firms other than manufacturers have a production function. Banks produce financial services, hospitals produce medical care, legal firms produce legal services, and symphonies produce musical enjoyment. Such a broad interpretation was made in Chapter 3 when the general model of the firm was presented. The model described how input resources are transformed into output resources. This transformation is the production function.

It is easier to see the universality of the marketing function. Every organization that provides products or services must sell them to their customers. Most organizations have marketing departments, and these include nonmanufacturing types such as banks, insurance companies, colleges, military branches, and churches.

So, it can be accepted that practically all types of organizations include manufacturing and marketing. The functional approach therefore provides a good general model of organization that can be applied in many situations. Perhaps this explains, in part, its widespread adoption—it fits practically all kinds of organizations.

There is a third functional area not yet mentioned. That function is finance—an important part of any organization. Finance lends support to the other two functions by assuring that sufficient operating funds are available and by controlling the use of those funds. It takes money to run any type of operation; therefore the financial function exists in all organizations.

Functional organization versus the flow network concept

In Chapter 2, the systems approach to organization recognized flows of basic resources (men, material, etc.). While the flow network approach has not been embraced by the real world of business as an organizational method, it can be used to explain the roles of the three functions.

The two concepts are not totally dissimilar. The financial function is concerned with the money flow. The manufacturing and marketing functions represent the material flow. Material, in this description, includes both products and services. The marketing function determines what material should flow from the firm to its customers, and the manufacturing function creates that material flow.

Only the machine and manpower flows lack representation in the functional structure. This is because both of these resources are used in all three functional areas. They are not employed separately. Very often a firm has a personnel function, but it is responsible only for certain parts of the manpower flow. And, no firm has a separate organizational unit that has sole responsibility for all the machines used throughout the company.

So, a close parallel exists between the two approaches, but not an identical one. Both the money and material flow can be seen quite readily in a functional structure. But, the manpower and machine flows become diffused throughout all functional areas.

Functional Information Systems

Any single business organization encompasses a multitude of varied activities. These activities comprise the physical system of the firm and usually are grouped according to the major functions as shown in Figure 10–1. When an effort is made to implement a conceptual information system to reflect the physical system, it is difficult to ignore the functional influence. It is only natural for the information system also to be organized functionally (Figure 10–2).

This is what has happened. The conceptual information system representing the physical marketing system has been named the marketing information system. The same logic has created a financial information system and a manufacturing information system. A review of business literature will yield a number of references to these functional information systems—especially in the marketing area.[2]

When information systems are organized functionally, a question arises concerning the information needs of the chief executive officers—the chairman of the board, the president, the executive vice-president, the administrative vice-president, etc. These positions do not fit within any function, but tie them together at the top level. This problem could be solved by organizing the information systems by management level. There could be a strategic management information system as well as those for the tactical and operational levels. This approach makes a great deal of sense. The information needs of these management levels are different, and separate information systems could be created for each. (See Figure 10–3.)

A major problem with this approach is that business firms are not organized that way. The strain of functionalism would exist within each level, causing the system to become too fragmented. The strain should not be too strong on the strategic level where the welfare of the entire firm is of prime importance. But on the lower levels, functional interests tend to supersede those of the firm.

Although other structures are possible for an information system, the one

2. See, for example, James C. Stephenson and Harvey Smith, "A New Marketing Information System," *Management Accounting*, August 1974, pp. 11–14, and Arthur F. Brueningsen, "Kodak's Financial and Reporting System," *Management Accounting*, September 1975, pp. 21–24.

Figure 10–2   Functional information systems represent functional physical systems.

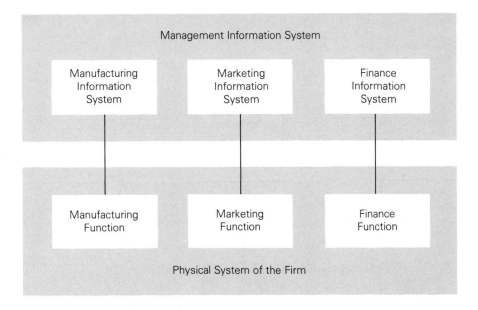

Management Information System

| Manufacturing Information System | Marketing Information System | Finance Information System |

| Manufacturing Function | Marketing Function | Finance Function |

Physical System of the Firm

most readily accepted by business firms is the functional one (Figure 10–4). For this reason it will be the structure presented here. A concept of information management is presented based on functional subsystems representing functional physical systems. A separate information system is not described for the chief executive officers. It is assumed that their information is a distillation and synthesis of that produced by each functional information system.

There is a point of major importance that must be appreciated as this functional approach is presented. Functional information subsystems do not

Figure 10–3   Information systems by management levels

Strategic
management
information system

Tactical management information system

Operational management information system

Figure 10–4   Users of functional information output

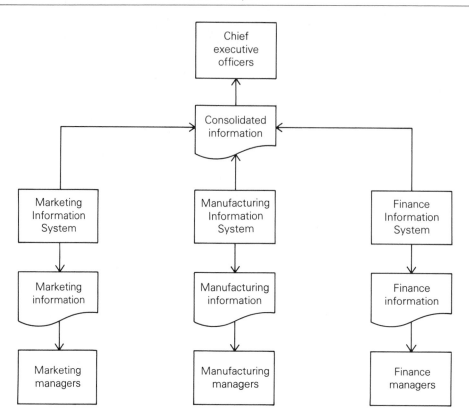

diminish the importance of an integrated overall system for the firm, i.e., the MIS. The functional subsystems must work together. They must share a common data base and model base; decisions made in one area must be compatible with those made in others and with overall firm objectives. Figure 10–5 illustrates this principle.

The remainder of this chapter will introduce each of the three functional subsystems. The information needs of the managers in each area will be identified, as will the primary sources of the information. These information inputs and uses will be used to construct a graphical model of each subsystem. The purpose of these models is to provide a structure to facilitate an understanding of what each subsystem can include. Then, in the following three chapters, each subsystem will be described in greater detail.

Marketing Information Systems

The marketing information system will be described first. This is not because it is more important, but because its composition is better defined than the

Figure 10–5   Functional subsystems must be integrated into a total MIS.

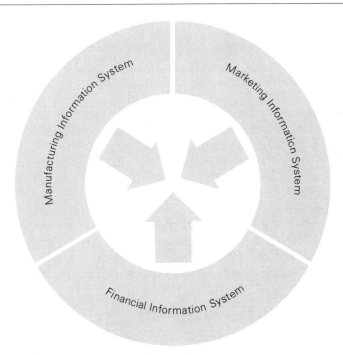

others. Marketers have spent considerable time studying the subject of the marketing information system and have developed some excellent models of how it should be constructed.

Marketing and the marketing concept

Many people think of marketing in very narrow terms—as including selling and advertising only. Marketing spokesmen, on the other hand, define it very broadly. E. Jerome McCarthy, author of a leading marketing text, defines marketing as:

> The performance of business activities which direct the flow of goods and services from producer to consumer or user in order to satisfy customers and accomplish the firm's objectives.[3]

The years since World War II have seen a large number of firms move toward a marketing orientation. This attitude means that the entire organization is dedicated to the mission of marketing—the satisfaction of customer

---

3. Jerome McCarthy, *Basic Marketing*, Fifth Edition (Homewood, Ill.: Richard D. Irwin, Inc., 1975), p. 19.

wants and needs at a profit. This is called the *marketing concept*. It is important in terms of the opportunity it offers to the firm to contribute to the increasing standard of living and also to meet its social obligations. More importantly here, the marketing concept has a special significance to the subject of information systems as well.

Much has been said in previous chapters about the importance of the firm acting as an integrated system. In reality, this integration has been very difficult to achieve. One of the most demanding tasks of the chief executive officer is to integrate the functional elements of the firm into a smoothly operating unit. What the marketing concept implies is that this integration is achieved through marketing goals. It does not mean that the marketing function dominates the company. It does mean that everyone in the organization works toward the same basic goal as the marketing function: satisfaction of customer needs.

Both businessmen and academicians, writing on the subject of the management information system, have commented consistently on the rather dismal outlook for the complete integration of effort within the firm, so critical to the success of the MIS. There is a real possibility that the marketing concept will provide the vehicle to achieve this integration, and resultantly, the MIS.

Sources and uses of marketing information

One model of a marketing information system has won widespread attention. It is the model developed by respected marketing authority Philip Kotler.[4] Kotler's model provides a subdivision of the parts based on the sources of management information and how it is used. He sees the information system as consisting of four separate subsystems: internal accounting, marketing intelligence, marketing research, and marketing management science (Figure 10–6). Each of these subsystems interfaces with both the environment and the marketing executive.

By including the *internal accounting system*, he recognized the symbiotic, or dependent, relationship between the functions of the firm. In fact, it is the internal accounting system that provides a common bond throughout the firm, gathering data describing actual operations and employing that data in the preparation of basic accounting documents and management reports.

The *marketing intelligence system* is concerned primarily with dissemination of information that alerts the manager to new developments in the marketplace. The marketing intelligence system differs from the accounting system in that the input data usually is gathered from the environment, rather than from within the firm. Also, the output information is oriented toward the future, rather than the present or the past. Information of this

---

4. Philip Kotler, *Marketing Management: Analysis, Planning, and Control,* third edition. (Englewood Cliffs, N.J.: Prentice-Hall, 1976) pp. 419–442.

Figure 10–6 Kotler's model of the marketing information system. (From Philip Kotler, *Marketing Management: Analysis, Planning, and Control,* 1972, Second Ed., p. 295.)

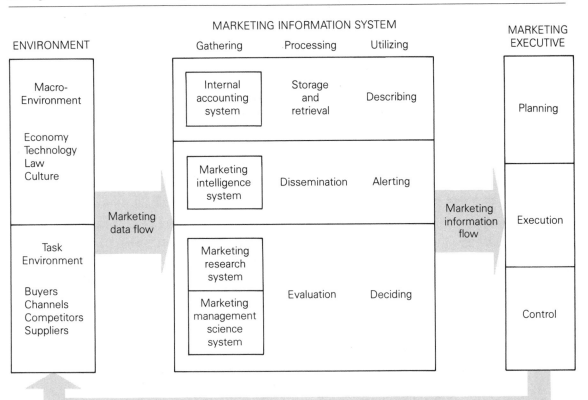

nature, such as an announcement that a competitor is developing a new product, is used mainly in planning.

The systems that evaluate alternative strategies and either decide which alternative is best or provide information to the manager so that he or she might make this decision, are the marketing research system and the marketing management science system.

Marketing research is a twofold activity carried on in many firms. It involves gathering current data that describes all parts of the marketing operations, and presenting the findings to management in a form that facilitates decision making. The emphasis is on the timeliness of the information; it usually is necessary to design and conduct projects for the purpose of gathering data describing what is happening currently. The techniques used for analyzing the data most frequently are quantitative in nature, although some analysis is qualitative. The quantitative techniques can be either basic or complex.

In *marketing management science*, the emphasis is on the use of only sophisticated quantitative techniques, such as simulation. The data sources can be either the marketing research system or the internal accounting system.

The marketing research and marketing management science systems therefore represent the most modern methods of analyzing data with the purpose of assisting the manager in problem solving. As seen in the model, the marketing manager uses the information output for the basic process of planning, executing, and controlling.

Kotler has produced a good structure that identifies the primary methods for generating marketing information. It is not so effective, however, in providing an understanding of the types of problems solved by the marketing manager with the aid of an information system. Most of the problem solving is accomplished by two of the subsystems: marketing research and marketing management science. Some finer breakdown is needed.

The marketing mix

The marketing manager, just like any one else, recognizes that he or she has a variety of resources with which to work. The objective of the manager is to derive strategies that enable these resources to be used in marketing the firm's products and services. The marketing strategies derived consist of a mixture of ingredients that has been termed the *marketing mix*.

The marketing mix is the offering presented to the prospect (or consumer) as a means of satisfying felt needs and wants. The ingredients of the marketing mix consist of the "four P's"—product, promotion, place, and price. *Product* is what the customer buys to satisfy the felt need or want. Although the product is most often something that exists physically, it can also be some type of service. *Promotion* is concerned with all the means of encouraging the sale of the product, including advertising, personal selling, and a variety of miscellaneous techniques and devices. *Place* deals with the means of physically distributing the product to the customer. This includes transportation, storage, and distribution on both the wholesale and retail levels. *Price* consists of all the elements relating to what the customer must pay for the product or service, including discounts and bonuses.

Marketing mix subsystems

The manager is concerned primarily with achieving an optimum mixture of these ingredients to meet the needs of a particular target market. Therefore, an approach to the study of marketing information systems based on the ingredients of the marketing mix appears logical. The overall information system can be segmented into subsystems for each of the mix ingredients. Also, a subsystem can be provided to integrate the ingredients in an optimum manner. A model of such an approach is presented in Figure 10–7.

The information-producing activities of the marketing information system may be classified in terms of the model pictured in Figure 10–7. The needs of the manager for product information are supplied by the product

Figure 10–7   Marketing mix subsystems of the marketing information system

subsystem, for promotion information by the promotion subsystem, and so on. Figure 10–7 views the marketing information system in terms of the decisions the manager must make.

Input subsystems

In building a structural model of the marketing information system, it also is necessary to recognize the *sources* of the data used to provide the needed information. Kotler's model identified the three main sources—the internal accounting system, the marketing intelligence system, and the marketing research system. The marketing management science system emphasized the processing of data more so than the gathering of it. When the three data sources are added to the basic mix subsystems, the result is a model that views the marketing information system in terms of both its output information and its input data sources. This model can be seen in Figure 10–8. The arrows in the model indicate the dependence the *output subsystems* have on the *input subsystems* for data.

This model provides a finer breakdown for the study of how information systems assist in solving marketing problems. For this reason, it will serve as the basis for the discussion of the marketing information system in the next

Figure 10–8   Marketing information system

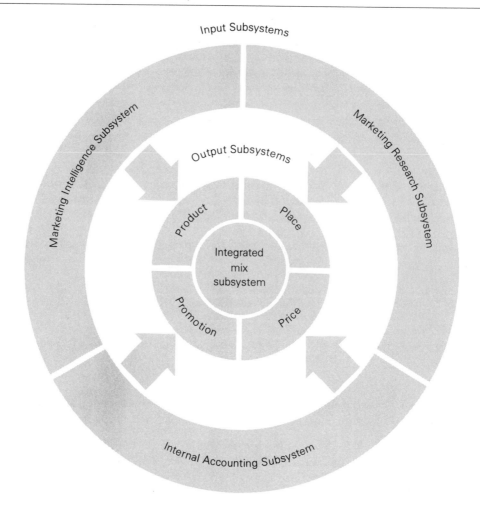

chapter. Its basic structure of input and output subsystems will also be used in describing the manufacturing and financial information systems.

Each subsystem in Figure 10–8 consists of computer programs residing in the model base. These programs have the responsibility of either entering data into the data base or converting data in the data base into information. This option is illustrated in Figure 10–9.

There seems to be more interest in marketing information systems than any other type of functional MIS. This certainly is supported by business publications. While marketers are writing about this subject, however, they have the least evidence of real accomplishment. This lack is due undoubtedly to the enormity of the task, including solution of problems difficult to define

Figure 10–9   Relationship of subsystem models to the data base

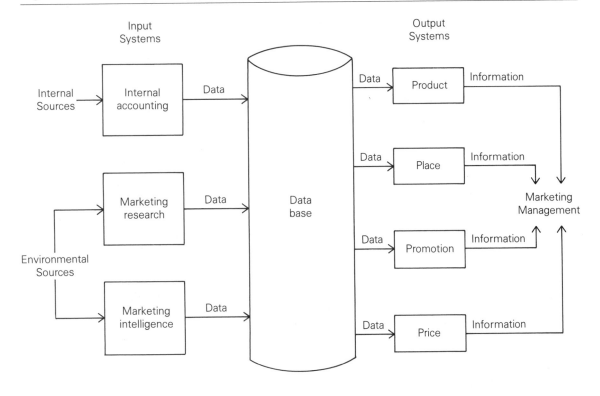

and to quantify. There appears to be greater potential for information system use in marketing than in either manufacturing or finance. Much remains to be done.

Manufacturing Information Systems

The manufacturing manager is concerned mainly with material flow from vendors, through the transformation process, and to marketing for distribution. Both manpower and machines are used to expedite and facilitate this flow and transformation. In a manufacturing firm, most of the employees work in the manufacturing function. Also, much use is made of machines that move material by conveyors, cranes, and trucks, and that transform raw materials into finished goods. Many of these machines now are controlled by computers.

The manufacturing manager must create the physical system that transforms input materials into finished goods. He or she must also obtain information describing the performance of the physical system so that decisions can be made when necessary. The model of a system that can supply the manufacturing manager with such information is illustrated in Figure 10–10.

Figure 10–10 Manufacturing information system

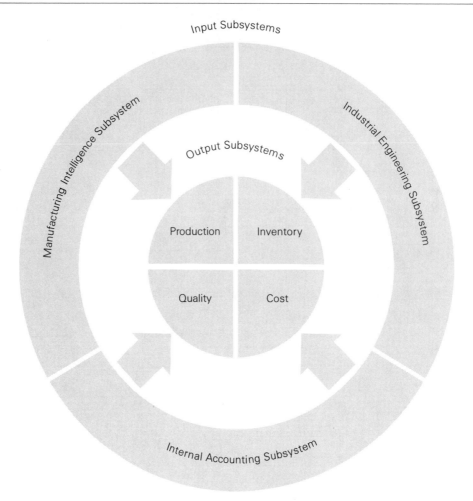

Input subsystems

The *internal accounting subsystem* appears again. It also will be included in the financial information system. The accounting system provides the strong tie between these three functional subsystems of the MIS. It provides a reservoir of data that can be used by each.

Very often, special machines are used in the production area to gather data describing the use of material, machine, and manpower resources. This gathering activity is called *data collection* and has become highly computerized. Some data collection devices are terminals; others are minicomputers. These data collection sensors record the movement of material through the plant and the expenditure of both manpower and machine resources in the transformation process. This data collection can be regarded as a part of the firm's internal accounting system, although the data has uses in addition to those of an accounting nature. The data provides a current status of the manufacturing process to planners, controllers, schedulers, and dispatchers.

The *manufacturing intelligence subsystem* gathers data from the environment. The two elements in the environment of particular interest to the manufacturing manager are vendors and labor. The vendors provide both material and machine resources; they also provide information in the form of catalogs and sales literature. In addition, the firm can generate much information as a result of past vendor performance in terms of quality, price, and service.

Data describing the labor element in the environment is much less formal and specific. This data can be gathered by reading newspapers and union publications, through personal contact with employment agencies and government commissions, and through personal discussions with lower level managers. Such data rarely finds its way into the computerized portion of the MIS, but instead is communicated orally and in the form of typed documents.

The *industrial engineering subsystem* is like the marketing research subsystem in that it relates to special data gathering projects. The subsystems are dissimilar in that the industrial engineering subsystem gathers data from inside the firm, rather than from the environment. Industrial engineers (or IEs) study the manufacturing operation and make recommendations for improvement. They frequently use stopwatches to shave seconds from a production step. The seconds add up to significant savings as the step is repeated many times during the process of creating a quantity of products.

Output subsystems

The manufacturing manager must both design and use production systems. An information system must provide an understanding of how this physical system functions. The *production subsystem* describes each phase of the transformation process, from the ordering of raw materials from a vendor to the release of the finished goods to marketing. A great many different activities therefore are tracked by this subsystem—purchasing, receiving, materials handling, and the production process itself. This subsystem reports on everything that is done to the material flow through the firm.

As the material flows, the manager wants to know how well the objectives of quantity, quality, and cost are being met. The *inventory subsystem* reports on quantity by keeping a record of how much material flows from one step to the next—from raw materials to work in process, and finally to finished goods. A special *quality subsystem* is used to assure that the quality level of raw materials received from vendors meets the required standards. Then this subsystem reports on the quality level at each critical step of the transformation process. Statistics play an important role in this quality control process.

Many problems worked in college statistics classes deal with the measurement of production quality.

The *cost subsystem* tells the manufacturing manager exactly what the transformation process is costing. While all managers are, or should be, concerned with costs, such costs can be reported more easily to the manufacturing manager than to many others. This is because the costs of labor, materials, and machines can be reported very specifically in production units or even in seconds. The data collection input devices record the exact time a worker or a machine starts a job and the exact time the job is finished. The same devices can also report exactly how much material is used. The data can be reported to the manufacturing manager and compared with predetermined standards. Excessive costs call for decisions that make the material flow and transformation process more efficient.

More has been done to develop manufacturing information systems than any other type of MIS. The reason for this achievement is that many of the problems facing the manufacturing manager can be expressed quantitatively. The major variables influencing the problem can be identified and their relationships expressed in a mathematical model. This capability applies to problems of production system design as well as operation. A great many of the major decisions made by manufacturing managers can be computerized. It is unlikely that such thorough use of the computer ever will be achieved in the other functional areas.

Financial Information Systems

Efforts have been directed toward the development of mechanized financial information systems for 50 or more years. Punched card machines were used primarily by the financial function. Actually, the use was generally restricted to the processing of accounting data, and little attention was paid to the information needs of management—even financial managers. When computers were developed, they too were applied to these same accounting problems. It wasn't until the mid-1960s that financial information systems were developed beyond the basic accounting tasks.

The financial function is concerned with money flow through the firm. First it is necessary to acquire enough money to support the manufacturing and marketing activities. Then it is necessary to control those funds to assure that they are used in the most effective way.

Information describing the money flow—both anticipated and actual—permits managers in all functional areas to meet their financial responsibilities. This information is provided by the financial information system. The function of this system is to identify future money needs, assist in the acquisition of those funds, and control their use. These three tasks are represented as output subsystems in the financial information system. The model of this system is illustrated in Figure 10–11.

Figure 10–11   Financial information system

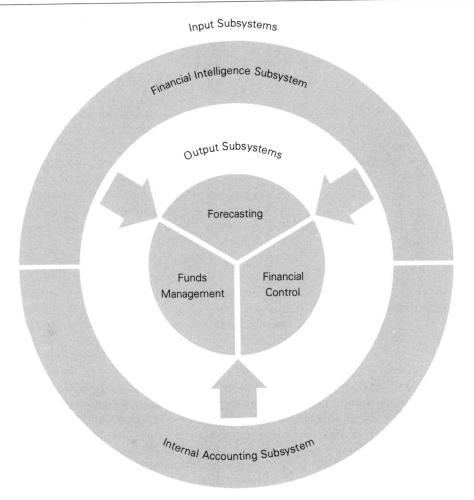

Output subsystems

The *forecasting subsystem* projects the activity of the firm for a period of up to 10 years. The activity for the coming year is influenced primarily by market demand and internal constraints such as size of the sales force, production capacity, and available finances. As the forecast period lengthens, the importance of the environment becomes greater. Changing needs of consumers must be anticipated, as should the climate of the national economy. Recent years have shown the necessity of considering government controls, as well as the availability of resources such as energy, in future planning. Forecasting models have been developed that include both internal and environmental data in providing a basis for immediate and longer term planning. These models compose the greater portion of the forecasting subsystem.

The *funds management subsystem* uses projections of company activity to determine the flow of money into and out of the firm. The manager can simulate several strategies designed to achieve the best balance in the inflow and outflow during a future period, such as the coming year. Balanced flows lessen the need to borrow operating capital and increase the return on invested surplus funds.

The use of available funds is controlled by the *financial control subsystem*. This subsystem primarily uses data gathered by the internal accounting subsystem to produce reports showing how monies are being spent. The reports compare actual financial performance to a budget, and provide ratios between financial figures as a measure of good performance. As business becomes more competitive and the costs of operations increase, good budget performance becomes increasingly important. It often is just as important to be under budget as it is to be over operational objectives such as sales or production quotas. The control subsystem enables managers to track their cost control activity.

Input subsystems

The model of the financial information system in Figure 10–11 includes only two input subsystems. One, the *internal accounting subsystem*, is responsible for gathering data from within the firm. This data describes how the manufacturing and marketing processes are being performed. The other, the *financial intelligence subsystem*, gathers data from the environment, primarily from stockholders, the government, and the financial community. Data gathered from the financial community represents the main input to the funds management subsystem. It identifies the best sources of additional financing, if such is required, and the best investment possibilities for surplus funds. All five of these input and output subsystems will be described in more detail in Chapter 13.

Summary

The objective of this chapter has been to provide a structure or format that can be followed in studying the MIS. The MIS has been discussed previously in general terms, and it is necessary to be more specific in how it is used by management. Since organizations, and managers, are grouped according to the functional areas of finance, manufacturing, and marketing, the uses of the MIS can also be grouped the same way.

A functional approach to the MIS probably is the most realistic, because that type of organization is so prevalent in the business world. Constructing the MIS as a composite of these subsystems, however, should not imply that a total integrated MIS is neither possible nor necessary. The end objective of every firm's information program should be the attainment of an integrated MIS in which all parts work in harmony. If the parts of the information system do not work together, the MIS will not be effective. And it is doubtful that the physical system of the firm can be any more efficient. The two systems must work together. An efficient physical system demands an efficient information system, and vice versa.

The main functional areas identified in this chapter are marketing, manufacturing, and finance. It is assumed that all managers, except the chief executives, fit within one of these three areas. Functional information systems are developed for each area, and all of the managers—including the chief executive officers—derive their information from them. It is logical to subdivide the MIS into functional information systems. The managers in these areas have unique information needs and the functional information systems meet these needs.

The models and the subsystems described in this chapter present only a single approach to the study of functional information systems. Others are possible, but they should describe the same activities, perhaps using different groups and terminology.

This rather tidy categorization of input and output activities should not mislead the reader into thinking that firms are organized this way. While there most certainly are accounting and marketing research departments, one might be hard pressed to find a door labeled "marketing intelligence" or "industrial engineering subsystem." These simply are names given to jobs that must be done within an information framework. If the reader understands what these jobs are, and why they are needed, other groupings and terminology can be taken in stride.

Important Terms

Marketing Information System

Marketing Concept

Internal Accounting System

Marketing Intelligence System

Marketing Research

Marketing Management Science

The Marketing Mix

The Four Ps

Output Subsystem

Input Subsystem

Product, Place, Promotion, and Price Subsystems

Integrated Mix Subsystem

Manufacturing Information System

Manufacturing Intelligence Subsystem

Industrial Engineering Subsystem

Production Subsystem

Inventory Subsystem   Financial Intelligence Subsystem

Quality Subsystem   Forecasting Subsystem

Cost Subsystem   Funds Management Subsystem

Financial Information System   Financial Control Subsystem

Important Concepts

An MIS must be adaptable to a functional organization since that is the most popular type of organizational structure.

The manufacturing function can exist in all types of firms when that function is defined very broadly.

There is some parallel between a functional organization and a flow network organization.

Functional information systems have been developed to meet unique information needs of functional managers.

The functional information systems must be integrated into an MIS that supports all of the firm's managers.

The chief executive officers receive a distillation of information from each of the functional information systems.

The marketing concept can be the stimulus that will facilitate achievement of an integrated MIS for the firm.

Each functional information system can be regarded as a composite of data-gathering input subsystems and information-producing output subsystems.

The internal accounting subsystem provides input data describing internal operations to all three functional information systems.

Each functional information system includes an intelligence subsystem that gathers environmental data and information.

Important People

Philip Kotler

Questions

1 What is the most popular form of organization structure for business firms? Why?

2 What types of firms include a marketing function? A manufacturing function?

3 Where does the information systems department fit in a functional organization?

4 In which functional area are these managers located?

> Director of Budgets
> Controller
> Manager of Programming
> Manager of Engineering
> Director of Purchasing
> Manager of Product Planning

5 Which functional area handles the money flow of a firm? What does manufacturing handle? What about marketing? What resource flow is handled by the personnel department? Where does the personnel department fit in a functional organization?

6 If the concept of the MIS is one of a "single information system for the entire firm," doesn't the idea of functional information systems defeat this purpose? Why?

7 What is the source of information for strategic level managers (the chief executive officers)?

8 What concept can possibly be the key in the achievement of an integrated MIS?

9 Who developed the first model of a marketing information system? Why is this a good model? Does it have any limitations? What are they?

10 Which functional information system contains the internal accounting subsystem?

11 What is the difference between marketing intelligence and marketing research?

12 Why is an integrated mix subsystem needed?

13 In which subsystem of the manufacturing information system would data collection terminals be located?

14 Why has the manufacturing information system been developed to the greatest extent of the functional information systems?

Problems

1 Figure 10–9 shows how the subsystems of the marketing information system relate to the data base. Draw a similar model for the manufacturing information system.

2 Draw the above model for the financial information system.

3 Draw a functional organization chart for your college administration. Do this without gathering any real data, but draw the chart the way you believe the structure exists.

4 Go to your library, look in the *Business Periodicals Index* (under "computers"), and list 10 articles that have been written on information systems.

Chapter 11

Marketing Information Systems

The concept of functional information systems was presented in the previous chapter. In this chapter, the marketing information system is analyzed in greater detail. This information system is selected for study before those of the manufacturing and financial functions for two reasons. First, more has been done in marketing to develop a description of a functional information system. Second, the marketing information system is concerned with that element of the environment that should represent the point of origin for everything the firm does, i.e., the customer.

The Model of the Marketing Information System

The second marketing information system model developed in Chapter 10, the one including input and output subsystems (Figure 11–1), will provide the basis for this chapter. All of the subsystems, except that of internal accounting, will be addressed separately. The accounting subsystem will be discussed in Chapter 13 when the financial information system is studied.

Marketing Intelligence Subsystem

In Chapter 4 the discussion focused on the different elements in the environment of the firm. It was recognized that certain functional areas within the firm have prime responsibility as far as each of the elements is concerned. The two elements identified with the marketing function are the customers and the competition.

Marketing has no responsibility to establish a communication flow *to* the competition, but is required to establish an incoming flow. The activity associated with this gathering of *competitive* information is termed *marketing intelligence*. This term possibly brings to mind visions of spying—an activity

Figure 11–1   The marketing information system model

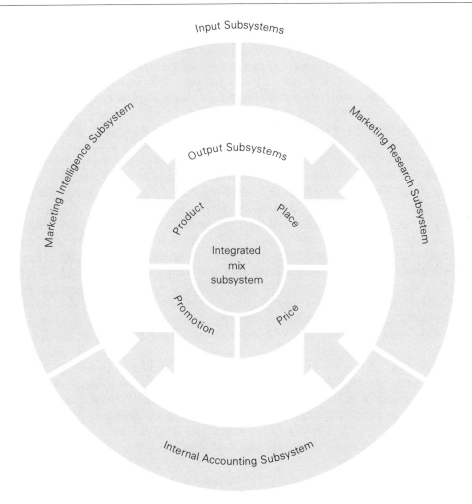

called "industrial espionage." A certain amount of such undercover work surely must exist in the competitive world of business, although few instances have been reported. This lack of publicity probably is because the need for such espionage activity is not as great as it might seem. One firm can obtain a large amount of information on the activities of another without spying. The term *marketing intelligence* refers to the wide range of ethical and aboveboard activities that may be used to gather information about competition, and not to those of an unethical or clandestine nature. And, marketing intelligence data and information usually are gathered through informal search. Formal gathering activities come under the heading of "marketing research."

   Much information about competitive firms is revealed by the communications media, especially those specializing in business news. If the executive reads *The Wall Street Journal*, a wealth of information can be gleaned on activities of competitive firms. The trade press of the different industries provides additional, and usually more detailed, descriptions of such activities. Table 11–1 contains a partial list of publications specializing in industry-oriented information. These publications do not contain all the information a manager would like to have on a subject, but they do provide the initial signal that some type of activity is underway. Additional information-gathering efforts, also conducted in an aboveboard manner, can provide more facts to fill out the picture. For example, marketing intelligence might trigger a marketing research project. A firm learning that a competitor is test marketing a new product can design its own research project to evaluate the degree of success being realized by the competitor.

Information-gathering efforts, in addition to exposure to mass circulation media, can take the form of attending stockholder meetings and reading stockholder announcements such as the annual report, attending open house celebrations to dedicate new facilities or announce new products, purchasing competitive products for engineering and design analysis, and visiting competitive stores to learn what is being sold and what prices are being charged.[1]

The sales force of the firm is also expected to play an important role in this feedback of competitive information. The salesperson is expected not only to communicate information from the firm to the marketplace, but also to communicate information back to the firm. When the salesperson establishes a good relationship with the customer, it is possible to learn much about competitive activity. The customer can pass along information just obtained from competitive salespersons. When this system works as it should, competitive operations can be monitored practically in realtime.[2]

And finally, it is possible to purchase competitive marketing information. Organizations such as A. C. Nielsen, Market Research Corporation of America, and Brand Rating Index Corporation gather information about certain types of activity such as retail food or drug sales, and prepare periodic reports.

Many of these intelligence efforts are conducted only when specific information needs arise. They are not ongoing. Consequently, little of this information finds its way into the computer. The information is disseminated either by word-of-mouth or by typed reports. The intelligence subsystem is an important part of the firm's marketing information system, and should be recognized as such. Only rarely, however, does marketing intelligence become a part of the *computerized* information system.

---

1. In the Fort Worth/Dallas area, four housewives, named the "Kroger Shoppers," report periodically on TV the result of their comparisons of Kroger prices with those of other supermarkets.

2. A few studies of the effectiveness of salesperson feedback have been less than encouraging. Certain companies have "planted" news stories in the field. In many cases, the information never was communicated by the salespersons back to their headquarters, or it was late or distorted. Specific steps must be taken to prevent these types of breakdowns.

Table 11–1   Some industry-oriented publications

Aerosol Age	House and Home
Air Conditioning, Heating & Refrigeration News	Industry Week
American Druggist	Iron Age
Automotive Industries	Journal of Purchasing & Materials Management
Aviation Week & Space Technology	
The Banker	Journal of Retailing
Best's Review—Life/Health Insurance and Property/Liability Insurance Editions	Labor Law Journal
	Merchandising Week
Broadcasting	Modern Packaging
Chain Store Age Executive	National Petroleum News
Chemical Week	Oil and Gas Journal
Computers and People	Personnel Journal
Credit and Financial Management	Pipeline & Gas Journal
Datamation	Progressive Grocer
Drug & Cosmetic Industry	Public Utilities Fortnightly
Electronic News	Pulp & Paper
Factory	Quick Frozen Foods
Financial World	Railway Age
Fleet Owner	Textile World
Food Processing	Transportation Journal
Forest Industries	Vending Times
Fuel Oil & Oil Heat	World Oil

Marketing Research Subsystem

The efforts employed by a firm to gather information about customers are much more formal and concerted than are similar efforts about competitors. Firms have long been aware of the necessity to understand their customers and their needs. These formal efforts to study the *customer* are termed *marketing research.*[3] Actually, marketing research can be concerned with gathering information about the entire marketing system and its environment. Up to this time, however, emphasis has been placed almost exclusively on learning about the customer.

Means of gathering data

It is difficult to find a person who is unfamiliar with marketing research. When asked about marketing research, the common response is "Oh yes, you mean surveys." Almost everyone has been approached at one time or another, in person, by mail, or by telephone, for information about shopping habits, product preference, brand loyalty, and so on.

Actually, the survey is only one method of gathering data through marketing research. A *survey* is conducted when the same questions are asked of a number of persons, by whatever method (personal interview, telephone, or mail). The number of persons surveyed may be relatively small, say 30, or quite large, say several thousand.

When different questions are asked of a small number of people, such as three or four, the technique is known as an *in-depth interview*. The time devoted to the interview is much longer than that spent with any single survey participant. Also, the emphasis is on probing for information explaining why the customers behave as they do. This approach is based largely on similar techniques developed in psychology.

Another technique from the behavioral sciences is that of *observation*. It presumes that the best way to learn of behavior is either to observe that behavior taking place or to obtain traces indicating that the behavior has occurred. The technique has been used quite effectively in anthropology and sociology, and has been adopted by marketers. Marketing researchers note license plate numbers in a shopping center parking lot in order to learn how far people have driven to patronize the center. Or, they set up movie or television cameras in supermarkets to record the response of shoppers to displays. A marketing research firm in England obtains information about customer purchases by sifting through people's garbage to note which packages and containers are being discarded.

Marketers even have adopted the technique of the *controlled experiment* of the physical and behavioral sciences, and both the real marketplace and the classroom serve as laboratories. Very often college students serve as subjects in experiments designed to measure the effect of a particular treatment (say a certain type of ad) on behavior (the ability to recall the ad).

---

3. The origin of marketing research can be traced back to 1911 when Charles Coolidge Parlin was named manager of commercial research for the Curtis Publishing Company. The first book on the subject, written by Dr. C. S. Duncan, appeared in 1919.

"According to our research department, our public opinion polls, our sampling of potential users, our forecasts of marketing trends, our estimates of consumer reaction, and our statistical model manipulations, we overcooked the vegetables."

© DATAMATION®

Information gathered from research

The marketer is interested in learning *what* the customer is doing and *why* it is being done. Some of the means of gathering information answer one question and some answer the other. Surveys and observations disclose what is happening or has happened. Marketers use this information to project what is likely to happen in the future. Even though these projections can prove quite accurate, the manager realizes that the real cause of the behavior is still undetermined.

The only methods successful in identifying why behavior occurs are the two developed by psychologists: the in-depth interview and the experiment. The number of customers involved in these activities is small compared to those in observations and surveys. For this reason the progress toward obtaining information that can be applied to large market groups is both slow and expensive.

All business firms know the importance of understanding their customers. Some, however, make a greater effort than others to gather data describing their own customers. Many use data gathered by other organizations, such as the federal government. Other firms conduct their own research projects. A variety of data-gathering techniques are available to help understand the many and complex dimensions of the customer.

Relationship of marketing research to MIS

While marketing research has been around for a long time, the MIS concept is quite new. As this concept evolved, there was some confusion within marketing as to how MIS related to marketing research. Some authorities believed MIS to be simply what had been known all along as marketing research. This was especially the case when the term *marketing information system* was used.

Most authorities now seem to regard marketing research as a subset of the marketing information system, which, in turn, is a subset of the management information system. The marketing research subsystem has the responsibility of interfacing the MIS with that important element in the environment—the customer.

There is one important difference between marketing research as normally conducted and MIS as conceived. This difference can provide an additional means of distinguishing between the two. The definition of MIS offered in the first chapter referred to a *continuous* flow of information. Marketing research, on the other hand, is primarily concerned with special information-gathering projects. The firm will have a need for a certain type of information, and a research project will be designed to provide what is needed. Usually, no effort will be made to maintain the information in an up-to-date manner once the information is gathered. One marketer compared marketing research to a flashbulb, and MIS to a candle. The information provided by marketing research is quite vivid as it relates to a particular area, like the illumination provided by a flashbulb. MIS does not provide as much information on any given topic; but the information is available for a wider area and for a longer period of time, as is the light given off by a candle in a room.

This concludes the discussion of the two marketing-oriented input subsystems. The remainder of the chapter will be concerned with the four output subsystems corresponding to the ingredients of the marketing mix, and to the integrated mix subsystem.

Product Subsystem

The product is usually the first ingredient in the marketing mix to be specified. The firm decides to provide a product to satisfy a particular market need. Subsequently, the remaining ingredients (place, promotion, and price) are identified and described.

It must be kept in mind that each of these marketing mix decisions assumes the existence of corporate goals. The firm must know where it is and where it wants to go. The goals, along with the resources available, are the primary constraints at each step of the decision-making process. For example, a firm may have an overall goal of providing equipment and supplies to the medical profession. In this case, the firm would not consider any activity outside of that field. The goals of the firm dictate the activity area.

The resources of the firm also play an important role. A firm usually develops both a production and a marketing capability for a particular product or family of products. An attempt to manufacture and market a completely different type of product could prove extremely difficult. For example, what problems would be created if the Head ski company decided to get into the frozen food field?

The product life cycle

The marketing manager is concerned with developing strategy and tactics for each ingredient in the marketing mix and then integrating these into an overall marketing plan. A framework exists to guide the manager in making these decisions; this framework is called the *product life cycle.* The product life cycle, as the name implies, charts the evolution of the product from introduction, or birth, through various growth and developmental stages, to deletion, or death. Names have been given to four stages in the life cycle: introduction, growth, maturity, and decline. The cycle, with the stages identified, is shown in Figure 11–2.

Although the product life cycle consists of four stages, there are three time periods during which the marketing information system assists the marketing manager in making product-oriented decisions. The first period is prior to the introduction of the product when a decision must be made whether to develop and market the product. The second period is during the introduction, growth, and maturity stages when the product is healthy. The final period is the time when product deletion must be considered.

A number of techniques have been developed to provide the manager with information needed for these product-oriented decisions. The one selected for discussion here helps the manager decide which product should be selected for introduction to the market. Techniques such as this, plus others relating to product decisions, compose the product subsystem of a firm's marketing information system.

Product development

The decision to develop a new product should be a carefully considered one, with a sound financial basis and made by the top corporate management. Prior to the decision, information should be available that will indicate, with a good degree of certainty, the profit potential of the proposed product. Many firms have developed an orderly and systematic approach to the consideration of new products that considers a variety of factors, such as profitability and utilization of resources, expressed both quantitatively and qualitatively. With both production and marketing resources of the firm identified, the extent to

Figure 11–2   Stages in the product life cycle

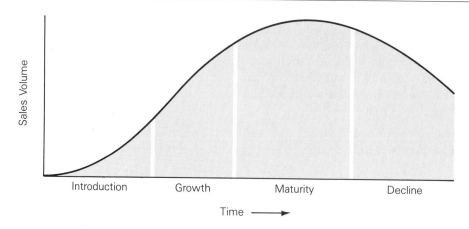

which each will be utilized in a potential new product can be measured (Figure 11–3). Scores can be computed for products under consideration, and management attention can focus on products with the best scores.

Figure 11–3 illustrates this quantitative approach to new product evaluation. In this example, new products are evaluated on both their marketing and their production features. A product selected for introduction would score high in both categories. The decision criteria are listed for both production and marketing considerations along with a weighting (criterion weight) that reflects the relative importance of each. The center portion of the tables consists of ratings that each criterion receives, from very good to very poor. The ratings each have values from a high of 10 for very good to a low of 2 for very poor. In the column beneath each rating is listed the probability (P) of the new product scoring such a rating on the specific criterion. For example, the probability of the new product receiving a rating of very good on the criterion of plant capacity (in Figure 11–3a) is .2. This probability is multiplied by the rating value of 10 to obtain an "expected value" (EV) of 2.0. The second column from the right contains a summation of the expected values for each criterion, and these are multiplied by the appropriate criterion weight to obtain the figures in the rightmost column. The total of these figures represents the "total production resources value" of 6.52 for the new product. The table reflecting the marketing consideration (Figure 11–3b) is constructed in the same manner. Both the production and marketing resource utilization scores are multiplied by respective weights (to reflect the relative importance of production and marketing considerations for the new product), and the weighted values are added. The final score of 6.70 represents the company production and marketing resource utilization for the new product (Figure 11–3c). Similar scores would be developed for other products under consideration to aid the management in selecting the new product to be produced and

Figure 11–3 Quantitative evaluation of a new product
   a. Utilization of production resources (proposed new product JXL5005)
   b. Utilization of marketing resources
   c. Utilization of firm resources

A--UTILIZATION OF PRODUCTION RESOURCES (PROPOSED NEW PRODUCT JXL5005)

DECISION CRITERIA	CRITERIA WEIGHT	VERY GOOD (10)		GOOD (8)		AVERAGE (6)		POOR (4)		VERY POOR (2)		TOTAL	CRITERION EVALUATION (TOT. EV X WEIGHT)
		P	EV	P	EV	P	EV	P	EV	P	EV		
PLANT CAPACITY	.20	.2	2.0	.6	4.8	.2	1.2	0	0	0	0	8.0	1.60
LABOR SKILLS	.30	.2	2.0	.7	5.6	.1	.6	0	0	0	0	8.2	2.46
ENGINEERING KNOW-HOW	.30	0	0	.2	1.6	.2	1.2	.6	2.4	0	0	5.2	1.56
EQUIPMENT AVAILABILITY	.10	0	0	0	0	.7	4.2	.3	1.2	0	0	5.4	.54
MATERIAL AVAILABILITY	.10	0	0	0	0	.1	.6	.6	2.4	.3	.6	3.6	.36

TOTAL PRODUCTION RESOURCES VALUE · 6.52

B--UTILIZATION OF MARKETING RESOURCES

DECISION CRITERIA	CRITERIA WEIGHT	VERY GOOD (10)		GOOD (8)		AVERAGE (6)		POOR (4)		VERY POOR (2)		TOTAL	CRITERION EVALUATION (TOT. EV X WEIGHT)
		P	EV	P	EV	P	EV	P	EV	P	EV		
PRODUCT COMPATABILITY	.20	0	0	.2	1.6	.5	3.0	.2	.8	.1	.2	5.6	1.12
SALES KNOWLEDGE	.20	.1	1.0	.5	4.0	.3	1.8	.1	.4	0	0	7.2	1.44
DISTRIBUTION FACILITIES	.30	.3	3.0	.5	4.0	.2	1.2	0	0	0	0	8.2	2.46
LONG-TERM DEMAND	.30	0	0	.2	1.6	.6	3.6	.2	.8	0	0	6.0	1.80

TOTAL MARKETING RESOURCES VALUE · 6.82

C--UTILIZATION OF FIRM RESOURCES

RESOURCE	VALUE	WEIGHT	WEIGHTED VALUE
PRODUCTION	6.52	.40	2.61
MARKETING	6.82	.60	4.09
TOTAL · · · · · · · · · · · · ·			6.70

marketed. The products with the highest scores would receive the most consideration.[4]

In order to use such an approach, it is necessary to quantify a number of essentially subjective measures. Numbers must be assigned to criterion weights, probabilities of performance, and relative weights of production and marketing. The managers assigning these numbers must recognize the limitations of the approach. It is extremely difficult to quantify these estimates. Even so, such an approach has inherent value. It forces the manager to identify the factors influencing the decision and to consider the relative significance of each.

A computer program can be written to accept the manager's criteria

---

4. Perhaps the first published description of the technique of quantitative evaluation of new products was John T. O'Meara's article, "Selecting Profitable Products," that appeared in the January–February 1961 issue of the *Harvard Business Review*, pages 83–89. A more recent description of the technique can be found in Stewart H. Rewoldt, James D. Scott, and Martin R. Warshaw, *Introduction to Marketing Management*, 3rd ed. (Homewood, Ill.: Richard D. Irwin, Inc., 1977), pp. 253–262.

ratings, perhaps from a terminal, and make the necessary computations. Output can be displayed on the terminal or printed in report form. With such a model, several managers can evaluate a large number of products in a short time.

Place Subsystem

Firms must make their products and services available to their customers. This distribution is accomplished by channel systems. Channels can be short, as with a firm like the Fuller Brush Company that sells direct to the customer, or long, as in making farm products available in supermarkets. When the channel of distribution includes more than the manufacturer and the customer, the intermediate links are known as *middlemen*. Wholesalers and retailers are middlemen.[5]

The method by which the firm makes its products available to the customer is identified as the "place" ingredient in the marketing mix. Place decisions fall into two categories: (1) the establishment of channel systems, and (2) the performance of the distribution functions.

Establishment of channel systems

In most cases, it is the manufacturer who must establish the channel. The manufacturer has created a product and must deliver it to the market. In creating a channel system, the manufacturer sees a need for information about the activity of the product at each step. It is not sufficient, though, for the feedback to the manufacturer to stop when the product has been delivered to the wholesaler. Just because the wholesaler bought the product does not assure that it will appeal equally well to the retailer. The same can be said of sales at the retail level—there is no assurance that the consumer will buy. If the manufacturer is to know what is happening in the channel, feedback must be obtained from each channel link—and in many cases, from the consumer as well.

If the manufacturer expects feedback from the channel members farther down the line, something must be offered in return. Quite possibly this need only be information—a type of *feedforward* to the wholesaler and the retailer. Just as the manufacturer has a need for information *after* the physical product flow occurs, the wholesaler and the retailer have a need for information (announcements of new products, selling and promotion aids, forecasts of demand, etc.) before the flow begins. If the participants in the channel system realize the value of the information flow and the improved performance that

---

5. These middlemen were the focus of the farmers' strike in late 1977 and early 1978. The farmers believed that too much of the end cost of farm products was added by the middlemen.

Figure 11–4 Resource flow through the channel

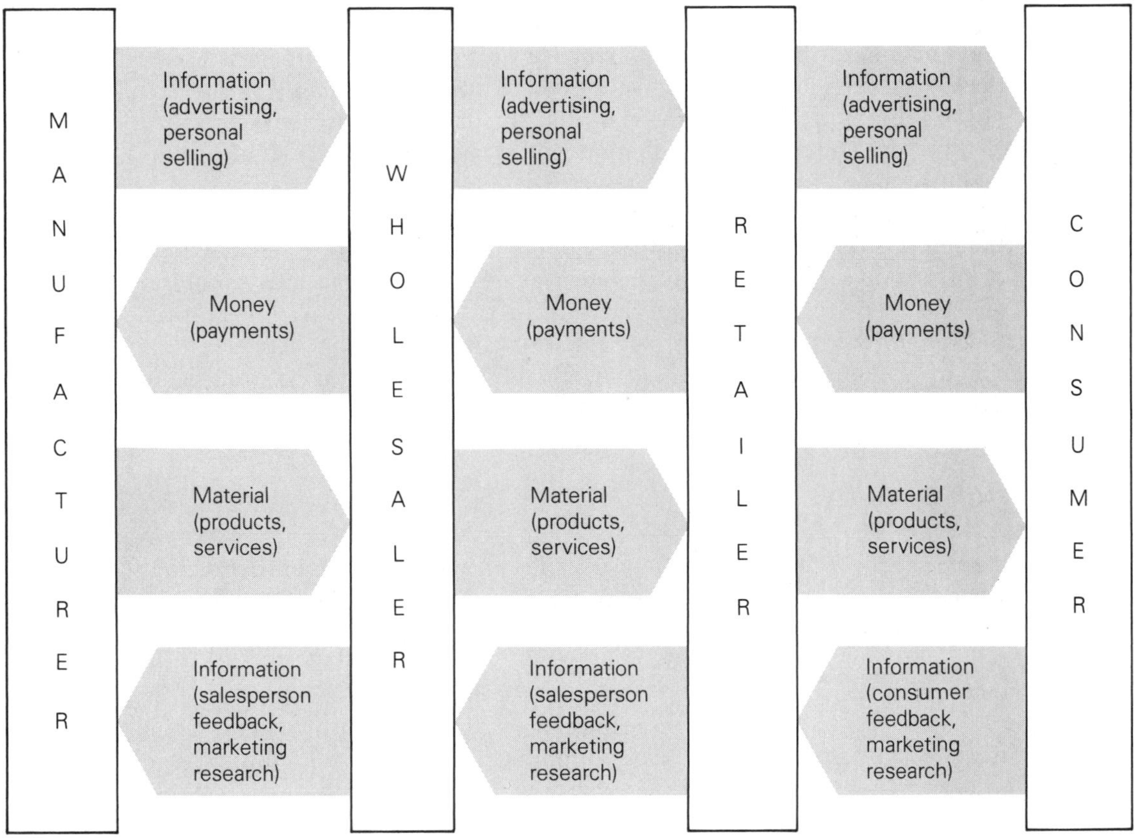

the system will realize when the flow is present, then an efficient interfirm information system will be possible.

It is important to understand that information is one of the resources flowing through the channel. It flows in both directions, as shown in Figure 11–4. These flows are accomplished in various ways. Sales representatives of the channel members have a responsibility to prepare written reports and to communicate information by word-of-mouth. Very often information or data is transmitted by punched card, magnetic tape, or data terminals. A channel system that permits information to flow freely among the firms provides an edge over competitive systems with a lesser capability.

Performance of distribution functions

Once the systems have been established, it is necessary to put into motion machinery that will facilitate the flow of resources along the channel. In probably no other area of the firm's marketing operations has the computer been applied so successfully. Physical distribution, or logistics (the names given to the physical flow) has greatly improved during the past decade through application of the computer and quantitative problem-solving techniques. The main reason for this success in solving physical distribution problems is that these are largely deterministic—not probabilistic. The variables usually are physical in nature (not people) and their interrelationships can be specified very clearly. The physical distribution part of marketing is very similar to the manufacturing function in this respect.

A great many tasks or functions are performed as a part of the distribution process. They offer a wide variety of problems to be solved, and a number of quantitative solution techniques are available to the manager. One problem will be discussed here, that of determining the optimum location of warehouses. Other functions performed as part of the place activity are determination of inventory levels, layout of merchandise in the warehouse, routing of delivery vehicles, and determination of the number of retail sales clerks required and their work schedules.

Choosing a warehouse location

A firm that distributes its output over a wide area is faced with the decision of where to store those goods until they move to the wholesale or retail level. A firm can have a single warehouse, in which case it would most likely be at the headquarters location. Advantages of such an arrangement include low cost of space, utilities, security, etc. In addition, the information system would be completely centralized, with no requirement for data communications facilities or decentralized operations such as billing. There also are disadvantages to the centralized approach and these relate mainly to customer service. When customers are dispersed, it can take a long time to get the merchandise to them from a central point, and shipping costs can be high. This situation calls for consideration of two or more warehouses. These are just a few of the factors that management must consider when making the warehouse location decision.

To illustrate how the marketing information system can assist the manager in making a decision of this type, assume that a beer distributorship has been awarded to a firm for the Fort Worth-Dallas metroplex area. Dallas represents the larger market area, but Fort Worth is by no means small. Since the cities are approximately only 30 miles apart, two alternatives appear feasible. As shown in Figure 11–5a, a single warehouse could be located midway between the two cities, in Arlington, with both cities served from this point. Real estate costs should be lower, but the warehouse would not be in either of the two dense market areas. The other alternative would be to consider two locations, one in each of the cities. This alternative is pictured in Figure 11–5b. The shaded areas in both of these maps indicate areas of equal distribution cost. The costs increase with the distance from the warehouse, but within a given shaded area they are roughly the same. This similarity means

Figure 11–5 Distribution costs increase with distance from warehouse.
a. One warehouse located midway between Fort Worth and Dallas
b. Two warehouses, one in each of the two cities

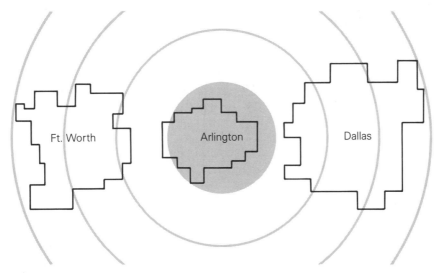

a. One warehouse located midway between Fort Worth and Dallas

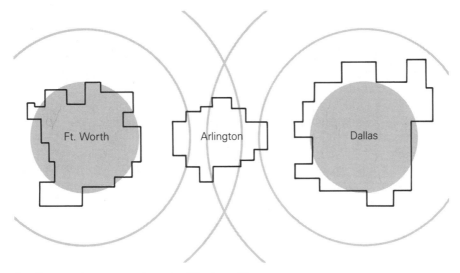

b. Two warehouses, one in each of the two cities

that the manager has a rather broad geographical area in which to locate, somewhat reducing the margin for error.

The place subsystem can provide the mathematical technique to identify the optimum solution. This technique is linear programming. Before the linear programming model can be used, however, there must be available complete and accurate data describing both the costs and the returns of each alternative. This data must come from the data base; and the internal accounting system is largely responsible for its generation. For example, it is necessary to determine the number of delivery trips that must be made from each location during a time period, say a year. The accounting system provides data such as annual sales dollars by customer and average delivery truck cost per mile. With the addition of information such as average product bulk per sales dollar and average truck capacity (provided by the transportation department), the average number of deliveries per time period for each customer can be determined. Costs of distributing merchandise to each customer from any warehouse location, or locations, then can be determined.

Projections of future sales levels also can be made using federal census data. Because the warehouse location decision is a long range one, considering the real estate investment, construction costs, etc., the analysis should not be limited to current conditions. It would be poor judgment for the beer distributor to make a warehouse location decision in the Dallas-Fort Worth area without considering the dynamics of population growth, income distribution, age distribution, etc.

Linear programming will consider all of these factors and identify the alternative that meets the objective of either economical distribution operation or quality customer service. In this example, the goal is minimum cost. Assuming that the input data is accurate, the decision is an optimum one and cannot be improved upon by the manager without introducing additional factors not considered by the mathematical model.[6]

Promotion Subsystem

Promotion, consisting of both personal selling and advertising, is an important ingredient in the marketing mix. However, it has been extremely difficult to harness the power of computerized information systems in this area. Companies have had salesperson-reporting systems for years, but these systems provide only a record of past performance. Even less has been accomplished in advertising. Some of the larger advertising agencies have developed models to help clients select media and apportion budgeted funds among them. These

6. Additional information concerning facility location can be obtained by reading Richard A. Johnson, William T. Newell, and Roger C. Vergin, *Operations Management: A Systems Concept* (Boston: Houghton Mifflin Company, 1972), pp. 128–136.

models have enjoyed only limited success and use. The reason for this relative lack of creative solution to some very important problems is that both advertising and selling are extremely dependent on the behavior of the prospect or customer. They are both "people-oriented" activities. Such actions are extremely difficult to predict and almost impossible to control.

Decisions must be made relative to both advertising and selling, but care must be taken to realize that these decisions cannot be made separately. The promotion ingredient should represent an integrated strategy, capitalizing on the effective and coordinated use of both techniques.

Decisions relating to advertising include whether it should be used, the budget, the theme, the selection of media such as TV or newspapers, and the layout of the ads. As with each of the mix subsystems, these decisions are influenced by the goals of the firm, the target market the firm is trying to reach, available funds, and a variety of other factors.

Personal selling decisions relate to the manner in which the sales force will be employed. Some decisions of this type include determination of how many salespersons are needed, where they should be located, the routes they should follow in covering their territory, how they can be motivated, and how they can gather data for entry into the firm's information system. This last decision is discussed below as an example of how a part of the firm's promotion subsystem might function.

Salesperson-reporting system

The Pillsbury Company has received nationwide publicity for their computerized sales-reporting systems. The first system was called SOAR—Store Objectives and Accomplishments Report.[7] SOAR required about six years to develop and became operational in the early 1970s. In late 1974, SOAR was replaced by another system, called REACH—Retail Achievement Report.[8] REACH covers a wider area of salesperson activity than SOAR, and deals with quarterly, rather than monthly, goals.

SOAR was unique in at least two respects. First, it was developed specifically for operational level managers—the sales managers. The information output was of interest to the salespersons, but the sales managers were the real users. Second, the system was based on the use of OCR call report forms. This is an example of how computer hardware can overcome problems of volume and time. Pillsbury used the system for its 525 salespersons to record the results of their calls on 220,000 customers. If the same data was collected in other ways, the process would have been extremely time-consuming for the

7. Lloyd M. Deboer and William H. Ward, "Integration of the Computer into Salesman Reporting," *Journal of Marketing*, January, 1971, Vol. 35, No. 1, pp. 41–47.

8. James M. Comer, "The Computer, Personal Selling, and Sales Management," *Journal of Marketing*, July, 1975, Vol. 39, No. 3, pp. 27–33.

salespersons. (They are intended to spend the majority of their time selling—not filling out forms. An OCR-based reporting system accomplishes this effectively and easily.)

Pillsbury has participated in publicizing SOAR and REACH, but only in general terms. While samples of the OCR call report form are not available, the items on the form have been identified by Pillsbury. These items are arranged in a page format in Figure 11–6 to illustrate an OCR call report form.

An OCR call report, such as that developed for SOAR, would most likely be preprinted on the line printer, with information describing each call to be made. The preprinting relieves the salesperson of copying this data. The top of the form pictured in Figure 11–6 contains standard information about each call.

The body of the form enables sales management to vary sales emphasis from one month to the next. The system is flexible and responsive. Up to 15 priorities can be identified, and the salesperson indicates (with a mark) the extent to which each is accomplished. Also, up to five questions can be asked facilitating feedback to company headquarters of market status information. These are multiple-choice questions, where the salesperson again makes a mark.

Figure 11–7 is a system flowchart, illustrating how questions and priorities are entered by the sales manager, the OCR forms are completed by the salespersons, and the management reports are prepared.

The information output from a reporting system such as SOAR and REACH is intended to help the manager, and the format of the reports reflects management by exception. Of the five basic reports prepared by SOAR, only one is not of the exception type, and it is the monthly account recap. This report consists of an entry for each account, describing the activity during the month. Accounts are listed in sequence by sales volume, so that management quickly can identify those representing extremely large and small sales volumes. The other reports reflect only the information demanding attention by the sales management and the sales representatives. Basically, the reports enable those involved to evaluate the extent to which goals have been met. Sales reporting systems such as SOAR and REACH, therefore, provide for the fundamental job of management—employment and motivation of resources toward established goals.

Price Subsystem

In the price subsystem the manager establishes the price for each product in the product line. As with the other ingredients in the marketing mix, manipulation of price affects the rate of sales. The graphical model, drawn by economists, shows the effect that price has on demand—and on sales. At a high price, demand is low; at a low price, demand is high. This concept is reflected in the demand curve of Figure 11–8.

However, the pricing decision is not made solely to increase sales. Other objectives include reducing the risk of loss, reducing indebtedness, increasing

Figure 11–6   Preprinted customer call report for OCR entry

STORE INFORMATION SECTION

REGION NO. _____3_____ : NAME ___WESTERN___

TERRITORY NO. __32__ : SALESPERSON NO. __7070__

STORE ___A & P SUPERMARKET___

___THUNDERBIRD SQUARE___

___WACO, TEXAS 76550___

STORE NO. _1223_: CALL CLASS _2_: DOLLAR VOLUME _$12,750_

DIRECT ACCOUNT NO. __55__ : NAME ___GREAT A & P TEA COMPANY___

ADVERTISING GROUP NO. __10__ : NAME ___PACIFIC COAST___

COUNTY NO. ___5254___ : NAME ___MCCLENNAN___

PRIORITIES SECTION

	PRESENTED	ACCOMPLISHED	QTY. SOLD
1			
15			

STORE DATA AND CALL SECTION

STORE DATA MAINTENANCE: CALL:

_____ DELETE   _____ BUYER OUT

_____ STORE, NEW   _____ RESET

_____ STORE, CHANGE   _____ EXTRA

_____ STORE DATA   _____ SPECIAL

                                 _____ RETURN FORM

DATE AND TIME SECTION

MONTH_____ : DAY_____ : TIME: HOURS_____ MIN._____

SPECIAL REPORTING SECTION

QUESTION	ANSWERS				
	A	B	C	D	E
1					

COMMENTS:

Figure 11–7   The SOAR reporting process

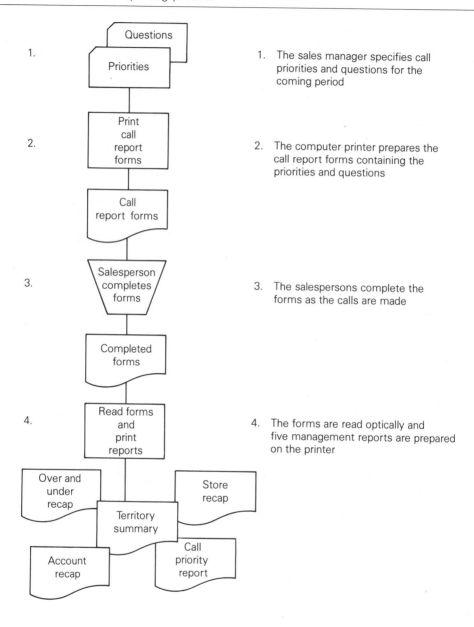

1. The sales manager specifies call priorities and questions for the coming period

2. The computer printer prepares the call report forms containing the priorities and questions

3. The salespersons complete the forms as the calls are made

4. The forms are read optically and five management reports are prepared on the printer

profit, increasing prestige for the product or service, and so on. Each of these objectives has an effect on some element in the firm's environment, such as stockholders or customers.

In addition to the effect that price has on the environmental elements, the elements in turn exercise certain constraints on the pricing decision.

Figure 11–8   The demand curve

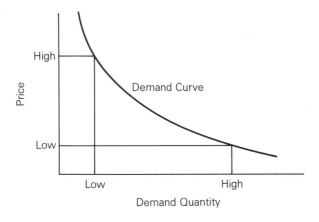

While stockholders press for increased earnings that apparently could be achieved through higher prices, such an increase would bring retaliatory measures by competition and possibly the government. Price is usually very sensitive to such environmental pressures, and the manager seeks to establish a level that keeps these relationships in balance.

If the pricing decision is influenced by the environmental elements to such a degree, it is apparent that the manager must have information on the anticipated impact of the decision. This information must describe the situation both within and outside the firm. The internal accounting subsystem provides the former type, and the marketing research and intelligence subsystems the latter.

All of this information, or data, can be made available to a *pricing strategy model* that will project the possible impact of various strategies on the environmental elements and on the firm's financial condition. This model (Figure 11–9) can be interactive in nature, providing the manager the opportunity to explore alternate pricing strategies.

Figure 11–10 illustrates a part of the dialog that can occur between the manager and the pricing model. The questions or commands from the model are underlined; the responses by the manager are not.

By entering appropriate codes in the terminal, the manager notifies the computer that a model is to be executed. The computer then asks for a specification of which model is to be executed. The manager types in PRIC-ING, and that model is entered into main storage from the model base. The model is then executed as the manager, on cue from the model, provides additional specifications.

After all the specifications have been entered, the computer simulates the effect on profit. In the figure, profit (and loss) amounts are printed for a

Figure 11–9   The pricing model simulates results of different pricing strategies.

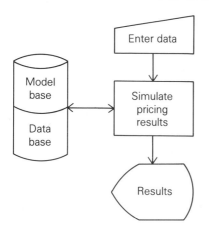

1. The manager enters data such as price, expected demand, etc.

2. The computer, using a pricing model from the model base and data from the data base, simulates expected results from the pricing decisions

3. The results are displayed on the manager's CRT or are printed on a typewriter terminal or line printer

three-year period. If the manager is dissatisfied with the results, other simulations can be made using modified values for one or more of the variables.

Of all the decisions facing the marketing manager, pricing is the most difficult. This observation is supported by the relatively small number of documented solutions to the problem, especially solutions involving quantitative techniques and information systems. This appears to be the area of the marketing information system where the potential for modeling is greatest. The value of modeling should be at its maximum as the problem becomes complex, and that is the situation in the pricing portion of the marketing mix.

Integrated Marketing Mix Subsystem

Simply because each of the marketing mix subsystems was described separately does not mean that they are separate and nonrelated decision areas. A decision cannot be made in one area without considering the effects on the other ingredients. It is necessary that the marketing manager concoct an integrated mix representing an optimum strategy of the firm. In the process of building such an integrated model, however, it is first necessary to consider the requirements and workings of each of the mix subsystems. This is what has been done up to this point. Now it becomes time to integrate each of the mix subsystems into a coordinated overall model.

The best examples of such integrated models, in terms of thorough documentation and widespread use, are the various *marketing management decision games* used by students to develop decision-making skills. There are many of these—some general in nature and some aimed at specific situations.

Figure 11–10 Partial output from interactive pricing model

```
WHICH MODEL DO YOU WISH TO EXECUTE

?PRICING

IDENTIFY THE PRODUCT GROUP

?SKIING-ACCESSORY

WHAT PRICE WILL BE CHARGED TO DEALERS?  ENTER DOLLARS AND CENTS WITH NO DOLLAR

SIGN OR COMMAS

?35.00

WHAT WILL BE THE SUGGESTED DEALER MARK-UP?  ENTER PERCENT

?100

HOW MUCH WILL BE BUDGETED FOR DEALER PROMOTION DURING YEARS 1, 2, 3?

ENTER DOLLARS

?10000,  8000,  5000

HOW MUCH WILL BE BUDGETED FOR CONSUMER PROMOTION DURING YEARS 1, 2, 3?

ENTER DOLLARS

?5000,  3000,  2500

WHAT ARE MINIMUM AND MAXIMUM PRODUCTION CAPACITIES IN ANNUAL UNITS

?10000,  60000

WHAT IS THE FORECASTED ANNUAL DEMAND DURING YEAR 1 AT THE PRICE LEVEL OF

$35.00?  ENTER UNITS

?7500

IF DEMAND WILL INCREASE (+) OR DECREASE (-) DURING YEARS 2 AND 3, ENTER

THOSE AMOUNTS IN UNITS

?+2500,  +5000

IF PRICE WERE LOWERED 5% (TO $33.25) WHAT WOULD BE THE DEMAND DURING YEARS

1, 2, 3

?10000,  15000,  20000

IF PRICE WERE INCREASED 5% (TO $36.75) WHAT WOULD BE THE DEMAND DURING YEARS

1, 2, 3

?5000,  7500,  10000

SHOULD STANDARD OVERHEAD COSTS BE ALLOCATED

?YES

ENTER ANY VARIABLE COSTS NOT PREVIOUSLY REQUESTED

?NONE

BASED ON THE DATA ENTERED, NET PROFITS BEFORE TAXES DURING YEAR 1, 2, 3

ARE PROJECTED TO BE:

        YEAR 1 --   $29,182 LOSS

        YEAR 2 --     5,263 GAIN

        YEAR 3 --    17,620 GAIN

DO YOU WISH TO EXECUTE THE MODEL AGAIN

?NO

DO YOU WISH TO EXECUTE ANOTHER MODEL

?NO

HAVE A NICE DAY.
```

[1]Responses provided by the manager are preceded by a question mark.

One of the more interesting ones is the Hinkle-Koza simulation of the skiing industry.[9]

In the Hinkle-Koza model, decisions are made concerning price, sales force size and use, advertising budget, number of products in the line, production volume, and inventory. The computer model determines the combined effect of these decisions on the sales of each firm in the industry. In addition to the effect of a firm's decisions regarding the mix ingredients on its sales level, the decisions of competing firms also have an influence. The model is a dynamic one with the mix decisions of the different firms all exerting an effect on the outcome.

Figure 11–11 contains an example of the output received by each firm in the simulated skiing industry. The upper portion reports accounting information by product; the lower portion presents a consolidated income statement for all products.

Business firms can develop their own models of a similar nature for use in decision making. Obviously, such models require a good understanding of the firm and its competitive environment. They take time and money to develop, but they can provide creative management with an ability for improved decision making.

Summary

The marketing information system has the important responsibility of interfacing the firm with the environmental element—the customers—that it intends to serve with its products and services. Input subsystems provide the data describing the customers and also the competition. This data is entered in the data base of the firm for use by the different processing routines that comprise the model base of the marketing information system. In this chapter, these processing routines were grouped according to the ingredients of the marketing mix. All of the routines, programs, or models helping the manager make product-related decisions are a part of the product subsystem. Composition of the place, promotion, and price subsystems is determined in the same way.

There are no set rules concerning which managers will use which subsystems. This policy is determined by the unique interests and capabil-

9. Charles L. Hinkle and Russell C. Koza, *Marketing Dynamics: Decision and Control* (New York: McGraw-Hill Book Company, 1975). Some other examples of marketing management decision games are the *Business Simulation*, developed by Westinghouse Information Systems Laboratory; *Complete: A Dynamic Marketing Simulation* by Business Publications, Inc.; the *M.I.T. Marketing Game*; and the *Purdue Supermarket Management Game*.

Figure 11–11   Output from skiing industry model
   a. Financial information by product
   b. Consolidated income statement for the firm

```
         VIKING CORPORATION

         INCOME STATEMENT-COMPANY 2 IN INDUSTRY  3 FOR TIME PERIOD   4
                                                                          86120.00
BRAND  14    NET SALES
             COST OF GOODS SOLD-
                BEGINNING INVENTORY                        713160.00
                VARIABLE COSTS                    .00
                OVERTIME                           .00
                INVENTORY CHARGES            71316.00      71316.00
                GOODS AVAILABLE FOR SALE                   784476.00
                ENDING INVENTORY                           627040.00      157436.00
             GROSS MARGIN CONTRIBUTION                                    -71316.00

BRAND  17    NET SALES                                                   2301844.00
             COST OF GOODS SOLD-
                BEGINNING INVENTORY                              .00
                VARIABLE COSTS             1477535.00
                OVERTIME                      5530.00
                INVENTORY CHARGES               .00      1483065.00
                GOODS AVAILABLE FOR SALE                 1483065.00
                ENDING INVENTORY                               .00      1483065.00
             GROSS MARGIN CONTRIBUTION                                    818779.00

BRAND  12    NET SALES                                                    856548.00
             COST OF GOODS SOLD-
                BEGINNING INVENTORY                        278810.00
                VARIABLE COSTS              276360.00
                OVERTIME                     39480.00
                INVENTORY CHARGES            27881.00      343721.00
                GOODS AVAILABLE FOR SALE                   622531.00
                ENDING INVENTORY                               .00       622531.00
             GROSS MARGIN CONTRIBUTION                                    234017.00

BRAND  21    NET SALES                                                   2359980.00
             COST OF GOODS SOLD-
                BEGINNING INVENTORY                        135642.50
                VARIABLE COSTS             1437500.00
                OVERTIME                         .00
                INVENTORY CHARGES            13564.25     1451064.00
                GOODS AVAILABLE FOR SALE                  1586706.00
                ENDING INVENTORY                            65377.50     1521328.00
             GROSS MARGIN CONTRIBUTION                                    838652.00

BRAND  18    NET SALES                                                    105550.00
             COST OF GOODS SOLD-
                BEGINNING INVENTORY                        898950.00
                VARIABLE COSTS                    .00
                OVERTIME                          .00
                INVENTORY CHARGES            89895.00       89895.00
                GOODS AVAILABLE FOR SALE                   988845.00
                ENDING INVENTORY                           793400.00      195445.00
             GROSS MARGIN CONTRIBUTION                                    -89895.00
```

a.   Financial information by product

```
         GROSS MARGIN                                                    2329892.00
         OPERATING EXPENSES
            ADMINISTRATION                                150000.00
            ADVERTISING
               BRAND 14                        3000.00
               BRAND 17                       24000.00
               BRAND 12                       20000.00
               BRAND 21                       25000.00
               BRAND 18                        3000.00
               BRAND 15                       20000.00
               BRAND  0                           .00
               BRAND  0                           .00     95000.00
            SALES FORCE
               FIELD SALESMEN               100000.00
               TRAINEES                          .00
               SEPARATIONS                       .00     100000.00
            MARKET RESEARCH                                    .00
            PRODUCT CONVERSION                               .00
            BRAND START-UP                               200000.00
            DEPRECIATION                                  15000.00     560000.00
                         SUB-PROFIT                                   1769892.00
            OTHER EXPENSES                              332340.00
                         PROFIT BEFORE TAXES                          1437552.00
```

b.   Consolidated income statement for the firm

Table 11–2 Users of the marketing information system

User	Product	Place	Promotion	Price	Integrated mix
			Subsystem		
Chief executive officer	X	X	X	X	X
Vice-president of marketing	X	X	X	X	X
Sales manager			X	X	
Advertising manager			X	X	
Manager of marketing research	X	X	X	X	X
Manager of product planning	X				
Other managers	X	X	X	X	X

ities of the personalities involved. However, some general pairings can be made between subsystems and likely users. This is done in Table 11–2. Note that the chief executive is included, and that he or she uses all subsystems. As stated earlier, the subsystem output used at this level is of a highly summarized form. The chief executive officer and the vice-president of marketing have the greatest interest in the integrated mix subsystem.

Of course, other functional managers could use output of the marketing information system as well. For example, an engineering manager could use the new product evaluation model, and a financial officer could use the pricing model.

The marketing information system will play an increasingly important role in the information system of the firm. Since problems relating to customers are essentially probabilistic in nature, they will take much time to solve. As the firm becomes better attuned to the task of meeting the needs of the customer, more resources will be directed to understanding this critical element in the environment. This focus will demand greater active participation by marketing management, both line and staff, in the design and implementation of marketing information systems. These managers, in addition to understanding the operation of their firm as a system, also must understand the environmental influences on that system. In addition, they must understand the task of management and how modern-day techniques and devices can be applied. Much remains to be accomplished in the area of marketing information systems. Perhaps that is the greatest indication of its importance.

Important Terms

Industrial Espionage

Survey

In-Depth Interview

Observation

Controlled Experiment

Product Life Cycle

Middlemen

Feedforward

SOAR (Store Objectives and Accomplishments Report)

REACH (Retail Achievement Report)

Pricing Strategy Model

Marketing Management Decision Games

Important Concepts

Much information about competitors is available without the need for special data- or information-gathering activities.

Marketing intelligence information seldom is the product of computer analysis.

There are several basic ways in which marketing research can gather data about customers.

Marketing research is not the same as a marketing information system.

The product life cycle can define the types of product information a marketing manager needs.

Quantitative evaluation of new products is an example of how the MIS helps the manager solve problems that are not completely structured.

All resources, including data and information, flow through the distribution channel.

Place problems usually are structured and can be represented with deterministic models.

Use of a problem-solving technique such as linear programming requires input data from several sources—some internal and some environmental.

Product, promotion, and price problems usually are very unstructured, and many can be represented by probabilistic models.

The marketing manager can analyze each of the mix ingredients separately, but they must be synthesized into an integrated mix subsystem.

Managers on a strategic level use information from all of the output subsystems; tactical and operational level managers use information relating to their own areas of responsibility.

Important Organizations

A. C. Nielsen

Market Research Corporation of America

Brand Rating Index Corporation

Pillsbury

Questions

1 Why is the literature of business so bare in terms of material on industrial espionage?

2 Why does marketing intelligence information seldom find its way into the computer?

3 What is the difference between marketing research and marketing intelligence?

4 What are the four basic ways of gathering data by marketing research?

5 Which of the above data-gathering techniques answer the question "What"? Which answer the question "Why"?

6 If a firm has a good marketing research system, could it be referred to as the firm's marketing information system? Why?

7 How could the product subsystem signal to the marketing manager that a product is going from the growth to the maturity stage, and from the maturity to the decline stage?

8 Who in a firm would rate a new product on the various criteria listed in Figure 11-3? What would be the basis for the ratings (probabilities) assigned to each of the criteria?

9 If a channel of distribution is comprised of "middlemen," who or what is on each end of the channel?

10 Which of the basic resources do not flow through the channel? Which of the resources flow in both directions as a general rule?

11 In Chapter 4 a model of the environment was presented (see Figure 4–7). When is a wholesaler considered by the firm to be a customer? When is it not?

12 Is warehouse location an example of a mix or a routing problem?

13 In the warehouse location problem, what are the alternatives?

14 How could Pillsbury's REACH system be used to report marketing intelligence information?

15 In an earlier chapter, several approaches to data processing (batch, realtime, etc.) were identified. Which one would be best for the pricing strategy model? What computer output device should be used to provide the pricing information to the manager? Would any of the other processing approaches be acceptable?

16 Why is an integrated mix subsystem necessary?

17 Why is the manager of marketing research interested in the output of all subsystems in the marketing information system? (See Table 11–2.)

Problems

1 Go to your library and read a copy of *The Wall Street Journal.* Does it contain any articles that might be considered examples of marketing intelligence? Write down the titles of six such articles. You might have to look at more than one issue.

2 From the following data, calculate the "total marketing resource value."

Decision Criteria	Criteria Weight	Probabilities				
		Very Good (10)	Good (8)	Average (6)	Poor (4)	Very Poor (2)
Product compatibility	.10	.5	.3	.2	.0	.0
Sales knowledge	.20	.2	.2	.2	.2	.2
Distribution facilities	.35	.0	.0	.1	.4	.5
Long-term demand	.35	.0	.1	.3	.4	.2

Chapter 12

Manufacturing Information Systems

Computer-Controlled Production

This textbook is not specifically about computers, although they serve as the basis for the information systems described. Even though computers are used for jobs other than providing information, those uses are not addressed. To do so would unnecessarily complicate this study of information systems. One computer use in the manufacturing area, however, should be recognized. This is the control of machines and processes. It is an application that is playing an increasingly important role in the transformation process.

In the early 1960s manufacturers began to use computers to operate various machines in the production area. As an example, a computer punched a paper tape to control a metal-cutting machine. The tape did work previously performed by an operator, e.g., positioning the metal so that multiple parts could be cut from it. The result was an increased level of quality due to the added precision, and a reduced cost through lower labor requirements and less scrap. This operation is called *numeric control* (*NC*) and represents an offline use of the computer. The computer is not connected to the machine, but communicates with it by means of the paper tape. Numeric control remains a popular use of the computer in manufacturing.

By the late 1960s technology was sufficiently advanced that computers could be connected directly to one or more production machines (Figure 12–1). This process is called *direct numerical control* (*DNC*). Initially the controller was a single, large computer. Later, as it increased in popularity, the minicomputer began to be used for the control function.

Minicomputers are being used for DNC at General Motors for testing carburetors, at Polaroid for producing film, and at Philip Morris for making cigarettes. Other tasks include insertion of electronic components on circuit

Figure 12–1   Computer control of production machines

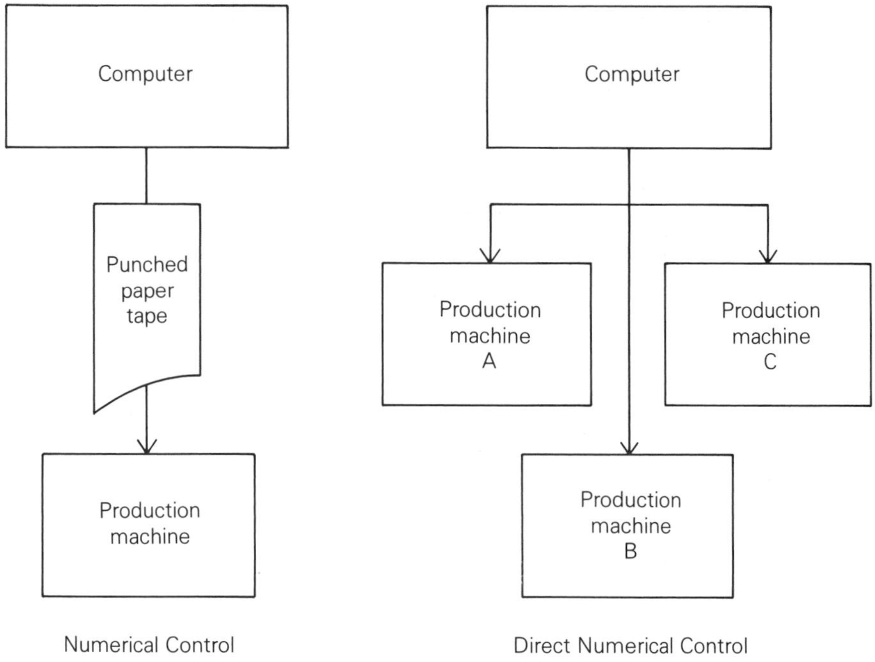

boards, control of plating tanks, operation of molding machines, and movement of raw materials and finished goods through the plant.[1]

The control of production machines by computer is an example of *automation* in the factory. The work is done entirely by machine without the need for manual effort. Automation is not the same as *mechanization*, where people use machines such as drills, sanders, saws, etc., in the performance of a job. Many production processes have become automated, and practically all are mechanized.

The Model of the Manufacturing Information System

The model of the manufacturing information system presented in Chapter 10 contains the same basic structure as the one for marketing. There are three

---

1. For additional information on computer control of production machines, see D. A. Van Cleave, "How Three Builders Made Better Milling Machines," *Iron Age*, July 4, 1977, pp. 43–46; "Praise Be For NC," *Economist*, August 6, 1977, p. 70; and J. B. Pond, "Fairfield Is Recognized as a Pioneer in DNC," *Iron Age*, August 29, 1977, pp. 68 ff.

"We got him from Disneyland. He was there three years before they found out he wasn't automated."

input subsystems used mainly for gathering data. One of these subsystems is internal accounting. Although internal accounting is a subsystem of the financial information system, a part relates directly to manufacturing. This part is concerned with collection of production data. Another input subsystem is manufacturing intelligence; it obtains data and information from environmental elements interfacing with the manufacturing function. This subsystem is very similar to the marketing information subsystem in this respect. The final input subsystem is that of industrial engineering; it focuses on the collection of internal data relating to the efficiency of the production process.

Figure 12–2   The manufacturing information system model

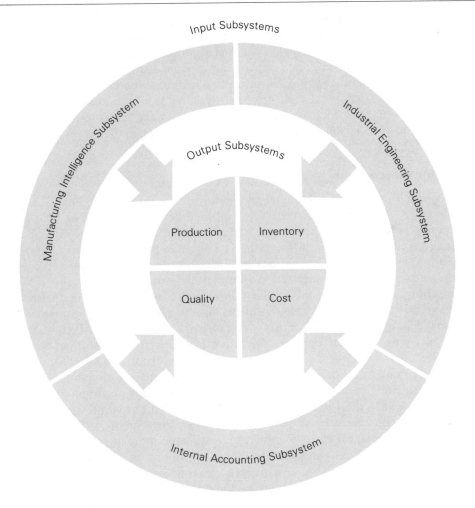

Data gathered by these input subsystems is processed by four output subsystems to prepare information for management use. Most of the use is made by manufacturing managers, but the chief executive officer and other functional managers can use the output when appropriate. The four output subsystems relate to four basic dimensions or characteristics of the production process: quality, cost, inventory control, and the process itself. Figure 12–2 illustrates the manufacturing information system model.

The remainder of this chapter will describe each of these manufacturing-oriented information subsystems.

Manufacturing Intelligence Subsystem

The two environmental elements of particular importance to the manufacturing function are labor and vendors. All production organizations make some use of manpower. Even in highly automated processes such as power generation, petroleum refining, and papermaking, some manpower is needed to initialize, maintain, and monitor the automated machinery. And, all organizations make some use of input resources acquired from vendors or suppliers. The manufacturing manager must remain aware of the status of these manpower and material sources so that they might flow through the firm as needed.

Labor information

In many firms the environmental manpower resource is organized into labor unions. A contract or agreement is established between the firm and those employees who belong to the union. Some firms must deal with more than one union, and a contract exists for each. The contract provides the basic information describing the expectations and obligations of both the firm and the union members. This contractual information provides the guidelines or constraints the manager must follow. Information describing actual performance of the firm and the union members must be gathered. This information usually is obtained by supervisory-level managers as a part of their daily contact with the union members. The supervisors forward this information to higher level managers by personal contact or written report. The firm's industrial relations department can play a vital role in this information flow— initiating and expediting it throughout the manufacturing organization. Very seldom does this information enter the computerized information system, but the information must be available for effective management.

For nonunion manpower, attention is directed more at sources of new employees than at relationships with those already on the job. Information must be gathered from employment agencies, colleges and universities, trade schools, and government agencies to provide for a continuing source of nonunion employees. Managers in the personnel department are primarily responsible for initiating and maintaining this information-gathering activity.

Vendor information

Substantially more data and information are gathered about the firm's material sources than those of manpower. For one reason, firms have many material suppliers, or vendors. And transactions involving those vendors occur each day. Another reason for the greater volume of input is that several of the firm's employees gather and use vendor data and information. These employees are called *buyers*, and they work in the purchasing department. Most purchasing departments have several buyers, and they usually specialize in contacts with

Figure 12–3   Input to vendor records

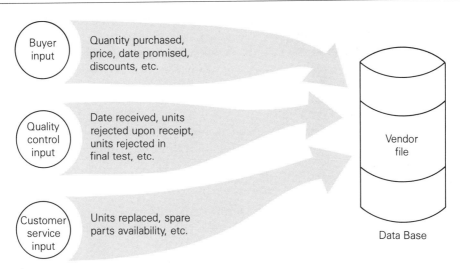

certain classes of vendors. As an example, one buyer will specialize in procuring electronic components and he or she will gain good awareness of those electronics suppliers. Another buyer will specialize in adhesives, another in maintenance supplies, and so on.

The buyers get much of their information from the vendors themselves. The vendors' sales representatives make personal calls on the buyers and furnish them with manuals and catalogs. Also, the buyers frequently contact the vendors by telephone to ask specific questions.

When a firm obtains materials from a vendor, a record is created describing the results of that transaction. These records can be kept in the data base (see Figure 12–3), with a record for each vendor in a vendor file. Such records contain information describing prices paid, shipping dates met, and material quality.

Information from a number of sources is necessary if the vendor records are to tell a complete story. The record is established when the buyer decides to obtain material of a certain quantity and quality from a vendor. The record is supplemented by the firm's quality control department as the material is received and used in the production process. Finally, the firm's customer service department reports on the performance of the material in the final product.

Buyers can retrieve this vendor information from the data base while considering a vendor for a possible order. More will be said about vendor selection in a later section.

Industrial Engineering Subsystem

Most everyone knows that firms use "efficiency experts" to study their manufacturing operations. These people conduct *time and motion studies,* often with the aid of a stopwatch, to eliminate unnecessary steps and to arrange steps in the best sequence. This type of analysis has been in use since the early 1900s, and people such as Frederick W. Taylor and Frank and Lillian Gilbreth (portrayed in the movie "Cheaper by the Dozen") gave the movement its start.

Today, these production analysts are known as *industrial engineers.* College programs, offered by engineering schools, prepare men and women for this work. These industrial engineers (IEs) work for the manufacturing firms or for consulting firms. While they can study any type of business operation to increase its efficiency, their main attention is usually directed at all processes in the manufacturing area.

Information provided to managers by IEs is used in two basic ways. First, it is used in the design of production systems. The IEs recommend designs that will operate most efficiently. Second, the information is used to establish acceptable standards of performance. As the system functions, actual performance is compared with the standards to determine whether management attention is required. Data describing actual performance is provided by the third input subsystem: the internal accounting subsystem.

Internal Accounting Subsystem

Internal accounting is usually identified with the financial function. However, a part of internal accounting relates directly to the manufacturing function. This part is the data collection network, and it is the main source of input data describing production activities.

Data collection terminals were described in Chapter 8 (see Figure 8–10). These terminals accept input from punched cards, plastic badges, or keyboard entry, and transmit the data to a computer. This flexible data-gathering ability enables the terminals to serve as "sensors" throughout the manufacturing area (Figure 12–4). Each time an action is initiated or completed, an entry can be made in a nearby terminal. The central computer uses this input to update the data base so that it reflects the current nature of the physical system.

Figure 12–4 shows 12 data collection terminals located throughout a factory. Terminal 1 is the receiving area. When raw materials are received from vendors, this is signaled by entering data in the terminal. All material receipts then undergo a quality control inspection, and the results are recorded on terminal 2. As the accepted receipts enter the raw materials inventory, that action is logged on terminal 3. That same terminal also is used to record the release of materials to the production process. Terminals 4 through 10 are used by production employees to signal the start and completion of each step of the production process. When the final product has been finished, terminal 11 is

Figure 12–4 Location of data collection terminals

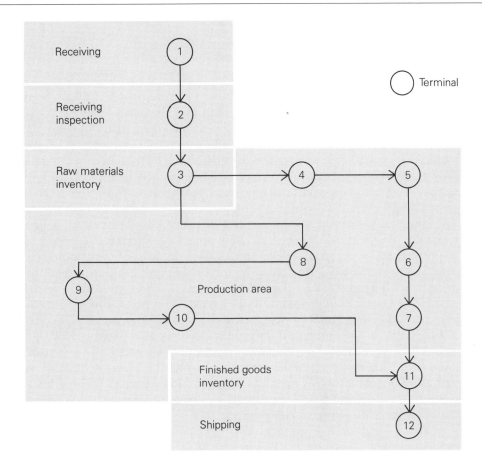

used to show that those goods now reside in the finished goods inventory. Terminal 11 also signals release of finished goods to the shipping department. When the goods are shipped to customers, that action is recorded on terminal 12.

The data collection terminals track the flow of materials through the plant every step of the way. In addition to reporting material flow, the terminals also record the use of manpower and machine resources. The same terminals can be used for *attendance reporting*, with the workers using their plastic badges to "punch in" in the morning and "punch out" in the afternoon. Also, as production steps employing machines are started and completed, the computer can determine how long the machines are in use.

Since the data collection system records the use of the three main manufacturing resources (material, manpower, and machines), it "senses" every important production action. Manufacturing management can use this data to monitor, on a realtime basis, the activities of the entire production system.

Inventory Subsystem

In well-managed organizations, manufacturing management has always been responsible for inventory. Records have been kept that show increase of the on-hand balance with receipts from vendors and decrease with shipments. In addition, physical counts have been made periodically to assure that the conceptual system accurately reflects the physical one. The conceptual system can employ manual methods, keydriven machines, punched card machines, or computers. This maintenance of inventory records is known as *inventory control.*

With the rather recent attention to reduction in operating costs, managers have given attention to another aspect of inventory. This is the reduction of its cost to the lowest possible level consistent with acceptable performance. This is an area where quantitative techniques have proven successful, and the name describing this use in the inventory area is *inventory management.*

The annual cost of maintaining or carrying an inventory can be as much as 25 percent of its value. So, if the raw material storeroom contains $1,000,000 in inventory, this inventory can generate an annual cost as great as $250,000.

These maintenance, or carrying, costs vary directly with the inventory level; the higher the level, the higher the costs. And the inventory level of an item is influenced primarily by the number of units ordered from a vendor at one time. In simplified terms, the average level is considered to be one-half of the order quantity plus any safety stock.

Safety stock is that quantity maintained to prevent an out-of-stock condition. It is a reserve that the firm never intends to use, but it is available in emergency situations.

The model in Figure 12–5 shows the effect of order quantity on average inventory level. A reduction in order quantity from 20 to 16 lowers the average level by 2. If the item happens to be an expensive electric motor, costing $5000, the reduction in annual maintenance costs could be $2500 (2 × $5000 × .25).

In the upper example, a quantity of 20 is ordered from the vendor. Sometimes (just after receipt) there are 25 units in inventory. Sometimes (just before receipt) there are 5 units on hand. On the average, there are 15 units in inventory. The sawtooth appearance of the graphs illustrates how the balance on hand is reduced gradually after receipt.

In the lower example a smaller quantity is ordered and the average level drops accordingly. This effect would seem to identify lower order quantities as the best goal for the manager. Such an assumption would be true except for another cost that *increases* as the order quantity decreases. This is the purchasing cost. It costs a fixed amount to prepare a purchase order, maybe $30,

Figure 12–5 Order quantity affects inventory level.
  a. Order quantity of 20, average level is 15.
  b. Order quantity of 16, average level is 13.

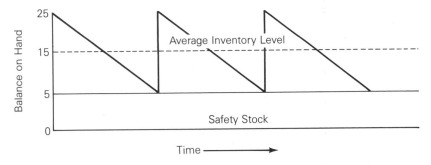

a. Order quantity of 20; average level is 15

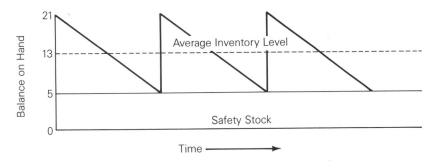

b. Order quantity of 16; average level is 13

regardless of the number of units ordered. Therefore, the fewer the units, the higher the *per unit* purchasing cost. If the firm orders one unit at a time, the per unit purchasing cost is $30. This cost can be reduced to $15 per unit when two are ordered, to $10 when three are ordered, etc.

A mathematical formula, called the *EOQ* (*economic order quantity*) *formula,* balances these two inventory costs and identifies the lowest combined cost. Both the graphical and the mathematical model of this technique are included in Figure 12–6.

An EOQ can be established for each item in raw materials inventory. This quantity is always ordered from the vendor. Another economic quantity can be used for the finished goods inventory if the firm produces its own finished goods. This is the *economic manufacturing quantity* (*EMQ*), and it balances the costs of carrying the inventory with costs of production inefficiencies.

These quantities—EOQ and EMQ—are optimum. They cannot be im-

Figure 12–6   The EOQ represents the lowest total cost:
    a. Graphical model
    b. Mathematical model

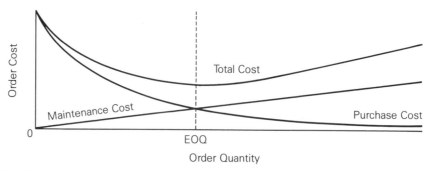

a.   Graphical model

$$EOQ = \sqrt{\frac{2PS}{M}}$$

where *P* = purchase cost (in dollars)
        S = annual sales (in units)
        M = maintenance cost (in dollars)

b.   Mathematical model

proved upon without changing the costs involved. The manager therefore is relieved of decisions on how much to order. The order decision becomes a completely structured one.

   Another example of a structured decision was described in Chapter 4. This was the decision of when to order replenishment merchandise. An order point can be calculated for each item to trigger a purchase order to the vendor (in the amount of the EOQ) or a production order to the factory (in the amount of the EMQ).

   These two decisions, *when* to order and *how much* to order, represent the two key decisions in inventory management. They can both be made by the inventory subsystem without the need for management intervention. Once these quantities have been established, the manager need not get involved until they need to be updated. The manufacturing manager can be informed of changes to the different ingredients (purchase cost, maintenance cost, annual sales, lead time, wage rate, etc.), as the changes occur.

Quality Subsystem

Quality standards normally are established for the products manufactured by a firm. The customers of the firm in effect establish these standards by creating a profitable market for a product of a certain quality. These standards are communicated to the firm by the marketing function and are adopted as manufacturing standards.

It is not sufficient to establish quality controls on only the finished goods output. If the end product is unacceptable, where does the manager look for a solution? The fault could be anywhere in the system. The manager must establish quality control checks at each key point in the system. One vital checkpoint is the input function, where raw materials are received from vendors. If the output products of the firm are to meet an expected quality level, the input materials must be of equal or higher quality. There is no way to make a quality product from substandard materials.

Most manufacturing firms have several potential sources of supply for each item purchased. This practice affords a certain amount of security against a complete lack of availability if a sole supplier is shut down by strike or other reason. This is one way that the firm can protect against environmental impacts. Another reason for seeking multiple vendors is that they are likely to bid against one another to get the order. Competition keeps the cost down.

Buyers in the purchasing department have the job of selecting the best vendor for a particular order. This decision has always been largely nonstructured because of the frequent changes in the variables. Vendors go out of business, new ones come on the scene, prices change, etc.

Each time a buyer must make a vendor selection, the quality subsystem can provide information to be used as a basis for the decision. The past performance of each potential vendor can be reported in a format that facilitates comparison and evaluation. Numeric scores can be computed for each vendor, and the ones with the highest scores are given prime consideration for the order.

Most of the vendor data is provided by the internal accounting subsystem. Included are measures of material quality, ability to make shipments without backorders, promptness in filling orders, and policies for handling credits and returns.

Additional vendor information is provided by the manufacturing intelligence subsystem. This information relates to future trends, such as anticipated price changes and scarcity of supply. Also, information is gathered on vendors who have had no previous business transactions with the firm.

As an example of how the quality subsystem functions, assume that a retailer of radios and TVs has identified three important measures of vendor performance: product quality, speed of delivery, and quality of service. Further, these measures are weighted as follows:

> 60—Product Quality
> 30—Speed of Delivery
> 10—Service Quality

The quality of the products obtained from the vendor represents 60 percent of the measurement. In this example, service apparently is of relatively low importance, representing only 10 percent.

Each vendor is measured on all three factors based on past performance. The formulas for the three factors are:

$$\text{Product quality}^2 = 60 \times \frac{\text{number of orders accepted}}{\text{total number of orders}}$$

$$\text{Delivery speed} = 30 \times \frac{\text{number of delivery promises met}}{\text{total number of orders}}$$

$$\text{Service quality}^3 = 10 \times \frac{\text{number of items repaired}}{\text{number of repair orders}}$$

One of the vendors supplying portable radios to the retailer has compiled the following performance record:

> 36 of 40 orders have been accepted.
> 5 of 15 promised delivery dates have been met.
> 16 of 20 repair orders have been completed.

This vendor's performance score is computed:

$$\text{Material quality} = 60 \times \frac{36}{40} = 54$$

$$\text{Delivery speed} = 30 \times \frac{5}{15} = 10$$

$$\text{Service quality} = 10 \times \frac{16}{20} = 8$$

$$\text{Total performance score} = 72$$

The score can be compared with those of other vendors of portable radios. The buyer can use this information in selecting the vendor, or vendors, to supply the next shipment.

Other quantitative measures of quality can be computed as the materials flow through the plant. These measures can be used as the basis for an incentive wage plan for the production workers. The workers with high scores receive a bonus. The data used in calculating these scores can be obtained from the data collection system.

---

2. Items ordered from the vendor are inspected for quality upon receipt. Orders not meeting the quality standards are rejected. A high percentage of orders accepted indicates a high quality level.

3. This example assumes that defective products can be returned to the manufacturer for repair. Each returned item is accompanied by a repair order. A high percentage of orders repaired indicates a high service level.

Production Subsystem

The production subsystem is the most complex of the output subsystems. It is concerned with all of the actions performed on the material flow. These actions are performed by two other basic resources: manpower and machines. The production subsystem is therefore a conceptual representation of how these three resources (material, manpower, and machines) are used together to create finished products.

Decisions affecting the physical production system of the firm must be made on all management levels. The decision to create such systems is made on the strategic level. These are decisions to build a new plant, enlarge a plant, or change the layout of a plant. It then becomes the job of the tactical level managers to plan how these changes in the physical system will be made. If a decision has been made to build a new plant, a determination must be made where the plant will be located and how it will be arranged. Once the system has been designed and created, the operational level managers have the responsibility to make day-to-day decisions affecting system performance.

System design decisions

Making changes in the physical production system and deciding how these changes will be made are regarded as system design decisions. Many factors must be considered and some are difficult to measure. As an example, the expected attitude of local citizens toward the new plant will be important. A firm wouldn't want to locate a plant in a community that is critical of the plant's effect on the environment or the quality of life. Also, the firm wouldn't want to locate a plant in an undesirable living area if skilled workers (and their families) must be recruited to move to the new location.

Although subjective considerations such as these exist, it is likely that the production subsystem can help the managers make the system design decisions. Many of the variables such as land cost, taxes, shipping distance, labor costs, and so on can be quantified. Quantitative techniques can be used to consider these factors and determine good locations for the plant and good arrangements or layouts. In the previous chapter, linear programming was used to decide where a liquor warehouse should be located. The same technique can be used to locate a plant and also to arrange the layout.

For an example of a system design decision, assume that a manufacturer of electrical products has determined that a new plant is needed and has selected a site. What remains is to decide how the layout should be arranged. Several alternatives can be considered but they all consist of a flow from a raw materials area, through a production area, and to a finished goods area. It is possible to determine the sizes of these areas from the volume of activity planned and the number of production processes to be performed. Figure 12–7 illustrates three alternatives that might be considered. They differ only in the location of the storerooms and the paths the material follows during the

Figure 12–7   Evaluation of alternate plant layouts

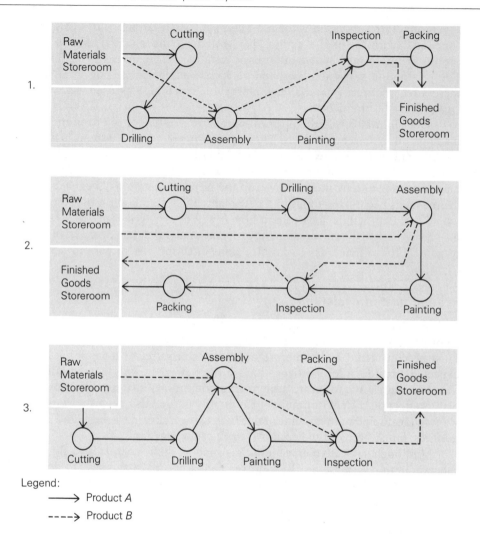

Legend:

———→ Product *A*

----→ Product *B*

assembly process. These alternatives can be evaluated quantitatively and the best one identified. Evaluation can be based on some specific objective, such as minimum distance the materials must travel during the assembly process.

While linear programming is an effective way to arrange the layout of a production area, a great deal of preliminary work must be performed. This work is performed by the industrial engineers who supply the linear programming model with the objective function (such as minimum material movement) and the constraints (such as the number and sizes of the separate work areas). Given this input information, the linear programming model can specify the optimum layout.

Figure 12–8   Sample product—bicycle flashlight

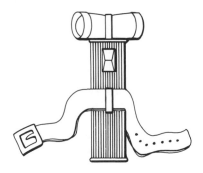

System operation decisions

System design decisions are not made often. Perhaps a firm has to decide whether to build a new plant only once every 5 years. But, once the plant is built, decisions about its operation are made practically every day. The operation decisions are concerned with which job to do next, whether to work overtime, which machine to use, and so on. Since many decisions of this type are made, many opportunities to use the information system exist.

For an example of some of the uses of the production subsystem in system operation, assume that an electrical manufacturer creates many products in its single factory. One product is a flashlight that can be strapped to a bicycle rider's leg. As the rider pedals, the light bobs up and down, warning oncoming motorists. This product is pictured in Figure 12–8.

The firm receives orders for the flashlight from wholesalers across the nation. Ideally, these orders are filled from finished goods inventory. This permits immediate shipment. However, if enough lights are not in inventory, the plant must make some more. This is where the production subsystem comes into use.

It first is necessary to decide how many lights to produce. The economic manufacturing quantity (EMQ) identifies this quantity. Assume that the EMQ is 2200.

Next, it is necessary to determine what resources will be required. One resource is materials. The lights are constructed from a number of separate parts. It can be assumed that the plant purchases all of the parts from vendors and simply assembles them into the finished products. The list of parts used in the production process is called a *bill of material* (Figure 12–9). Only single quantities of each part are used, except for batteries. Each light uses two batteries.

If the plant is to produce 2200 flashlights, raw materials sufficient for 2200 bills of material will be required. The process of multiplying the manufacturing quantity times each item on the bill of materials is called *exploding the bill of materials*. This process is illustrated in Figure 12–10. The total quantity

Figure 12–9   Bill of materials for bicycle flashlight

Part	Quantity
Plastic cylinder	1
Plastic top	1
Strap	1
Switch	1
Spring	1
Reflector	1
Bulb	1
Lens, red	1
Lens, clear	1
Battery	2

required for each part is known as the *gross requirement.* These numbers appear in the right column.

Since 2200 flashlights must be assembled, does this mean the plant must purchase 4400 batteries and 2200 of the other parts? Not necessarily. Some of these parts might already be on hand—in raw materials inventory. The production subsystem checks the inventory status of each part to determine the *net requirements* (gross requirements minus those on hand). This process is shown in Figure 12–11.

It can be seen that all of the parts are available in the needed quantities except two: switches and bulbs. The firm has only 800 switches on hand, and 2200 are needed. Thus a purchase order must be sent to a vendor for at least

Figure 12–10   An exploded bill of materials

Part	Qty. per Final Product		Number of Final Products		Gross Requirement
Plastic cylinder	1	x	2200	=	2200
Plastic top	1	x	2200	=	2200
Strap	1	x	2200	=	2200
Switch	1	x	2200	=	2200
Spring	1	x	2200	=	2200
Reflector	1	x	2200	=	2200
Bulb	1	x	2200	=	2200
Lens, red	1	x	2200	=	2200
Lens, clear	1	x	2200	=	2200
Battery	2	x	2200	=	4400

Figure 12–11 Net raw-material inventory requirements for flashlight parts

Part	Gross Requirements	Inventory on Hand	Net Requirements
Plastic cylinder	2200	3000	0
Plastic top	2200	2250	0
Strap	2200	6000	0
Switch	2200	800	1400
Spring	2200	2999	0
Reflector	2200	2204	0
Bulb	2200	0	2200
Lens, red	2200	3625	0
Lens, clear	2200	5500	0
Battery	4400	5005	0

1400 switches. If the EOQ is more than 1400, say 1750, the firm will order 1750 switches.

An order also must be placed for bulbs. There are no bulbs in raw materials inventory, so 2200 must be ordered. If the EOQ is greater, say 2935, a purchase order will be sent to a bulb vendor for 2935 bulbs.[4]

It is possible that additional purchase orders will be triggered by the net requirements computation. These orders are for items still in stock, but with a balance below the reorder point. The reflector might be one of these items. There are enough reflectors on hand, but only four will be left after the flashlights are produced. The requirement for the flashlights could have dropped the balance on hand below the reorder point. In this case, an order will be placed in the EOQ amount so that reflectors will be available for future production runs.

The production subsystem uses the raw material file in the data base to determine the net requirements. The inventory subsystem then uses the EOQ and the net requirements to determine the quantity to order. The specific vendor is selected by the quality subsystem. In this manner, all the subsystems work together to satisfy the decision needs of the manufacturing manager.

Production cannot start until all the parts are available. When the switches and bulbs are received, the production subsystem notifies the manufacturing management. The notification can be accomplished by transmitting the needed data to the central computer from terminals located in the receiving and the receiving inspection areas. The computer then notifies the appropriate managers, such as the schedulers and dispatchers, by transmitting messages to terminals in their offices.

The assembly of the flashlight requires a series of steps. The item is

4. In some situations the order quantity is increased slightly (5–10%) to allow for breakage or malfunction.

Figure 12–12   Flow of job through the plant

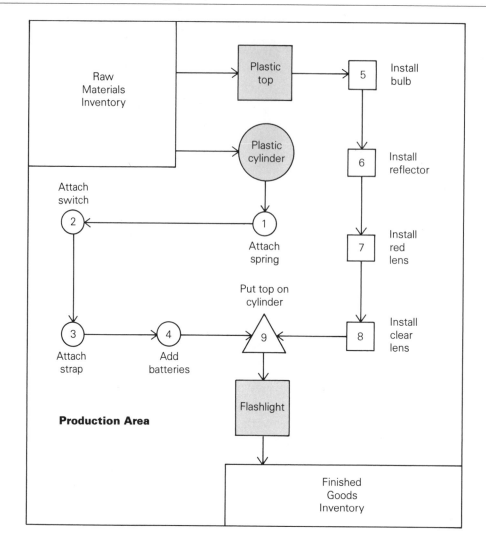

assembled a step at a time from the required parts. The item moves from one workstation in the plant to another as the assembly process is performed. Figure 12-12 shows this flow through the plant. The layout of the plant, facilitating this flow, could have been designed by the production subsystem as described earlier.

The production flow starts with release of the raw materials from inventory. In this example there are two main flows: one for assembly of the cylinder and one for the top. Work can be accomplished simultaneously on both the cylinder and the top to reduce length of time required for the job. The

Figure 12–13 Computation of machine and labor requirements

```
            MACHINE AND MANPOWER REQUIREMENTS

PRODUCT--BICYCLE FLASHLIGHT
PRODUCTION QUANTITY--2200

                  -------MACHINE------      -------EMPLOYEE------
      STEP        TYPE  STD•  TOT• TIME      TYPE   STD•  TOT• TIME

   1--ATTCH SPRG   129  •16    352           O-129  •16    352
   2--ATTCH SW     402  •30    660           O-402  •30    660
   3--ATTCH STRP   ---  ---    ---           ASSY   •10    220
   4--ADD BATTS    ---  ---    ---           ASSY   •08    176
   5--INST BULB    202  •16    352           O-202  •16    352
   6--INST REF     ---  ---    ---           ASSY   •30    660
   7--INST LNSR    602  •20    440           O-602  •20    440
   8--INST LNSC    604  •20    440           O-604  •20    440
   9--ATTCH TOP    ---  ---    ---           ASSY   •16    352
```

steps in the cylinder flow are numbered 1 through 4 and are circled. The steps for the top are numbered 5 through 8 and are enclosed in squares. In step 9 the top assembly is attached to the cylinder assembly and the result is a finished flashlight that then enters the finished goods inventory.

The production subsystem can compute the machine and manpower requirements by multiplying the production quantity times standards for each resource for each step in the production process. For example, if the first step is the attachment of a battery spring to the plastic flashlight cylinder (step 1 in Figure 12–12), a special spring insertion machine can be used. The machine must have an operator. The standard insertion time of 0.16 minute means that 352 minutes of both machine and operator time will be required to attach 2200 springs.[5] Similar computations can be accomplished for each remaining step of the process, thus producing total machine and manpower requirements.

The computations can be seen in Figure 12–13. Some steps (1, 2, 5, 7, and 8) require machines and operators. The others are assembly processes performed manually. Specific types of machines and employees are identified.

The production subsystem has now determined all of the requirements. These can be matched to the resources available to prepare a production schedule.

The schedule is a conceptual representation of what the physical system

---

5. This standard time includes allowances for expected delays in the routine, such as rest breaks, machine maintenance, etc.

should achieve. It spells out the optimum way the resources should be used. Therefore the production scheduling decisions of the manufacturing manager are of a structured type. It is left to the manager to control the production processes to assure that the schedule is met.

A date and a time of day are printed on the schedule (see Figure 12–14) for the release of each of the 10 parts from the raw materials inventory. The parts are not released until they are needed. When they are released, they are transported to the workstation where they will be used.

The nine production steps also are listed, along with a start date and time for each. A production step is scheduled to begin not later than 30 minutes after the raw materials have been delivered to the workstation. Steps 5 through 8 require a total of 1892 minutes of production time compared with 1408 minutes for steps 1 through 4. The start time for the cylinder assembly (steps 1–4) is therefore delayed so that the tops can be attached (step 9) as soon as the cylinders are assembled.

The production subsystem triggers the production process. Information is prepared for employees in the inventory and production areas, telling them what to do, when to do it, and (if necessary) how to do it. One approach is for the computer to transmit signals to the appropriate terminals as the actions are scheduled to begin. Another approach calls for the computer to print all of the information on forms that are contained in a folder called a *shop packet*. The shop packet accompanies the job as it moves through the plant. The timing of the actions is specified on the separate, printed production schedule.

As work begins on a step in the production process, the worker uses the terminal at his or her workstation to advise the computer of:

- Job identification
- Step number
- Workstation
- Employee identification
- Start time

The first three items are entered from a punched card or by keying the data into a keyboard. The employee can be identified by inserting his or her plastic badge. Start time is recorded by the computer as the message is received.

When the job step is completed, the worker advises the computer by use of the terminal. Again the computer enters the time of day. In this way the computer can calculate the time required to complete the step (stop time minus start time).

The production subsystem can include a programmed routine that will compare the actual time for each step with the predetermined standard. This comparison can be made as each step is completed. Upper and lower boundaries can be assigned to each standard time. When the actual exceeds a boundary, a signal can be sent to management advising of the exceptional performance. If a step took too long to complete, subsequent steps possibly will be delayed. Perhaps management can take action to prevent the delay. If a step is

Figure 12–14   Example of a production schedule

```
                        PRODUCTION SCHEDULE

   JOB NAME=BICYCLE FLASHLIGHT
   JOB NO. 79=133

     RAW           RELEASE      PRODUCTION      START        COMPLETION
    MATLS        DATE  TIME      STEP         DATE  TIME      DATE  TIME

   CYLINDER      10=24 0800
   SPRING        10=24 0800    1=ATTCH SPRG 10=24 0838      10=24 1430
   SWITCH        10=24 1430    2=ATTCH SW   10=24 1500      10=26 0900
   STRAP         10=26 0930    3=ATTCH STRP 10=26 0950      10=26 1330
   BATTERY       10=26 1345    4=ADD BATTS  10=26 1404      10=26 1700
   TOP           10=23 0900
   BULB          10=23 0900    5=INST BULB  10=23 0930      10=23 1522
   REFLECTOR     10=23 1530    6=INST REF   10=23 1600      10=25 1000
   LENS RED      10=25 1030    7=INST LNSR  10=25 1100      10=26 0920
   LENS CLEAR    10=26 0930    8=INST LNSC  10=26 1000      10=26 1620
                               9=ATTCH TOP  10=27 0800      10=27 1352
```

completed earlier than scheduled, it might be possible to speed up the completion time for the job so that an earlier shipping date can be realized for the customer.

The production subsystem is able to assist the manager in two ways. It makes the structured decisions, and it provides information to be considered and used in making decisions of the nonstructured variety.

Cost Subsystem

Inventory costs can be minimized through the use of economic order and manufacturing quantities. Production costs can be controlled through the use of accurate cost standards.

On a periodic basis the manufacturing manager can receive a report showing how the actual production costs compare with the standards. An example is shown in Figure 12–15.

The manager can key an inquiry into a terminal, and cost data for each department can be displayed. The computer program compares total standard hours with total actual hours and calculates the variance. When the actual hours exceed the standard, the job numbers contributing to that excess are printed. In the figure, the painting department exceeded the standard by 35 hours on jobs 79-283 and 79-291.

If the manager wants more information on the excess, another inquiry can be made and the data can be reported by employee. Figure 12–16 is an

Figure 12–15 Production cost report

```
              PRODUCTION COST REPORT
                   BY DEPARTMENT

              WEEK ENDING 10-22-78

DEPARTMENT      STD.    ACT.    VAR.     SEE JOB      JOB
                HRS.    HRS.             NUMBERS      VAR.

WELDING         1090    1085    -5

PAINTING         330     365    35       79-283       10
                                         79-291       25

PLATING          523     522    -1

INSPECTION        78      85     7       79-303        7

ASSEMBLY        2027    2423   396       79-292       23
                                         79-295      107
                                         79-298       47
                                         79-313      219

CLEANING         293     278   -15
```

Figure 12–16 A second production cost report

```
              PRODUCTION COST REPORT
            BY DEPARTMENT AND BY JOB

              WEEK ENDING 10-22-78

DEPARTMENT      JOB     EMP.    STD.    ACT.    VAR.
                NO.     NO.     HRS.    HRS.

PAINTING       79-283   3124      11      13      2
                        3309      18      18      0
                        4119      62      65      3
                        7218      42      40     -2
                        7301      10      11      1
                        8514      73      79      6

               TOTALS . . . . . .  216     226     10
```

example. Analysis of this data indicates employee 8514 accounted for a 6-hour overage on job 79-283. Now the manager has the information needed to determine the cause. The foreman of the painting department can meet with the employee to discuss what happened on job 79-283. Once the causes are identified, action can be taken to eliminate or minimize them in the future.

The two required ingredients for such an effective cost control program are standards of comparison and accurate reporting of actual costs. The data collection network of the production subsystem enables both requirements to be achieved. Data describing actual job performance is collected, and over a period of time this data is used in setting standards. When start and stop times are recorded for each step of the production process, accurate actual times can be computed. When the conceptual system is able to track the flow of resources through the physical system in the manner described, the manager is able to control all dimensions of acceptable performance: quality, time, quantity, and cost.

Summary

The manufacturing function of the firm primarily involves the flow of material resources. Managers in this area must design and operate a system to handle this flow.

Computers have been applied in the manufacturing area in two basic ways: to control production processes and machines and as information systems. The manufacturing information system can be used in both the design and operation of the production system. Design decisions are not made frequently, but they are important in terms of commitments of large sums of money for long periods of time. These decisions are of the nonstructured type and are made on upper management levels. Most likely, the information system cannot supply all of the information the manager would like in making these decisions. Much information can be provided, however, and some parts of the decision can even be structured.

Operational decisions are of a different type. They are made on a daily basis and can be structured to a great extent. This is because most of the important variables can be identified and measured in quantitative terms.

The model of the manufacturing information system includes three input and four output subsystems. The output sybsystems can be used in both design and operation of the production system. The information from the output subsystems is used by different managers in the manufacturing area, and by others as well. This usage is shown in Table 12–1.

As with the marketing information system, the chief executive officer receives information from all output subsystems in a summary

Table 12–1   Users of the manufacturing information system

User	Subsystem			
	Inventory	Quality	Production	Cost
Chief executive officer	X	X	X	X
Vice-president of manufacturing	X	X	X	X
Plant superintendent	X	X	X	X
Manager of planning and control	X		X	
Manager of engineering		X	X	X
Manager of quality control		X		
Manager of physical distribution	X		X	
Director of purchasing	X	X		X
Manager of inventory control	X			
Other managers	X	X	X	X

form. Both the vice-president of manufacturing and the plant superintendent also use highly summarized output, describing the entire operation.

It is probable that managers in marketing and finance will also make use of the output. Marketers will be interested in all aspects of production (cost, quality, and availability) since they influence the product that is to be sold. Financial managers will have a special interest in output of the cost subsystem.

Much has been accomplished in applying information systems to problems of manufacturing management. These systems are a vital part of modern manufacturing techniques and account to a large extent for the stream of quality products made available to consumers and users around the world.

Important Terms

Numerical Control (NC)

Direct Numerical Control (DNC)

Automation

Mechanization

Buyer

Time and Motion Study

Industrial Engineer (IE)

Attendance Reporting

Inventory Control, Inventory Management

Safety Stock

EOQ (Economic Order Quantity)

EMQ (Economic Manufacturing Quantity)

Bill of Material

Gross Requirements

Net Requirements

Shop Packet

Important Concepts

Computers, including minis, can be used to control machines in the production area. This is an example of automation.

The manufacturing function has primary responsibility for two environmental elements: labor and vendors.

Labor information permits the manager to use the manpower resource effectively.

An internal accounting subsystem using data collection terminals can track the flow of work through a factory, almost in real time.

Quantitative techniques have greatly simplified the task of maintaining profitable inventory balances.

Vendor quality information is pro-

duced from both internal accounting and manufacturing intelligence data.

Identification and evaluation of vendor alternatives is a good example of computer solution of a structured problem.

Production facilities can be designed using the computer and quantitative techniques such as linear programming.

The planning and control of the production process—from exploding the bill of materials to tracking each production step—can be largely computerized.

Different managers use different parts of the manufacturing information system, depending on their interests and responsibilities.

Questions

1   What is the difference between mechanization and automation?

2   What is the difference between NC and DNC?

3   Is labor information usually computerized? Why or why not?

4   What about vendor information? Name as many sources of vendor information as you can.

5   Why are industrial engineering studies usually restricted to the manufacturing area of the firm?

6   What resource, or resources, does the data collection network track in a manufacturing operation?

7   What is the difference between inventory control and inventory management?

8   When would a manufacturing organization use the EMQ? the EOQ?

9   What are the two key questions that an inventory management system must answer?

10 Is a plant layout problem a structured or an unstructured one? What about plant location?

11 Where do the standards come from that are used to compute machine and manpower requirements?

12 How can data collection terminals be used in providing the manufacturing manager with cost information?

13 Name the two basic ways that computers have been applied in the manufacturing area.

Problems

1   Calculate the average inventory level when order quantity and safety stock have the following values:

Order Quantity	Safety Stock	Average Level
6	1	
10	2	
28	6	
50	10	
100	12	
200	18	

2 Calculate the EOQ when:

$$\text{Purchase cost } (P) \quad = \$25.00$$
$$\text{Sales } (S) \quad\quad\quad = 100 \text{ units}$$
$$\text{Maintenance cost } (M) = \$2.00$$

3 Your company's factory layout is pictured in Figure 12–4. As administrative assistant to the plant manager, you have been asked to specify where quality control inspections should occur in order to control each step of the production process. Do you have any ideas? Can the data collection terminals be used? If so, generally in what way?

4 Calculate vendor performance scores for the following vendors:

Vendor	Product Quality (Weight = 60)	Delivery Speed (Weight = 30)	Service Quality (Weight = 10)	Total Performance Score
1	$^{50}/_{50}$	$^{8}/_{10}$	$^{60}/_{100}$	
2	$^{40}/_{50}$	$^{7}/_{10}$	$^{50}/_{100}$	
3	$^{45}/_{50}$	$^{9}/_{10}$	$^{80}/_{100}$	

5 What would be the order quantity if:

$$\text{Gross requirements} = 1200$$
$$\text{Inventory on hand} = 1050$$
$$\text{EOQ} \quad\quad\quad\quad\quad = \ \ 300$$

What if the inventory on hand equals 600?

Chapter 13

Financial Information Systems

Importance of Accounting Data

Had this book been written 20 years ago, it would have dealt primarily with the internal accounting system of the firm. This is because that system was *the* conceptual information system until a more complete treatment of management information was developed.

The accounting system is still important, even though it is but a single part of the MIS. Accounting is important because it provides a detailed record of the activity of the firm. Accounting tells what the firm has done in the past, and in certain instances, what is happening now. It is important for the manager to have this understanding, but it also is necessary to project what is likely to happen in the future. Techniques more sophisticated than those of accounting must be used to provide the manager with information about what lies ahead.

The internal accounting system provides a common data base that links all three functional information systems. Each system shares in gathering and using this data. A good accounting system is a prerequisite to an MIS (Figure 13–1). Without one, an MIS can never be achieved.

The Model of the Financial Information System

The remainder of this chapter will be devoted to a discussion of the five subsystems of the financial information system (Figure 13–2). These subsystems include those providing for data input (internal accounting and financial intelligence subsystems) and for information output (forecasting, funds management, and financial control subsystems).

Figure 13-1　Accounting data provides the foundation for the MIS.

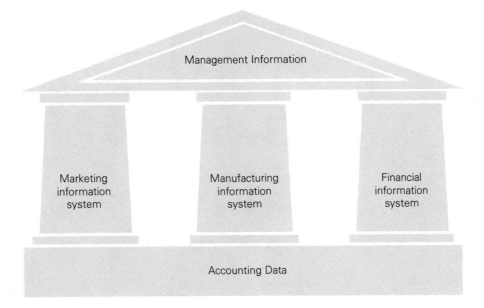

Internal Accounting Subsystem

Accounting data provides a record of everything of monetary importance that happens in the firm. A record is made of each transaction, describing the important facts—what happened, when it happened, who was involved, how much money was represented, etc. The usefulness of this data is that it can be analyzed in various ways to meet the unique information needs of management. If a wholesaler wants to learn more about customers who have bought more than $25,000 of merchandise in the past month, those accounting records can be selected. If a retailer wants to know how sales fluctuate by day of the week, that information, too, can be provided. Virtually any type of information can be produced from this accounting data.

Three features of accounting data must be recognized. First, it deals only with the firm and the activities of environmental elements dealing with the firm. The firm must be directly involved. If information is needed about environmental elements never involved in the firm's business transactions, the accounting system cannot provide it.

Second, the data represents thousands of facts, which, presented separately, would only confuse management. This data must be processed to convert it into information. This is the task of the MIS.

Third, the data is largely historical. In no way does it describe everything

Figure 13–2   The financial information system model

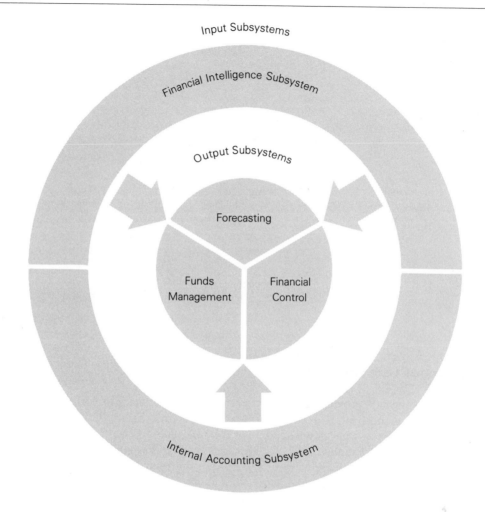

happening now. This situation is not due to the slowness of the data processing, but to the delay in entering the data into the system. Modern data-
gathering techniques, using optical character recognition, magnetic ink character recognition, remote terminals, and similar innovations, are doing much
to make accounting data more nearly current. The data collection terminals
located in the manufacturing area are an example of how accounting data can
be gathered without delay.

Each day, hundreds or thousands of transactions occur within a firm.
Even though there are a lot of these transactions, many are of the "chain
reaction" type, with one or more triggered by a single activity. A large number
are triggered by a customer order. This fact is not surprising, since all of the

Figure 13-3 Subsystems in the internal accounting system

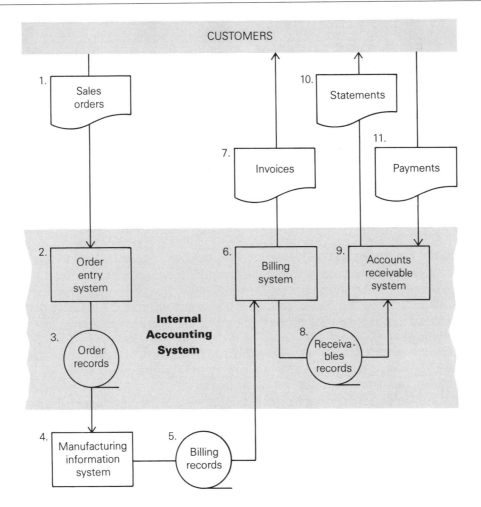

firm's subsystems are intended to respond, in one way or another, to customer requests for products and services.

A number of accounting systems handle the type of transactions initiated by a customer order. These are subsystems within the overall internal accounting system. One internal accounting subsystem is the *order entry system*, which enters the orders into the accounting system. Another is the *billing system*, which sends bills or invoices to the customers. A third is the *accounts receivable system*, which collects the money. Figure 13-3 shows how these systems interface with the customer and how they are linked with the manufacturing information system. The numbers in the figure are keyed to the numbers in the explanation below.

1. Sales orders. When a customer such as a wholesaler or retailer decides to purchase something from the manufacturer, some type of *order form* is prepared. In many cases, a salesperson for the manufacturer will complete the form. Such a form is pictured in Figure 13–4.

The order form identifies the customer, the salesperson, the items ordered, the quantities of each, and the prices to be paid. Other data completes the description of the sales order.

2. Order entry system. When the sales order is received by the firm, several processes occur. Since most sales are on credit, rather than for cash, a credit check can confirm the customer's ability to pay. The decision whether to grant customer credit is a structured one, and can be programmed. Usually a credit limit in dollars is established for each customer, and the amount of money owed the firm must remain within this limit. As long as the customer pays its bills to the firm, the firm will continue to accept the customer's orders for amounts within the credit limit.

Another process performed by the order entry system establishes a control over orders received. A record is made of the important data for each order. Data, such as customer number, order number, and order date, is keyed into a terminal. An order suspense record is created from this data and entered into the data base. A program checks each suspense record daily to assure that the order is filled within a reasonable time. If an order is not filled within a specific period, a signal is generated by the system. An employee in the order department can then investigate the cause of the delay. This is an example of how the conceptual information system can make structured decisions to improve the performance of the physical system.

Other order data must be entered in the system, in addition to that used for control; this includes identification and quantity of each item ordered. This data can also be entered from a terminal, or it can be keypunched or read optically.

The output from the order entry system is a file of order records. In Figure 13–3 these records are on magnetic tape, but they could just as easily be on a disk. The figure also illustrates a condition that should not go unnoticed. The systems and subsystems are connected by data files. One system creates a file and passes it on to another for additional processing.

3. Order records. The order records include the data from the sales order that will be needed to complete the processing. All that is required is the customer identification, a specification of what was ordered, and how much. At this point, the firm doesn't know whether these orders can be filled or not. Perhaps some of the items are not in stock. These records simply reflect what the customers have ordered.

4. Manufacturing information system. In the previous chapter, it was explained that the inventory subsystem of the manufacturing information system determines whether the order can be filled. This is the point in the

Figure 13–4   A sales order form. (Courtesy of Waples-Platter Companies)

WHITE SWAN, INC.   AUSTIN/DALLAS/LUBBOCK   JUNE 13, 1978   WAPLES PLATTER   PAGE 1

PACK	SIZE DESCRIPTION	ITEM#	PRICE	PAR LEVEL MIN./MAX.	UNIT	WEEK 1 ON HAND/ORDER	WEEK 2 ON HAND/ORDER	WEEK 3 ON HAND/ORDER	WEEK 4 ON HAND/ORDER	WEEK 5 ON HAND/ORDER	LINE #
12	6 3/4OZ NESTEA 1 JAR YLD 10 GAL4450	026005	23.16		1.93						1
50	3/4OZ 1GAL POUCH NESTEA 4457	026104	11.45		.23						2
24	3.75OZ 5GAL POUCH NESTEA 4467	026203	25.28		1.05						3
4	1 GAL REALEMON LEMON JUICE #15140	066605	13.03		3.26						4
6	10 RANCH STYLE BEANS-NET WT 6# 12OZ	078006	12.31		2.05						5
6	10 WSR TOMATO PASTE 6#14OZ	124685	18.27		3.05						6
2	12/2 OZ MCILLHENNY TABASCO SAUCE	140681	11.89		5.95						7
1	4 GAL WSB MUSTARD POLY CAN	141507	4.37		4.37						8
1	4 GL WSB SALAD DRESS 31% OIL 5% EGG	142562	10.22		10.22						9
4	1 GAL FIGARO LIQUID SMOKE	143362	16.49		4.12						10
3	1M WS/SWEET N LOW SUGAR SUBSTITUTE	159566	13.93		4.64						11
2	12/2 OZ MCILLHENNY TABASCO SAUCE	140681	11.89		5.95						12
24	6 OZ WSR LOUISIANA HOT SAUCE	140806	6.02		.25						13
4	1 GAL WSR WORCHESTERSHIRE SAUCE	144402	6.71		1.68						14
1	100 LB WSR PINTO BEANS	180208	26.35		26.35						15
1	25# TEX-TRA TEINE-TVP CARAMEL COLOR	237941	10.93		10.93						16
6	1GAL WSR WHITE PICKLNG VINEGAR 50GRN	238808	6.70		1.12						17
6	10 WSR KOSHER DILL SPEARS 70/90 CT	255182	13.26		2.21						18
6	10 LA COMIDA JALAPENO PEPPERS	254466	12.19		2.03						19
1	5 GAL WSR SWEET RELISH-POLY	255745	14.66		14.66						20
4	1 GAL WSR ITALIAN PEPPERS	256289	15.66		3.92						21
4	1 GL WSR MLD SWT CHERRY PEPPER GLASS	256248	11.36		2.84						22
4	1 GL WSR STUF MANZ OLIVE340/360#4192	253641	36.50		9.13						23
4	1 GL WSR STUF MANZ OLIVE240/260#4190	253567	36.50		9.13						24
4	500 KFT 8LB WHITE PAPER BAG	261529	20.11		5.03						25
2	500 KFT 16LB WHITE PAPER BAG	261644	16.22		8.11						26
20	50 CONT 8SFC CHINA THERM SQUAT CONTR	271239	15.39		.77						27
20	50 CONT 16CE CUP 16OZ CHINA THERM	271403	18.82		.94						28

ORDER GUIDE   CASE QUANTITY / LINE # / ITEM #

process where this determination occurs. The inventory record for each ordered item is obtained from the finished goods inventory file, and a check is made to determine if sufficient stock is on hand. If so, the order will be filled and shipped. If not, the manufacturer will have to produce additional stock, as described in the previous chapter.

The finished goods inventory file can be on either magnetic tape or DASD. If on tape, the order records must be sorted into the file sequence before processing. If transaction processing is being used, the order records can be in random order.

When the finished goods inventory record is obtained from the data base, the needed data is extracted. This includes item description, price, and the location in the warehouse where the item can be found. Any computations, such as checking the reorder point or determining backorder quantity, are also done at this point.[1]

5. Billing records.   The manufacturing information system communicates with the billing system by means of a file of billing records. These records represent the items on the order that can be filled. If a customer orders four items and three can be filled, those three will be included in this file. The record for the single item that cannot be shipped is retained by the manufacturing information system as a backorder and will trigger a production process.

The billing records include only the important data relating to the transactions: customer identification, item identification, and quantities and prices of items to be shipped. It is not necessary that descriptive data relating to the customer (customer name and address, shipping instructions, etc.) be included. That data can be extracted from the data base by the billing system when it is needed.

6. Billing system.   At this point, it is known which items will be shipped to the customers. However, no activity has occurred within the physical system. All has been accomplished within the conceptual information system. Conceptual data files confirmed the customer's credit ratings and the availability of items in inventory. The actual filling of the orders in the storeroom remains to be done. This activity is triggered by the billing system.

7. Invoices.   The outputs of the billing system are used in three vital tasks. Printed *invoices* are sent to the customers (Figure 13–5), advising them of the items shipped and the financial obligations to the firm that have been incurred.

A copy of the invoice also is sent to the finished goods storeroom or warehouse. This copy serves as a *picking ticket*, or list of items to be selected

---

1. A *backorder quantity* is a quantity ordered but not filled because of lack of stock. The quantity will be filled when stock becomes available.

Figure 13–5   A customer invoice. (Courtesy of Waples-Platter Companies)

WHITE SWAN, INC. P.O. BOX 30505 DALLAS, TEXAS 75230	*a symbol of finer foods*	DELIVERY RECEIPT

WAPLES PLATTER
P O BOX 1350
FT WORTH   TX76101

** CWD **

PAGE NO.	INVOICE NO.	INVOICE DATE	CUSTOMER NO.	TRUCK STOP	ORDER	A/R NO.
1	66989	6/15/78	46880	1K00	00001	

OFFICE TELEPHONE NUMBER 214-263-3411
071   JODY ROWE   214-255-6178

8   T70-33   NO. COPIES 2

QUANTITY FULL PACK / PARTIAL	PRODUCT DESCRIPTION	UNIT TAX	UNIT PRICE	EXTENSION	ITEM CODE NUMBER	
2	50 3/4OZ 1GAL POUCH NESTEA 4457		11.45	22.90	026104	
1	4 1 GAL REALEMON LEMON JUICE #15140		13.03	13.03	066605	
1	6 10 RANCH STYLE BEANS-NET WT 6# 12OZ		12.31	12.31	078006	
1	6 10 WSR TOMATO PASTE 6#14OZ		18.27	18.27	124685	
1	2 12/2 OZ MCILLHENNY TABASCO SAUCE		11.89	11.89	140681	
1	2 12/2 OZ MCILLHENNY TABASCO SAUCE		11.89	11.89	140681	
1	1 4 GAL WSB MUSTARD POLY CAN		4.37	4.37	141507	
1	4 1 GAL FIGARO LIQUID SMOKE		16.49	16.49	143362	
1	4 1 GAL WSR WORCHESTERSHIRE SAUCE		6.71	6.71	144402	
1	1 25# TEX-TRA TEINE-TVP CARAMEL COLOR		10.93	10.93	237941	
1	4 1 GL WSR STUF MANZ OLIVE240/260#4190		36.50	36.50	253567	
1	6 10 WSR KOSHER DILL SPEARS 70/90 CT		13.26	13.26	255182	
1	1 5 GAL WSR SWEET RELISH-POLY		14.66	14.66	255745	
1	4 1 GL WSR MLD SWT CHERRY PEPPER GLASS		11.36	11.36	256248	
1	2 500 KFT 16LB WHITE PAPER BAG		16.22	16.22	261644	* NON FOOD ITEM *
1	20 50 CONT 16CE CUP 16OZ CHINA THERM		18.82	18.82	271403	* NON FOOD ITEM *
3	1 5 GL GOLDEN CHEF OIL35#GOLD-N-SWT*		19.75	59.25	323485	
1	5 100 WS A-200 PLASTIC APRONS 28X46	2.47	49.45	49.45	790303	* NON FOOD ITEM *
	-THE FOLLOWING ITEMS REQUIRE -					*** FREEZER ITEMS ***
	-STORAGE IN A FREEZER AREA -					
2	1 10# WSR T-BONE STEAKS 16/10 OZ		35.64	71.28	932202	
	-THE FOLLOWING ITEMS REQUIRE -					*** REFRIGERATOR ITEMS ***
	-STORAGE IN A REFRIGERATED AREA -					
2	3 8#WSR COLE SLAW SALAD #36509		13.19	26.38	995845	

* NON FOOD TOTAL AMOUNT   84.49
****

25 PIECES

TERMS: NET ** CWD **
All past due accounts are payable at Dallas County, Dallas, Texas

TOTAL BEFORE TAX	445.97
STATE SALES TAX .050	2.47
INVOICE TOTAL	448.44

CWD

In the absence of protest in writing within forty-eight (48) hours after delivery of merchandise, that the party signing for the merchandise on behalf the buyer, had no authority to do so, it shall be agreed and understood that the party had full authority to agree to all terms and conditions of this invoice on behalf of the buyer. Reasonable attorney's fees and other expenses incurred by the Seller shall be borne by the buyer when delinquent accounts are placed in the hands of an attorney for collection or suit brought thereon.

RECEIVED BY – SIGNATURE

from the shelves and bins. The computer can list the items in a particular sequence, thus facilitating an efficient selection process. All of the items in one area of the storeroom are printed together on the invoice. The inventory clerks do not waste time by moving back and forth unnecessarily across the storeroom floor.

This is the point in the process where the physical system becomes involved. The physical system responds to signals generated by the conceptual information system. The conceptual information system determines what should be done, and the physical system does it. If a firm is to place such faith in its conceptual system, that system must be accurate. It is the conceptual system that determines if the physical system can fill the order. For the procedure to work smoothly, the conceptual system must be an accurate reflection of the physical system. Otherwise, chaos will result.

8. Receivables records. The third important output of the billing system is the communication to the accounts receivable system. This communication can be in the form of a magnetic tape or disk. It is a file of *receivables records*, or records representing transactions where money is owed the firm. A single record is included for each invoice, giving the vital data—invoice number and date, customer identification, and amount due.

9. Accounts receivable system. This system has the responsibility of collecting all money owed the firm. In many cases, the customers will send their payments upon receipt of the invoice, or within 30 days. Very often a discount will be allowed for such prompt payment.

10. Statements. Some customers, however, do not pay when they should. They must be reminded. The document that serves as the reminder is the *statement* (Figure 13-6).

A line is printed in the body of the statement for each invoice on which an amount is owed. The amounts can be printed in separate columns based on the length of time they have been due. Amounts due over 90 days represent critical receivables situations demanding management attention. Credit managers can receive notice of these past-due amounts for follow-up action. An overdue receivables report can be prepared weekly, listing those customers with amounts due over 90 days. Such a report was illustrated in Chapter 9. See Figure 9-3.

11. Payments. When payments are received, the corresponding amounts due are removed from the receivables file. The receivables file therefore contains only records of outstanding customer debts; the file is an inventory of money owed the firm.

It is common for some type of turnaround document, such as a punched card or optical reading slip, to accompany the payment. This computer-readable input relieves the firm of the necessity of keying the payment into a terminal or other keydriven machine. The turnaround document was described in Chapter 6 and illustrated in Figure 6-10.

The three systems described above are just a sampling of those included in the internal accounting system. Another group of systems interfaces with the firm's vendors. These systems are involved with purchasing, receiving, and accounts payable, and are triggered by the manufacturing information system when a need for replenishing raw material is detected. Still other systems handle transactions with stockholders, the firm's personnel, and the government.

These internal accounting subsystems make a number of structured decisions. The subsystems determine whether or not a customer's order is to be accepted, which discounts apply, and when collection activities should be initiated. This process relieves the manager of this decision-making responsibility, and assures that the decisions are made accurately and in accordance with rules that the manager establishes.

Figure 13–6 A customer statement. (Courtesy of Waples-Platter Companies)

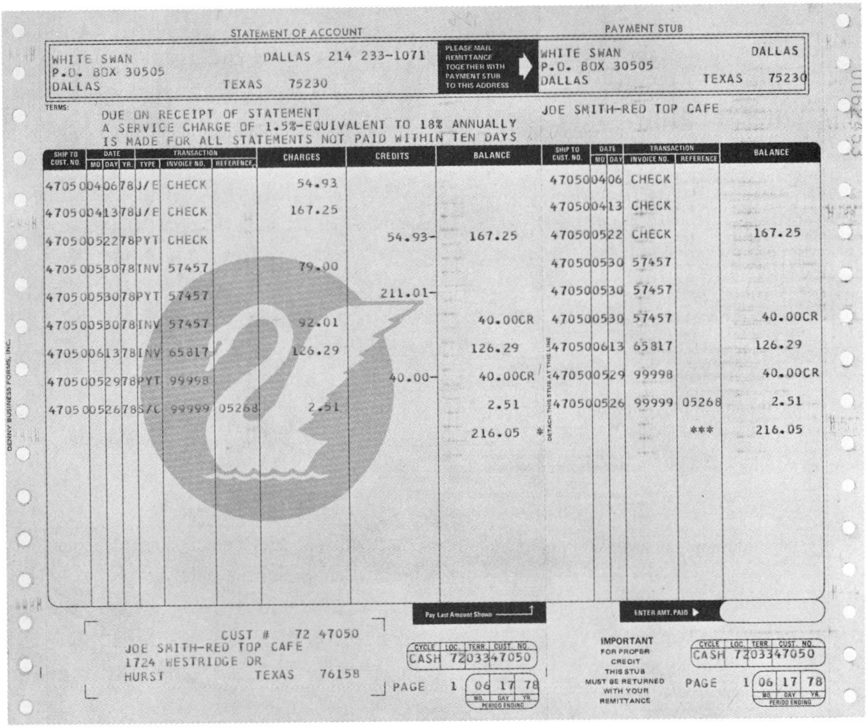

STATEMENT OF ACCOUNT

WHITE SWAN DALLAS 214 233-1071
P.O. BOX 30505
DALLAS TEXAS 75230

PLEASE MAIL REMITTANCE TOGETHER WITH PAYMENT STUB TO THIS ADDRESS

TERMS: DUE ON RECEIPT OF STATEMENT
A SERVICE CHARGE OF 1.5%-EQUIVALENT TO 18% ANNUALLY
IS MADE FOR ALL STATEMENTS NOT PAID WITHIN TEN DAYS

SHIP TO CUST. NO.	DATE MO	DATE DAY	DATE YR.	TRANSACTION TYPE	TRANSACTION INVOICE NO.	TRANSACTION REFERENCE	CHARGES	CREDITS	BALANCE
47050	04	06	78	J/E	CHECK		54.93		
47050	04	13	78	J/E	CHECK		167.25		
47050	05	22	78	PYT	CHECK			54.93-	167.25
47050	05	30	78	INV	57457		79.00		
47050	05	30	78	PYT	57457			211.01-	
47050	05	30	78	INV	57457		92.01		40.00CR
47050	06	13	78	INV	65817		126.29		126.29
47050	05	29	78	PYT	99998			40.00-	40.00CR
47050	05	26	78	S/C	99999	05268	2.51		2.51
									216.05 *

CUST # 72 47050
JOE SMITH-RED TOP CAFE
1724 WESTRIDGE DR
HURST TEXAS 76158

Pay Last Amount Shown

CYCLE	LOC.	TERR.	CUST. NO.
CASH	72	03	3 47050

PAGE 1 06 17 78 (MO. DAY YR. PERIOD ENDING)

DETACH THIS STUB AT THIS LINE

PAYMENT STUB

WHITE SWAN DALLAS
P.O. BOX 30505
DALLAS TEXAS 75230

JOE SMITH-RED TOP CAFE

SHIP TO CUST. NO.	DATE MO	DATE DAY	TRANSACTION INVOICE NO.	TRANSACTION REFERENCE	BALANCE
47050	04	06	CHECK		
47050	04	13	CHECK		
47050	05	22	CHECK		167.25
47050	05	30	57457		
47050	05	30	57457		
47050	05	30	57457		40.00CR
47050	06	13	65817		126.29
47050	05	29	99998		40.00CR
47050	05	26	99999	05268	2.51
				***	216.05

ENTER AMT. PAID

IMPORTANT FOR PROPER CREDIT THIS STUB MUST BE RETURNED WITH YOUR REMITTANCE

CYCLE	LOC.	TERR.	CUST. NO.
CASH	72	03	3 47050

PAGE 1 06 17 78 (MO. DAY YR. PERIOD ENDING)

DENNY BUSINESS FORMS, INC.

The real value of these internal accounting subsystems to the manager is the wealth of data they provide in making unstructured decisions. Since each monetary transaction of the firm is recorded in detail, that data can be screened, selected, and summarized to provide accurate descriptions of internal processes.

Other data input subsystems, such as the functional intelligence subsystems and the marketing research subsystem, provide environmental input data. Data provided by the internal accounting subsystem, therefore, assumes an important role in the day-to-day management of the firm.

Financial Intelligence Subsystem

The financial intelligence subsystem has the responsibility of gathering data and information from the elements of the environment involved in the money flow. These elements include the financial community, stockholders, and the government. Although vendors and customers also are involved in this flow, they are the responsibility of the manufacturing and marketing information systems, as described earlier.

Since the financial function controls the money flow through the firm, information is needed that can expedite this flow. The day-to-day flow of money from customers and to vendors is controlled by the internal accounting subsystem. The financial intelligence subsystem is concerned with flows other than those of a daily operational nature. This system seeks to identify the best sources of additional capital and the best investments of surplus funds.

When a firm needs to acquire additional capital for large-scale expenditures, such as plant expansion or development of new products, two avenues can be followed. In *debt financing*, money is borrowed from a bank or other institution, usually to cover short-term, or temporary, needs. Needs of a longer duration are usually met by selling a part of the ownership of the firm. In a corporation this is called *equity financing*, and money is received from the sale of stock.

Stockholder information

All but the smallest corporations have a stockholder relations department within the financial function. This department is concerned with the flow of information between the firm and its stockholders. Most of the information flows from the firm to the stockholders in the form of annual and quarterly reports (Figure 13–7). These reports are prepared by the stockholder relations department working closely with top management. They contain information in a highly summarized form.

Stockholders have an opportunity to communicate information (complaints, suggestions, ideas, etc.) to the firm through the stockholder relations department. Also, once a year an annual stockholders meeting (Figure 13–8) is held to enable stockholders to learn firsthand what the firm is doing. Very often, stockholders use these meetings as an opportunity to aim communications directly at top management.

Information gathered informally from stockholders is seldom entered into the computerized information system, but is disseminated by verbal communication and written memo to key executives in the firm.

Financial community information

The relationship between the firm and the financial community receives much more attention from the financial management. There should be a balanced flow of money through the firm, but this equilibrium is not always achieved. At times, additional funds are needed or investments of surplus funds are desired. It is the responsibility of the financial intelligence subsystem to compile information on sources of funds and investment opportunities for use when needed.

An important indirect environmental effect influences this money flow through the firm. The federal government controls the money market of the

---

Figure 13–7   Reports to stockholders inform them of the firm's activities. (Courtesy of Electronic Data Systems)

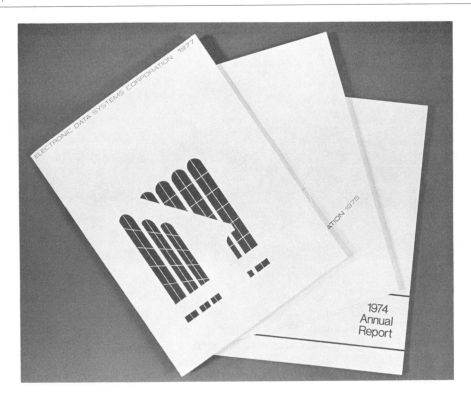

country through the Federal Reserve System. There are various means to release the controls when the money flow is to be expedited and to tighten the controls when the flow is to be reduced.

The firm therefore must gather information from both financial institutions and the Federal Reserve System. This information permits the firm to remain current on national monetary policies and trends and possibly to anticipate future changes. A variety of publications can be used for this purpose. They are prepared by both the financial institutions and the government. Two examples are the *Monthly Economic Letter*, prepared by the First National City Bank of New York, and the *Federal Reserve Bulletin*, prepared by the Federal Reserve System.

In addition to the need to acquire funds, the firm frequently must invest surplus funds on either a short- or long-term basis. These funds can be invested in a number of different ways: in United States Treasury securities, commercial paper, and certificates of deposit (CDs). Since the terms and rates of return for some vary over time, it is necessary to continually monitor these investment opportunities so that the optimum ones may be used when needed.

Figure 13–8   An annual stockholders' meeting. (Photo courtesy of Recognition Equipment Incorporated)

This gathering of information from the financial environment is the responsibility of the financial intelligence subsystem. As with the other two functional intelligence subsystems, such information usually is handled outside the computer system. An opportunity exists for improved use of the computer in this subsystem area.

Forecasting Subsystem

Most business managers have always recognized the need to forecast the future performance of the firm. As a result, a large variety of forecasting techniques have been developed.[2] Many of these techniques are informal and depend to a great extent on the knowledge, experience, and intuition of the manager. Others involve the use of quantitative methods to project sales and other types of activity for the firm.

Quantitative methods were used in forecasting long before they were applied to other areas of the firm's operations. However, the power of the computer and more sophisticated quantitative methods such as simulation have recently improved the accuracy with which managers can forecast the

---

2. For a good comparison of different forecasting techniques, see John C. Chambers, Satinder K. Mullick, and Donald D. Smith, "How to Choose the Right Forecasting Technique," *Harvard Business Review*, July–August 1971, pp. 45–74.

future. For example, one of the early users of computer simulation in forecasting, Sun Oil Company, was able to achieve an accuracy within 1 percent for its total operations.[3]

Who does forecasting?

Forecasting very often is accomplished by marketing. In these instances, the objective is to forecast sales. These sales forecasts serve as the basis for planning all phases of the firm's activity for the near future, such as the coming year. Based on the estimates of the firm's sales, the manufacturing function determines the manpower, machine, and material resources needed to accomplish the production of the needed products. Likewise, the marketing function determines the required marketing resources, and the financial function determines the financial resources. The financial function uses these requirements to identify the total money needs of the firm for the future period. In this manner, the planning for each functional unit is directed at assuring that the firm meets its sales objectives.

The sales forecast serves as the basis for short-term planning in most firms. Many firms, however, need to plan activity for a longer period of time—sometimes 8 or 10 years in the future. When such a long planning horizon is assumed, much of the firm's success depends on environmental influences. This demands that attention be given the national economy and the effect it can have on the firm. Long-range forecasting of this type normally is done by the financial function.

Forecasting methods

Forecasting techniques can be divided into two categories—quantitative and nonquantitative. All techniques, however, are based on projections of what has happened in the past.

A nonquantitative approach is one that does not involve computations of data. The manager says something like, "We sold 2000 units last year, and we should be able to improve on that. So, I think we will sell 2500 next year." Forecasts such as this can have little or no basis, or they can result from an informed firsthand knowledge of the situation. As long as these forecasts satisfy the user, it is almost impossible to sell the user on a different approach. Many managers are extremely adept at the use of the nonquantitative approach, and in those cases it appears unnecessary to complicate matters with computations.

Not all managers are so gifted, however, and many businesses are too complex for such a simple approach. In these situations the manager can use a

3. George W. Gershefski, "Building a Corporate Financial Model," *Harvard Business Review*, July–August 1969, pp. 61–72.

Figure 13–9   Relationship of sales to number of salespersons

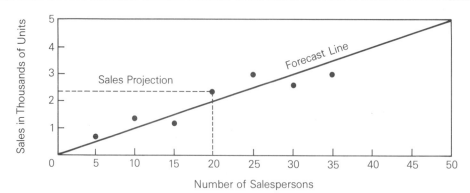

variety of quantitative techniques to assure the most accurate forecast using the available data.

One such technique is regression analysis. It involves the relationship of the activity to be forecast, such as sales, to some other activity, such as the number of salespersons. This relationship can be seen in Figure 13–9.

Seven points are plotted on the graph. They represent the relationship between the two variables during previous periods, say the past 7 years. For example, in one year 20 salespersons were employed and sales were approximately 2,300 units (dotted lines). It is apparent from the plot of points on the graph that a positive relationship exists between the two variables—the more salespersons the firm employs, the higher the sales.

Regression analysis permits the use of a mathematical model to specify the relationship very exactly. When the model is executed, a regression line can be drawn through the points so that the total distance from each of the points to the line is at a minimum. This line is the "best fit" to the points. The management can then use this regression line to forecast sales based on some particular number of salespersons. For example, if the firm employed 50 salespersons, it could assume that sales would approximate 5000 units.

This example involves only two variables: an *independent variable* (salespersons) and a *dependent variable* (sales). Sales "depend" on the number of salespersons. This type of regression is known as *bivariate regression*—only two variables are involved.

Many business activities, such as sales, are sufficiently complex to defy prediction based on a single independent variable. In those cases more than one can be used; this technique is called *multivariate regression.* For example, it might be necessary to relate sales to (1) the number of salespersons, (2) advertising budget, (3) number of retail outlets, and (4) number of customers.

Several years ago, Kristian Palda developed a multivariate regression equation (Figure 13–10) to reflect the sales history of Lydia Pinkham's Vege-

Figure 13–10   Lydia Pinkham regression equation

$$Y = -3649 + 0.665X_1 + 1180 \log X_2 + 774X_3 + 32X_4 - 2.83X_5$$

where

Y = yearly sales in thousands of dollars

X_1 = yearly sales (lagged one year) in thousands of dollars

X_2 = yearly advertising expenditures in thousands of dollars

X_3 = dummy variable, 1908-1925 = 1; 1926-1960 = 0

X_4 = year (1908 = 0; 1909 = 1; etc.)

X_5 = disposable personal income in billions of dollars

table Compound.[4] This equation, containing five independent variables, accounted for 93 percent of the fluctuation in sales over the years—a very high percentage. While the equation has no practical value (the product no longer is being produced), the influence of multiple independent variables is demonstrated.

Econometric models

Recent fluctuations in the national economy have emphasized the effect of environmental influences on the firm's activity. In 1969, record sales were being forecast in many industries for the seventies. The economic slump that followed caused most of these predictions to fall short. The reason was not due to major weaknesses in the firm's strategies or tactics, but rather to the poor condition of the economy.

The models that consider economic influences on the firm's activity are called *econometric models,* since they combine techniques from economics, statistics, and mathematics. These models relate data describing the firm to that of the economy to predict how the firm will react to economic influences. Therefore, if a firm is to engage in this type of forecasting, internal data, economic data, and an econometric model must be available.

The accumulation of economic data and the creation of the model

4. Kristian S. Palda, *The Measurement of Cumulative Advertising Effects* (Englewood Cliffs, N.J.: Prentice-Hall, Inc., 1964), pp. 67–68.

represent a major undertaking by a firm. While many firms have developed their own, other firms have purchased models and data from special service organizations. One such organization is Data Resources, Inc. of Lexington, Massachusetts.

Data Resources offers a timesharing service to its clients. The manager of the client firm can use a terminal to communicate with the model and data bases located at the central computer facility. Data Resources furnishes a data base of economic data, plus a selection of forecasting models. The models relate the economic data to data provided by the firm. Included in the economic data base are 6500 series of economic variations plus over 100,000 series of international, regional, and national data.

The manager first creates a regression equation relating the firm's sales to several economic variables. An equation for an electronic parts manufacturer might look like this:

$$S = a + bG + cK + dM$$

where

S = sales

a, b, c, d = computer-calculated weights that relate the three independent variables to sales

G = gross national product (GNP)

K = consumer durables spending

M = military spending

This equation is developed by fitting the firm's past sales curve to various economic series such as GNP and military spending. Once created, the manager can use the equation to forecast sales for a 2-, 5-, or 10-year period.

When sales have been forecast, the next step is to forecast other activities, such as the manpower, money, machine, and material resources needed to meet the sales objective. The same general approach is followed.

Use of an econometric model such as this enables the manager to take advantage of a wealth of economic data and to relate it to the firm's activities. The result is a forecast compatible with the predicted influences of the environment.

Funds Management Subsystem

The general systems model of the firm shows how resources flow from the environment, through the firm, and back to the environment. One of these flows is money. This flow is important in that it makes possible the other resources; and, in the form of profits, it reflects the ability of the firm to meet its responsibilities to the owners.

The flow of money from the environment, through the firm, and back to the environment is circular. The money itself does not remain in the firm very

Figure 13–11   Fluctuating sales influence monthly profit.

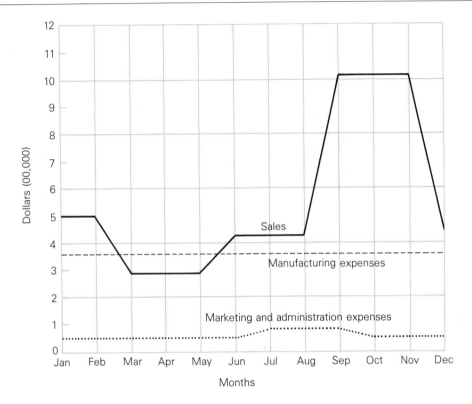

long. As soon as money is received it is redirected to the environment in the form of payments of debts, returns on stockholder investments, investments that will earn interest, taxes, etc. Only enough cash is retained to meet the day-to-day operating requirements and most of that is deposited in banks.

The limitation on the size of the money flow presents a major constraint on the activities of the firm. Activities can be pursued only when they can be adequately financed.

This money flow can be managed, or controlled, and the financial manager strives to achieve two goals: (1) to assure that the inflow in the form of sales revenue is greater than the outflow in the form of expenses, and (2) to assure that this condition remains as stable as possible throughout the year. It would be possible for a firm to show good profit on the year's activities, yet have periods during the year when expenses exceed revenue. This situation can be seen in Figure 13–11 where a manufacturer of garden equipment enjoys high sales in the fall and low sales in the spring.

During March through May, monthly sales of $300,000 are not high enough to cover monthly manufacturing expenses of $360,000. Money outflow

Figure 13–12   An unbalanced money flow

	JAN.	FEB.	MAR.	APR.	MAY	JUN.	JUL.	AUG.	SEP.	OCT.	NOV.	DEC.	TOTAL
MONEY INPUT													
SALES	$500	$500	$300	$300	$300	$400	$400	$400	$1000	$1000	$1000	$500	$6600
MONEY OUTPUT													
MANUFACTURING													
EXPENSES													
WAGES	82	82	82	82	82	82	82	82	82	82	82	82	984
MATERIALS	220	220	220	220	220	220	220	220	220	220	220	220	2640
OTHER MFG.													
EXPENSES	58	58	58	58	58	58	58	58	58	58	58	58	696
TOTAL MANU-													
FACTURING													
EXPENSES	360	360	360	360	360	360	360	360	360	360	360	360	4320
MARKETING AND													
ADMIN. EXP.	26	26	26	28	28	28	40	40	40	30	30	30	372
NET CHANGE IN													
MONEY	+114	+114	-86	-88	-88	+12	0	0	+600	+610	+610	+110	1908

PROJECTED MONEY FLOW

during March through May exceeds inflow of $262,000, even though profit for the year is $1,908,000.

The funds management subsystem can prepare a report such as that in Figure 13–12, showing money flow for the next 12-month period. The report can be printed by a mathematical model that uses the sales forecast plus expense projections as the basis for the calculations.

While the annual results are good, the money flow throughout the year is anything but stable. Since the sales to middlemen are made mostly in the winter months, there is a big inflow of money from September through February. But, the plant operates at a fixed output throughout the year and this puts a drain on money from March through August. This feast-or-famine condition presents problems for financial management. What can be done with the surplus during the winter months? And what about the deficit during the summer?

The manager can use the systems approach, plus the model, to solve the problem. The problem has been identified as unbalanced money flow, and data has been gathered describing why this condition exists. The manager would like to consider alternative strategies in balancing the flow, and the model will permit this to be done.

First simulation—variable production schedule

One alternative is to develop a new product that would increase sales revenues during the first part of the year. Because such a development program normally

Figure 13–13   Modified production schedule

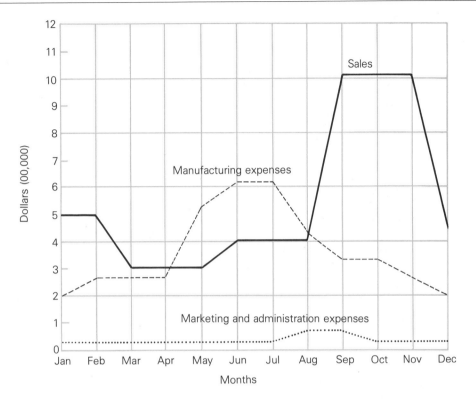

spans a period of several years, it will not be considered as a feasible alternative for the immediate problem.

Another way to achieve a better balance between sales and expenses is to match production to sales, rather than spend constant amounts for wages, materials, and manufacturing expenses as in Figure 13–12. The financial manager schedules production output in one month to equal the sales forecast for the next. Of course this change would have to be approved by the manufacturing manager. This new strategy is illustrated in Figure 13–13.

The figure shows a peak manufacturing period during the summer, creating the products for fall sales. The effect of this strategy is provided by the money flow model in the form of the report shown in Figure 13–14. The report can be printed or displayed on a CRT terminal.

Second simulation—delayed materials payments

It is clear that the above change helped the situation during the first 4 months, but the money drain during May through August increased. The main reason for these negative balances is the high materials expenses for May–July of

Figure 13–14   Effect of production changes on money flow

PROJECTED MONEY FLOW

	JAN	FEB*	MAR*	APR*	MAY	JUN*	JUL*	AUG*	SEP*	OCT*	NOV*	DEC*	TOTAL
MONEY INPUT													
SALES	$500	$500	$300	$300	$300	$400	$400	$400	$1000	$1000	$1000	$500	$6600
MONEY OUTPUT													
MANUFACTURING EXPENSES													
WAGES	44	44	60	60	60	150	150	150	74	74	74	44	984
MATERIALS	120	160	160	160	400	400	400	200	200	200	120	120	2640
OTHER MFG. EXPENSES	46	46	50	50	50	80	80	80	56	56	56	46	696
TOTAL MANUFACTURING EXPENSES	210	250	270	270	510	630	630	430	330	330	250	210	4320
MARKETING AND ADMIN. EXP.	26	26	26	28	28	28	40	40	40	30	30	30	372
NET CHANGE IN MONEY	+264	+224	+4	+2	-238	-258	-270	-70	+630	+640	+720	+260	1908

$400,000 per month. If the manager can shift these expenses to months with high sales revenues, the negative balances can be eliminated or reduced. It probably would not be practical to shift the acquisition of the materials to an earlier or later period, but the payment might be delayed. Materials could be acquired for the May–July production peak, and payment delayed until September–November. Vendors would have to approve a 120-day delay in payment without an interest charge. Assuming that vendors would be receptive to such an arrangement, the finance manager can simulate that solution. The results are illustrated in Figure 13–15.

This strategy, combined with the earlier one of matching production to sales, creates the most balanced money flow of the three examples. The manager might be satisfied with the results and take action to implement the decision. Or, additional alternatives might be tried. For example, the effect of speeding up customer payments by 30 days could be simulated.

The money flow model enables the manager to simulate the effect of alternate strategies to achieve the best use of money available. The finance manager can use the model to evaluate strategies, and then work cooperatively with other functional managers to select and implement the optimum strategy.

Control Subsystem

One of the basic management functions is control. Managers compare actual performance with predefined standards to assure that overall objectives are being met. This occurs on all management levels.

Figure 13–15 Effect of delayed materials payments on cash flow

```
                                PROJECTED MONEY FLOW

                  JAN   FEB•  MAR•  APR•  MAY   JUN•  JUL•  AUG•   SEP•   OCT•   NOV•   DEC•  TOTAL

MONEY INPUT
  SALES          #500  #500  #300  #300  #300  #400  #400  #400  #1000  #1000  #1000  #500  #6600

MONEY OUTPUT
MANUFACTURING
EXPENSES
  WAGES            44    44    60    60    60   150   150   150    74     74     74    44    984
  MATERIALS       200   200   120   120   120   160   160   160   400    400    400   200   2640
  OTHER MFG•
  EXPENSES         46    46    50    50    50    80    80    80    56     56     56    46    696
  TOTAL MANU-
  FACTURING
  EXPENSES        290   290   230   230   230   390   390   390   530    530    530   290   4320

MARKETING AND
ADMIN• EXP•        26    26    26    28    28    28    40    40    40     30     30    30    372

NET CHANGE IN
  MONEY          +184  +184   +44   +42   +42   •18   •30   •30  +430   +440   +440  +180   1908
```

Managers have operational objectives to achieve, such as producing or selling a certain value of items. Managers are given an amount of money to use in meeting these objectives; this money is called the *operating budget* (often simply called the "budget"). The budget usually provides the operating funds for a fiscal (financial) year.

The establishment of the budget is not a completely structured decision. The managers must enter into the process and prepare a budget that will be realistic and yet stimulate efficient operations.

Each organizational unit has its own budget. Together, these budgets comprise the budget of the entire firm. The managers on all levels are evaluated, based not only on how well they meet their operational objectives, but also on how well they stay within their budgets.

The budgeting process

The econometric model discussed earlier can provide a starting point for the budgeting process. The model can produce a forecast of sales that is then revised or approved by top management. The same model, or another one especially prepared for the purpose, can then determine the resource requirements by organizational units to meet the forecast sales level. For example, if the firm is to sell 230,000 units next year, eight new salespersons must be hired, a new drill press must be purchased, two new accounting clerks must be added, etc.

These programmed projections by the model are then evaluated by each of the managers of the units to which they apply. These managers use their

knowledge of the business to increase or decrease (very infrequently) the budgeted amounts. Each manager works in conjunction with his or her superior in arriving at an acceptable budget. Finally, the organizational budgets are approved by chief executive officers. A model of the budgeting process is shown in Figure 13–16. The two-directional arrows between steps 4 and 5 represent the "give and take" that often exists between top management and functional management before the budget is finalized.

Budget reports

A manager thus has an amount of money to spend in a certain way over the time period of a year. Once set, the budget rarely is changed. Each month the manager receives a report from the information system comparing actual financial performance to the budget. A sample of such a report is illustrated in Figure 13–17.

The report is for the Midwestern Region sales office, and shows the performance on eight budget items. The left side of the report shows the performance for the current month, and the right shows the cumulative (year-to-date) performance since the beginning of the fiscal year. Actual expenses are compared with budget and the variance in dollars is shown. Variance also can be shown as a percentage.

This office was below budget by $625 for the month of March, but is $670

Figure 13–16   The budgeting process

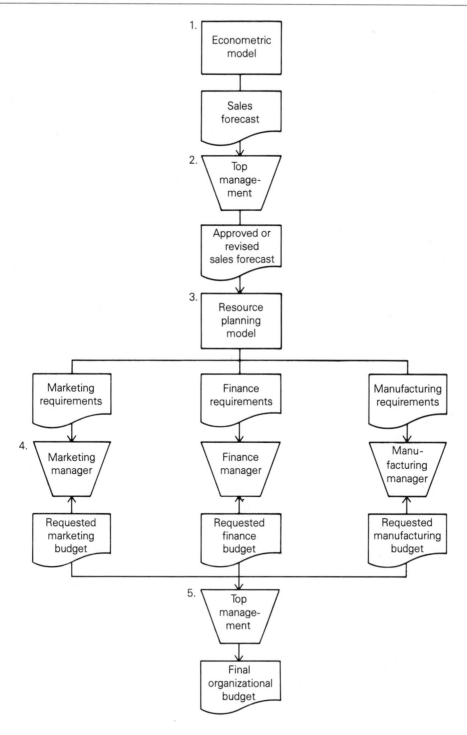

Figure 13–17   Sample budget report for a regional sales office

```
                                    BUDGET REPORT
                                 AS OF JANUARY 31, 1979
                                   MIDWESTERN REGION

                     CURRENT MONTH                    YEAR-TO-DATE
      ITEM        BUDGET   ACTUAL    DOLLARS      BUDGET   ACTUAL    DOLLARS

SALARIES         $23,500  $22,000  -$1,500      $59,000  $54,250  -$4,750
TRAVEL             8,250    9,000  +   750       23,500   28,100  + 4,600
ENTERTAINMENT      1,400    1,635  +   235        4,200    5,100  +   900
TELEPHONE            200       85  -   115          600      225  -   375
RENT                 535      535        0        1,605    1,605        0
FURNITURE              0        0        0          420      505  +    85
SUPPLIES             625      410  -   215        1,875    1,320  -   555
MISC.                400      620  +   220        1,200    1,965  +   765

TOTAL            $34,910  $34,285  -   625      $92,400  $93,070  +   670
```

over budget for the year. The manager can identify items requiring attention
and can take action to keep the expenses under control. If additional information is desired on any of the expense items, another inquiry can be made and
more detailed information can be provided.

Performance ratios

In addition to the budget, the control subsystem produces a number of ratios
that enable management on all levels to compare their performance with
internal standards and also with those accepted as desirable by financial
analysts. Many industries also have standards that member firms seek to attain
if they are to remain competitive. These ratios are computed using summary
totals of accounting transactions. On a periodic basis these totals can be
computed and stored in the data base for use in answering inquiries, or they
can be incorporated in reports.

Three of these ratios are described below.

1. Current ratio—the ratio of assets easily convertible into cash (current
assets) divided by the money the firm presently owes (current liabilities).
Financial analysts believe that this ratio should be 1.0 or greater (assets are
greater than liabilities).

$$\frac{\text{Current assets}}{\text{Current liabilities}}$$

2. Average collection period—the number of days required to collect money owed the firm by its customers. This is a measure of the collection ability of the firm. A period in excess of 30 days is generally undesirable.

$$\frac{\text{Accounts receivable}}{\text{Average daily credit sales}}$$

3. Inventory turnover—the number of times the inventory of finished goods is "turned over" (sold) to account for the firm's annual sales. A high ratio indicates an ability to achieve sales success with a minimum investment in inventory. The value of the goods sold annually is named "cost of goods sold." This figure is divided by the average value of inventory on hand at any given time. This latter figure can be estimated by dividing the order quantity by 2 for each item and adding the safety stock (see page 326). Generally, the higher the ratio the better; but ordering costs can get out of hand if an EOQ is not used.

$$\frac{\text{Cost of goods sold}}{\text{Average inventory value}}$$

Managers control operations by assuring that operations remain within prescribed limits. Both the ratios and the budget serve as yardsticks of acceptable performance.

Summary

The financial information system assists the manager in achieving an efficient flow of money through the firm. The heart of the system is the internal accounting subsystem, providing details of transactions to all three functional information systems. Many of the internal accounting systems are closely interrelated. Three of these systems (order entry, billing, and accounts receivable) are concerned with handling customer orders. These systems communicate with each other, using files of data.

The other input subsystem, financial intelligence, gathers information and data from the environment. Stockholders, the financial community, and the national economy are the primary sources of financial intelligence.

The data and information gathered by the input subsystems are used by the forecasting subsystem to project the status of the firm's environment for longer-term planning. Econometric forecasting models combining advanced mathematical and statistical techniques with files of economic data can be designed by the firm or obtained from service orga-

Table 13–1   Users of the financial information system

User	Forecasting	Subsystem Funds management	Financial control	Accounting
Chief executive officer	X	X	X	X
Vice-president of finance	X	X	X	X
Controller	X	X	X	X
Manager of accounting			X	X
Manager of financial planning	X			X
Director of budgets			X	X

nizations. Many of these models permit management input from terminals.

A second output subsystem, funds management, provides an estimate of the money flow into and out of the firm for the near future. Expected excesses or shortages of funds are flagged before they occur. Alternate strategies can then be considered to realize the best use of available funds. This is a good opportunity to combine modeling with the systems approach for problem solution.

Finally, the control subsystem enables the manager to measure the degree to which the financial objectives are being met. The operating budget and ratios enable this measurement to be accomplished. This application is a rather straightforward use of the computer, for example, comparing accounting data with established standards of acceptable performance.

These subsystems are used by managers throughout the firm. The reason for this popularity is the fact that the subsystems deal with an important resource—money. Money not only is necessary to obtain other resources but provides the basic measure of success.

The chief executive officer makes use of selected information from each of the three output subsystems plus the input subsystems as well.

Top managers in the financial area, the vice-president of finance and the controller, also make use of all subsystems. Lower level financial managers tend to favor those subsystems relating to their area of responsibility. This "match" between subsystems and managers is shown in Table 13–1.

For years, the internal accounting system dominated data-processing activities in the firm. Today, accounting data is regarded as an important input to the MIS. Financial information is being created from both this internal data and that from the environment, using a wide variety of techniques. Managers in all areas, and on all levels, make use of this information in practically every decision-making situation.

Important Terms

Internal Accounting Subsystem

Order Entry System

Billing System

Accounts Receivable System

Order Form

Backorder Quantity

Invoice

Picking Ticket

Receivable Record

Statement

Financial Intelligence Subsystem

Debt Financing

Equity Financing

Forecasting Subsystem

Regression Analysis

Independent Variable

Dependent Variable

Bivariate Regression

Multivariate Regression

Econometric Model

Funds Management Subsystem

Control Subsystem

Operating Budget

Current Ratio

Average Collection Period

Inventory Turnover

Important Concepts

Internal accounting is a subsystem of all three functional information systems.

Although accounting data is important, it has limitations that

must be overcome through the use of data from other sources.

A group of accounting systems work together to process a customer order. These systems are linked by data files, and are linked to both the customers and the manufacturing information system.

The financial intelligence subsystem gathers data and information from the environment (financial community, stockholders, and government) that can be used to control the money flow.

Information to stockholders (annual reports) comes from the data base; information from stockholders seldom is computerized.

Both the government and private financial institutions disseminate information relating to present and future money flow.

Short-term sales forecasting is performed by marketing, and seldom is based on economic data.

Long-term forecasting must consider economic influences, and usually is performed by the financial function.

Forecasting can be performed with a minimum of quantitative analysis, but a large number of quantitative techniques are available.

Both econometric models and data bases of economic data are available from software service organizations.

The funds management subsystem controls money input and output to achieve a balanced flow.

The operating budget originates from the sales forecast and provides the basis for projecting functional resource requirements.

Managers use periodic budget reports and ratios to control financial performance.

Managers throughout the firm use parts of the financial information system to control financial performance within their areas of responsibility.

Questions

1 What are the limitations of accounting data.

2 Identify the input and the output of the following systems:

Input	System	Output
	Order entry	
	Billing	
	Accounts receivable	

3 Who prepares the order form?

4 In what ways does the computer assist in processing orders?

5 What is the minimum data that must be entered into the computer in order for it to process an order?

6 What is the difference between an invoice and a statement?

7 Is "sales" always the dependent variable? Explain your answer.

8 Could a bank use an econometric model? For what? What about a supermarket chain? What about a hardware store?

9 If annual profit is the excess of revenue over expenses, why is it a good practice to balance money inflow and outflow?

10 What manager, or managers, in the firm would likely use the money flow simulation? *Hint:* Look for these people in Figure 10–1.

11 The final form of the money flow simulation (Figure 13–15) still contains some negative flows in June, July, and August. Can anything else be simulated that could remove these negative flows?

12 When the sales forecast is used as a basis for the operational budget, does the forecast represent what marketing thinks it can sell or what top management wants it to sell?

Problems

1 Go to your library and search through the current business periodicals on display. List those titles that you feel would provide a source of financial intelligence information.

2 Draw a graph similar to Figures 13–11 and 13–13, showing the data presented in Figure 13–15.

3 Prepare a regression equation that a student could use to forecast a course grade. The grade (G) will be based on four tests (X_1 through X_4), each representing an equal part of the grade.

4 Calculate a current ratio for Alcoa, using 1977 data from Figure 9–2.

5 If Alcoa averages $22.5 million per day in credit sales, what is its average collection period? (Use Figure 9–2.)

6 Calculate the inventory turnover for Product PZ04 at Pickwick Papers, Inc. when:

$$\text{Cost of goods sold} = \$100 \text{ million}$$
$$\text{Safety stock} \quad\quad = \$ \ \ 5 \text{ million}$$
$$\text{Order quantity} \quad = \$ \ 30 \text{ million}$$

Part Five

Development and Control

At this point, three major topics have been discussed. They include the theoretical basis of systems, computing equipment, and functional uses of the computer. Only one major topic remains: how a firm can develop an MIS. This remaining topic is the subject of Part Five.

The following four chapters describe the process of MIS development. As this development unfolds, two key points must be understood. First, the process is accomplished in steps. Second, both the users of the information and the information specialists work together.

The organization of the chapters is intended to convey this step-by-step process. Each chapter deals with a major step. Planning the MIS project is described in Chapter 14. The analysis and design work leading to the specifications of the MIS is the subject of Chapter 15. The implementation of the MIS in the firm is treated in Chapter 16. The control of the operating MIS concludes the discussion, in Chapter 17.

Therefore, the MIS has a life cycle consisting of four major phases. But, unlike other life cycles, MIS development is a never-ending affair. Attainment of an MIS does not mean the end of management attention to the subject. At some future time the newly attained MIS will become deficient and the process will have to be repeated. This circular effect is shown in Model 1, on the following page.

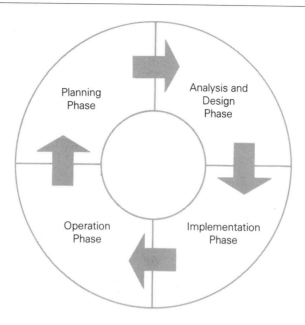

The second key point is emphasized in the following chapters with a series of graphical models. Each model illustrates how the responsible managers work with the members of the information systems staff. The diagram of Model 2 is a summary of the relationship described in more detail by the separate models.

Upon completion of this final part, the most important material relating to the MIS will have been presented. The reader will have an introductory description of the MIS in terms of its theoretical basis, how it uses computing and communication equipment, how it is used by managers, and how it is developed. There is much more to learn about MIS than the material presented on these pages. But, that additional knowledge will come later as the reader completes the educational process and becomes an active part of an information system.

Model 2   The cooperative development process

Phase	Responsible Development Manager	Information Specialists
Planning	Plan	Support
Analysis and design	Control	Conduct system study
Implementation	Control	Implement
Operation	Control	Operate

Chapter 14

Information Systems Development:
The Planning Phase

Importance of Planning

Chapter 2 described the management functions identified by Henri Fayol. As explained, these are activities in which every manager engages, and they include planning, organizing, staffing, directing, and controlling. All are important, but the first, planning, is the key to satisfactory performance of the others. For this reason, managers have learned that time spent in planning pays dividends at the time the other functions are performed.

The efforts of a firm to implement an MIS represent a large scale activity involving many people and facilities, much money and equipment, and considerable time. The MIS project can require as many resources as the development of a new product, construction of a new plant, and entry in a new market. Therefore, the MIS project should receive the same management attention as any expensive, time-consuming project.

Difficulty of the Task

This chapter deals with the planning that must be done *after* a decision is made to consider implementation of an MIS and *before* work begins to design and implement such a system. It is important that this planning be accomplished before work on the project actually starts. If not, it is likely that much of the work will be misdirected and have to be redone. Such an event delays the time in which the organization can realize the benefits of the MIS, and adds to the cost (that will be great, even when the work is performed efficiently).

The difficulty of the development will depend on several factors. While there are many influences, three appear especially critical. These are (1) the attitude of the employees toward the MIS, (2) the availability of good objec-

Figure 14–1   Difficulty of the MIS development

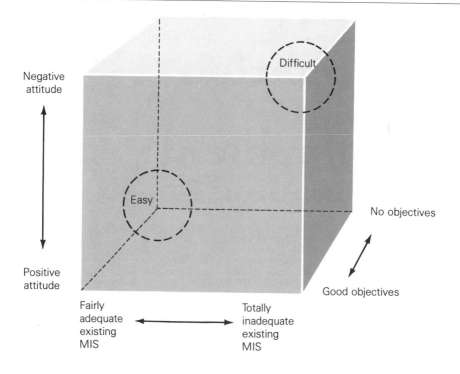

tives for the firm, and (3) the degree of adequacy of the existing information system. These three influences are illustrated in Figure 14–1.

When the firm's employees have a positive attitude toward the MIS, when the existing system is fairly adequate, and when the firm has good objectives, the development can be relatively easy. This fact does not reduce the importance of planning, but should reduce the time that management spends on it. When the three conditions do not exist, the development will be difficult and much time must be devoted to planning.

Responsibility for the MIS Project

Someone within the organization must have overall responsibility for the MIS *project.* This will *not* be the manager, such as the vice-president of information systems,[1] who has responsibility for the computer. Rather, it will be a high-level manager representing the users of the information system output.

---

1. In this and the following chapters, the title *vice-president of information systems* will be used to identify that individual having overall responsibility for the firm's MIS. It is recognized that not all firms establish this responsibility at the vice-president level.

There is nothing wrong with the president of the firm having this responsibility. In fact, that would be the ideal situation. The MIS will provide information needed by all types of managers on all levels. The importance of this system to the success of the firm is such that the president's involvement is justified. However, the president might not have the time to devote to the MIS project that it deserves. In this case, the president delegates primary authority for achieving the MIS to a key top-level executive.

Positions within a firm lending themselves to the type of direction needed are the executive vice-president and administrative vice-president. Generally, a functionally oriented executive, such as the vice-president of finance, should not be selected as that approach could impede achievement of a total MIS serving all areas of the firm. The executive could be tempted to devote primary attention to his or her own area, to the disadvantage of the others. This is only a general rule, however, and must be considered in light of the management resource available.

The *executive vice-president* usually is the senior executive with overall responsibility for assuring that the firm meets its operational and tactical objectives. This assignment frees the president to concentrate on long-range strategic planning. The executive vice-president therefore can represent *all* of the interests of the firm in terms of needs of both its physical system and its conceptual information system. And, since the information system should support the physical system, the executive vice-president has the best understanding of these total information needs.

If the firm does not have an executive vice-president or if that person cannot assume responsibility for the MIS project for one reason or another, the logical second choice is the *administrative vice-president*. This person occupies a staff position responsible for providing administrative support to the entire firm. However, no responsibility or authority exists for the physical system. This person's scope of activity, therefore, is more limited than that of the executive vice-president. But, the administrative vice-president can represent the firm as a whole, in terms of meeting its administrative and information needs. Figure 14–2 shows where these positions generally are located within a firm. Solid lines indicate superior/subordinate relationships. The dotted line indicates the staff relationship of the administrative vice-president to the other executives.

In this discussion it will be assumed that the executive vice-president has primary responsibility for the MIS project. *This title is used only to simplify the discussion; in no way is it implied that this individual should have, or does have, responsibility in all cases. Designation of this responsibility depends entirely on the conditions within a particular firm.*

MIS responsibilities of the executive vice-president

The executive vice-president is responsible for determining what the MIS will do, and then for assuring that it is done. This task involves communication with other executives and managers in the firm to determine their *general* information needs. The executive vice-president, assisted by the vice-president

Figure 14–2   Executive positions within a firm

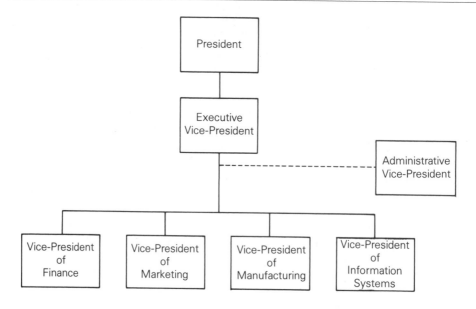

of information systems, meets with the president and the functional vice-presidents to determine the major subsystems of the MIS. This information then is augmented with more specific details provided by lower level managers.

MIS responsibilities of the functional executives

The vice-presidents of finance, marketing, and manufacturing do not escape involvement in the MIS project. First, they communicate with the president, executive vice-president, and vice-president of information systems in developing the overall description of the MIS. Then, the functional vice-presidents work with the vice-president of information systems in developing the overall description of their functional information systems.

MIS responsibilities of the vice-president of information systems

During the preimplementation period, when the firm is considering an MIS, the vice-president of information systems assists the other managers in identifying their information needs. When the decision is made to implement an MIS, the vice-president of information systems directs the efforts of the information systems staff in design and implementation. Once the MIS is implemented, and its performance approved by the executive vice-president, the vice-president of information systems is responsible for maintaining the performance of the MIS.

The responsibilities of these executives are summarized in Table 14–1.

Table 14–1   Executive responsibility for the MIS

Executive	Preimplementation period	Implementation period	Postimplementation period
President		Final responsibility for the MIS	
Executive vice-president	Primary responsibility for the design and implementation of the MIS		Approve the perfor- mance of the MIS
Vice-president of finance	Design of overall MIS. Design of financial information system	Implementation of financial information system	Make suggestions for improvement
Vice-president of marketing	Design of overall MIS. Design of marketing information system	Implementation of marketing information system	Make suggestions for improvement
Vice-president of manufacturing	Design of overall MIS. Design of manufactur- ing information system	Implementation of manufac- turing information system	Make suggestions for improvement
Vice-president of information systems	Design of overall MIS. Design of functional information systems	Implementation of the overall MIS and its functional information systems	Operation and mainte- nance of the MIS

The MIS committee

Most firms make liberal use of committees. Committees exist on practically every management level. They are used to pool knowledge that is to be directed at a specific project or problem and to improve communication.

The MIS project is the type where an executive committee is justified. Many companies have followed this approach. The membership of the *MIS committee* includes the executive vice-president, the functional vice-presi- dents, and the vice-president of information systems. The executive vice- president is chairperson and keeps the president informed of the committee activities. The other members serve in an advisory capacity.

The initial responsibility of the committee is to agree on what the MIS should do, in general terms, and to approve expenditure of funds for the development of the project. During the project, the committee monitors the progress. Once the MIS is implemented, the committee formally approves its performance in terms of meeting its objectives. When such a committee is not formed, these responsibilities are held by the key executive assigned to the project, such as the executive vice-president.

Summary of MIS responsibility

Responsibility for design and implementation of the MIS therefore exists in two general areas: (1) managers who will use the MIS output, and (2) the information systems staff who will create the MIS. In addition, responsibility exists on several levels dealing with the overall MIS, the functional subsystems, and parts of the functional subsystems.

A top executive, the president or executive vice-president, has responsibility for the overall effort and is assisted by the other managers who will use the MIS output. The vice-president of information systems lends support when and where needed. The implementation of an MIS, therefore, is a team effort.

Benefits of Planning the MIS

Managers engage in planning to facilitate achievement of certain goals, such as the development of an MIS. Managers expect the time invested in planning to pay off in benefits not realized when planning is bypassed or done poorly. In terms of the MIS project, good planning is expected to have the following benefits:

1. Identify tasks necessary for goal achievement. The scope of the project is defined. Which activities or subsystems are involved? Which are not? *In general terms*, what types and amounts of work will be necessary? This information provides management with an initial idea of how many resources will be required.

2. Recognize potential problem areas. Good planning will point out things that might go wrong. It is better to know of potential problems than to wait for them to appear. In most cases, the problems can be eliminated before they become serious, or the project can be planned so that its success is not impaired by existence of the problem constraints.

3. Arrange sequence of tasks. Most likely, hundreds of separate tasks will be necessary to implement an MIS. These tasks are arranged in a logical sequence based on information priorities and the need for efficiency. For example, a sales forecasting model is of such importance to the firm that its implementation would be scheduled earlier than another of lesser importance, such as a warehouse location model. Also, the sequence of tasks has an impact on efficiency. One task usually follows another. The computer should not be scheduled for delivery until the room has been prepared, as an example.

Table 14–2 Alternative approaches to planning

Type of firm	Objective orientation	Problem orientation
New	Establish objectives and design an MIS to assist in their achievement.	
Existing	Evaluate existing objectives and improve when needed. Use as a basis for MIS design.	Identify problems and design an MIS to assist in their solution.

4. Provide a basis for control. If the executive vice-president is to have control over the project, the manner by which that control will be achieved and maintained must be identified in advance. Certain project goals and methods of performance measurement must be specified. When the time comes for company resources to be directed at the MIS effort, the executive vice-president, assisted by the other managers, will have a good understanding of what is to be done, who will do it, and when it will be accomplished.

These planning benefits enable the manager to understand what is to be done. The project can then be executed in the most efficient manner and the manager can maintain continuous control.

Alternative Planning Approaches

There are two basic ways to initiate an MIS project. One is to begin with objectives and one is to begin with problems. A new firm will begin with objectives, as there has been no opportunity to encounter problems. An existing firm, however, can take either approach. Table 14–2 presents both approaches.

The new firm has no choice. An objective orientation must be followed. Objectives are established for the firm, and an MIS is designed to help the firm meet those objectives.

The existing firm does not merely select between the two approaches; it follows the route dictated by the situation. (See Figure 14–3.)

If an existing firm does not have good objectives, these must be defined before proceeding further with MIS planning. The question is then asked if the firm is meeting these objectives. If so, there is no need to develop a new MIS. The existing one is doing its job.

When the firm is not meeting its objectives, then it must choose which

Figure 14–3   Determination of MIS approach

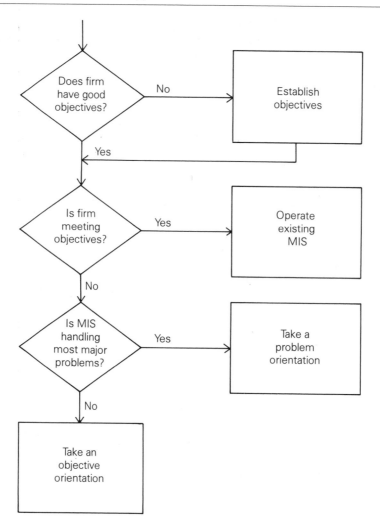

path to follow. The choice depends on how well the MIS is handling most of the major problems encountered. If the MIS is doing a good job, a comprehensive redesign is unnecessary—the existing system need only be modified to correct its minor flaws. If, on the other hand, the MIS has serious faults, a fresh approach following an objective orientation is needed.

Objective orientation

There is a direct relationship between what the MIS is to do and what the firm is attempting to accomplish. What the MIS is to do—its performance criteria—is determined by objectives. This relationship is illustrated in Figure 14–4.

Figure 14–4   Relationship between objectives, information needs, and MIS performance criteria.

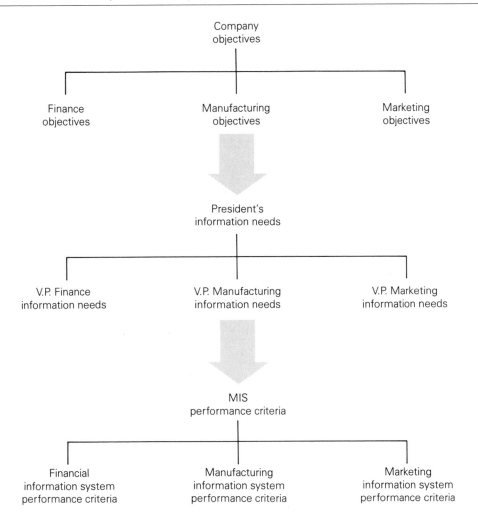

The figure shows that the information needs of the managers on different levels determine the performance criteria. And, the information needs are determined by the objectives that exist on each management level. Information need, therefore, is an intervening variable connecting the objectives with what the MIS is to do.

Problem orientation

If a firm designs an MIS to solve particular problems, it does not do so in the absence of objectives. A good set of objectives must exist and a physical system for achieving those objectives must be present. The situation is one where specific problems are preventing the firm from achieving its objectives. The assumption is that the problems can be solved with the right kind of information. It then is up to the MIS to provide that information—the performance criteria.

Similarities of the approaches

While the point of origin for the two approaches is different, there should be no difference in the end product. An MIS should be created to support the firm's objectives. And, regardless of the approach, the performance criteria for the MIS are based on objective attainment, as shown in Figure 14–4.

Further, it should be pointed out that redesign of an old MIS requires that the same steps be taken as the creation of a new one. The only difference is the scope of the effort. A redesign effort limits the scope of the project to only that part of the MIS being improved. In some cases, redesign can be more demanding than a fresh approach. This is true when the old system suffers from many weaknesses that must be identified before improvement can be attempted. Also, it generally is often more difficult to cut over from an old system to a revised one than to a completely new one.

In the discussion that follows, it is assumed that a completely new MIS is to be designed and implemented.

Planning Steps

The executive vice-president and the vice-president of information systems (assisted by the information systems staff) work together in a series of steps to plan the MIS project. The information specialists support the executive vice-president during the initial stages, prepare a study project proposal for approval, and work jointly with the executive vice-president to establish a control mechanism. These steps, illustrated in Figure 14–5, represent the systems approach to planning an MIS. The seven steps provide a finer breakdown of the first step of the systems approach, "define the problem," as discussed in Chapter 4.

1. *Recognize the problem.* This step is taken when a problem orientation is being followed. When an objective orientation is followed, the process begins with step 3.

It is the responsibility of the executive vice-president or functional vice-presidents to recognize the problem, or problems. The problems affect his or her organizational unit, but they need not necessarily originate there. Problems in one area may originate in another. This means that managers of the different areas must work together to solve problems that cross departmental boundaries.

A manager can become aware of a problem in various ways. Simply encountering one during the course of the day-to-day activities is an *informal*

Figure 14–5   Steps in the planning process

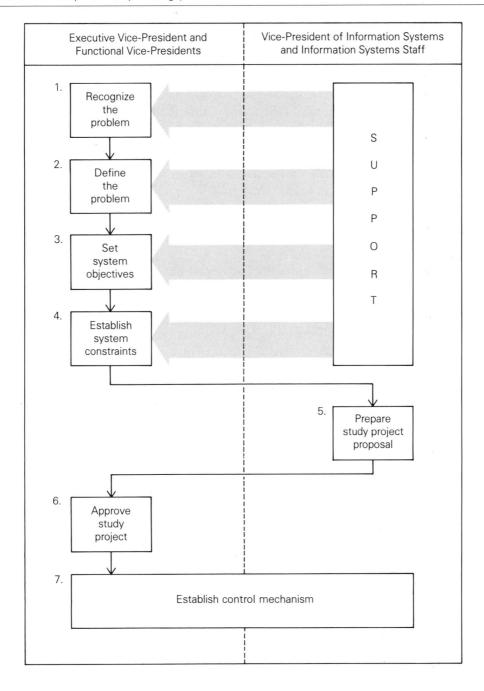

approach. The manager does not actively look for problems, but neither does he or she try to avoid them. Also, the manager has no set procedure for identifying problems. Many problems are encountered in such an informal manner.

It is possible to follow a particular procedure that will identify problems when, or before, they occur. Use of such a procedure represents a *formal* approach. This assumes the manager has some type of information system that can identify problems. Essentially, this information system advises the manager of actual performance of subsystems within the firm. When this actual performance varies from the plan by a significant amount, the manager initiates a problem-solving action.

The manager also can have different attitudes toward problem identification. A problem doesn't always deal with something bad. It can relate to something that is good, but could, or should, be better. This is the underlying principle of management by exception and represents a *positive attitude* toward problem recognition. When the manager is concerned only with things going wrong, the attitude is a *negative* one.

2. Define the problem. Once the manager (the executive vice-president or functional vice-president) realizes that a problem exists, he or she must understand it well enough to pursue a solution. At this point the manager doesn't attempt to gather all of the information describing the problem. That would require a full-scale systems analysis effort. The manager is interested only in understanding the problem well enough to direct an effort aimed at solution. As a minimum, the manager should know where the problem exists. Which management level is involved? Perhaps there is more than one level. Which functional area is involved? Again, the problem may exist in more than one area. In addition, the manager should know which system or subsystem is deficient and what the general difficulty is.

Most likely the manager will be assisted by the analyst in defining the problem in these terms. Once there is agreement on the problem, its location, and its general nature, the findings should be put in writing. This written description can serve as a useful guide for the work that follows.

3. Set system objectives. The objectives the MIS should achieve (its performance criteria) are specified next. The functional vice-presidents play key roles in identifying these objectives, since the MIS should meet the needs of their areas. Lower level managers most likely will be called upon to participate at this point. An MIS must be designed to meet the needs of the potential users.

4. Establish system constraints. The new MIS will operate under many constraints. Some are imposed by the environment, such as the demand by the government for certain tax reports and the demand by customers for billing information. Other constraints are imposed by the firm's management, such as limits on computer cost or response times.

It is important that these constraints be established before work on the MIS actually begins. In this way, the MIS design will fall within the constraints. Otherwise, the system might have to be redesigned to conform to the constraints at the time they are made known. These initial constraints will be supplemented with others as more is learned about the new system.

5. Prepare study project proposal. Before a new MIS can be designed, a systems study must be conducted. This study will provide the *detailed* basis for the design of the new system in terms of what it does and how it does it.

The systems study will be conducted by the analyst or a team of analysts and will require several weeks or months of effort. As such, the study will require a substantial outlay of cash. The executive vice-president must approve this expense and should have some basis or support for the go-ahead decision. The study project proposal serves this purpose.

Figure 14–6 is a sample outline of the study proposal. Both the executive vice-president and the vice-president of information systems realize at this point that the report does not offer a complete treatment of the topics. However, it does represent the best information available at this early stage.

Sections 1 through 3 of the proposal are developed jointly by the information specialists and the executive vice-president during the first four steps of the planning.

The information specialists develop sections 4 through 7, using their general knowledge of systems work, their experience with the firm, and personal interviews with the top managers in each functional area. The purpose of the interviews is to identify the subsystems of the functional information systems and the major models to be included in each subsystem.

Section 4 recognizes that there are several alternative system solutions. Each is described in general terms. The specialists then select the one appearing to be the best suited for the firm. The reasons for this selection are included in section 5 along with an explanation of what will be needed. Section 6 describes the effects, both positive and negative, on the firm and its operations. Section 7 presents a general implementation plan.

Section 8 relates only to the system study project leading to the MIS. The system study is the next step in the development process, and the proposal represents a request to take that step.

6. Approve study project. In preparing the proposal, the analyst must be careful not to "sell" an unjustified study. The facts should be reported honestly, with equal attention given to the reasons why the study should not be conducted and to weaknesses in the design. The executive vice-president must decide whether to continue the project, and this decision must be based on the best information available.

The executive vice-president weighs the pros and cons of the proposed project and the system design and takes one of three actions. The first question the executive vice-president asks is, "Do I have enough information?" If the answer is "no," the analyst is told what additional information is needed.

Figure 14-6   The study project proposal

1. Introduction—reason for the proposal

2. Problem definition

3. System objectives and constraints

4. Possible alternatives

5. Recommended course of action
   a. Tasks to be accomplished
   b. Resource requirements
   c. Time schedule
   d. Cost recap

6. Anticipated results
   a. Organizational impact
   b. Operational impact
   c. Financial impact

7. General implementation plan

8. Study project objectives
   a. Tasks
   b. Budget

9. Summary

When this information is obtained, the review process is repeated. The executive vice-president will not reach a final decision on the project until all of the necessary information is at hand.

Once the executive vice-president feels that sufficient information is available, the "go/no go" decision is made (Figure 14–7). If the decision is "go," the project proceeds to the study phase. If the decision is "no go," both the executive vice-president and the information specialists turn their attention to other matters of importance.

As the manager considers approval of the project, two key questions must be answered:

1. *Will the proposed system solve identified problems, or enable the firm to meet its objectives?* These are the performance criteria. This will be the basis for evaluating the performance of the MIS once it is implemented; it also should be the basis for evaluating the proposed MIS.

2. *Is the proposed study project the best way to determine the specific*

Figure 14–7 The "go/no-go" decision

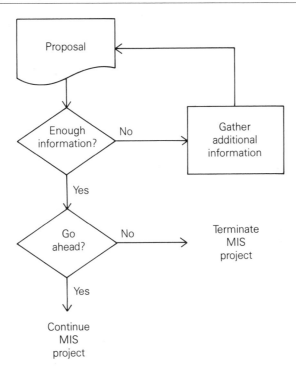

design of the proposed MIS? There is no pat answer to this question. The executive vice-president must be assured that the information specialists have considered all of the feasible approaches to the study effort. If the executive vice-president is to have this assurance, a good understanding of the MIS concept and computer implementation is necessary. One reason why managers must learn about computer processing is that they must approve the expenditure of large sums of money for computer projects. This approval cannot rest on an insufficient understanding of the subject or an uninformed acceptance of another person's recommendation.

The purpose of this textbook and the course of study in which it is being used is to help the students of management and computer science develop the basic understanding necessary to perform this and other related tasks.

*7. **Establish a control mechanism.*** Before the study effort begins, the executive vice-president must take steps to establish control over the project. This executive has overall responsibility for the final system and the efforts leading to it, and responsibility cannot be delegated to the information specialists. The executive vice-president must assure that all persons involved in the project—information specialists and others as well—perform in the prescribed manner.

Project control must be developed in phases. Complete control depends on a detailed specification of the work to be done, and no such specification exists at this point. Only a general specification exists, but it is adequate for establishing an initial control. Once a detailed specification is accomplished, complete control can be achieved.

General Project Control

The executive vice-president and the vice-president of information systems must work together closely in establishing the control mechanism. A thorough understanding of the task ahead is necessary, and this can be provided by the vice-president of information systems.

Throughout the project, both executives must receive progress reports showing how actual performance compares with the plan. For this to be possible, two tasks must be completed before the end of the planning phase. First, performance standards must be determined; second, a progress reporting system must be created.

1. Performance standards.   Standards of acceptable performance are established for three dimensions of the activity: time, cost, and quality. At this stage, these standards can only be established in general terms. This especially is true for the standard of quality. What the executives seek at this point is some control over the first part of the project. Rough standards can serve this purpose and can be refined as soon as more is known about the work to be done and the expected end-product.

2. Progress reporting.   The executive vice-president must remain up-to-date concerning progress of the MIS project. It is the responsibility of the vice-president of information systems to keep the executive vice-president current, and this is done through scheduled meetings. The meetings usually are held weekly, but can be supplemented by special sessions as the need arises. The meetings take the form of progress reports by the vice-president of information systems. Quite often, visual aids are used to acquaint those in attendance with what has been accomplished, what has not been accomplished and why, upcoming activities, and possible trouble spots. As a minimum, the meetings include the executive vice-president and the vice-president of information systems. If an MIS committee is formed, that group is in attendance. At times managers from functional areas and members of the information systems staff are invited to participate. The meetings employ management by exception in that the managers do not dwell on things going as planned, but devote their attention to critical areas.

Detailed Project Control

Once the basic components of the MIS have been specified, it is necessary to be more detailed about the work to be done. As much detail as possible must be assembled on what is to be done, who is to do it, and when it is to be done.

1. *What is to be done?* The preliminary planning meetings between the top managers and the members of the information systems staff should produce a list of jobs for the MIS to perform. For example, in the marketing information system the jobs could include:

> *Product Subsystem*
>   New Product Evaluation Model
>   Product Deletion Model
>
> *Place Subsystem*
>   Warehouse Location Model
>   Warehouse Layout Model
>
> *Promotion Subsystem*
>   Territory Assignment Model
>   Advertising Media Selection Model
>
> *Pricing Subsystem*
>   Pricing Model

2. *Who is to do it?* The vice-president of information systems next decides who will be responsible for designing each of the subsystem models. For example, in the marketing information system, analyst A might be assigned to the two product models, analyst B to the place models and the advertising media selection model, and analyst C to the sales territory assignment model and the pricing model.

It is possible that an adequate systems staff does not exist to do all of the specified work. In that case, new employees must be recruited and hired. If so, the general design specifications identify the type, or types, of employees needed. As an example, the two warehouse models and the advertising media selection models likely will use linear programming. If a linear programming specialist is not presently on the staff, one will have to be added. Therefore, personnel are assembled who have the skills necessary to achieve the MIS.

3. *When will it be done?* It is necessary to establish a time schedule for the MIS project. Certain things will have to be done at specific times. For example, new computing equipment might have to be scheduled for delivery. The firm will want the computer delivered when it can be used—not before and not after. If a new disk file is required for the customer master file, delivery should coincide with completion of work in building the file and in debugging those programs using the contents of the file.

Assignment of responsibility

The project schedule is based on the time required to do the different tasks. Once the tasks have been identified and assigned to persons or teams, an estimate can be made of the time required to do each subtask. As an example, the following subtasks might be required to develop the product deletion model:

1 Identify criteria for deleting products.
2 Identify information requirements of the manager making the deletion decision.
3 Identify input data necessary to produce the required information.
4 Prepare a program flowchart[2] of the computer processing to convert input data to information output.
5 Code the program.
6 Test the program.
7 Obtain manager approval of program performance.
8 Implement the model.

The vice-president of information systems then determines who will perform each of the subtasks, and how long each should take. Table 14–3 illustrates how responsibility is distributed for the product deletion model, and how time estimates are made for each subtask.

The assignment of responsibility is usually not too difficult. The nature of the system to be designed and the nature of the design work specify personnel or types of personnel that should have the responsibility. The estimation of time duration is something else. At this stage of the project, these estimates can be only broad approximations. They are based on the experience of the people involved. The vice-president of information systems and the systems analysis staff are expected to provide this experience. For example, it might be estimated that the product deletion model will require approximately 750 program instructions. If work standards indicate that a programmer can code 50 instructions per day, the total time duration should be 15 working days.

Monitoring project progress

Once the MIS project has been defined in terms of the models or programs to be prepared, who is responsible for them, and when the work should be done,

---

2. Flowcharting is explained in the Appendix.

Table 14–3   Detailed subtask planning

	Functional System: Marketing Subsystem: Product Model: Product Deletion		
Subtask	**Responsibility**	**Time Estimate (person days)**
1. Identify deletion criteria	Systems analyst and product manager	5
2. Identify output information requirements	Systems analyst and product manager	3
3. Identify input data requirements	Systems analyst	4
4. Prepare program flowchart	Systems analyst	5
5. Code program	Programmer	15
6. Test program	Programmer and operations staff	10
7. Approve program performance	Product manager and vice-president of marketing	3
8. Implement model	Operations staff	5

the executive vice-president has a basis for control. The next step is to document the project plan in a manner facilitating control as the work is accomplished.

There are a number of documentation techniques. The one selected is the one with which the executive vice-president and the vice-president of information systems feel most comfortable. One technique is the *Gantt chart*, or bar chart, showing when work on each subtask is to be performed. Figure 14–8 is an example.

The Gantt chart illustrates how the work on the seven marketing models is phased over time. During the progress report meetings, the managers can use charts such as this to compare actual performance with planned performance. These charts make it easier to "see" what is happening.

Figure 14–8   Bar chart of marketing information system activity

Activity	Time Period										
	1	2	3	4	5	6	7	8	9	10	11
1. Approve system composition	▓										
2. Create product evaluation model		▓	▓								
3. Create product deletion model				▓	▓						
4. Create warehouse location model		▓	▓								
5. Create warehouse layout model				▓	▓						
6. Create territory assignment model			▓	▓							
7. Create media selection model								▓	▓		
8. Create pricing model					▓	▓	▓				
9. Approve system performance											▓

The main shortcoming of the bar chart is that it doesn't show how the activities are interrelated. It doesn't show that work on the seven models (steps 2–8) cannot begin until the system composition is approved (step 1). Also, it doesn't show that the same information systems specialist is going to create both of the product models (steps 2 and 3).

These interrelationships can be represented by another documentation technique—*network analysis.* In network analysis, activities are represented by arrows, interconnected to show how one relates to another. In Figure 14–9, the bars in the Gantt chart have been redrawn as interconnecting arrows.

The network diagram shows that activity 9 cannot be started until activities 3, 7, and 8 are completed. Activity 3 cannot be started until activity 2 is completed, and so on.

An added bonus of network analysis is that data for each activity can be entered in the computer and a "calendar" printed showing when each activity can be started and completed.[3] The computer even can print a diagram such as that in Figure 14–9. This is especially easy with a graph plotter, but a line printer also can be used.

---

3. Data for each activity includes the identification of leading and following activities, and estimated activity completion time.

Figure 14–9 Network diagram of marketing information system activity

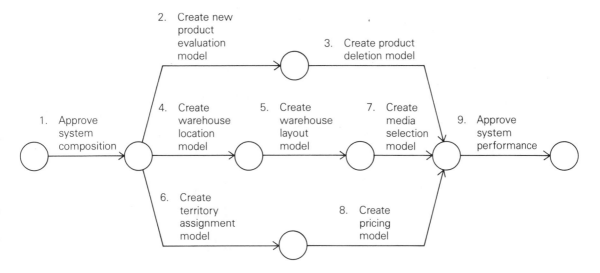

When the computer determines the dates for each activity, it also can identify the critical path through the network. The *critical path* is that series of activities requiring the greatest time to complete. The critical path in Figure 14–9 is comprised of activities 1, 4, 5, 7, and 9. This is based on the time requirements used in Figure 14–8. Identification of the critical path enables the executive vice-president and the vice-president of information systems to focus attention on the most critical activities throughout the project period.

Figure 14–9 only shows a small portion of the activities involved in an MIS project. The value of network analysis increases as the project becomes complex. Figure 14–10 (on the following page) is a network diagram of an MIS project, and the extent of the interrelationships of the activities can be seen.

As with the Gantt charts, the network diagram and associated computer information can be used to monitor the progress of the MIS effort. These documents provide a good basis for the discussion of progress at the regularly scheduled meetings of the managers.

Summary

This chapter has been concerned with planning. It is necessary that responsibility for planning the MIS project be placed in the hands of a top executive. This executive must understand what is to be done so that the needed resources can be allocated, and the effort controlled.

Figure 14–10 (a) Network diagram of an MIS project. (b) Network schedule. (Courtesy of Electronic Data Systems)

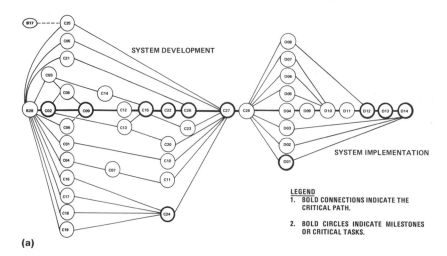

(a)

TASK NUMBER AND SHORT TITLE	DATES START	COMPLETE	MAN-DAYS
C01 INITIATE PROCUREMENT PROCESS	28MAR79	06APR79	5
C02 CODE SYSTEM MODIFICATIONS	30OCT78	11JAN79	650
C03 PROVIDE TEST DATA	27DEC78	11JAN79	15
C04 CONTACT CLIENTS	21FEB79	28FEB79	10
C05 CONDUCT INSTRUCTION	29MAR79	12APR79	40
C06 TESTING DOCUMENTATION CRITERIA	28DEC79	11JAN79	16
C07 PROCUREMENT SCHEDULE	28FEB79	05MAR79	6
C08 CONSTRUCT UNIT TESTING FILES	11JAN79	18JAN79	15
C09 CONDUCT PROGRAM & UNIT TESTING	11JAN79	08FEB79	80
C10 VERIFY ON-SITE READINESS	06APR79	12APR79	4
C11 PROCUREMENT TRAINING	05MAR79	12APR79	36
C12 TRANSFER SYSTEM	08FEB79	22FEB79	50
C13 PREPARE OPERATIONS DOCUMENT	08FEB79	22FEB79	45
C14 PREPARE SYSTEM TEST FILES	08FEB79	22FEB79	20
C15 CONDUCT SYSTEM TESTING	22FEB79	22MAR79	140
C16 CLERICAL OPERATIONS TRAINING	12MAR79	09APR79	30
C17 FINANCIAL ACCOUNTING TRAINING	22MAR79	09APR79	41
C18 PRODUCTION TRAINING	02APR79	09APR79	12
C19 DISTRIBUTION TRAINING	26MAR79	09APR79	10
C20 DATA PROCESSING TRAINING	29MAR79	12MAR79	20
C21 ACCEPTANCE TEST GUIDLINES	19MAR79	22MAR79	6
C22 APPROVE TEST RESULTS	16MAR79	22MAR79	2
C23 APPROVE SOURCE PROGRAMS & JCL	05APR79	12APR79	5
C24 APPROVE USER TRAINING	09APR79	12APR79	3
C25 IMPLEMENT ORGANIZATION CHANGES	29MAR79	12APR79	10
C26 CONDUCT ACCEPTANCE TESTING	22MAR79	12APR79	140
C27 APPROVE ACCEPTANCE TEST RESULTS	12APR79	18APR79	6
C28 MODIFY PROJECT SCHEDULE	13APR79	18APR79	2

(b)

It is important to understand why planning and controlling the MIS project are the responsibility of a top executive. The size of the project is such that high level attention is necessary. The responsible person should not be the manager of the computer facility, but should be someone who can represent the users of the MIS output. The only purpose of the MIS is to help managers manage. For this reason, a manager, or managers, should decide what the MIS will do and assure that it is done. The ideal person to have this responsibility is a top executive with total-firm interests and involvement. Such a person is the executive vice-president.

Planning an MIS project requires some knowledge of what the MIS will do. Some assumptions must be made about system design, and these provide the basis for the planning. As more information is gained about design, the plans can be updated. Before the actual analysis and design efforts get underway, the plans are based on some general assumptions.

As a minimum, the managers must know whether the MIS will be designed to solve specific problems or to help the firm meet certain objectives. Then, it must be decided if the existing MIS is to be redesigned or a completely new one created. Discussions with functional vice-presidents then identify the subsystems of each functional information system. With this basic knowledge, the executive vice-president or the MIS committee can set the specifications and authorize a systems study. The study, described in the next chapter, will shed new light on the MIS and will provide the basis for continuing the project.

Planning an MIS project requires that the executive vice-president and the vice-president of information systems follow seven steps. The first four determine the objectives of the MIS and identify its constraints. These steps are the responsibility of the executive vice-president, but assistance is provided by the vice-president of information systems. A study project proposal is then prepared that serves as the basis for proceeding with a systems study. If this proposal is approved, a control mechanism for the project is established jointly by the two vice-presidents. Each task is subdivided into subtasks, responsibility is assigned, and time estimates are made. These details provide the basis for project control. Graphical techniques, such as Gantt charts and network diagrams, provide a useful means of tracking progress of the MIS effort.

Important Terms

Vice-President of Information
  Systems

Executive Vice-President

Administrative Vice-President

MIS Committee

Objective Orientation

Problem Orientation

Informal Problem Recognition   Gantt Chart

Formal Problem Recognition   Network Analysis

Study Project Proposal   Critical Path

Important Concepts

Development of an MIS can vary in difficulty, depending on the situation.

Control of the MIS project must be established at the top management level, with either a single person or a committee.

Implementation of an MIS requires the cooperative efforts of both the managers who will use the system and the information specialists.

Planning takes time, but it provides benefits that make the time spent worthwhile.

Without a plan, control can be achieved only by accident.

Planning can follow either an objective or a problem orientation.

There is a direct relationship between the objectives of the physical system, the information needs of the managers, and the performance criteria that an MIS should meet.

The steps of the MIS planning process are a detailed means of accomplishing the first step of the systems approach: define the problem.

The main task of the information specialists during the planning process is to support the responsible project manager.

The study project proposal documents the findings of the planning process and represents the key to proceeding to the next phase.

The responsible project manager must assume that a system is defined that will solve the problems or meet the objectives, and that a project is defined that will permit the system to be achieved.

At this early point, control of the remainder of the MIS project can only be established in general terms, but this is better than no control at all.

Project control is based on two ingredients: standards of acceptable performance, and a system of reporting progress.

As project control becomes more detailed, it answers the questions: What is to be done? Who is to do it? When will it be done?

An effort is made during the planning phase to assign responsibility at the subtask level, rather than the task level.

Progress reporting is made more effective by using visual aids such as a Gantt chart or a network diagram.

Questions

1   What conditions make MIS implementation a difficult task?

2   Should the manager of the MIS project be a different person than the one who will manage the MIS operation? Why or why not?

3   Is the decision to implement an MIS a strategic, tactical, or operational one? What about the implementation itself—on what level does it fall?

4   Is the executive vice-president a strategic or a tactical manager? What about the administrative vice-president?

5   What responsibilities does the executive vice-president have that the administrative vice-president does not?

6   Is the executive vice-president always in charge of the MIS implementation project?

7   What are the benefits of forming an MIS committee? Are there any disadvantages?

8   Why do managers plan?

9   Could a new company take a problem orientation to planning? Explain.

10   Should any work begin on development of an MIS if the firm doesn't have a good set of objectives? Why or why not?

11   What is the difference between recognizing the problem and defining the problem?

12   Which is better: a formal or an informal approach to problem recognition?

13   Who imposes constraints on an MIS design?

14   Should information specialists attempt to "sell" the systems study when it appears to be absolutely necessary? Explain.

15   How are performance standards established for an MIS project when the firm has never been involved in such a project?

16   On what basis are people assigned responsibility in the MIS project?

17   What are the similarities between a Gantt chart and a network diagram? What are the differences?

Problems

1   As vice-president of marketing for Pickwick Papers, your responsibility is to assure that customer orders are processed rapidly. You have difficulty in seeing to it that this is always done. Identify what types of information you need and the performance criteria of the MIS.

2   The finance division of your company is planning to implement a financial information system. Since you made an A in a college Gantt chart course, you have been asked to prepare such a chart showing how the implementation work will be spread over time. Only a single information specialist will be involved, and each subsystem except accounting will require 2 months of effort. Accounting will take 3 months. Accounting will be done first, followed by financial intelligence, forecasting, money flow, and control.

3 Draw a network diagram illustrating how a breakfast of bacon, eggs, toast, and milk can be prepared in the least amount of time.

Activity	*Time (seconds)*
Put toast on plate	5
Fill pot with water	10
Butter the toast	15
Cook bacon in skillet	300
Remove bread from pantry	10
Get plate, glass, and silverware from cabinet	20
Put silverware on table	15
Put bread into toaster	5
Sit down to eat	2
Remove eggs, bacon, and butter from refrigerator	25
Toast the bread in a toaster	120
Put bacon on plate	20
Put eggs into water	5
Boil the eggs	240
Put eggs on plate	20
Put filled glass on table	10
Put bacon into skillet	5
Pour milk into the glass	5
Put filled plate on table	10
Remove milk from refrigerator	10

Chapter 15

Information Systems Development:
The Analysis and Design Phase

A Shift in Emphasis

In the previous chapter, the role of the firm's manager in planning and controlling the MIS project was described. In this chapter, the emphasis shifts to the work performed by the information systems staff. This is the work that creates an MIS to meet the objectives identified by the firm's management. It is the responsibility of the vice-president of information systems to see that this work is carried out in the prescribed manner and that the schedule is followed. As the work is performed over a period of months, the vice-president of information systems reports the progress to the executive vice-president or the MIS committee. As problems are encountered, actions are taken to get the project effort back on course.

Although this chapter focuses on the information systems staff, it is important to understand that their work is aimed at creating an MIS that meets the managers' needs. And those managers, through the executive vice-president or MIS committee, exercise control over the work.

In addition to playing a role in the planning and control of the MIS project, the managers also play an active part in the analysis and design of the MIS. It is necessary that the managers communicate to the information systems staff their exact information needs. If this communication is to be carried out effectively and efficiently, the manager must understand the tasks of the information systems staff. The purpose of this chapter is to provide that understanding. After this goal is accomplished, the manager's perspective again will be taken.

The Impact of the Computer on Employment

When the computer was introduced to the business scene in the late 1950s, there was considerable fear of widespread unemployment. Certainly, many jobs were eliminated, but they were generally of a low-level, repetitive, and monotonous nature. Examples of persons losing their jobs to computerization were billing clerks, factory timekeepers, and inventory recordkeepers. The actual impact of the computer was less than anticipated, mainly because of the restricted range of computer applications. During the first and second computer generations, the computers were used largely for basic accounting tasks. The new devices therefore had little effect on the employees in other parts of the firm.

In situations where employees' jobs were eliminated by the computer, those persons were rarely terminated. Invariably, there were other jobs in the firm that needed to be done. These jobs were frequently more challenging and demanding and represented an increase in status and pay. Employees not retrainable or transferable were allowed to leave the firm through normal attrition. Of course, the good fortune of a healthy economy with high productivity during this period also contributed to the minimum effect of the computer on unemployment. This cushioned impact did much to dispel the fears. Mass unemployment simply did not happen.

Instead of a situation of unemployment, the computer actually created thousands of new jobs. An entire new industry was established—one concerned with designing, manufacturing, selling, repairing, and using the new devices. Computer manufacturers offer jobs in hundreds of categories ranging from janitorial workers to receptionists and secretaries to sales representatives and electronics engineers. All of these jobs have been made possible by the computer revolution.

Moreover, for every single computer manufacturer, there are thousands of users.

The Information Systems Staff

Most of the computer-related jobs in organizations using computers fall within three broad categories: operations, programming, and systems analysis.

The operator

The computer, just as any machine or device, must be operated. A small computer requires only a single *operator*, while a large one can require three or four. The operators communicate instructions to the computer through the console, place appropriate card files in the card reader, mount and dismount tape reels and disk packs, and put the correct paper forms in the line printer.

The operators are a part of the computer operations department. This department, under the supervision of an *operations manager*, is responsible primarily for running the different jobs on the computer. Most firms operate their computer as a *closed shop*. This practice means that users do not have access to the computer room. Access is available only to operations personnel. Some computer installations, however, operate on an *open shop* basis where the users operate the equipment. These situations normally involve a highly trained users group, such as scientists or engineers.

In addition to those working directly with the computer, other members of the operations department operate keydriven data input machines, maintain controls over computer input and output, schedule jobs on the computer, and maintain library files of tapes and disk packs.

The programmer

The persons preparing the programs are the *programmers*. Programmers have available a variety of special computer languages to use in writing programs. Choice of a language is determined by the type of problem and the manner in which it is to be solved. A mathematical problem most often is solved with FORTRAN (FORmula TRANslator). A similar problem can be solved through use of a data terminal with BASIC (Beginner's All-purpose Symbolic Instruction Code). A business problem can be solved with COBOL (COmmon Business Oriented Language). These are only three of many such languages.

The programmer has the important responsibility of communicating with the computer. If the computer is to do what is expected, the program must be accurate. Before a program is put into operational use, the programmer subjects it to many tests to assure that it contains no errors, or "bugs."

Firms usually have more than one programmer. In some cases, these persons specialize in writing certain types of programs. Perhaps a firm will have a programmer who specializes in writing programs for marketing or for accounting.

The programmers are supervised by a *programming manager.*

The systems analyst

It is the responsibility of the *systems analyst* to define the approach to a computer solution to a problem. The systems analyst must gain an understanding of the problem from the manager. The manager has a problem that requires information for solution, and this need is communicated to the analyst. In some cases, the manager recognizes this need independently. In other cases, the analyst serves as a catalyst by informing the manager of the kinds of information available. Obviously, the analyst must have a good understanding of the manager's responsibilities and duties in order to identify information needs.

Typically, the manager and the analyst engage in long discussions. These discussions provide the analyst with a sufficient understanding of the needs to develop a computer approach to the solution.

Once the approach is defined, it is communicated to the programmer.

This communication is accomplished both verbally and in writing. Much of the written communication incorporates diagrams and tables.

The systems analysts in a firm are directed by a *systems analysis manager.*

The analyst programmer

The jobs of systems analyst and programmer are not separated in all firms. One person often performs both jobs. This situation exists in small firms where the information systems staff is not large enough for specialization. Perhaps the firm has only a single person available to do the analysis and design work. That person becomes the *analyst/programmer.*

In many large organizations one person does both jobs. These are usually companies where the systems being designed are not overly complex. Banking and manufacturing are good examples. It is not unrealistic to expect a person to develop an adequate understanding of the system being designed, such as a checking account system or inventory control, and an understanding of how to program its solution on the computer. In other industries, such as insurance, the systems are so complex as to require specialization. Here, different individuals usually function as analysts and as programmers.

The combined analyst/programmer approach benefits the programming task. A communication and coordination link is eliminated. It is not necessary that two people work together. However, the combined position works to the detriment of the systems analysis. There is less opportunity to develop the deep understanding of the problem when responsibility also is shared for programming.

Organization of the information systems staff

The information systems staff consists of systems analysts, programmers, and operators. All of these people play important roles in the MIS project. The manner in which they participate depends on the size of the staff. Figure 15–1 illustrates one way to organize a large information systems staff.

This approach of grouping analysts and programmers by functional subsystems enables the specialists to develop a better understanding of the information needs of the managers. If an analyst and a programmer have an educational background in one of the areas, that background can be augmented with experience gained on the job. This approach can do much to overcome the communication barrier too often existing between managers and the information systems staff.

Other specialized organizational structures are possible. Analysts and programmers can be grouped within the firm by departments: accounting, inventory, personnel, advertising, and the like. Or they can be grouped by technical specialty: modeling, forecasting, data base maintenance, and report generation. It also would be possible to group these personnel by information system level: strategic, tactical, and operational. Most likely, multiple analysts

Figure 15–1 The information systems staff

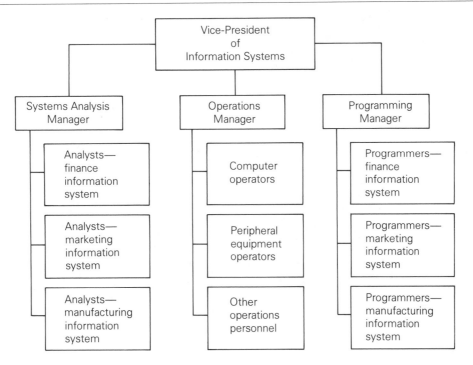

and programmers will be grouped in some manner within the information systems department to realize the greatest efficiency.

A trend to decentralization

As the needs of the functional areas for management information increase, there is a trend to decentralize the location of the specialists. In other words, the analysts and programmers are a part of marketing or manufacturing or finance, not of the information systems department. This arrangement should ease the communications barrier within a functional area and contribute to the development of effective functional information systems. However, its effect on the single, integrated MIS has yet to be understood. It is possible that this trend will do more harm than good in achieving a balanced and unified use of the computer by the functions. Only time will tell. But there is definitely a trend in this direction.

Whatever the organizational arrangement, the information systems staff must interface with managers on different levels and in different functional areas. Figure 15–2 illustrates interactions between functionally organized teams of information specialists and managers.

As shown in the figure, the vice-president of information systems works

Figure 15-2 Relationship between information systems staff and other executives and managers

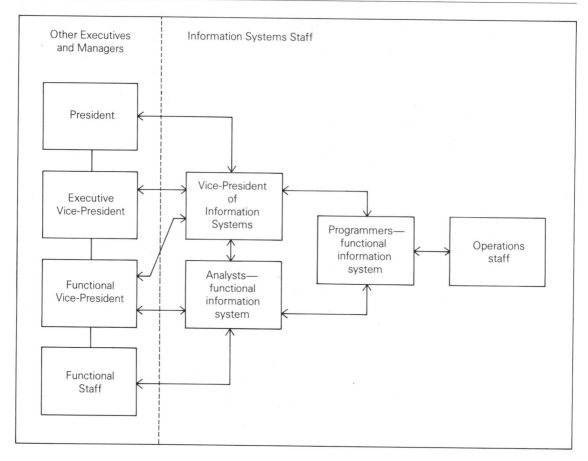

with the president, the executive vice-president, and the functional vice-presidents in developing the specifications for the MIS. The appropriate analysis team works with the vice-president of the functional area, such as marketing, and with the staff managers in that area, such as the sales manager, advertising manager, and the like.

All of the arrows in the diagram are bidirectional, indicating the two-way communication that must take place.

Once the analysts have developed the detailed specifications for a functional information system, the specifications are communicated to the appropriate functional programming group for development of the needed computer programs. It is then the task of the operations staff to run these programs on the computer to generate the output information.

Figure 15–3 The communication process

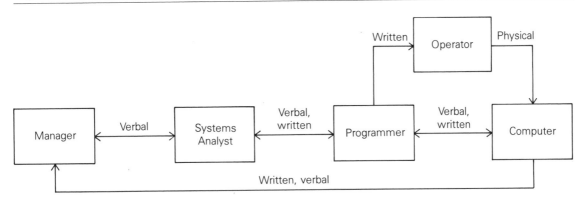

The Communication Process

The process of developing a computer solution to a problem is one of communication. It begins with the manager and ends with the computer. In between are the information specialists—the analyst, the programmer, and the operator. Figure 15–3 illustrates this communication flow.

The manager has a need for information and verbally communicates this need to the analyst. The analyst prepares the basic computer approach and communicates it verbally and in writing to the programmer. The programmer creates the detailed computer approach and communicates it to the computer in the form of a written program. The programmer also prepares written instructions for the operator to follow in running the job on the computer. The communication from the operator to the computer is physical, in the form of switch settings and keyed instructions. Finally, the communication from the computer to the manager usually is in written form, either as a printed report or as in information displayed on a CRT terminal. When the computer configuration includes an audio response unit, output can be in the form of a verbal message.

The communication problem

The design of an MIS requires two broad types of knowledge: management and information systems. The manager furnishes the management knowledge; and the systems analyst, the information systems knowledge. Representatives from these two areas must communicate and this is not always easy. Both areas have their separate jargon, educational and career development paths, and professional interests. At some point, however, these two bodies of knowledge and experience must be shared, at least to the extent necessary for the realization of an MIS.

Figure 15–4   Communication between manager and systems analyst

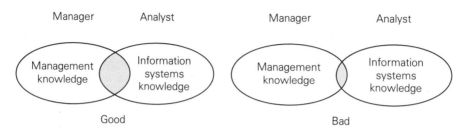

The point where this knowledge and experience come together is the verbal communication between the manager and the systems analyst in Figure 15–3. This is potentially the weakest link in the chain. If this link breaks down, the remaining communications do not happen.

Both the analyst and the manager can take steps to assure that the communication link between them is not broken. They both can learn as much about the other's job as possible. This provides a shared knowledge that can form the basis for a strong communication tie.

Figure 15–4 illustrates examples of both good and bad communication between the manager and the systems analyst. The factor differentiating "good" from "bad" is shared knowledge (the shaded area). If the two groups are to communicate, the manager must know something of information systems, and the analyst must know something of management responsibilities and duties. Much of this shared knowledge can be gained in college and university programs in management and computer science. The remainder is gained through experience by jointly solving real-world business problems.

Analysis and Design of the MIS

In the previous chapter, it was explained that the MIS can be designed to help the firm meet certain objectives or to solve particular problems. This is the basic decision that influences what the MIS will do. That decision during the planning phase defined the general approach to be taken. With the knowledge of the approach, the vice-presidents were able to make some assumptions about what the MIS will achieve and what will be required for implementation.

Now that it is time to perform the detailed analysis and design work leading to the MIS, it is necessary to specify the exact method by which the design is to be achieved.

Approaches to MIS design

There are three basic approaches to the design of an MIS. One is the *top-down approach* in which the specifications for the MIS are defined on the strategic level and then are filtered down through the management layers. This approach works best with the objective orientation. The top managers know the objectives, and design an MIS that will support attainment of those objectives. The problem is that an MIS is imposed on lower level managers that might not satisfy their needs.

This problem is solved by taking another approach—the *bottom-up approach*. When this is followed, operational level managers design an MIS to help them meet their objectives or solve their problems. It is likely that the problem orientation will be predominant since the firm's objectives often become obscured by day-to-day problems. Whatever the orientation, the manner in which these lower level systems operate will have a restricting influence on upper level systems.

There is a third approach that can overcome the limitations of the other two when performed correctly. This is an *integrative approach* that permits managers on all levels to influence the design. Activity starts on the top level with identification of an MIS structure that will enable the firm to meet its objectives. This design is presented to lower level managers for approval or modification. The managers on the lower level make changes, additions, or deletions, and return the design to the top level for approval. The revised design is evaluated on the top level and perhaps sent down again in a modified form for further consideration. This evaluation, modification, and approval process continues until a design is achieved that is satisfactory to all levels.

The pursuit of the integrative approach is the most costly in terms of management time, and it demands input from all levels. However, the potential benefit is great. All managers have a voice in the design and therefore are more likely to participate in other steps of the MIS project and to use the information output.

What is systems analysis?

Analysis is another word for study. In an MIS project the firm as a system is studied. In an ongoing firm, the study aims at the physical system and its conceptual information system. Some information system exists, and the question is whether it meets the needs of the managers of the physical system. The analysis job requires the systems analyst to gain some understanding of the physical system. The analyst spends time in the production area, in the warehouse, and in the sales office in order to understand what is happening. The analyst talks with the various managers to become familiar with what they do and what information they need. Sometimes, this familiarization process takes weeks, or even months.

The systems analyst rarely becomes involved in making improvements to the physical system. That is the work of the industrial engineer. The analyst only tries to become familiar with the physical system, not to change it. As the analyst studies the existing physical system, attention is devoted to its conceptual information system. Is this information system adequate? If not, what is needed?

In a new firm, there is no information system to study. One must be created. The emphasis is on understanding the operation of the planned physical system so that the anticipated information needs might be met. Perhaps there is not yet a factory, warehouse, or sales office. In that case, the analyst meets with the people who will be managing those operations in order to learn of the planned work and its demand for information.

In the discussion that follows, it is assumed that a systems study is being conducted in an existing firm.

What is systems design?

After interviewing the managers in the study process, the analyst has secured enough information to design the MIS. During the planning phase, the subsystems of the functional information systems were identified. Now the analyst knows what the managers will need from each subsystem in terms of information output.

As the analyst seeks to design these systems and subsystems, he or she considers different designs. The one that best enables the firm to meet its objectives is selected. This design is documented in detail, using graphic, as well as narrative, descriptions.

When the documentation has been prepared, it is given to the programmer for coding. The work of the programmer can be considered a part of system design or implementation. In this discussion, programming and the role of the operations staff in testing the programs and building the data files are included in the implementation phase. Thus, of the three information staff positions, only the analyst is involved in analysis and design.

An example of the systems approach

The manner in which the systems analyst learns about information needs and then designs an MIS is an example of the systems approach. The analyst first defines the problem by discussing it with the managers. Then, the analyst considers alternative solutions or system designs.

The analyst doesn't have to follow the systems approach. There must have been many instances when a system was designed before the problem was defined or understood, or when an inferior alternative was selected. Some of these efforts might have met with success, but the odds of failure were greater. The systems approach doesn't guarantee success, but it offers the best likelihood of it.

The Analysis and Design Phase

The previous chapter described the planning by the executive vice-president and the vice-president of information systems. A study project proposal was prepared and approved, and a control mechanism was established. It is now time to perform the analysis and design. The executive vice-president retains overall control, but the work of the information systems staff is the responsibility of the vice-president of information systems. Figure 15–5 illustrates how these two executives continue to work together.

The bulk of the work in this phase is performed by the systems analysts. A systems study is conducted in steps 3 and 4 to define the needs, and then a system is designed in steps 5 through 8 to meet those needs. When the design work is completed, the analysts, under the close direction of the vice-president of information systems, prepare a second proposal. This proposal recommends continuation of the project through the implementation phase.

Although it is unlikely that a firm would get this far and then decide to drop the project completely, it is possible. In the beginning, very little is known about the MIS and what it will do for the firm. As more is learned, the management might decide the results do not justify the cost. The process of implementing an MIS is a series of two key go/no go decisions. One determines if the firm will go through the expensive and time-consuming analysis and design phase. The other determines if many of the firm's resources will be harnessed in an implementation effort. The information systems staff must provide the justification for proceeding from one phase to another.

The following paragraphs correspond to the numbered steps in Figure 15–5.

1. Announce the study project.   Possibly no project affects as many employees in a company as does an MIS effort. All managers should be involved, and many workers will participate in the analysis and design effort and will perform important roles in the MIS.

It is important that the project not have a negative effect on morale so that the cooperation and participation of these employees is obtained. Nothing is more fearful than the unknown, and it is easy to generate rumors about the effect of the MIS on jobs. For this reason, *top* management must keep the employees informed of what is planned.

In the case of larger firms, a computer probably has been in use for several years, most likely as a data (rather than information) processing system. If this is the situation, the employees have come to accept the computer as a positive resource and not as a device aimed at replacing people. Management then only has to explain the new use of the computer as an information system, and ask for the employees' support. This announcement should present no big problems.

In the case of a firm with no computer history, the situation is different. Here, management must explain what the computer is intended to do in order to overcome any employee fears.

A company meeting can be called, with the president presiding. His or her comments can be supported by the executive vice-president and the vice-president of information systems. The presentation is not technical; it simply summarizes, in very general terms, what the MIS will do and what it will take to achieve the MIS. This announcement can be supplemented by an article in the company newspaper, and perhaps by departmental meetings. The tone of these communications should not be one of "Here is what we have

Figure 15–5   The system study project

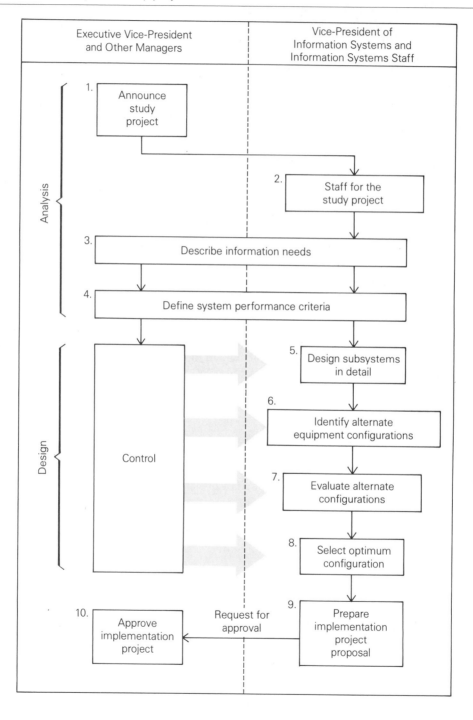

decided to do, and you can take it or leave it." Rather, the message should be an appeal for cooperation and input. Each employee should be encouraged to participate and to make suggestions. The MIS cannot attain its highest level of performance without this support and input from the rank and file of employees.

2. Staff for the study project. Before the system study can begin, all of the needed resources (primarily systems analysts) must be acquired and made ready. Perhaps some training will be necessary, and teams or work units must be formed.

If all of these manpower resources presently are not working for the company, they must be obtained from the environment. New employees can be recruited, and perhaps temporary help can be acquired from consulting firms, or even computer vendors. Some vendors, IBM for example, make analyst and programmer help available to their customers for a fee.

Many of the members of the information systems staff will have specialized skills. Programmers might be needed who are proficient in a particular language, say COBOL. Analysts might be needed who have experience with an industry (airlines) or with a subsystem (accounting) or with a technique (computer simulation).

Since only the analysts are to be involved in the analysis and design phase, the programming and operations staff need not be brought into the project at this time. Additional programming and operations resources are acquired as they are needed. Sufficient leadtime must be allowed, however, for them to receive any orientation or training before they begin their work in the next phase: implementation of the MIS.

3. Describe information needs. The analysts must now gather information describing the information needs of the managers. This is done primarily through personal interview. In interviewing the manager, the analyst asks questions such as:

1 What decisions do you regularly make?
2 What information do you need to make these decisions?
3 What information do you get?
4 What information would you like?
5 What specialized studies do you request?
6 What magazines and trade reports would you like to have routed to you on a regular basis?
7 What specific topics would you like to be informed of?
8 What do you think would be the four most helpful improvements that could be made in the present information system?[1]

---

1. Adapted from Philip Kotler, *Marketing Management: Analysis, Planning and Control* (Englewood Cliffs, N.J.: Third Edition, Prentice-Hall, Inc., 1976), p. 423.

Getting answers to these questions is not easy. Several meetings spanning several weeks might be necessary to get the answers from a single manager. The analyst first has to gain the manager's confidence if an open and honest dialogue is to take place. During the interviewing period, the analyst assists the manager by helping him or her think through information needs in a logical manner.

In addition to personal conversation, the analyst also gathers information by observing (spending several days in the department watching the activity), by studying historical records, and even by conducting surveys. This analysis work is concluded when the specific information needs of the managers are known.

4. Define system performance criteria.   For the first time in the project, the specific needs of the managers are known. Up to this point, the needs have only been defined in general terms, and some have been assumed. It is now possible to specify in exact terms what the MIS should accomplish. These are the performance criteria that were stated in general terms during the planning phase.

For example, a marketing manager might want a certain level of performance from a pricing model. The manager can insist that it consider a 5-year projection of the national economy, probable reactions by competitors based on the past 5 years' performance, and production and marketing costs. Further, the manager might specify that the model require no more than 5 minutes of simulation time, and that the resultant accuracy (projected results compared with actual) be within 5 percent.

Of course, what the manager wants and what he or she gets can be two different things. Perhaps the firm cannot afford a computer configuration that can provide the needed information. Or, perhaps the information is not available due to environmental constraints. Finally, and most importantly, manager requests must be evaluated in terms of how they support the firm as it attempts to meet its objectives.

If acceptable, the specifications become the performance criteria for the pricing model. How well the pricing model does its job will be determined by comparing the model with these criteria. Efforts are made to establish similar criteria for each part of the MIS and for each computer program. These criteria should be quantitative, rather than subjective, so that performance can be measured precisely.

5. Design subsystems in detail.   Systems analysis is now completed and it is time to design the MIS. This task will be done in a series of steps. The first is to document each computer program in terms of its inputs, processes, and outputs. This documentation includes, as a minimum, the following:

Figure 15–6 A program description

```
                    CREDIT RESPONSE PROGRAM


          This program accepts customer number as input,
       selects the appropriate customer master record,
       and provides the following information:
            1. Customer number
            2. Customer name
            3. Customer credit limit
            4. Amount due
            5. Additional authorized credit
```

1 Program description
2 System flowchart
3 Input record layout(s)
4 Output record layout(s)
5 Program flowchart

A set of these materials for a program is called a *program documentation package*. It is created by the analyst, and more materials are added by the programmer during the implementation phase. The package is kept up-to-date as long as the program resides in the model base.

The *program description* of a program answering a request from a credit manager for a description of a customer's credit record appears in Figure 15–6.

This is simply a brief description of what the program does. Someone examining the package can glance at this description and gain a quick understanding of the contents.

A graphical diagram of the overall system containing this program is called a *system flowchart*. It is the "big picture" of the system, with no detail. The flowchart is drawn with a plastic flowchart template, such as that shown in Figure 15–7.

Each shape in the template has a special meaning. These meanings are explained in the Appendix. The system flowchart for the credit response system is shown in Figure 15–8.

The symbols either have general or specific meanings. The parallelograms used for the inquiry and the response are general symbols representing input or

Figure 15–7 Flowchart template. (Courtesy of International Business Machines)

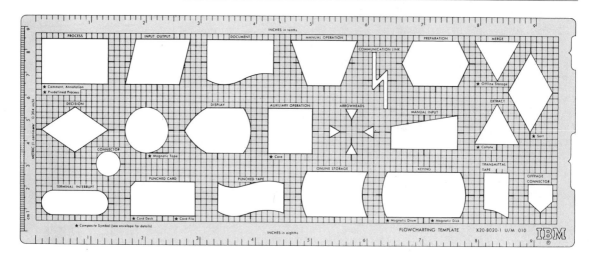

Figure 15–8 System flowchart of credit response system

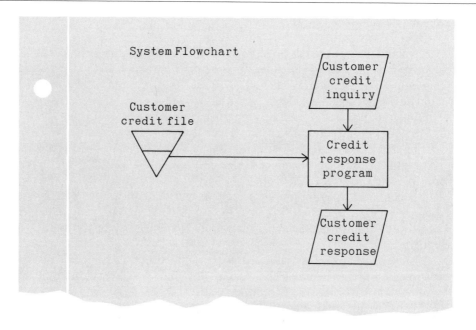

Figure 15-9 Input record layout of credit response system

```
                        Input Record

      Data Element           No. Positions      Type

      Customer number              8             N
```

output. The inverted triangle with the line through it represents a file. The rectangle represents the computer program. At this point, the exact media used for input, output, and the file are not known; they will be specified later. For that reason, only general symbols are used.

The system flowchart shows that a program will accept an inquiry, obtain data from the customer credit file, and answer the inquiry. This is a simple system flowchart. Most are more lengthy, showing a series of computer programs required to perform the tasks required of the system. See Appendix for an example.

The analyst next specifies the exact form of the input and output by using record layout forms. The *input record layout* (Figure 15-9) shows the data fields contained in the record, in the sequence they will be entered in the computer. The input record layout for the credit response system only contains a single element, the customer number; this is an eight-digit numeric ("N") field.

At this time it has not been determined whether the number will be entered through a terminal keyboard or perhaps punched into a card. That choice will be decided later.

Many management information systems are characterized by a small amount of input data. Limited input data makes it easier for the manager to use the system. Many data processing systems, such as payroll or billing, have lengthy input data records.

The credit response will be displayed in some form. It might be printed by the line printer or a typewriter-style terminal. Or, it can be displayed on a CRT terminal. It is even possible that the response can be communicated verbally by an audio response device. The *output record layout* (Figure 15-10) shows what information will be contained in the response, and in what sequence or format. Both horizontal and vertical alignment of the data elements is usually illustrated on the layout.

Figure 15–10   Output record layout of credit response system

---

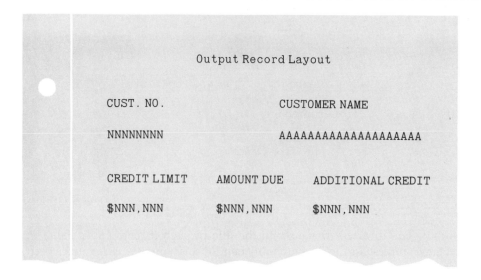

Output Record Layout

CUST. NO.   CUSTOMER NAME

NNNNNNNN   AAAAAAAAAAAAAAAAAAAA

CREDIT LIMIT   AMOUNT DUE   ADDITIONAL CREDIT

$NNN,NNN $NNN,NNN $NNN,NNN

The output record layout shows that the computer will display the customer number and name (up to 20 alphabetic letters; "A" means alphabetic), along with the three dollar amounts.

The analyst now has specified what the program will do in general terms, what it uses as input, and what it produces as output. The only remaining documentation is a detailed description of what the program will do. This description is shown in a *program flowchart* (Figure 15–11).

The program flowchart contains the symbols on the left and a brief narrative on the right that explains each step. The ovals represent points of entry into and exit from this program. As in the system flowchart, the parallelograms represent input and output. But, the rectangles represent computer processing steps—not separate programs as before.

The credit response program is designed to function as a foreground program (see page 124). The computer will interrupt what it is doing, handle the credit inquiry, and then return to the interrupted program.

The program documentation reflects the detailed knowledge of the information problem to be solved, with a solution that can be adapted to various computer configurations. The documentation will provide the basis for considering alternate configurations in the next step, and in coding the programs in the implementation phase.

System documentation is very important to the success of the MIS. The documentation enables the systems analyst to *understand* the system so that it might be designed and, at a later date, improved. The documentation also facilitates an understanding by new analysts as they learn about the firm's MIS.

Figure 15-11   Program flowchart of credit response system

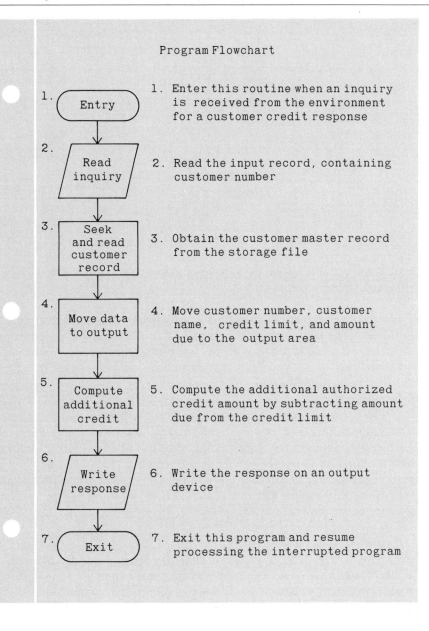

Program Flowchart

1. Entry

   1. Enter this routine when an inquiry is received from the environment for a customer credit response

2. Read inquiry

   2. Read the input record, containing customer number

3. Seek and read customer record

   3. Obtain the customer master record from the storage file

4. Move data to output

   4. Move customer number, customer name, credit limit, and amount due to the output area

5. Compute additional credit

   5. Compute the additional authorized credit amount by subtracting amount due from the credit limit

6. Write response

   6. Write the response on an output device

7. Exit

   7. Exit this program and resume processing the interrupted program

Figure 15–12   Feasible equipment alternatives

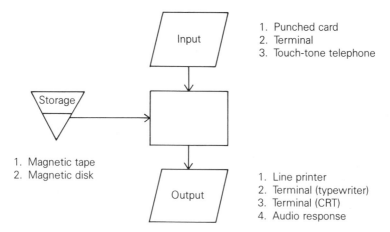

1. Punched card
2. Terminal
3. Touch-tone telephone

Storage

1. Magnetic tape
2. Magnetic disk

1. Line printer
2. Terminal (typewriter)
3. Terminal (CRT)
4. Audio response

In addition, documentation permits the analyst to *communicate* the design to both programmers and managers.

6. *Identify alternate equipment configurations.* It is now time to think about the computer configuration. All of the required computer programs have been documented in the above manner. Or, as a minimum, flowcharts exist for each program. A configuration must be selected that allows the programs to function efficiently. The needs of the programs will determine the configuration.

This is a sequential process starting with an identification of the different configurations that can execute each program. As an example, the credit response program can function with input from one of three sources (punched card, terminal, or Touch-Tone telephone), with the customer credit file on either magnetic tape or disk, and with output prepared on one of four devices (line printer, typewriter terminal, CRT terminal, or audio response). These alternatives are shown in Figure 15–12.

7. *Evaluate alternate configurations.* The analyst evaluates each alternative in terms of its pros and cons. For example, a disadvantage of punched card input is its slowness. An advantage is low cost. The analyst then consults with the manager who will use the output, and the pros and cons are discussed. A configuration is selected that offers the best performance to the manager, within cost constraints. The credit manager might prefer Touch-Tone input, magnetic disk storage, and audio response.

The preferred program configurations then are pooled and evaluated. The objective is the selection of a computer configuration that best satisfies the needs of all of the programs at lowest cost. In an effort to control cost, the configurations of some programs might have to be changed.

Table 15–1   Preferred equipment configurations for major programs in the marketing information system

Program	Input Devices					Storage		Output Devices						
	Card reader	OCR	Terminal	Badge reader	Paper tape	Magnetic tape	Magnetic disk	Card punch	Line printer	Terminal—CRT	Terminal—	Typewriter	Audio	Graph plotter
New product-evaluation model	X					X			X					
Product deletion model		X					X					X		
Warehouse location model	X					X								X
Warehouse layout model	X					X								X
Sales territory assignment model	X					X			X					
Advertising media selection model	X					X			X					
Pricing model		X					X		X					

Table 15–1 contains a grid of preferred program configurations for the marketing information system.

Similar grids also are prepared for the other functional systems.

8. *Select optimum configuration.* Different computer configurations are considered based on how well the needs of each program are met. If the two warehouse models above are the only programs requiring graphical output, it might not be economical to include a plotter in the configuration. The model output would have to be prepared another way, such as on the line printer.

As the programs are considered in terms of their equipment requirements, prime attention is given to the most important programs. Every effort is made to select a computer configuration that enables these important programs to operate at maximum efficiency.

At the conclusion of this final step of the system design, a computer configuration has been selected. The selection has been based on the combined needs of each program and the preferences of the managers who will use the program output. A particular brand of computer has not been identified. Selection of the computer vendor is a completely different process that will be described in the next chapter.

When the computer configuration has been selected, the documentation for each of the programs is reviewed and updated to reflect the specific types of computer equipment used.

9. Prepare implementation project proposal.

9. *Prepare implementation project proposal.* Although much has been accomplished toward achieving an MIS, considerable work remains. None of the computer programs have been coded at this point, for example. But before additional funds are allocated to the implementation phase, management requires as much information as possible to justify continuation. Now that the system has been designed, it is possible to provide this information.

The information systems staff prepares an implementation project proposal outlining the work to be done, the expected benefits, and the costs. The format of this proposal is similar to the one prepared for the study project. Figure 15–13 is an outline that can be followed.

Sections 2, 3, and 5 of the figure represent updated versions of corresponding sections in the study project proposal (Figure 14–6). More is known about these sections now, and the information can be less general and more specific.

The study project proposal described possible alternatives the firm might follow. That is not done here. The selected design and computer equipment configuration are presented in section 4 along with the performance criteria. The anticipated results of that design are described in section 5.

Where the study project proposal contained a general implementation plan, that plan now is presented in a detailed form. Since that plan is such an improvement over the old one, new documentation of the implementation phase should be prepared—new bar charts, network diagrams, and so on.

10. *Approve the implementation project.* The vice-president of information systems reports the progress of the information systems staff throughout the systems study. These reports are made periodically to the executive vice-president or the MIS committee. The key executives in the firm are therefore able to intervene and take appropriate action as problems are encountered. At the conclusion of the study, the managers not only have an understanding of the work that has been done, but have a genuine satisfaction from having actively participated. This is a healthy situation when proposal review time rolls around. The executive vice-president (or the MIS committee) is reviewing his or her proposal, not one produced entirely by the information systems staff.

In some cases, approval might be conditional, requiring changes to the design or the implementation plan. If the executive vice-president (or MIS committee) has been kept informed of the progress throughout the analysis and design phase, it is unlikely that approval to continue will not be given.

Figure 15–13 The implementation project proposal

1. Introduction—reason for the proposal

2. Problem definition

3. System objectives and constraints

4. System design
   a. Summary description
   b. Performance criteria
   c. Equipment configuration

5. Anticipated results
   a. Organizational impact
   b. Operational impact
   b. Financial impact

6. Detailed implementation plan
   a. Objectives
   b. Tasks to be accomplished
   c. Resource requirements
   d. Time schedule
   e. Cost recap

7. Summary

Upon approval, the information systems staff proceeds with the implementation phase.

Summary

The information systems staff is composed of systems analysts, programmers, and operations personnel. This staff has the responsibility of developing an MIS. This development includes analysis of the existing system, and design and implementation of the new MIS. The work of the staff is directed by the vice-president of information systems, but the overall control is exercised by the executive vice-president, or the MIS committee if one is employed.

This chapter describes the analysis phase. This work is performed by the systems analysts. The programmers and the operations personnel perform their work during the implementation phase.

The general system design can be influenced primarily by top executives (the top-down approach), by the operational level managers (the bottom-up approach), or by interaction between managers on all levels (the integrative approach). Although the latter approach is the most effective in meeting the information needs of the total management, all three approaches require the analyst to understand the manager's needs. The analyst gains this understanding by employing a variety of information-gathering techniques, but with emphasis on the personal interview. This process of gaining an understanding of the existing system and the manager's information needs is called *systems analysis*. When this understanding is gained, the different approaches to the new MIS are defined and evaluated. The selection of the design believed to best enable the firm to meet its objectives concludes the *systems design*.

As in the planning phase, systems analysis and design require a series of steps. The steps are: (1) announce the study project, (2) staff for the study project, (3) describe the information needs, (4) define system performance criteria, (5) prepare the detailed subsystem design, (6) identify alternate equipment configurations, (7) evaluate alternate configurations, and (8) select the optimum configuration.

The analyst seeks to understand the manager's information needs by asking a series of questions. This understanding enables the analyst to document each alternate approach. This documentation, including a program description, record layouts, and system and program flowcharts, is called a *program documentation package*. First, each program is documented without attention to specific equipment configurations. When the optimum configuration is selected for the combined programs, the documentation is updated to reflect the final configuration.

The analysis and design phase is concluded with the preparation and approval of an implementation project proposal. The management authorizes expenditure of funds for the final phase in the development of the MIS.

Important Terms

Open Shop

Operator, Programmer, Systems
    Analyst

Analyst/Programmer

Top-Down Approach

Bottom-Up Approach

Integrative Approach

Systems Analysis

Systems Design

Documentation Package

Program Description

System Flowchart

Input Record Layout

Output Record Layout

Program Flowchart

Important Concepts

Computer-using firms employ people in three computer-related areas: operations, programming, and systems analysis.

Programmers and analysts usually have only limited or restricted access to their firm's computer room.

The trend is toward decentralization of the systems analysis task.

Analysts and programmers can be organized based on the users of their output (functional area or management level) or based on their primary skills (linear programming, etc.).

The vice-president of information systems represents the MIS activity on the top management level; the analysts and programmers represent the activity on lower management levels.

The task of providing information for management can be regarded as a communication process involving the manager, the computer, and the information specialists.

The communication problem in MIS design involves the manager and the systems analyst.

The system study includes both analysis and design.

Staffing for the study project usually involves acquisition of only analysts; programmers and operators are not needed until later.

The most thorough definition of management information needs is based on analyst interviews of managers performed during the system study.

An effort should be made to define quantitatively acceptable system performance while the system is being designed.

All of the description of a system design is assembled by the analyst in a documentation package.

The analyst engages in the documentation process as a means to better understand the system being designed and to communicate that design to the programmer.

Varieties in central processing, input/output, and auxiliary storage units permit a large number of possible computer configurations.

The selected computer configuration is not based entirely on management preferences; but these provide a starting point and receive consideration.

The implementation project proposal provides a record of accomplishments achieved during the system study, and a definition of what is needed for the MIS development process to proceed.

Questions

1 What two basic types of firms offer computer-related jobs?

2 What three types of computer jobs exist in firms that use computers?

3 In what situations will the job of analyst and programmer be combined? What is the main advantage of this method?

4 Why is a communication problem created between the manager and the analyst but not between the analyst and the programmer?

5 Is it easier for the manager to learn about information systems or the information specialist to learn about management? Can one person be proficient in both areas?

6 Which approach to MIS planning is best: top-down, bottom-up, or integrative?

7 When does systems analysis stop and systems design begin?

8 Is programming a part of analysis, design, or implementation?

9 Why would employees resist development of an MIS if the firm has been using a computer for years as a data processing system?

10 Chapter 11 described marketing research techniques of survey, in-depth interview, observation, and controlled experiment. Which technique does the analyst use the most in identifying the manager's information needs? Which would be used the least?

11 What items are included in the program documentation package?

12 What are the two main reasons for the program documentation package?

13 What is the difference between a system flowchart and a program flowchart?

14 Who prepares the program flowchart: the analyst or the programmer?

15 What do the following flowcharting symbols represent: a parallelogram? a rectangle? an inverted triangle?

16 What type of computer unit will produce the data described on the output record layout?

17 How many computer configurations are possible when there are two possible input methods, one storage method, and one output method? What about two input, two storage, and two output methods?

18 Why does the implementation project proposal contain some of the same sections as were included in the study project proposal?

Problems

1 You are a systems analyst for Pickwick Papers. Before you leave on your summer vacation to the Bahamas, you must interview the plant superintendent to determine information needs. You begin by asking, "What decisions do you regularly make?" The superintendent replies, "Oh, I don't know. I don't keep a record. I couldn't begin to tell you what all I do. Every day is different. I suppose my secretary could answer that question the best. Why don't you check with her, and I'm sure she will tell you anything you need to know about my daily activities." What do you say to the superintendent?

2 Draw a general system flowchart to represent the following procedure:

a. New account cards are sorted into customer sequence by the computer. The output is recorded on magnetic tape as a new account file.

b. The records from the new account file are read, in sequence, and are added to the customer master file on DASD. A printed report is prepared, listing the additions to the file.

3 Draw a general system flowchart to represent the following procedure:

a. Checks and deposit slips are encoded with MICR characters.

b. The encoded documents are read by the MICR reader sorter and the data is written on a DASD.

c. After being read, the documents are placed in the current month suspense file.

d. The computer updates the customer master file with check and deposit data recorded on DASD in step b above.

e. As the customer master file is being updated, an activity report is printed on the line printer.

Chapter 16

Information Systems Development:
The Implementation Phase

Significance of the Final Approval

The approval by the executive vice-president or MIS committee of the implementation project proposal is the final go-ahead signal for realization of the MIS. This approval indicates that the firm's management is sufficiently satisfied with the system design and its anticipated benefits to authorize an additional expenditure of funds.

Much work has been accomplished up to this point, and perhaps this work has been the most difficult part of the project. The systems analysts have been able to communicate with the managers to identify their information needs. This is never easy, since it requires a positive and cooperative attitude mixed with a good portion of creativity and ingenuity.

Once the MIS is designed, implementation tends to be more automatic. Certain tasks remain to be done, and they are important. These tasks can be planned and executed with considerable precision. If the firm has reached this point in the MIS project, a high level of competence by the management and the information systems staff is indicated. Recognition of that competence should give the firm's management confidence that the implementation will be carried out successfully.

Implementation of an MIS

The implementation phase includes all of the tasks necessary to convert the MIS design to a working system. The analysis and design phase describes the new system and how it will work. The description exists only on paper; it is a model of the planned MIS. What is necessary now is a conversion of that model to the real thing: the MIS. The MIS will be a physical system consisting of machines (the computer and peripheral or auxiliary equipment), manpower (managers, employees, and the information systems staff), and materials (tapes, disks, cards, paper forms, etc.). *Implementation* is the acquisition and integration of these resources to form a working MIS. Once this operational status has been achieved, the MIS enters its fourth and final phase: operation.

The MIS: a physical or conceptual system?

Earlier in the book, a distinction was made between a physical and a conceptual system. As pointed out above, an MIS is a physical system. However, it also is a conceptual system. It represents a physical system: the total firm. The storage units of the computer contain data representing the firm. This data is processed to create the information that managers use in controlling the performance of the physical system of the firm.

The implementation phase, therefore, is concerned with creation of this physical system (the MIS) that can function as a conceptual representation of the firm.

Implementation tasks

Many separate tasks comprise the implementation effort. These tasks involve practically everyone in the firm in the MIS project, where the planning and the analysis and design phases involved primarily the managers and the systems analysts. The implementation phase involves these same people, plus lower level employees throughout the organization and the remainder of the information systems staff.

The tasks involved in implementation include:

1 Programming
2 Computer selection
3 Physical installation of computer facilities
4 Education (management and employee)
5 File creation
6 Cutover to the new system

A flowchart illustrating these tasks of the implementation phase appears in Figure 16–1. As in the previous phases, the executive vice-president controls the activity. This flowchart is different from those used previously, however, where a series of activities were performed, one following another. Here, several activities are being performed simultaneously. The completion of some is required before the initiation of others, but several are ongoing at the same time.

The following paragraphs correspond to the numbered activities on the figure.

Figure 16–1   The implementation phase

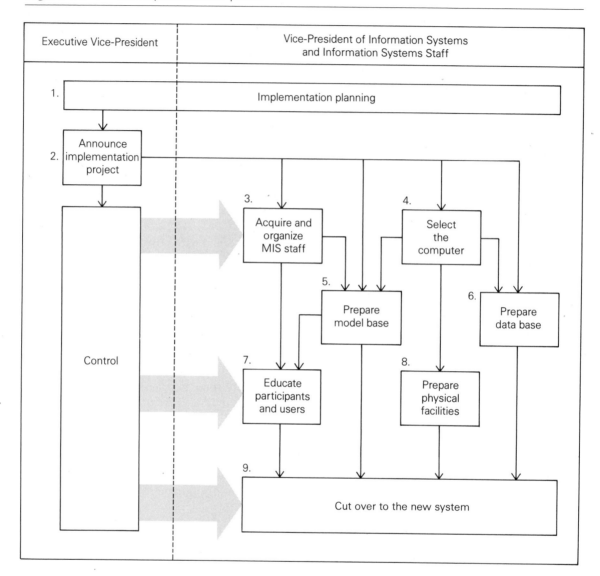

Implementation Planning (1)

Each of the implementation tasks can be planned separately. Then the plans can be integrated to form a coordinated implementation phase. The planning should be more effective for this final phase, since most of the details of the MIS have been determined.

Task 1: Programming

Each of the computer programs has been designed and documented. Perhaps additional programs, not recognized in the planning phase, have been identified as necessary. Other programs may have been eliminated or modified. An accurate list now exists for all of the programs that will be required. This list can be used to update the planned programming effort.

The relative complexity of each program can be estimated rather accurately. The program flowcharts provide a picture of the work each program is to do. These flowcharts can also be used to estimate the time required to prepare each program.

In addition to the better knowledge of the required programs, the firm also has a better understanding of the resources that will do the work: the programmers. Quite probably, the programming staff has been assembled. Their numbers and capabilities are known. Specific programmers can be assigned to specific programs.

An understanding of programmer capabilities and experience, along with a measure of programming complexity, makes possible a plan of the programming effort that is much more detailed and accurate than the initial one.

Tasks 2 and 3: Computer selection and installation

A specification for a computer configuration was not available in the planning phase. It now exists. This specification provides a good basis for planning the activities surrounding computer selection. The configuration makes it possible to identify the vendors that will be given an opportunity to submit bids. Also, the time allotted to each vendor for bid preparation can be better estimated.

The computer configuration also provides a good basis for planning the physical installation. The size of the computer room, along with the air conditioning and power needs, can be estimated accurately.

Task 4: Management and employee education

An important element in the MIS consists of the people who make it work. They will be responsible for putting into the system data that describes the activities of the firm. Factory employees will enter data through terminals or on keypunch forms. All this data must be accurate, and the employees must be trained to do the work correctly.

The users of the MIS output—the managers—also must be oriented in proper use of the information. These managers have defined their information needs, but they must be able to understand how to interpret the output. Now that a design exists for the system, these training and orientation needs can be planned in greater detail.

Task 5: File creation

The system design includes an identification of all the required data files, as well as their contents. Some of these files might currently exist in computer-readable form, such as punched card or magnetic tape. Perhaps they will remain as is, or they may be converted to another form, such as magnetic disk. Whatever the file medium, there is a good chance that additional data will be required and must therefore be added. Also, there is a good chance that completely new files will have to be created. This likelihood is especially great for files of environmental data that may not have existed previously. The system design permits a detailed plan of this file-building activity that will provide the data base for the MIS.

Task 6: Cutover to the new system

The system design also permits the development of a plan of how the firm will cut over to the new system. This cutover must be accomplished with as little disruption to the daily operations as possible. At this point, the effect of the new system on the existing one can be specified. Problems can be identified and plans made to solve them.

All of the problems will not be internal. The new system is likely to place additional demands on the communication between the firm and its environment. Environmental elements, especially customers and vendors, must be integrated into the new information flow, and this activity must be planned carefully.

Summary of implementation planning

The control mechanism initiated in the planning phase can be updated to incorporate detailed plans for the above tasks. If a network diagram is used, it will be redrawn and serve as the basis for monitoring the implementation project. Periodic meetings will continue, thus providing the vice-president of information systems an opportunity to report progress and receive management participation in solving problems. From this point on, management attention shifts from planning to control. The final plan has been made; it is time to execute it.

Announce the Implementation Project (2)

Just as the analysis and design phase had to be announced to the employees, the top management must communicate the plans for the implementation phase. The impact of this communication should be less than the previous one. The rank and file of employees know of the management's interest in an MIS and probably expect the project to continue through completion.

Although all employees were not involved in the analysis and design phase, the communications were aimed at all levels. This approach was intended to stop rumors from spreading about negative impacts of the MIS on employment and duties. Now, however, most of these employees will be expected to play a role in the implementation. An appeal must be made for

Figure 16–2 Announcement of the implementation flows from top to bottom.

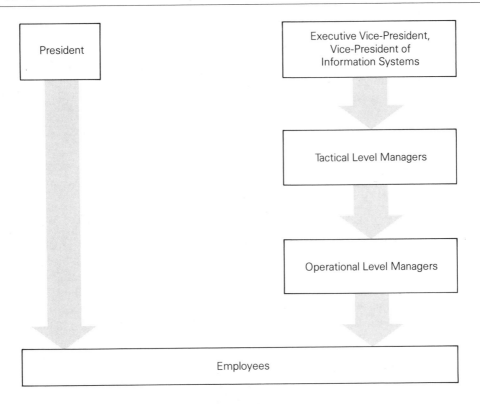

their cooperation. Some explanation should be offered of the roles they will play, and the benefits they will receive.

Since significantly more material must be communicated now, the announcement can be made in phases (Figure 16–2). The president can address the entire employee force (if possible) or can make a statement for the company's publication, explaining the plan in general terms. Then, the executive vice-president and the vice-president of information systems can meet with the key managers to discuss how each area will be involved. These managers next will meet with their staffs to acquaint them with the upcoming events. The final step includes meetings with each section and department to discuss in specific terms how the implementation will be handled. These meetings are not intended to educate the employees about their role in the operating MIS, although this might be covered briefly. The objective is to inform the employees of their role in implementation.

In Figure 16–2, the communication from the president to the employees is intended to prevent morale problems, such as negative attitudes toward the MIS. The employees must know of their importance to a successful system. This message best comes from the top. The communication flow on the right is intended to pass along information describing the role of each level in the implementation.

All of the communication, however, does not deal with implementation roles. At this time, management knows the impact the MIS will have on employment. The system design provides this understanding. If employees are to be transferred or terminated, they should be told as soon as possible. When the system design becomes common knowledge in the firm, those employees will know of the impact. Management must be the first to explain the situation. The employees benefit when they know of the effect before it takes place. This approach provides time for retraining, relocation, or job search.

Acquire and Organize the MIS Staff (3)

The systems analysts have already been acquired. They prepared the system design and will work with the programmers to assure that the programs perform as intended. They also will work with the operations staff in building the files, and with the firm's personnel department in training the employees in how to work with the system. In addition, they will explore additional computer applications not contained in the initial design.

The remainder of the information systems staff must be available to begin implementation activity. Programmers and operations personnel with the proper qualifications must be ready to start to work. Any training or orientation should already have been accomplished. In fact, that training can proceed as soon as the detailed design is finalized during the previous phase.

If the firm has been using a computer, many of these programming and operating resources exist as current employees. Additional persons might have to be added, however, to supply special skills required by the MIS.

When additional staff members are required, all existing employees can be given an opportunity to apply for the jobs. Aptitude tests can be administered that provide a good indication of a person's chances of success in programming or operations. Many computer personnel once worked in other areas of the company and received an opportunity for career improvement as a result of their firm's computer effort. Also, consideration of existing employees for the new staff positions does much to offset any damaging effects of job elimination. If the employees holding these eliminated jobs can find a place on the information systems staff, that is good. However, that is not a prime consideration in staff selection; consideration must be based on ability and potential, not on hardship.

These staff openings provide good employment opportunities for college men and women. Both operations and programming are open doors to a career in computing or management. College graduates are given top consideration. College students also frequently find part-time employment as computer and peripheral equipment operators.

Select the Computer (4)

The system design must be expressed in terms of a specific vendor's computer model before any remaining implementation steps can be taken. Although much compatibility exists between different vendors' equipment, there are enough differences to delay programming and file creation until the exact equipment is specified. Also, no work begins on physical installation until the exact environmental requirements of the equipment are known.

Requests for bids

The system design should be made available to the vendors offering all or any of the types of equipment in the configuration. Many vendors supply only certain units, like graph plotters, terminals, and OCR readers. Some of these units may be superior to similar devices supplied by vendors such as IBM, Honeywell, and Control Data Corporation, who offer complete configurations. The best configuration might be one that integrates hardware from more than one vendor. Since so many firms produce computing equipment, some screening process usually precedes the offering of invitations to bid.

Each vendor selected should be provided with a document called a *request for bid* or *request for proposal* (*RFP*). This document is a summary of the relevant parts of the system study and the implementation project proposals. Figure 16–3 is an outline of such a bid request.

The letter of transmittal explains to the vendor what is expected, including the type of proposal desired and the deadline for submission. Sections 2, 3a, 3b, and 3c are taken directly from the implementation project proposal (Figure 15–13). Section 3d includes the material from the documentation that will enable the vendors to understand what the equipment is intended to do. Sections 3e and 3f, plus the performance criteria, will enable the vendors to select specific hardware devices and prepare timing estimates and price quotations. Section 4 contains that portion of the implementation schedule specifying target dates for equipment installation.

Preparation of vendor proposals

The vendors review the request for bid and decide whether to respond. If a vendor chooses to compete for the order, the vendor representatives prepare a proposal describing how their equipment meets the performance criteria.

Most likely, the vendors will want to interview selected key managers and information system staff members to gain additional facts. Time is made available to the vendors to conduct these interviews, knowing that much of this onsite work is more sales than systems effort. The vendors recognize the value of getting to know the key people who will influence equipment selection. It is difficult not to grant them access to these people. The proposed

Figure 16–3   The request for bid

---

1. Letter of transmittal

2. System objectives and constraints

3. System design
   a. Summary description
   b. Performance criteria
   c. Equipment configuration
   d. Program documentation packages
      (selected portions)
   e. Estimated transaction volume
   f. Estimated file sizes

4. Installation schedule

equipment configurations are more likely to meet the needs of the firm when the vendors have a good understanding of the key people involved. If the request for bid adequately describes the planned MIS, the need for additional information gathering by the vendors will be minimal.

Presentation of vendor proposals

In practically all cases, the vendors prepare written proposals. Some proposals may be nothing more than a letter, while others may be lengthy volumes. An outline of a vendor proposal is shown in Figure 16–4.

Section 2 summarizes the recommendations of the vendor relating to type of equipment proposed and major benefits to be expected. This section does not elaborate, but condenses the relevant points of the proposal into a succinct management summary. Section 3 lists the advantages of selecting this vendor's equipment over that of another. Sections 4 and 5 identify the proposed computer system components along with their performance specifications (speeds, accuracy ratings, etc.) and their price. In section 6, the performance criteria are addressed, program by program. When included, this is the most lengthy section in the proposal. Finally, in section 7, the vendor quotes a delivery schedule that should meet the installation dates in the implementation plan.

Very often, the vendor also will make a formal oral presentation to the key executives or the MIS committee. This presentation gives the firm's executives an opportunity to ask questions about points unclear in the proposal.

Figure 16–4 The vendor proposal

1. Letter of transmittal

2. Summary of recommendations

3. Advantages

4. Equipment configuration

5. Equipment specifications
   a. Performance data
   b. Prices

6. Satisfaction of performance criteria

7. Delivery schedule

Selection of vendor

Vendor selection can be very easy or it can be practically impossible, depending on how well the firm has specified its needs. If the specifications are vague, each vendor will adapt their proposal to best highlight their advantages, perhaps at the cost of meeting the firm's needs. For example, one firm with a good key-to-disk device will recommend it for data entry, while another firm will recommend their superior OCR reader. The result is a comparison of "apples and oranges" that provides no common basis for selection.

A tight equipment specification and design documentation will permit an "apples to apples" comparison, making selection more straightforward. When all vendors propose the same types of equipment, selection primarily boils down to which one best meets the performance criteria at least cost.

The entire selection decision, however, is not based strictly on this quantitative proposal data. Consideration must be given also to the record of the vendor in meeting previous commitments. A quick survey of some of the vendor's customers can indicate the consistency with which promises of future performance are fulfilled.

Very often, the vendor provides implementation assistance in the form of programming help, computer time for program testing and file building, and physical installation consultation. These services may be included in the prices of the equipment or may be charged separately.

The executive vice-president and the vice-president of information systems, or the MIS committee, then select the vendor. This selection is approved by the president, and an order is placed.

Prepare the Model Base (5)

The term *data base* has been accepted widely among computer professionals. It, and its less formal and more widely used synonym, *data bank*, refer to the files of data used by a computer system. The term *model base* is less well known. It describes the set of models or programs that the computer uses. The programming effort, then, can be regarded as the preparation of this model base.

As a programmer goes about the task of creating a program for the model base, a series of steps are taken. These steps are illustrated in Figure 16–5 and discussed separately.

1. Understand the problem. Before the programmer begins coding the program, he or she must understand the problem being solved by the program. Most of this understanding is gained from reviewing the program documentation package prepared by the analyst. This inspection is augmented by discussions with the analyst and, perhaps, the manager who will use the output.

The programmer might see some way the program can function more efficiently than that described by the package. If so, this fact should be discussed with the analyst, and the changes made when warranted. Perhaps the arrangement or form of the data in the input or output records can be changed. Or the sequence of steps in the program flowchart can be modified. Maybe a different technique can be used to accomplish the results more efficiently. The programmer is concerned with computer efficiency, both minimizing input/output and processing time and conserving storage. The detailed knowledge of the computer and programming techniques enables the programmer to develop the most efficient approach to problem solution.

2. Code the program. The programmer usually codes the program, one instruction at a time, on special coding sheets for the language being used. Figure 16–6 illustrates a COBOL coding sheet.

In some situations, the programmer codes the program at a terminal. This technique bypasses the keypunch step. Some languages are more adaptable to this approach than others, although it is possible to code all languages in this manner. Much depends on the availability of terminals and the preferences of the programming manager.

3. Keypunch the source program. One card is punched for each line on the coding sheet. An alternative approach is to use a key-to-tape or a key-to-disk device to eliminate the need for cards. The program deck or file is called the *source program*. It exists in the source language, such as COBOL, used by the programmer.

4. Compile the program. The source program is entered into the computer, with appropriate control cards, and the computer attempts to convert it

Figure 16–5   The programming task

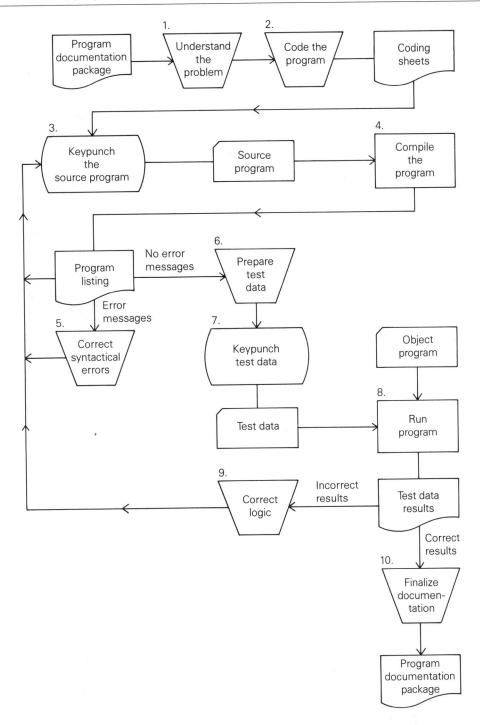

Figure 16–6 A COBOL coding sheet

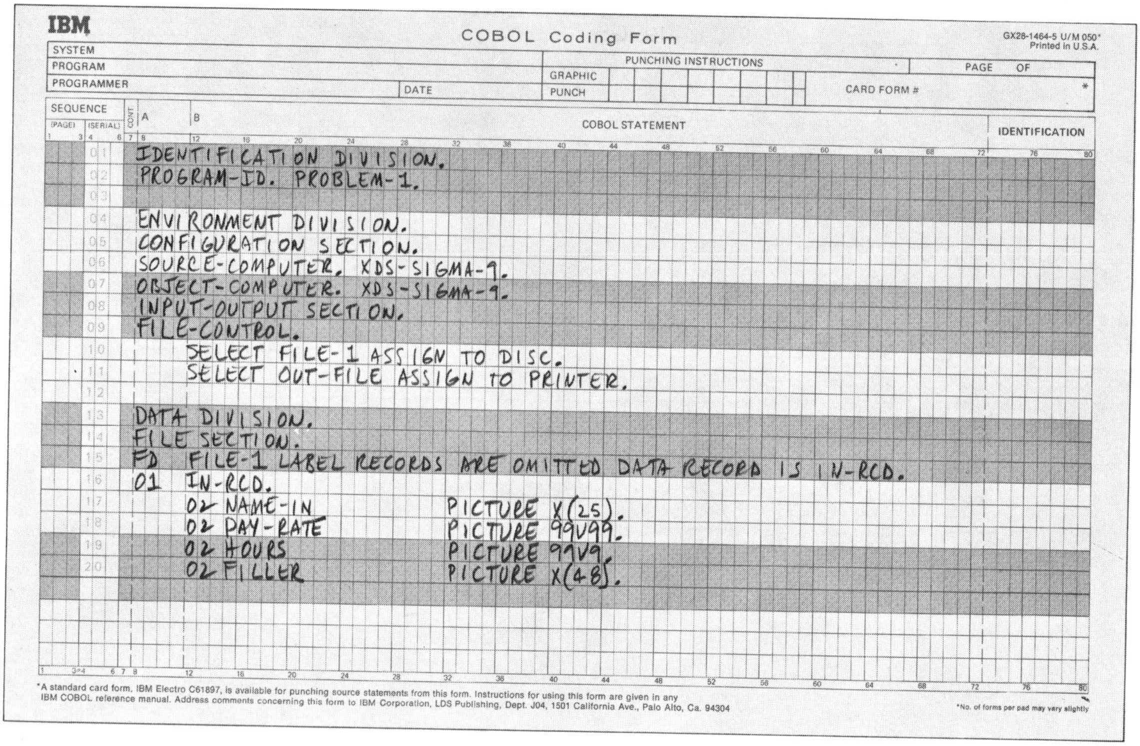

IBM COBOL Coding Form — GX28-1464-5 U/M 050* Printed in U.S.A.

SYSTEM / PROGRAM / PROGRAMMER / DATE / PUNCHING INSTRUCTIONS / GRAPHIC / PUNCH / PAGE OF / CARD FORM #

SEQUENCE (PAGE) (SERIAL) / CONT. / A / B / COBOL STATEMENT / IDENTIFICATION

```
01 IDENTIFICATION DIVISION.
02 PROGRAM-ID. PROBLEM-1.
03
04 ENVIRONMENT DIVISION.
05 CONFIGURATION SECTION.
06 SOURCE-COMPUTER. XDS-SIGMA-9.
07 OBJECT-COMPUTER. XDS-SIGMA-9.
08 INPUT-OUTPUT SECTION.
09 FILE-CONTROL.
10     SELECT FILE-1 ASSIGN TO DISC.
11     SELECT OUT-FILE ASSIGN TO PRINTER.
12
13 DATA DIVISION.
14 FILE SECTION.
15 FD  FILE-1 LABEL RECORDS ARE OMITTED DATA RECORD IS IN-RCD.
16 01  IN-RCD.
17     02 NAME-IN            PICTURE X(25).
18     02 PAY-RATE           PICTURE 99V99.
19     02 HOURS              PICTURE 99V9.
20     02 FILLER             PICTURE X(48).
```

*A standard card form, IBM Electro C61897, is available for punching source statements from this form. Instructions for using this form are given in any IBM COBOL reference manual. Address comments concerning this form to IBM Corporation, LDS Publishing, Dept. J04, 1501 California Ave., Palo Alto, Ca. 94304

*No. of forms per pad may vary slightly

to a language the computer can understand, or *machine language*. When the program is converted to machine language, the new form is called the *object program*. This program is the object, or end result, of the compile process. The computer cannot execute a program in source language. That language is only for the benefit of the programmer since it is easier to understand and use than machine language. Machine language represents everything in a coded form for the purpose of efficiency. Figure 16–7 illustrates machine language.

The term *compile* describes the conversion of a source program into an object program by a compiler program, such as a COBOL or FORTRAN compiler. A conversion of an assembly language program such as one in BAL (Basic Assembly Language) is called an *assembly process*. Step 4 also can be accomplished by an assembly process when the source program is written in such a language.

The main difference between a compiler and an assembler is the number of object instructions or program steps created from each source instruction. In an assembler, each source instruction is translated into one object instruction. In a compiler, the translation can produce more than one object instruction.

The compiler and assembler programs are important parts of the operating system, discussed in Chapter 5.

Figure 16–7   Sample of machine language

```
0B980    1404C12E    0000A75E    0010AB36    80000B21
0B984    0010B994    0000C12E    000B2DB6    0007020A
0B988    0000B9C4    00000000    03800000    00000008
0B98C    00000011    000B2DB6    00020000    048F0004
0B990    00000000    00FE0301    00180000    000C2BF6
0B994    01000308    02C3C540    40404040    40404040
0B998    C56BE3C5    C3C850C3    E4D3E340    40C54000
0B99C    648C0760    02000202    F2F1F0F0    F0F0F2C1
0B9A0    03000002    000C4000    0C404001    05000010
0B9A4    195E1301    195E0B01    21370F01    0A021202
0B9A8    019A2000    1334C015    C1404040    000C4040
0B9AC    40404040    40404040    40404040    40404040
0B9B0    40C54000    648C0760    121C4040    00000C00
0B9B4    0700000C    000C0000    000C4000    0C404001
0B9B8    195E1201    195E0B01    195E0B01    1F051001
0B9BC    0AB40F02    019A2700    14348016    761C4040
0B9C0    005CC2C1    04010002    000C4000    00000C10
0B9C4    03033C20    F0F0F0F2    C1F2F1F0    0BF70B01
0B9C8    00020A01    270F0701    11DB0402    00010301
0B9CC    082A0401    02940902    00020201    195E0B01
0B9D0    195E0101    195E0101    195E1401    195E1400
0B9D4    4E000001    00048800    05000000    0000A75E
0B9D8    0000AB36    80000011    0000B9EA    00000000
0B9DC    00000000    00058000    0000BA1A    00000000
0B9E0    00000000    00000000    00000000    00000000
0B9E4    00000000    00000000    00000000    00000000
0B9E8    00000000    00000000    01000308    03C3C5E2
0B9EC    40404040    40404040    00000000    00000000
0B9F0    00000000    00000000    00000000    02000202
0B9F4    F2F1F0F0    F0F0F2C1    03000002    00000000
0B9F8    00000000    06000010    00000000    00000000
0B9FC    00000000    00000000    00000000    00000000
0BA00    00000000    00000000    01AFB404    011AFB01
0BA04    0132402C    011AFB02    46390320    0CC2D6D3
0BA08    E3C54040    40404040    0700000C    C8D540C5
0BA0C    40404040    40404040    40404000    0000C00C
0BA10    0000000C    40404040    40404040    40404040
0BA14    404040D4    C1055030    1CE2F4C7    04010002
0BA18    404040C1    C0404040    40404040    40404040
0BA1C    40404040    40404040    000C011A    FE010121
0BA20    72020100    0114011A    FB04011A    FB03011A
```

5. *Correct syntactical errors.* Each programming language has rules that must be followed. Certain data must be punched in certain columns of the card; spaces should appear in certain positions and not in others; certain words can be used and others cannot; and the like. These rules are known as the *syntax* of the language. Violations of these rules are called *syntactical errors;* they are identified on the printout of the source program by *error messages* or *diagnostic messages.* Figure 16–8 illustrates some error messages.

When error messages appear, the errors must be corrected. This process is called *debugging* and occupies a significant portion of a programmer's time.

Figure 16–8 Error messages on the source program listing.

```
8-1  FOO    COBOL SOURCE, DIAGNOSTIC AND PROCEDURE-MAP LISTING      11:06 MAY 25, 1977    PAGE   1

        00000                COBOL LS,GO,SEQCHK,DIAG    ... SOURCE DECK FOLLOWS ...          .COBOL 4
        00001                IDENTIFICATION DIVISION.
        00002                PROGRAM-ID. P. O. REPORT.
        00003                ENVIRONMENT DIVISION.
        00004                CONFIGURATION SECTION.
        00005                SOURCE-COMPUTER. XDS-SIGMA-9.
        00006                OBJECT-COMPUTER. XDS-SIGMA-9.
        00007                INPUT-OUTPUT SECTION.
        00008                    SELECT P-O-FILE ASSIGN TO CARD-READER.
→ **** 014 **** REQUIRED PARAGRAPH OMITTED
→ **** 038 **** SOURCE WORDS BYPASSED
        00009                    SELECT P-O-REPORT ASSIGN TO PRINTER.
→ **** 038 **** SOURCE WORDS BYPASSED
        00010                DATA DIVISION.
        00011                FILE SECTION.
        00012                FD  P-O-FILE LABEL RECORDS OMITTED DATA RECORD IS P-O-REC.
→ **** 034 **** UNSELECTED FILE
        00013                01  P-O-REC.
        00014                    02 P-O-NO          PICTURE 9(6).
        00015                    02 P-O-DATE        PICTURE 9(6).
        00016                    02 VENDOR-NO       PICTURE 9(6).
        00017                    02 VENDOR-NAME     PICTURE X(20).
        00018                    02 DUE-DATE        PICTURE 9(6).
        00019                    02 P-O-AMT         PICTURE 9(5)V99.
        00020                    02 FILLER          PICTURE X(29).
        00021                FD  P-O-REPORT LABEL RECORD OMITTED DATA RECORD IS PRINT-LINE.
→ **** 034 **** UNSELECTED FILE
        00022                01  PRINT-LINE.
        00023                    02 FILLER          PICTURE X.
        00024                    02 NO-OUT          PICTURE 9(6).
        00025                    02 FILLER          PICTURE XXX.
        00026                    02 DATE-OUT        PICTURE 9(6).
        00027                    02 FILLER          PICTURE XXX.
        00028                    02 NAME-OUT        PICTURE X(20).
        00029                    02 FILLER          PICTURE XXX.
        00030                    02 AMT-OUT         PICTURE $99,999.99.
        00031                PROCEDURE DIVISION.
        00032                HOUSEKEEPING.
        00033                    OPEN INPUT P-O-FILE OUTPUT P-O-REPORT.
        00034                    MOVE SPACES TO PRINT-LINE.
        00035                MAIN-LOOP.
        00036                    READ P-O-FILE AT END GO TO END-OF-JOB.
        00037                    MOVE P-O-NO TO NO-OUT.
        00038                    MOVE P-O-DATE TO DATE-OUT.
        00039                    MOVE VENDOR-NAME TO NAME-OUT.
        00040                    MOVE P-O-AMT TO AMT-OUT.
        00041                    WRITE PRINT-LINE.
        00042                    GO TO MAIN-LOOP.
        00043                END-OF-JOB.
        00044                    CLOSE P-O-FILE P-O-REPORT.
        00045                    STOP RUN.
**** 159 **** EXTERNAL REFERENCE GENERATED

*** NUMBER OF DIAGNOSTIC MESSAGES    6 ***    HIGHEST SEVERITY LEVEL    7 ***
```

The programmer corrects the errors, and the source program is revised. Another compile is attempted, and this process is repeated until a "clean" compile is obtained, one with either no errors or only minor ones. The computer and its compiler program will not produce an object program until the critical errors are corrected.

When the object program is produced, it can be in various forms. The computer can punch an *object deck* in punched cards, or store the program on magnetic tape or DASD. In any of these forms, the object program can be used at a later date to process data without the need to recompile. Most debugged object programs are stored on some type of DASD for rapid retrieval by the computer's operating system when needed.

Another approach is to leave the object program in main storage and process the data immediately after compilation. This method is called *load and go*, and represents a popular way to process student programs. The end product is a computer solution to a problem, and not an object program to be added to the model base.

6. Prepare test data. It is the programmer's responsibility to produce a program that processes the data correctly. The best way to accomplish this task is to prepare a file of data records that can be processed by the object program, run the program, and then evaluate the results.

The file of test data does not have to be large. The important requirement is that the data allows the program to test all conditions or combinations of conditions that will be encountered when real data is used. Some of the data records should contain the types of errors the program is to detect. Safeguards against bad data can be verified along with processing accuracy.

After the data is created, but before the program processes it, the programmer simulates the computer results with a calculator or manual method. The programmer subjects the test data to the same logical tests the computer will make, and uses the calculator to perform the arithmetic. This simulation of the computer by the programmer is called *desk checking*.

Desk checking is intended to detect a second type of programming error: a *logical error*. This type cannot be detected by the computer as in the case of the syntactical error. The logical error is one where the syntax is followed correctly, but the wrong instructions are used or they are used in an incorrect manner. As an example, assume the programmer wanted to compute an employee's net pay by subtracting both withholding tax and social security tax from gross pay. Further, assume that an instruction is coded in COBOL as follows:

COMPUTE NET-PAY = GROSS-PAY − WH-TAX + SS-TAX.

The instruction complies with the COBOL syntax, but it will produce the wrong answer. Instead of adding the two taxes together and subtracting the total from gross pay, the first tax will be subtracted and the second added. This type of error can be detected through desk checking and the use of test data.

Either of the following corrections will eliminate the logical error:

COMPUTE NET-PAY = GROSS-PAY — (WH-TAX + SS-TAX).
COMPUTE NET-PAY = GROSS-PAY — WH-TAX — SS-TAX.

7. Keypunch test data. If a long data record is being tested, it is easier to key the data directly to a tape or disk. Key-to-tape or key-to-disk devices, or terminals, can be used for this purpose. Otherwise, an 80- or a 96-column card can be punched for each record.

8. Run the program. The object program is entered in the computer's main storage where it is executed. If the program is designed to produce an output report, that report is printed. Other output, such as punched cards, magnetic tape, or DASD records, can also be produced, but they too must be printed for examination by the programmer.

9. Correct logic errors. The programmer compares the computer results with those from the desk check simulation. Any differences are analyzed to determine the source of the error. Corrections are made to the source program and it is recompiled. Another try is made at processing the test data. This procedure is followed until the test data output is correct.

10. Finalize documentation. When the programmer is assured that the program handles the data correctly, it is necessary to finalize the documentation. A complete, accurate documentation package must exist for each operational program. If any changes were made to the record layouts or program flowchart, the layouts must be updated. Copies of the test data and the test data results are added to the program documentation package. In addition, instructions to the operations personnel are prepared to help them run the program on the computer. These instructions will be kept in the computer room and will identify any special equipment setup instructions or error procedures. For example, if the program produces punched card output, the operator is reminded to put blank cards in the card punch unit. The operators will refer to these instructions each time the program is run until they become familiar with it.

The program documentation package remains in the programming department. It is available for use in modifying the program at a later date, or for training new analysts and programmers.

The model base

All of the programs prepared to be run on the computer become the model base. Most of the programs may be written by the firm's programmers. These programs process customer orders, print payroll checks, project cash flows, and simulate price change results. Other programs in the model base are written by the computer vendor. These programs compile or assemble programs, sort and merge data records, convert punched card data to magnetic tape data, etc. Still other programs are written by outside firms, such as software houses or consultants. These programs usually perform sophisticated quantitative routines, such as simulations, regression analyses, or linear programming solutions.

Many "canned programs" are available to the computer user. It is foolish to incur the expense of writing a program when a similar one is available, probably at less cost. It is the responsibility of the programming manager to stay abreast of programming developments and sources of canned programs.

Prepare the Data Base (6)

Earlier discussions have explained the data base in terms of what it is, how it is organized, and how it is maintained (see Chapter 7). The discussion here centers on how the data base is prepared.

Preparation can be easy or difficult, depending on the circumstances. The task becomes difficult when (1) the firm is converting from a system of manual files to computer media, (2) the files are large, (3) the files contain data that is very old, and (4) some of the data is not being maintained presently. The degree to which any of these conditions exist determines the difficulty of the task. It can be just as difficult as preparation of the model base.

Preparation difficulties

Manual files create conversion problems because they usually contain errors, omissions, and inconsistencies. These flaws can go unnoticed in a manual system, but are not acceptable to the computer. As an example, if a programmer defines a salesperson number field in a record as consisting of eight digits, it must be exactly that. Each record must contain the salesperson number, it can be no larger nor smaller than the eight positions, and it can contain neither alphabetic nor special characters. Flaws such as these must be corrected before the data is acceptable to the computer.

Large files simply add to the size of the task. Conversion can take weeks or even months and demand large commitments of personnel and equipment that the firm may not have available.

Old files add yet another dimension to the difficulty. Over the years, forms and coding systems change, creating a hodgepodge of nonuniform data. Files with these variations must be converted to a standardized format. Any efforts to confirm the accuracy of data elements or to reconstruct missing elements are usually very difficult. The reason for this difficulty is because the source documents used to prepare the files probably have long been destroyed.

When data is *not maintained,* special data-gathering activities must be performed. This task can be expensive, especially when the data is gathered from the environment. Competitor plans and customer attitudes are examples of data that is difficult to obtain.

Figure 16–9   Preparation of the data base

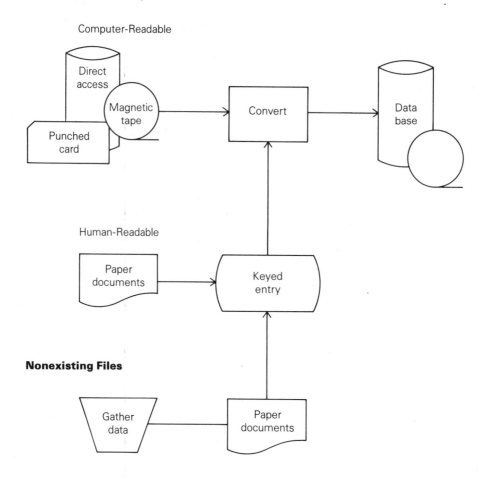

Existing Files

Computer-Readable

Human-Readable

Nonexisting Files

Basic routes to the data base

Figure 16–9 shows the three basic routes that can be followed in data base preparation. The most direct path is that from computer-readable media such as punched cards, magnetic tapes, and DASD. Data from these media is read into the computer's main storage, edited for accuracy, recoded when necessary, and arranged in the new format. The data is written on a data base medium, usually DASD or magnetic tape.

Very often data will be maintained, but not in a computer-readable form. Data in manila file folders is of this type. It is first necessary to enter this data into the computer using some keyed entry device (keypunch machine, terminal, or a key-to-tape or key-to-disk unit). Once the data is in the main storage of the computer, the same procedure can be followed for building the output files as described above. It is possible that OCR can be used to read data from paper file documents. Usually, however, poor condition of the paper and variations in the shape and location of printed characters prevent OCR use.

The third route to the data base shows the special data-gathering step required for new data. Data usually is recorded on a form especially designed for the purpose.

Planning and controlling data base activity

All of the activity leading to the data base can demand significant expenditures of time and money. The size of the task must be estimated and the necessary resources allocated. Estimates should include some margin for error since unforeseen problems inevitably arise.

Part or all of the data base project can be subcontracted to an outside organization, such as a consulting firm or software house. The costs of this approach at first might seem high, but tend not to be unrealistic when the expenses of data gathering, editing, correcting, and converting are all considered. If an outside organization is used, it is subject to the same system of progress reporting and controls that governs the rest of the implementation effort.

Importance of the data base

If the MIS is to provide the manager with information, a necessary prerequisite is accurate, complete, and current data. The task of creating this data base is more difficult in some industries than in others. Insurance and banking are noted for their difficult file conversion problems. The work in these industries is essentially one of maintaining customer master files over long periods of time, and such files easily become unwieldy. In other industries—manufacturing and retailing—file conversion is not so tedious, but should not be underestimated.

Educate Participants and Users (7)

The MIS will affect many people. Some will make the system work and others will use its output. All must be educated concerning (1) their role in the system, and (2) how the system will benefit them.

The education program is aimed at not only members of the firm, but at elements in its environment as well. Table 16–1 identifies the different groups that have a need for education and the type of education needed.

The only groups not receiving education concerning the expected benefits of the MIS are the members of the information systems staff and strategic level management. It is assumed that both already have received this information during their previous involvement with the system. If such is not the case,

Table 16–1   Structure of the MIS education program

	Group	Type of education
I N T E R N A L	Information systems staff	How to perform specific tasks.
	Other employees (clerical, production, sales, etc.)	How to perform specific tasks; how to interpret output; benefits.
	Operational and tactical level management	Departmental duties and responsibilities; how to interpret output; benefits.
	Strategic level management	How to interpret output.
E N V I R O N M E N T A L	Vendors	The role of the vendor in the system; benefits.
	Customers (industrial)	The role of the customer in the system; benefits.
	Customers (individual)	Changes to billing and collection procedures; benefits.
	Organized labor	The role of union workers in the system; benefits.
	Government, stockholders, local community, financial community	No specific education program required.

the situation must be remedied. All participants should have a good understanding of how the system will benefit *them.*

Lower level employees, such as clerical personnel, factory workers, and salespersons must learn how to do specific tasks. These tasks include filling out forms, operating terminals, and using output. This information can be communicated in the work area during regular duty hours. The sessions, usually not exceeding 1 hour per day, continue for as many days as necessary. The information can be communicated by supervisors, members of the information systems staff (systems analysts), instructors from the firm's personnel department, or outsiders such as consultants. This education is very detailed and specific. All these people must understand exactly how the system works.

Managers on all levels receive much less specific instruction. Departmental managers must understand the role of their departments, including the flow of data and information, how it is interrelated with that of other departments, and the effect on the system of not performing the work as specified. All managers also must understand how to interpret and use the information output. These educational sessions can be conducted by systems analysts, the firm's instructional staff, or outside consultants. Quite probably, some "hands on" training in the use of a terminal will be necessary. This training can be provided by representatives of the equipment vendors.

Education for internal employees is best handled in face-to-face situations where the opportunity for two-way communication exists. Education for members of the firm's environment is less elaborate.

Vendors and industrial customers (other firms buying the company's products) have a need for more information than the other groups. Both vendors and industrial customers must understand that they are participants in an interfirm information network (see Figure 11–4). The benefits accruing to all participating firms in the network should be stressed. This program should be communicated in person to key individuals by capable representatives in the firm's purchasing and sales departments. Direct mail can support these personal contacts.

Very often, the new MIS will cause a change in procedures relating to individual customers, or consumers. These changes usually affect the way the firm bills and collects for purchases. The customer can be informed of these changes with a letter inserted in bills or statements. Consumers have a need for this type of information. Not getting it has accounted for a great deal of resistance by the general public to the increasing role of the computer in their everyday lives. A simple and inexpensive education program can prevent most of this resistance. Figures 16–10 and 16–11 illustrate two letters mailed to customers of a men's clothing store, informing them of the firm's new computer system.

If the firm's workers are members of organized labor unions, the local union officials should be included in the education effort. There likely will be strong resistance if the MIS is to have any effect on jobs. No employees will likely be replaced by the MIS itself; however, work procedures will be changed. Employees might be asked to input additional data and operate data terminals.

These sessions with labor representatives are much like those directed at lower and middle level managers: they stress general procedures and benefits. These sessions can be conducted by members of the firm's industrial relations department, assisted by the vice-president of information systems.

There is no need for specific education programs for other members of the environment. Any information needs that may arise can be handled on an exception basis.

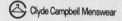
Clyde Campbell Menswear

Dear Customer: July 25, 1977

    This is your new computer statement. We hope you like it.

    As you know, we are not a big corporation--we are a small group of men's
specialty shops in Fort Worth, Dallas and Austin. And our main specialty,
being small, is personal service to you--your salesman knows you by name,
knows your tastes, your wardrobe, and probably has a record of your sizes.
If we get in something he thinks you will like, you'll usually get a phone
call or a note. We pride ourselves in doing things the giants can't do.

    Same with this statement. You'll find it's almost identical to the one
you've been getting with the charges, credits and balance in the right place.
You won't have to keep your original sales ticket to know what you've bought,
or find a number in the fine print on the back with a vague description.
You'll still get another copy of your signed ticket with your statement. You
won't be billed in the middle of the month--we will still close our books on
the 25th. You won't have to carry another credit card, or remember your
account number--your salesman will personally handle this when you make a
purchase. And your salesman's initials follow the ticket number on the face
of the statement.

    So ... we hope you will like this kind of old-fashioned statement.

    There's only one thing we're a little nervous about. In putting all of
our accounts on the computer at one time, we may have mispelled your name,
or perhaps gotten the wrong address. Will you please check this first statement very carefully and give us a correction on anything you find wrong. Be
sure to check your balance, too. We have taken every precaution in making
the changeover, but if there is any possibility of a mistake, we want to know
and correct it quickly, right now at the start. There's a place below for
you to tell us. Send it to us with your payment, or mail it now if you
prefer.

                          Sincerely yours,

                          Clyde Campbell Menswear

    "With you from College to Career to Chairman of the Board"

Correct Name and Address (please print)

_____

_____

_____

Anything else wrong?_____

_____

Figure 16–11   Letter reporting computer installation progress to customers. (Courtesy of Clyde Campbell Menswear, Inc.)

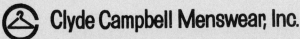

Clyde Campbell Menswear, Inc.

14175 Proton Road, Dallas, Texas 75240 • Dallas (214) 233-9797 Fort Worth-Dallas Metro 263-3903

                              WE'RE SORRY

    Our statements last month contained a number of errors, some of which
we corrected by hand prior to mailing, but many of which we missed. We're
Sorry. We and our computer (we have named it Hal) fouled up. Perhaps we
should take all the blame, but we strongly suspect the computer (Hal) has
a will of its own and sometimes does things without telling us about it.
We considered harsh action against Hal, but were afraid to make it mad.
No telling what it might do to us if that happens.

    This month's statements are better, but still probably not error free.
We will continue to work closely with Hal to minimize the inconvenience
to you.

    Our credit people report that our customers have been very understanding
and pleasant in pointing out the errors on their statements. For this we
are very grateful. It gives us a good feeling to receive this kind of
treatment.

Prepare Physical Facilities (8)

The work required to prepare the physical facilities for the computer equipment installation can vary from none to much. It depends on the amount of equipment needed. If only a few additional units are to be installed (disk drives, terminals, etc.), they probably can be housed in existing areas. If a new computer system is needed, a complete construction project may be necessary.

Such a project begins with specification of equipment environment requirements (power, temperature, space, and humidity) by representatives of the equipment vendor. These same representatives also recommend the best arrangement of the equipment units for operating efficiency. Once the layout of the computer area has been developed (Figure 16–12), attention is given to surrounding areas (offices, peripheral equipment rooms, libraries, etc.). Layout and design of these areas often is done by architects and interior designers. Finally, the design is implemented by a general contracting firm.

This activity should be one part of the implementation phase where the firm has previous experience. Construction of computer facilities is not unlike construction of facilities to house any piece of expensive equipment. Representatives of architectural and contractor firms, along with those of the computer manufacturer, can supply expert consultation on how the construc-

Figure 16–12   Layout of a computer area. (Courtesy of Electronic Data Systems)

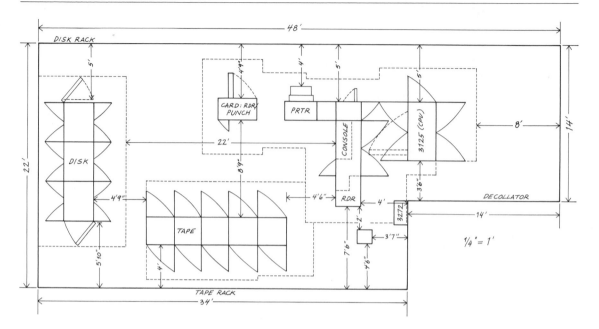

tion should be accomplished. All of these activities are incorporated into the overall implementation plan and are controlled in the same manner as work performed by the firm's own employees. It is very common for the manager of computer operations to have primary responsibility for representing the firm to the various outside groups.

Cutover to the New System (9)

When the previous implementation work has been completed, it is time to cut over to the new system. The larger the firm and the more complex its operations, the more difficult the cutover becomes. It is not unlike a human patient undergoing a heart or a kidney transplant: the total system must be kept alive while converting to the new vital organ. There is a large history of successful computer conversions by firms, and there is no reason to fear failure when these conversions are performed correctly.

Basic approaches to cutover

Cutover to the new MIS involves three basic approaches: immediate, phased, and parallel. The one selected will depend on characteristics of the firm (size, geographic distribution, etc.) and on money available to finance the conversion.

1. *Immediate.* The most simple approach is to convert from the old system to the new one on a given day. If this can be done, then this approach should be selected since it is the least expensive and time-consuming. This approach is feasible in smaller firms, but not in larger ones. As the scale of operation increases, the timing problems of an immediate cutover become too great. It is almost impossible to convert from all of the old procedures and files at one time.

2. *Phased.* If the entire system cannot be converted at once, it can be divided into subsystems and converted a subsystem at a time. This process prolongs the conversion period and introduces problems when one subsystem must be linked to another. However, these problems can be worked out, and this approach is very common. It can be followed within a single geographic location or among several locations. For example, at the firm's main plant site the order entry subsystem can be implemented first, followed by the finished goods inventory subsystem, and so on. Or, if the firm has suboffices located across the country, each can be converted to the new system in succession.

3. *Parallel.* This approach offers the greatest security against failure, but it is the most expensive. It requires that the old system be maintained until the new one is fully checked out. The firm actually operates two systems at the same time: the old one and the new one. A big advantage of the parallel approach is the ability to fully debug the new system, using live data, before the old system is scrapped. The expense is caused by the need to maintain two systems, including the people, equipment, supplies, etc. It is possible, however, to hire temporary help or contract with computer data centers to perform much of the duplicated work during the conversion period.

Summary

The implementation of an MIS requires the coordination of many activities. This coordination is achieved by development of a detailed implementation plan and continuous control. The executive vice-president (or the MIS committee) exercises this planning and control, but the vice-president of information systems plays a key role. This latter executive directs the activities of the information specialists, coordinates their interactions with the rest of the firm, and reports progress and problems to top management.

The implementation can take several months and involve most of the firm's employees and certain elements in the environment as well. It is a costly process, and the success depends on the cooperation of all con-

cerned. A good education program, aimed at meeting the specific information needs of the different groups, is one of the keys to success.

Management performs the important tasks of announcing the project
to the firm's employees, acquiring and organizing an MIS staff, and selecting the computing equipment. The computer selection follows a logical
process of identifying the equipment that best meets the performance criteria, at least cost.

Once the MIS staff is available, its two main tasks are preparation of
the model base and the data base. Both programmers and computer operations personnel perform the majority of this important work.

When the above steps have been taken and the physical facilities
have been prepared, the firm can cut over to the new system. Cutover can
be immediate, phased, or parallel. The firm can begin to enjoy the benefits
of the new MIS.

Important Terms

Request for Bid	Error Message, Diagnostic Message
Request for Proposal (RFP)	Debugging
Source Program	Object Deck
Machine Language	Load and Go
Object Program	Desk Checking
Compile	Logical Error
Syntax, Syntactical Error	

Important Concepts

Implementation of an MIS requires execution of several major
activities, some of which can be
executed at the same time.

Implementation planning at this
point in the life cycle of the MIS
can be much more detailed and
accurate than that done earlier.

When possible, the MIS staff
should be created internally
through employee transfer from
other areas.

Computer vendors should be
asked to propose equipment to accomplish specific, predefined tasks.

Computer vendors recommend certain computer configurations in written proposals and in oral presentation of these proposals.

Vendor selection is based on ability to do the specified job at the least cost; but much of the decision is subjective evaluation of vendor abilities—past, present, and future.

Both the model base and the data base must be created during the implementation phase.

Most of the programs in the model base have to be written by the firm's programmers following a well-defined step-by-step process.

Some programs in the model base can be acquired from outside sources, such as computer vendors, software houses, other firms, etc.

Data enters the data base from different sources, and undergoes a variety of processes to convert it into the final form.

Outside firms, such as service organizations, can be contracted to perform all or part of the data base creation activity.

Implementation of an MIS requires that most of the firm's employees, as well as selected elements in the environment, receive some special education.

A firm's approach to cutover—immediate, phased, or parallel—is determined by the size, geographic distribution, and available resources of the firm.

Questions

1 What are the six major tasks that are included in implementation?

2 Who performs implementation tasks: the information systems staff, the manager, or someone else?

3 What tasks must be completed before the model base can be prepared?

4 Does the computer have to be selected before participants and users are educated?

5 Why is time devoted to implementation planning, when that task was accomplished in each of the two preceding phases?

6 What type of information must be communicated to employees prior to implementation that was not communicated at the beginning of the system study?

7 What sections of the request for bid are taken directly from the implementation project proposal?

8 Do top managers read all of the vendor's proposals in their entirety? Who else in the firm should have an opportunity to read the proposals? Discuss.

9 Is computer vendor selection a structured or an unstructured problem? Can this problem be solved using the systems approach?

10 How does the programmer understand the problem to be programmed?

11 What two types of errors can a programmer make? How does the programmer know that these errors have been made?

12 Would a company use a "load and go" approach to payroll computing? Why or why not?

13 Who prepares the final version of the program documentation package?

14 Does the model base contain only mathematical models, such as those discussed in Chapter 9?

15 Is the data base maintained on magnetic tape or DASD?

16 How can the MIS affect jobs in the company?

17 Should a parallel cutover be used when the new system is completely different from the old one? Why or why not?

Problems

1 As the manager of the order department at Pickwick Papers, you are confronted by a very serious decision. The new computerized order entry system will read orders optically, bypassing the keypunch operation. The person who has been doing this work for 12 years, Sue Rankin, must be replaced by the OCR unit. Sue is bright, having completed a 2-year business course at a community college in Casper, Wyoming. However, her only business experience is that of keypunching. What should you do?

2 You have been asked by your boss, the vice-president of finance, to represent her at the proposal presentation by the Ace Computing Company. After the Ace sales representative introduces himself, he says: "I know that you have designed your order entry system to use key-to-disk machines, but we are recommending another approach. Our company has just announced a new OCR unit that outperforms anything else on the market. We have designed an order entry system with optically read sales order forms." Is this good or bad? Why?

3 The vice-president of information systems is on time for the scheduled meeting with the MIS committee to discuss the implementation plan. The vice-president says: "Gentlemen, the MIS conversion is not going to be as difficult as we feared. The system will not affect many people within the organization." Describe your reaction.

Chapter 17

Control of the Information System

The Importance of Control

In several previous chapters, reference has been made to Henri Fayol's management functions. Each reference to these has been related to the process of developing an MIS, as described in the previous three chapters. The *planning* of the MIS development effort was described in Chapter 14; the *organizing*, *staffing*, and *directing* of the various activities were the subjects of Chapters 15 and 16. The remaining function of *controlling* also received attention in the three previous chapters. Figures 14–5, 15–5, and 16–1 illustrate how management control of the development process can be exercised.

Considerable emphasis already has been placed on control. However, it is of such importance to the MIS that more needs to be said. That is the purpose of this final chapter.

Areas of Control

There are three areas within the MIS effort where management control is applied:

1 The development process
2 The system design
3 The system operation

The *development process* includes the steps taken in the three previous chapters leading to the realization of the MIS: planning, analysis and design, and implementation. Control of the development process simply assures that those steps are followed in an efficient and effective manner. When management controls the development process, as described in Chapters 14 through 16, the important first step is taken toward an MIS that will perform as intended. And, the development costs will be minimized.

The *system design*—both the computer equipment configuration and the programmed routines—refers to the MIS itself. All of the computer units have circuitry devoted to maintenance of accuracy. These circuits either prevent errors from happening, or they detect errors that are entered into the system or generated by it. The controls built into the computer units are called *hardware controls;* they are the responsibility of the computer manufacturer. They add to the integrity of the MIS, but do not assure perfect performance. Hardware controls must be augmented by controls built into the computer programs and the procedures using the programs. These are called *software controls* and are the responsibility of the computer user.

The *system operation* deals with the physical operation of the computer and its facilities. Control of operations assures that the procedures are carried out as designed and that the intended integrity of the system is preserved. These controls are the responsibility of the computer operations staff.

Methods of achieving and maintaining control

Management can exercise control in various ways and these are illustrated in Figure 17–1.

First, management can take direct control, evaluating progress and performance, and determining what corrective actions are necessary. This action requires substantial knowledge of computers and information systems. Such knowledge is gained by reading books such as this textbook, taking courses such as the one using this textbook, and learning through informal contacts with knowledgeable persons.

Second, management is represented indirectly in the design effort on a full-time basis by the vice-president of information systems. This person is an executive, who not only owes allegiance to the technical staff, but to the using managers as well. It is this person's main responsibility during the design effort to assure that the system design is acceptable to the users.

Third, management makes use of internal or external auditors to evaluate the system and influence its design from a technical standpoint. These specialists represent the management on a project basis and provide the computer expertise that the managers do not possess.

The Role of Auditors in Control

There are various kinds of auditors. The term first brings to mind the accounting variety. These auditors may work for the company (*internal auditors*) or they might be retained from auditing firms (*external auditors*). Firms such as Ernst and Ernst, Peat Marwick and Mitchell, Arthur Anderson, and Price Waterhouse provide external auditors. Such organizations traditionally have designed and examined the accounting procedures of a firm to confirm that they meet acceptable standards.

With the increased use of computerized accounting procedures, some

Figure 17-1   Control of the MIS effort

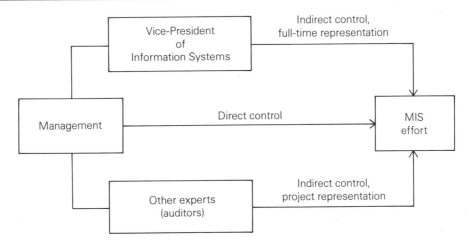

employees of accounting firms have become expert in computer use. These persons are called *EDP auditors. EDP* stands for electronic data processing—the computer. These persons specialize in providing an auditing service to computer-based systems.

Another source of external EDP auditors is provided by consulting firms. The firm might offer general management assistance in solving all types of problems, or it might concentrate only on computer or information systems problems. Booz, Allen, and Hamilton, and McKinsey and Company are examples of general management consulting firms. Electronic Data Systems (EDS) is an example of a firm specializing in computer consulting.

The above are examples of external EDP auditors. A firm can have its own staff of internal EDP auditors, and many such staffs have been formed. However, most of this activity has taken place since 1970.

A real need presently exists for more EDP auditors, and this promises to be an increasingly popular career path.

Responsibilities of EDP auditors

Regardless of source, EDP auditors can verify that the manager's needs are being met. Also, they vouch for the integrity of the system in terms of accuracy, appropriateness, and security. *Accuracy* deals with the data base and the procedures used to manipulate that data. Does data in the data base meet the required accuracy standards, and do the procedures maintain this level? *Appropriateness* deals with the degree to which the procedures conform to acceptable accounting practices. *Security* relates to the degree to which the contents of the data base and the entire MIS operation are safe from tampering, unauthorized access, embezzlement, and destruction.

The participation of auditors cannot begin too early in the MIS development process. They can provide valuable input during planning because of their experience with computer-based information systems. During the analysis and design and the implementation phases, they offer advice on design techniques and monitor the design effort. They also participate directly in the acceptance of the implemented system, and monitor the performance of the operational system.

Managers may elect not to make use of auditors. Perhaps the managers know enough about computers and information systems to perform the control function themselves. Or, a thoroughly competent information systems staff may be available. When either of these conditions are not met, however, the use of auditors should be considered.

Control of the Development Process

Management seeks to control the development of the MIS from the time initial interest is shown in the project until it is concluded. This control attempts to assure an acceptable MIS by accomplishing the following actions:

1 Establish overall project control.
2 Identify user requirements.
3 Establish performance criteria for the MIS.
4 Establish standards for the design and operation of the MIS.
5 Specify an acceptance testing program.
6 Specify a postinstallation review program.
7 Establish a procedure for maintaining and modifying the MIS.

Each of these control actions is taken at a specific point in the life cycle of the MIS, as shown in Figure 17–2. And, each action is taken before the system goes into operation.

1. Overall project control.   Top management takes steps to establish overall project control during the planning phase. The responsible top executive is assigned to the MIS project, a working relationship with the top information systems executive is established, an MIS committee is formed (if needed), the basic specifications of the MIS are determined, and some type of project control mechanism (such as network analysis) is created.

2 and 3. User requirements and performance criteria.   These two activities are addressed as the systems study is conducted. It is the responsibility of the systems analysts to identify these user requirements. Once defined, the requirements are expressed in terms of what the MIS must do to meet them, i.e., the performance criteria. The ultimate success of the MIS rests on how well these criteria are met.

Figure 17–2   Control actions in the MIS life cycle

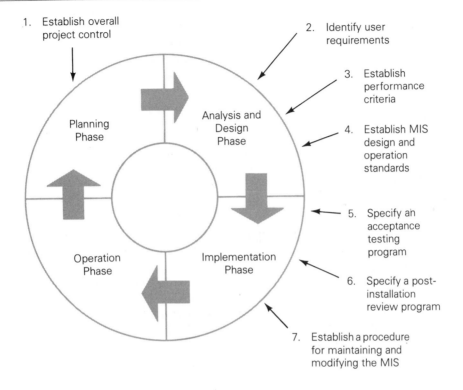

1. Establish overall project control

2. Identify user requirements

3. Establish performance criteria

4. Establish MIS design and operation standards

5. Specify an acceptance testing program

6. Specify a post-installation review program

7. Establish a procedure for maintaining and modifying the MIS

Planning Phase

Analysis and Design Phase

Operation Phase

Implementation Phase

4. Design and operation standards.   In the relatively brief history of computer use, a strong case has been made for standards in design and operation. The standards are the guidelines of acceptable performance by members of the information systems staff.

First, it must be made clear that there is no single set of official MIS or computer standards. There are many sources of standards that a firm can consider. There are *standards organizations,* such as ISO (International Organization for Standardization) and ANSI (American National Standards Institute, Inc.). The flowchart symbols pictured in Figure 15–7 are those accepted by ISO and ANSI. In addition, there are *user groups* of different manufacturer's equipment. The Cooperative Users of Burroughs Equipment (CUBE) is an example. Many of the names of these groups convey the spirit of cooperation and unity among the members, such as SHARE (IBM users) and EXCHANGE (Xerox users). However, none say it better than the Honeywell Users Group—HUG. Certain standards are also developed by the *computer manufacturers,* such as the format of data file labels and program control cards. A firm can evaluate these various standards and decide whether they are applicable. And, *the firm* can create its own standards when necessary.

It is a good idea to have a *standards manual* that spells out the conventions that the members of the information systems staff are expected to follow. This manual is developed as the different standards are devised and accepted. Standards are established for each area of MIS activity (systems analysis, programming, and operations). For example, a systems analysis standard would specify the contents of the program documentation package. A programming standard would specify names to be used for data files, records, and elements. An operations standard would describe the procedure to follow in case of equipment malfunction. Figure 17–3 contains a sample table of contents for a standards manual. The manual is developed by the information specialists under the guidance of the vice-president of information systems.

5. Acceptance testing program.   The requirements for approval of each computer program are spelled out in detail. This approval is necessary before individual responsibility for program development is satisfied and the program is entered into the model base.

6. Postinstallation review program.   The last chapter concluded with the cutover to the new MIS. With that accomplished, management could feel that the MIS project was completed, and turn their attention elsewhere. This would be a mistake. Is the MIS performing as intended? This question cannot be answered without a formal examination of the MIS by qualified persons, and this formal examination is the *postinstallation audit*.

   The audit has two main purposes. First, are management's needs for information being satisfied? Is the right information being supplied in a form that is accurate, timely, and complete? The managers can make this evaluation. Second, is the MIS satisfying acceptable standards of business operation and accounting? EDP auditors, internal or external, can answer this question.

   It is not a good idea for members of the information systems staff to conduct the audit of the system's capabilities. The real possibilities of unauthorized manipulation of the MIS by its staff of information specialists demand an audit by a reputable, unbiased third party.

   The postinstallation audit is first conducted shortly after cutover, perhaps 30 or 60 days later. This schedule provides all concerned with a chance to catch their breath after a long and demanding implementation process. Thereafter, an audit is conducted on a regularly scheduled basis, such as each year.

   The information systems staff can engage in the evaluation of the system's ability to satisfy the manager's information needs. Each manager in the firm can be contacted in person by a systems analyst, or information can be gathered by questionnaire. The sample questionnaire shown in Figure 17–4 can be printed by the computer. The questionnaire is addressed to each manager receiving computer output, and each output is listed separately. The manager can check the appropriate response boxes and return the form, along with any necessary explanations. The final question is intended to identify situations where information needs are not being met. A yes answer triggers an inquiry by an analyst to consider an additional MIS application.

   The audit of the system's accounting integrity, conducted by EDP

Figure 17–3 Table of contents for a standards manual

TABLE OF CONTENTS

auditors, should be extremely thorough. The audit procedures followed are outside the scope of this book and will not be addressed.[1] Simply stated, however, the procedures are intended to verify that the controls built into the

1. For a description of EDP audit procedures see *Systems Auditability and Control: Audit Practices*, (Altamonte Spring, Florida: The Institute of Internal Auditors, Inc., 1977).

Figure 17–4 MIS evaluation questionnaire

TO: F.A. AKERS
         MANAGER OF PRODUCT PLANNING

FROM: F.D. DRY
         VICE PRESIDENT OF INFORMATION SYSTEMS

SUBJECT: PERIODIC EVALUATION OF MIS PERFORMANCE

DATE: JUNE 30, 1980

LISTED BELOW ARE EACH FORM OF INFORMATION OUTPUT PRESENTLY BEING
SUPPLIED BY THE INFORMATION SYSTEMS DIVISION. PLEASE INDICATE
YOUR EVALUATION OF EACH OUTPUT BY CHECKING THE APPROPRIATE BLANK.
RETURN THE COMPLETED QUESTIONNAIRE BY JULY 15.

OUTPUT 1--NEW PRODUCT EVALUATION MODEL

1. THE ACCURACY OF THIS OUTPUT IS:
      ACCEPTABLE (NO EXPLANATION NEEDED)
   ___
      MARGINAL: EXPLAIN
   ___   _____
      UNACCEPTABLE: EXPLAIN
   ___   _____

2. THE TIMELINESS IS:
      ACCEPTABLE (NO EXPLANATION NEEDED)
   ___
      MARGINAL: EXPLAIN
   ___   _____
      UNACCEPTABLE: EXPLAIN
   ___   _____

3. THE COMPLETENESS OF THE INFORMATION IS:
      ACCEPTABLE (NO EXPLANATION NEEDED)
   ___
      MARGINAL: EXPLAIN
   ___   _____
      UNACCEPTABLE: EXPLAIN
   ___   _____

4. THE PRESENTATION MODE (PRINTED REPORT, CRT DISPLAY) IS:
      ACCEPTABLE (NO EXPLANATION NEEDED)
   ___
      MARGINAL: EXPLAIN
   ___   _____
      UNACCEPTABLE: EXPLAIN
   ___   _____

OUTPUT 2--PRODUCT DELETION MODEL

DO YOU HAVE ANY INFORMATION NEEDS THAT ARE NOT BEING MET
PRESENTLY?
      YES
   ___

      NO
   ___

system and its operation are followed. Those controls are described in the next two sections of this chapter.

After the MIS passes the postinstallation audit, management can rest assured that the system is meeting the current performance criteria. However, these performance criteria will change as the demands on the business firm and its managers change. A mechanism must be established to update the performance criteria, and to continually evaluate the MIS based on the revised criteria.

7. *Maintenance and modification of the MIS.* Many cases of computer fraud have been reported in which persons made unauthorized changes to operational programs or to contents of the data base. One bank programmer "rounded down" interest computations to the lower penny figure, and added the fractional amount to his personal account.

To either prevent such unauthorized changes, or to catch them when they are made, controls can be established on program changes. Some computer users have established *program change committees* to evaluate each request for change. The request is described on a special form, and all of the detailed documentation is attached. No change can be made to a program without this committee approval.

Formal procedures such as this should reduce the number of unauthorized changes, but will not eliminate them. Other controls also must be instituted, such as having the computer print out reports of unauthorized data requests or exceptionally high activity for certain financial accounts.

Control of System Design

It is possible to design an information system without any built-in controls. The design cost would be less than a system with controls. While that result might seem appealing, management usually is quick to spot the weaknesses. The penalties in operating such a system would outweigh the savings in design. The situation is like buying a car without a spare tire, a fuel gauge, bumpers, and doorlocks. The cost would be lower, but the reduced safety and security would present serious problems in using the car. The cost savings would not be worth the problems incurred.

Some subsystems of the MIS demand greater controls than others. Generally, those of a financial nature—where money is involved—demand the greater controls. A firm cannot afford to make a mistake in calculating an employee's payroll check or a vendor's payment. However, a nonmonetary subsystem, such as a report of sales statistics, might not be less useful if it contains some minor errors.

Computer control is based on a key point. Systems controls cost money. And a control should not be implemented if its cost exceeds its value. This is an important decision that must be made in systems design: what level of controls is justified in each subsystem? Management cannot make this decision alone: assistance must be provided by members of the information systems staff and auditors.

Areas of system design controls[2]

The MIS includes many subsystems, and most are unique in one way or another. Each one can be subdivided into basic parts, however, and controls considered for each part. Figure 17–5 illustrates these basic subsystem parts.

Over the years, a great many control techniques have been devised for each of these parts. The scope of this textbook does not permit all to be identified, much less described. The intent here will be to only explain them to a point that the thoroughness of such control possibilities is appreciated.

The first part of a subsystem is devoted to *transaction origination*. This procedure usually involves recording several data elements on some type of source document. The document might be a sales order form, a payroll time card, or a bank check. This origination is external to the computer equipment. It is not accomplished by the use of the computer, but precedes any computer processing.

After the transaction is originated, it is converted into some machine- or computer-readable form, a process called *transaction entry*. This subsystem part does involve the use of computer or data processing equipment. The transaction data may be keyed into a terminal or a keypunch or key-to-tape or key-to-disk unit.

In some subsystems, data is communicated from one location to another. This is the *data communication* part. In other subsystems, data is entered by transaction entry directly into the computer for processing.

Once the data is entered into the computer storage, it is processed by programs in the model base. In many instances, this *computer processing* results in data added to or taken from the data base.

When the processing has been completed, some *computer output* is created. This output can be information for management or data for use by another subsystem.

In the following paragraphs, each subsystem part will be addressed. Some examples of control for each part will be described briefly to provide an idea of the alternatives available.

1. Transaction origination.   Each subsystem part in Figure 17–5 can be subdivided further to identify specific control areas. In Figure 17–6, this is done for the subsystem part "Transaction Origination."

Controls of transaction origination start with the *source document*

---

2. This discussion of control areas is based on the classification developed for The Institute of Internal Auditors, Inc. by SRI International. More detail can be found in *Systems Auditability and Control: Control Practices* (Altamonte Springs, Florida: The Institute of Internal Auditors, Inc., 1977), pp. 45–86.

Figure 17–5   Basic subsystem parts

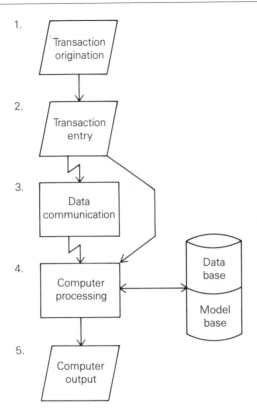

1. Transaction origination
2. Transaction entry
3. Data communication
4. Computer processing — Data base / Model base
5. Computer output

origination—the order form, the payroll card, or the check. These controls deal with procedures for (1) designing source documents for use, (2) assuring security of documents before use, and (3) handling of the documents.

Authorization controls describe how data entries are to be made to the documents and by whom. This action is accomplished by requiring signatures on source documents, involving several persons in the preparation of each document, devising written procedures, and establishing limits on the approval of certain transactions, such as customer credits.

Computer input preparation controls establish a means of identifying input records found to be in error, and assure that all input data is processed. Examples of controls of this type are maintaining transaction logs that serve as a record of transactions to be processed, and batching source documents into groups.

Error handling controls provide a systematic way of correcting errors and resubmitting those records for input. This control area is not concerned with

Figure 17–6   Transaction origination control areas

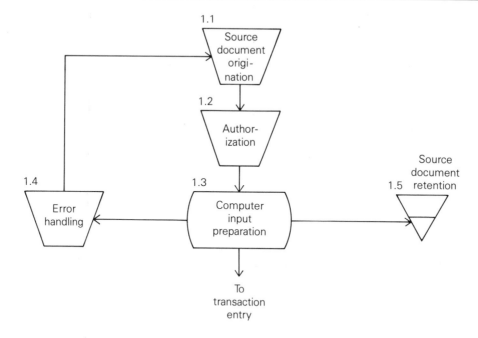

detecting errors, but in correcting them once they have been detected. Each subsystem part has such an error handling area.

Finally, controls of *source document retention* specify how the documents will be stored after use and under what conditions they will be made available to potential users.

2. Transaction entry. Transaction entry converts the data from a source document to some machine- or computer-readable format. The controls attempt to maintain the accuracy of data to be transmitted over a communication network or to be entered directly into a computer. Figure 17–7 shows how this subsystem part is divided into four control areas.

Controls over *data entry* can apply to either batch processes (such as keypunching) or terminal input. The controls exist in the form of written procedures and the input equipment itself. The equipment should be located close to the point of transaction origination to reduce delays in entry. Also, an effort should be made to capture the input on a computer-readable medium such as a cassette tape or floppy disk.

After the data is recorded on some type of machine-readable medium, it is *verified* for accuracy. The use of a key verifier machine is a good example of *data verification*. The data is keyed a second time and the key depressions are compared with holes in the card. An unequal comparison indicates an error. These errors are corrected by the *error handling* area.

Figure 17–7   Transaction entry control areas

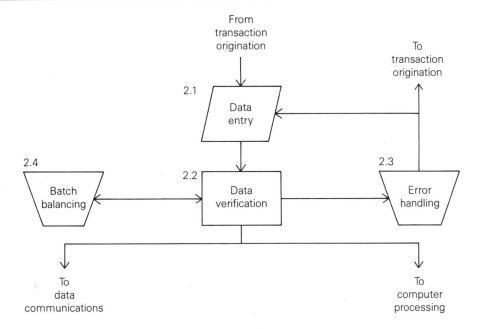

Control totals such as document count and dollar amounts are accumulated for each batch created previously in a *batch-balancing* process. These totals later are compared with similar totals prepared on the input data by the computer. An equal comparison indicates all transactions have been processed.

3. *Data communication.*   In those subsystems where data is transmitted over a communication network, there are three areas where controls are possible: message sending, the communication channel, and message receipt (Figure 17–8). Error handling is not a separate area, but is accomplished by the communication equipment in the other areas.

Control can be established over *message sending* by securing all phone equipment rooms to prevent wiretapping, by using a code to identify each terminal, and by restricting terminals to enter only certain approved transactions. In addition, a message log can be maintained of all transactions for periodic audit or follow-up.

Most of the controls of the *communication channel* are of a hardware, rather than software, type. Examples are sophisticated codes that permit detection and correction of data errors as they are being transmitted, and encryption techniques that scramble confidential data (Figure 17–9). For example, an employee pay rate data field can be scrambled during transmission to make its use difficult if intercepted by unauthorized persons during communication.

Figure 17–8 Data communication control areas

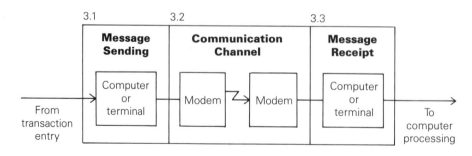

Controls of *message receipt* include automatic detection of errors by the receiving units and requests for resubmission. Errors can be detected when "check bits" or "check characters" are transmitted along with the data, and the bits or characters are inappropriate for the data received. For firms using dial-up lines, telephone numbers of the modems can be changed frequently and kept confidential. All calls can be intercepted by a computer operator, who obtains proper identification before permitting transmission.

4. Computer processing. Up to this point, all of the controls have been placed on entering data into the computer. With that now accomplished, controls can be built into the programs and the data base to maintain system integrity. These control areas are shown in Figure 17–10.

Data handling controls properly identify input transactions and assure accuracy of data manipulation and computation. Assume that three types of input transactions—identified by codes 1, 2, and 3—can be processed. Through programming, the computer can determine if a transaction is a code 1 or 2. If not, it is a mistake to assume the code is a 3. Perhaps an error was made in keying in a 1 code, and an A was entered instead. It is neither a 1 nor a 2, but it most certainly isn't a 3. Figure 17–11 shows examples of good and bad program logic to test the transaction code.

Figure 17–9 Encryption can confuse unauthorized data users.

In the above figure, a pay rate of $0,875.62 would be transmitted as 620758.

Figure 17–10 Computer processing control areas

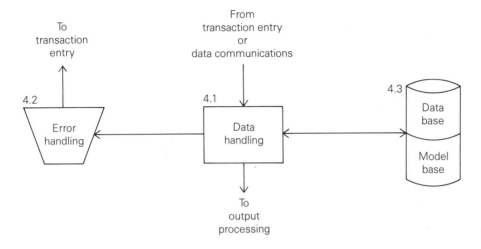

An example of a control of data manipulation and computation is one where the result of an arithmetic operation is tested for reasonableness. The monthly commission for a sales representative can be checked for a maximum limit, say $5000. Any exceptions can be flagged for follow-up to verify accuracy.

The *error handling* control area is concerned with reporting and correction of errors, and with reentry of correct data. When a transaction is found to contain one or more errors, processing of that transaction is suspended. The transaction record is entered into an error suspense file and held until it is corrected. An error report is printed by the computer, specifically identifying the error or errors. Errors in money data fields are corrected with proper debit and credit entries rather than deletion and replacement. If deletion and replacement were used, any figure could be entered as a replacement amount and an error could be difficult to detect. The error suspense file can be used periodically to prepare statistical reports on types of errors, frequency, and source.

Processing controls also can be established on changes to both the *data base* and the *model base.* No changes to data files or programs are permitted without a proper departmental security code and an individual password. Only certain types of changes are permitted for each code and password. A log of all changes to data and programs is maintained in auxiliary storage. The log identifies the date and time of the transaction, identification of the terminal (if used), security codes, and password.

A very common method of controlling the use of data files is by incorporating header and trailer labels into the files (Figure 17–12). Both magnetic tape and DASD files use these labels.

Figure 17–11   Good and bad approaches to code testing

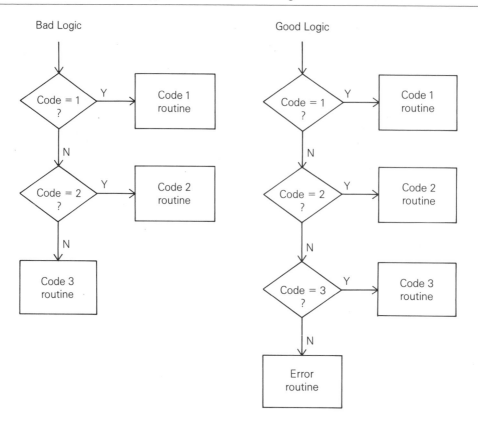

These labels are not the gummed variety frequently applied to tape and disk containers. They are data records that can be read by the computer. Header labels contain data such as file identification, creation date, retention period, and reel number. The program interrogates this data before processing the file. The header label assures that the proper file is in use. Trailer labels contain control totals. As the file is being processed, totals can be accumulated on important data, such as gross sales amount, discount amount, and sales tax. When the end of the file is reached, these totals are compared with the totals in the trailer label. Totals in balance indicate that processes involving file data match the file itself, all of the records have been handled, all amount fields have been processed, etc.

5. Computer output.   A computer facility is a type of factory. It produces a finished product (information) for its customers (such as the managers). This subsystem part has the responsibility of delivering the finished product to the customer. See Figure 17–13.

Figure 17–12   Header and trailer file labels

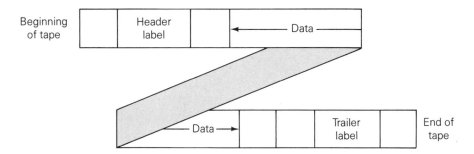

The *computer operations balancing* area verifies that all batches and transactions received from user departments are processed. This procedure is accomplished by balancing computer output totals to totals established at input. Additional controls can be established on money amounts. Computer reports also can be prepared on changes to programs and on transaction volume by terminal to detect unauthorized use.

Controls on report *distribution* attempt to assure that only the appropriate persons receive the output. A cover sheet identifying the recipient is attached to each report, and a log is maintained showing when each output is distributed. Only the correct number of copies is prepared. The recipient can be asked to acknowledge receipt by return of a special form. The thoroughness of these controls varies with the level of information distributed.

User department balancing also involves balancing computer output to control totals established when input data was prepared. This type of balancing usually is more thorough than that of computer operations. It is the responsibility of the user department to establish and maintain controls that guarantee system integrity.

Error handling consists of an error log maintained by a special control group. Errors are corrected, following written procedures, and the corrected transactions are re-entered. Upon acceptance by the system, the transactions are removed from the error log. Periodically the error log is scanned to identify transactions where correction is overdue.

The final area of *records retention* is a responsibility of the user department. The objective is to maintain proper security over computer output and to control waste disposal. Paper shredders of out-of-date reports and aborted computer runs represent a control of this type.

Control of System Operation

The two control areas discussed above deal with actions taken prior to cutover to the MIS. After cutover, when the MIS becomes operational, a third control

Figure 17–13 Computer output control areas

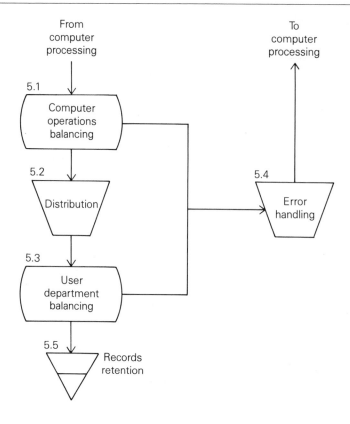

phase becomes necessary. This is the control over the actual operation of the MIS.

System operation controls are intended to achieve efficiency and security. Computer operations is a complex system composed of the computer, peripheral equipment, personnel, facilities, and supplies that must work together in a coordinated fashion. In addition, the operations are meant to be safe from disruption or abuse by unauthorized personnel both inside and outside the firm.

Controls that contribute to the desired efficiency and security can be classified into six areas:

1 Organizational structure
2 Input/output scheduling and control
3 Library control
4 Equipment maintenance
5 Environmental control and facilities security
6 Disaster planning

Figure 17–14 Organization of the operations department

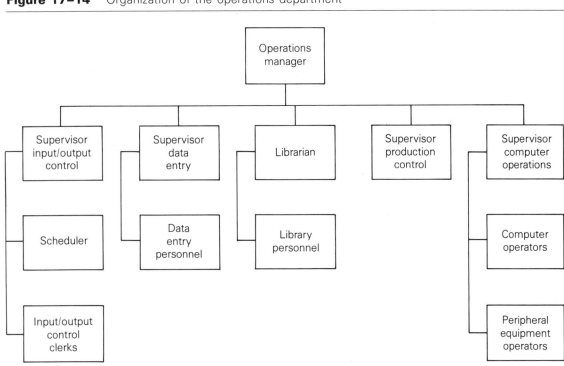

Organizational structure

The information systems staff is organized along lines of specialization. Analysts, programmers, and operations personnel are usually kept separate, and develop the skills required of their work area only. This structure contributes to the efficiency of the overall operation, and also to security. It is much more difficult to violate the system when cooperation of several individuals is required. Controls are built into the system by the analysts, programmers, and operations personnel. One type of employee (say a programmer) might be able to bypass his or her controls, but not those of the others.

In addition to the separation of operations from analysis and programming, it is desirable to separate the different areas within operations. The main areas are input/output control and scheduling, data entry, media library, production control, and equipment operations. In a department organized as in Figure 17–14, it is extremely difficult for user departments or operations personnel to violate the system.

Input/output scheduling and control

In the last section, computer operations was compared to a factory. Carrying this approach further, it is necessary to input raw materials into the factory,

Figure 17–15   Input/output control is an interface with batch users.

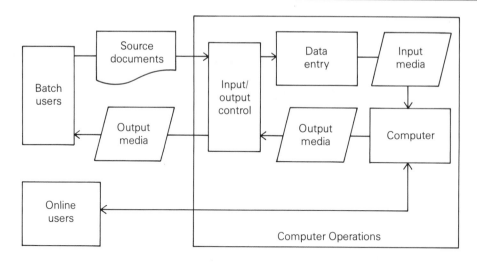

schedule the flow of materials through the production area, and distribute the finished output to the customers. In the computer operations "factory," these tasks are the responsibility of the input/output scheduling and control section.

Often, an important responsibility of this section is to serve as an interface between the computer and its users. This relationship is true in a batch environment, where users submit source documents to computer operations for data entry. The relationship does not exist in an online environment where users communicate directly with the computer, using terminals. Figure 17–15 illustrates these relationships.

The input/output control section performs the computer operations balancing activities described previously and illustrated in Figure 17–13.

In addition, input/output control schedules jobs on the computer. The jobs must be scheduled so that the data and information flow with minimum delay. This schedule is given each day to the production control section that has the responsibility of coordinating the schedule with computer operations. Separation of scheduling from production control makes it difficult to run unauthorized programs or make unauthorized changes to the data base. In an online environment, however, that possibility exists. Prevention must be achieved by the incorporation of controls (use of codes, passwords, etc.) into the programs.

Library control

A computer media library is very similar to the book variety. There is a librarian, a collection of data and information media, a place to store them, and a procedure for making them available to users.

The computer media include reels of magnetic tape and disk packs. These are stored in racks, some with locks for confidential material. The racks are housed in a walled area that is secure from unauthorized access. The same temperature and humidity controls exist in the library as in the computer room. Only library personnel are allowed in the library, and computer media are released only to computer operators.

Two types of records provide the basis for control: a record of each reel and disk pack, and a record of each data file. These records can be kept on index cards and filed by serial number of the tape reel or disk pack, or by file number. As reels or disk packs and files are checked out to computer operators, entries are made to the records. The records are updated upon return. The records reflect the location and use history of the items.

Duplicate copies of files and programs should be maintained, although not in the library. Another location is desirable as a hedge against a disaster of some type in the computer area. Additionally, it is common practice to maintain two generations of data files so that reconstruction can be performed if necessary.

In a batch environment, files are updated on a cycle basis, such as daily or monthly. The file created on Wednesday contains data from the Tuesday file plus Tuesday transaction data. Likewise, the Tuesday file was prepared from the Monday file plus Monday data. The Monday, Tuesday, and Wednesday files represent three generations of data. (This concept is illustrated in Figure 17–16.) The data on the Monday file is not erased until the Wednesday file is created. If anything happens to the Wednesday file, it can be reconstructed by again processing the Tuesday transactions against the Tuesday file. These batch files can be recorded on magnetic tape or DASD.

A different procedure must be followed in an online environment. Here, file changes can be made from terminals, and the files are recorded on a DASD. File backup is provided by "dumping" the DASD files periodically onto magnetic tape. The transaction data also is saved so that the DASD file can be reconstructed if necessary.

Equipment maintenance

It is the responsibility of the computer manufacturer to keep the equipment in running order. This service is included in the monthly lease charges, or is contracted separately.

The computer repairmen, called *customer engineers* (*CEs*) or *field engineers* (*FEs*), perform both scheduled and unscheduled maintenance. *Unscheduled maintenance* is performed when the computer develops unexpected problems, like an electronic component suddenly going bad. *Scheduled maintenance*, called *preventive maintenance* (*PM*), is designed to prevent problems. It is like changing the oil in an automobile or lubricating the chassis.

It is common practice to provide the FEs with a specific time each day on larger systems to perform PM, such as from 8 to 9 a.m. The frequency is less for smaller computers. It also is common for the FEs to be given a room to house

Figure 17–16 Three generations of magnetic tape files

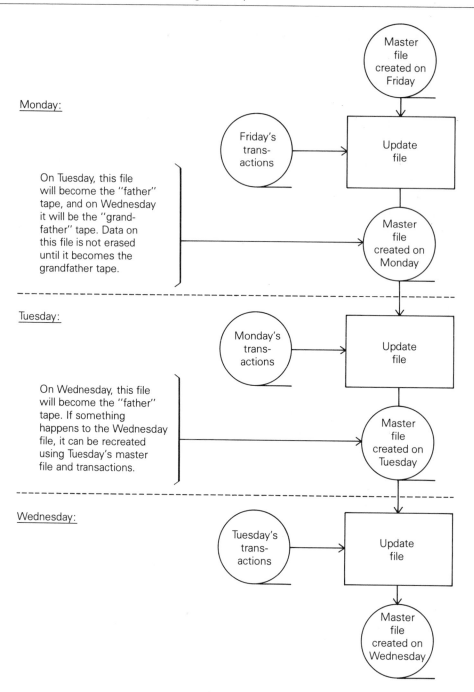

their test equipment, supplies, repair manuals, etc. In larger installations, one or more FEs can be assigned full-time to the installation.

The manager of computer operations should compile reports on computer performance, and use this information to keep the performance at an acceptable level. When the time of computer unavailability due to malfunction (called *downtime*) becomes excessive, action is taken. The operations manager must be aware continually of the status and condition of the system.

Time for PM, adequate FE facilities, and the computer performance reports are controls that contribute to good equipment operation.

Environmental control and facilities security

Computers are expensive pieces of equipment. They must be given special care to protect the investment and ensure against damage or malfunction. Computers require special environmental conditions: the computer room must be clean, and the temperature and humidity must remain within tolerance limits. Very often, backup electrical power is provided so that operation will continue even when normal electrical service is interrupted. For example, an insurance company in Texas installed two generators in the basement to provide backup electricity for their computer.

Some organizations even provide backup computing equipment, perhaps a second identical configuration. When something happens to the first, the second immediately is put into use. Organizations such as airlines and newspapers cannot afford for the computer to be "down," and thus recognize the value of dual equipment.

In the early years of computer use, the systems were regarded by many firms as showpieces. Computers frequently were located in sidewalk-level rooms with large viewing windows. Passersby could note the progressive nature of the firm.

The social backlash of the late 1960s changed all of that. Some computer centers were bombed or sabotaged. Now, the trend is to maximum security of computer areas. Equipment rooms are inaccessible to all except authorized persons. Those persons must use I.D. cards or doorlock combinations for entry. These measures protect the device that represents such an indispensable part of the firm's operation.

Disaster planning

When the firm establishes the above controls on system operation, a high level of performance can be anticipated. However, unforeseen disasters may occur. For example, a fire in another part of the building could destroy peripheral equipment, such as terminals. A program tape mistakenly could be erased; vendor supplies and services could be terminated because of strikes or a variety of reasons. Management should anticipate these possible disasters and devise a formal plan for handling them.

This type of planning is not uncommon in our society. Fire drills and evacuation plans in dormitories, military "alerts" where procedures are practiced for national crises, and mock drills at airports for treating crash victims are examples. The same precautions can be taken in computer operations. Formal plans can be designed and documented in writing. Employees can be trained in what to do if certain disasters strike. The plans must be reviewed periodically so that they remain current and an ability to react is guaranteed.

This is one area of operations control needing greater attention. In a recent mail survey of computer users, it was found that only 33 percent of the firms contacted had published disaster plans.[3] And, 29 percent of those plans had never been tested.[4]

Summary

This chapter has dealt with controls. Computer systems can be designed without these controls, but penalties likely will be paid. The penalties can be in the form of information output that is inaccurate, untimely, or misleading. Confidential company information can be leaked to outsiders, employee and customer rights to privacy can be violated, company funds can be embezzled, and computer equipment can be destroyed. Controls cost money, but lack of controls can cost more.

Many of the controls discussed in this chapter are technical in nature. The manager cannot be expected to know and understand them all. But, technical specialists such as the information systems staff and auditors can provide the expertise. Management must assemble a qualified team of specialists that will recognize the need for these controls and represent management in implementing them.

Important Terms

Hardware Controls	Electronic Data Processing (EDP)
Software Controls	EDP Auditor
Internal Auditor	Standards Organization
External Auditor	User Group

3. *Systems Auditability and Control: Control Practices*, p. 96.

4. Ibid.

Standards Manual

Postinstallation Audit

Program Change Committee

Father Tape, Grandfather Tape

Customer Engineer, Field Engineer
   (FE)

Unscheduled Maintenance

Scheduled Maintenance

Preventive Maintenance (PM)

Downtime

Important Concepts

Control must be exercised over the process of developing the MIS, how it functions (the design), and its use (the operation).

Management control is achieved directly, or indirectly through informed assistants.

EDP auditors can provide unbiased, informed counsel to the manager concerning MIS controls.

Development controls can be built into each phase, starting with planning and ending with implementation.

There are accepted standards of good MIS development, design, and operation, and these standards originate with several sources.

Controls should not be built into system designs unless the cost is less than the contribution.

All computerized systems do not require the same level of thoroughness in design controls.

Design controls can be built into five basic system areas: transaction origination, transaction entry, data communication, computer processing, and computer output.

Operations controls are of six basic types: organizational structure, input/output scheduling and control, library control, equipment maintenance, environment control and facilities security, and disaster planning.

Questions

1   What is meant by "control of the information system"?

2   Who is responsible for hardware controls? What about software controls?

3   What differentiates an external auditor from an internal one?

4   When should an EDP auditor be used? Where can they be found?

5   What type of control is established in the planning phase of the MIS life cycle?

6 What are three external sources of MIS standards? Do these standards have to be followed?

7 Who develops the firm's standards manual?

8 Is the postinstallation audit an example of acceptance testing?

9 When is a postinstallation audit conducted?

10 Would the membership of the program change committee be the same as the MIS committee? Explain.

11 Would system design controls more likely be found in the internal accounting subsystem or in output information subsystems?

12 Are system design controls considered expense items that drain profits? Explain.

13 What is the difference between transaction origination and transaction entry?

14 Are batch balancing controls established before data enters the computer, or after?

15 Where would encryption be found?

16 Why are detected money errors corrected with debit and credit entries, rather than replacement data?

17 What type of data is likely to be found in header labels? in trailer labels?

18 Does the combined analyst/programmer position make control more difficult or less difficult than separate positions?

19 Does the computer operations department have more control over batch or online users?

20 Is control of magnetic tape master files easier than DASD? Explain.

21 Are computer users doing a good job of anticipating disasters? In what way?

Problem

1 You are the manager of a new "fast food" restaurant being constructed across the street from the college. It is up to you to build controls into the procedures to prevent errors and employee thefts. You are mainly concerned with transaction origination and entry. Orders are to be written on order forms by clerks and the data then keyed into cash register terminals connected to an in-store mini. The mini will compute the amount of the bill, the tax, and the change. What controls would you consider?

Appendix

Flowcharting Techniques

Tasks performed by the computer can be complex. This complexity can confuse the person designing the system (the systems analyst) or the person preparing the computer program (the programmer). Also, confusion can arise as these people attempt to explain the system to each other and to other persons, such as managers.

It didn't take these computer professionals long to realize that diagrams or drawings of the systems could overcome much of the complexity. The diagrams, called *flowcharts*, consist of specially shaped symbols that identify the type and sequence of steps that solve a particular problem.

Basic Types of Flowcharts

There are two basic types of flowcharts. One is used by the systems analyst to illustrate how programs and/or noncomputerized processes are linked to form a system. This type of flowchart is the "big picture" of the system and is called a *system flowchart.*

The other type of flowchart is used by the analyst or the programmer to show the steps executed in a single program. College students enrolled in programming classes frequently draw flowcharts of this type. These flowcharts are named *program flowcharts.*

Flowchart Symbols

Both types of flowcharts are drawn with the template pictured in Figure 15–7. These symbols are internationally accepted standard shapes and represent a common language among computer professionals around the world.

Some of the shapes are used only with one type of flowchart, some are used only with the other, and some can be used with either. The remainder of this appendix will be devoted to an explanation of these symbol shapes.[1]

System flowchart symbols

Data or information processing systems (the procedures, not the equipment) consist of a series of *processes* linked by *files* of data or information.

1. Process symbols. There are three primary ways to process data: manually, with a keydriven device, and with a device such as a punched card machine or computer that can be programmed.

Processes performed *manually* are illustrated with this symbol:

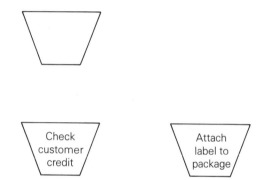

Examples are:

| Open the mail | Check customer credit | Attach label to package |

Appropriate lettering is entered in the symbol to provide more information about the exact process involved.

Processes performed by operating a *keydriven machine* such as a keypunch, a cash register, or a desk calculator are represented by:

Examples are:

| Keypunch sales cards | Verify sales cards | Accumulate batch totals |

---

1. Several books have been written about flowcharting. Some of these are Marilyn Bohl, *Flowcharting Techniques* (Palo Alto, Ca.: Science Research Associates, Inc., 1971), Michel H. Boillot, Gary M. Gleason, and L. Wayne Horn, *Essentials of Flowcharting* (Dubuque, Ia.: William C. Brown Co., 1975), and Nancy Stern, *Flowcharting: A Tool for Understanding Computer Logic.* (New York: John Wiley & Sons, 1975).

Finally, processes performed by the *computer* are illustrated by:[2]

Examples are:

Print payroll checks	Sort sales records	Print sales report

System flowcharts are prepared by arranging the processing symbols in the correct sequence (Figure A–1). For example, a procedure might involve (1) opening the mail, (2) keypunching sales cards from the orders received, (3) sorting the sales records, and (4) printing a sales report.

Symbols usually are arranged in a vertical sequence. Arrows show the direction of the flow, steps often are numbered, and a brief description can be

---

Figure A–1   Process steps

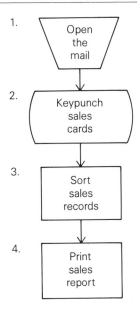

1. Open the mail
2. Keypunch sales cards
3. Sort sales records
4. Print sales report

---

2. Special symbols have been developed for each of the punched card machines. These symbols will not be explained here.

printed next to each step. The example does not include the accompanying description.

2. File symbols. It is common practice also to include symbols representing the files of data or information linking the process steps. These symbols can take approximately six forms, depending on the file media used.[3]

When the file symbols are added to the four process symbols linked in Figure A–1, the system flowchart is completed (Figure A–2).

File Medium	Symbol Shape	Example
Punched Card		Sales cards
Punched Paper Tape		Sales tape
Adding Machine Tape		Batch totals
Magnetic Tape		Inventory file
Direct Access Storage Device		Customer file
Printed Document		Sales report

---

3. There is less agreement on the symbols to be used for the more exotic file media such as microfilm, audio, and magnetic ink character recognition.

Figure A–2 System flowchart example

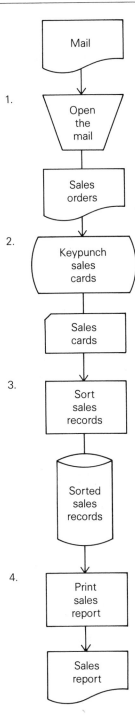

Program flowchart symbols

The analyst or the programmer must prepare a program for each of the computer steps in a system. In the example of Figure A–2, programs are prepared for steps 3 and 4.

While a large number of different computer instructions can be used in a program, they fall within one of four categories. These categories are (1) input, (2) data movement or manipulation, (3) logic, and (4) output.

An *input* or *output* instruction can be illustrated with:

Examples are:

The above are general purpose input/output symbols; they apply to any type of media. It also is acceptable to use specially shaped symbols to represent certain input or output forms. These are the same symbols used for files in the system flowchart.

For example, reading from a punched card file can be drawn as:

Printing a record on the line printer is illustrated by:

In addition, there are two special input/output symbols that were not presented above. These deal with terminal operations. Keyed terminal input is represented by:

And terminal output displayed on paper or a CRT is diagrammed as:

Data movement or manipulation instructions include the different types of arithmetic processes and also moving data elements from one location to another. The rectangle represents all of these.

Examples are:

Add sales to total	Multiply rate by hours	Compute square root	Move name to output

The *logical decisions* the computer makes usually involve selection of one of two alternatives. A condition either exists or it doesn't. A statement either is true or it is false. These decisions are illustrated with a diamond.

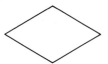

Examples of a yes/no decision are:

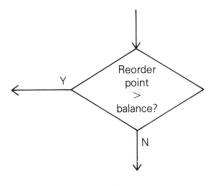

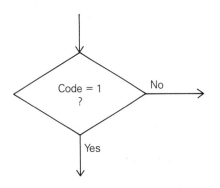

In both of these examples, a question is asked. The answer either is yes (Y) or no (N). One arrow leads into the diamond, and two exit from it. It makes no difference which points on the diamond are used.

Examples of a true/false decision are:

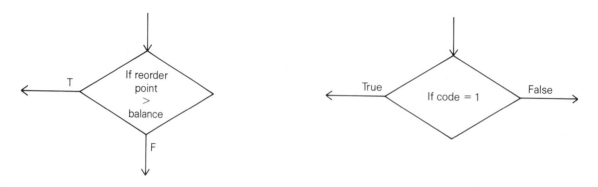

A statement is made, and the statement either is true or it is false. This technique is especially applicable to IF statements in programming languages.

The diamond is strictly a program flowcharting symbol, and is not used in a system flowchart.

There is another symbol that is limited to use in program flowcharts. It is the oval.

The oval represents a terminal point in a program: the beginning or the end of the program or a major subroutine within it. The beginning and end of the program are illustrated with:

Figure 15-11 provided an example of the use of the oval in a subroutine.

Program flowchart example

A program flowchart for the "Print sales report" program in the earlier system flowchart might be drawn as shown in Figure A-3.

In step 1, a single record is read from the sales file. The program only handles one record at a time, and repeats itself for each record in the file. This repeating process can be seen by the loop made with steps 1 through 5.

In step 2, the computer makes a logical decision. Have all records in the

Figure A–3   Program flowchart example

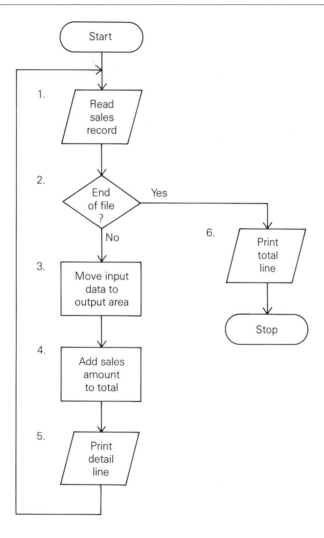

file been read? The computer can answer this question, using the results from step 1. When the computer is unable to read a record in step 1, it becomes apparent in step 2 that all of the records have been read and processed. In that case, step 6 follows step 2. When the end of the input file has not been reached, step 3 follows step 2.

In step 3, data elements from the record just read are moved to an output area in main storage for later printing. This sample program flowchart does not indicate the specific data elements moved. That can be explained in an accompanying narrative.

The arithmetic is performed in step 4 by adding the amount of the sales transaction to a total.

In step 5, a detail line is printed, showing the data for the transaction just processed. Data can include elements such as invoice number, date, customer number and name, and amount.

After printing the detail line, the program loops back to step 1 where another record is read, or an attempt is made to read another record (in the case of an end of file condition).

When all of the input records have been read and processed, the program branches from step 2 to step 6. There, a total line is printed with the amount accumulated from each transaction. Then the end of the program is reached.

Lengthy flowcharts

The system and program flowcharts above are greatly simplified versions. Those used by analysts, programmers, and programming students get more involved.

Some problems might require a flowchart too lengthy to fit on a single page. In those cases, some technique must be used to "connect" the lines on one page with those on another. A special symbol, the *off-page connector*, is used for this purpose.

If the flow goes from the bottom of page 1 to the top of page 2, a pair of off-page connectors makes the connection.

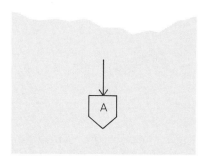
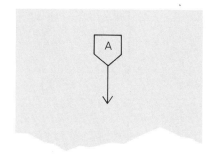

Bottom of Page 1   Top of Page 2

A letter or number is entered in both symbols to show the relationship. This permits the use of more than one set of connectors.

Another connector eliminates long connecting lines on a single page, and is called the *on-page connector*.

A pair of on-page connectors could have been used in Figure A–3 to eliminate the line looping back to step 1 from step 5.

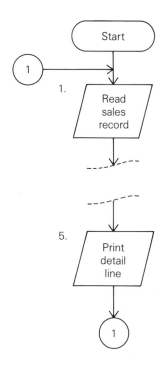

Either letters or numbers are entered in sets of related on-page connector symbols. If letters are used for off-page connectors, numbers can be used for on-page, or vice versa.

Flowcharting suggestions

Very often, students in computer programming classes will be required to draw flowcharts for assigned problems. The instructor will specify any particular requirements that must be met for a satisfactory grade. No attempt will be made here to list all of the possible do's and don'ts of flowcharting. Some suggestions will be offered, however, that should make the task easier and more productive, whatever the situation.

1 Draw the flowchart *before* designing the system or coding the program.
2 Use a template.
3 Draw a preliminary flowchart, using a pencil. Then draw a neat version (using pencil or pen) when the final form is certain.

4 Make the flow go from the top of the page to the bottom, and from the left to the right.

5 Use on-page connectors to eliminate long lines on the page.

6 Don't try to cram too many symbols on a page. Use off-page connectors to "overflow" to additional pages.

The instructor will identify which of the above suggestions should be followed, and may add others to the list.

Bibliography

This bibliography is not intended to be a complete list of all material relating to management information systems. While that might have been possible 10 years ago, it isn't now. And if such a list were possible, it would be inappropriate for an introductory textbook such as this one.

There appear to be several basic bodies of literature relating to the MIS. These are:

- Systems theory
- MIS concepts and issues
- Data base
- Functional information systems
- Quantitative decision-making techniques
- MIS development
- MIS control
- Computing equipment

Sources are identified in this bibliography for all of these areas except computing equipment. Such hardware information is best derived from the many fine introductory data processing textbooks, or from vendor literature.

The references presented here tend to originate in two sources: textbooks and business periodicals. The theory references, for the most part, have been described in textbooks. The references to MIS applications and developments originate primarily with business journals. Only the more recent of these journal articles have been selected.

Systems theory

Bertalanffy, L. von. "An Outline of General System Theory." *British Journal for the Philosophy of Science* 1 (1950): 134–165.

Bertalanffy, L. von. "General System Theory." *General Systems* 1 (1956): 1–10.

Bertalanffy, L. von. "General System Theory: A Critical Review." *General Systems* 7 (1962): 1–20.

Bertalanffy, L. von. "General System Theory: A New Approach to Unity of Science." *Human Biology* 23 (December 1951): 302–361.

Bertalanffy, L. von. "The Theory of Open Systems in Physics and Biology." *Science* 111 (1950): 23–29.

Boulding, Kenneth E. "General Systems Theory—The Skeleton of Science." *Management Science*, April 1956, pp. 197–208.

Hopeman, Richard J. *Systems Analysis and Operations Management.* Columbus, Ohio: Charles E. Merrill Publishing Co., 1969.

Johnson, Richard A., Fremont E. Kast, and James E. Rosenzweig, *The Theory and Management of Systems.* 3d ed. New York: McGraw-Hill Book Co., 1973.

Weinberg, Gerald M. *An Introduction to General Systems Thinking.* New York: John Wiley & Sons, 1975.

MIS concepts and issues

Ahlers, David M. "Management Information Systems, from Spyglass to Pocket Calculators." *Financial Executive*, July 1976, pp. 44–52.

Alter, Steven L. "How Effective Managers Use Information Systems." *Harvard Business Review*, November-December 1976, pp. 97–104.

Burch, John G., Jr., and Felix R. Strater, Jr. *Information Systems: Theory and Practice.* Santa Barbara, Calif.: Hamilton Publishing Co. 1974.

Carper, William B. "Human Factors in MIS." *Journal of Systems Management*, November 1977, pp. 48–50.

Couger, J. Daniel. "Top Executives Aren't On-line—Why?" *Data Management*, January 1978, pp. 19–20.

Davis, Gordon B. *Management Information Systems: Conceptual Foundations, Structure, and Development.* New York: McGraw-Hill Book Co., 1974.

Ein-Dor, Phillip. "Parallel Strategy for MIS." *Journal of Systems Management*, March 1975, pp. 30–35.

Floyd, Herbert F., and Robert W. Zmud, "Daily Information Reporting." *Business Horizons*, February 1976, pp. 39–44.

Herzlinger, Regina. "Why Data Systems in Nonprofit Organizations Fail." *Harvard Business Review*, January-February 1977, pp. 81–86.

Mace, Myles L. "Management Information Systems for Directors." *Harvard Business Review*, November-December 1975, pp. 14–16ff.

Mader, Chris, and Robert Hagin. *Information Systems: Technology, Economics, Applications.* Chicago, Ill.: Science Research Associates, Inc., 1974.

Mandell, Steven L. "Management Information System Is Going to Pieces." *California Management Review*, Summer 1975, pp. 50–56.

Mockler, Robert J. *Information Systems for Management.* Columbus, Ohio: Charles E. Merrill Publishing Co., 1974.

Murdick, Robert G. "MIS for MBO," *Journal of Systems Management*, March 1977, pp. 34–40.

Murdick, Robert G., and Joel E. Ross. *Introduction to Management Information Systems.* Englewood Cliffs, N.J.: Prentice-Hall, Inc., 1977.

Ross, Joel E. *Modern Management and Information Systems.* Reston, Virginia: Reston Publishing Co., Inc., 1976.

Schewe, Charles D., and James L. Wiek. "Guide to MIS User Satisfaction." *Journal of Systems Management*, June 1977, pp. 6–10.

Shio, Martin J. "New Look at MIS." *Journal of Systems Management*, May 1977, pp. 38–40.

Soden, John V. "Understanding MIS Failures." *Data Management*, July 1975, pp. 29–33ff.

Sprague, Ralph H., and Hugh J. Watson. "MIS Concepts." *Journal of Systems Management*, January 1975, pp. 34–37; February 1975, pp. 35–40.

Strassman, Paul A. "Managing the Costs of Information." *Harvard Business Review*, September-October 1976, pp. 133–142.

West, Glenn M. "MIS in Small Companies." *Journal of Systems Management*, April 1975, pp. 10–13.

Willoughby, T. C., and Richard A. Pye. "Top Management's Computer Role." *Journal of Systems Management*, September 1977, pp. 10–13.

Data base

Appleton, Daniel S. "What the Data Base Isn't" *Datamation*, January 1977, pp. 85–87ff.

Benbasat, I., and R. C. Goldstein. "Database Management Systems for Small Business Computers." *Business Quarterly*, Spring 1977, pp. 66–72.

Chow, John V. "What You Need to Know about DBMS." *Journal of Systems Management*, May 1975, pp. 22–27; June 1975, pp. 28–35.

Curtice, Robert M. "Outlook for Data Base Management." *Datamation*, April 1976, pp. 46–49.

Dyke, Ruth F. "Data Base Master Plan." *Journal of Systems Management*, July 1976, pp. 11–13.

Kroenke, David. *Database Processing.* Chicago Ill.: Science Research Associates, Inc., 1977.

Lewis, Charles J. "Understanding Database and Data Base." *Journal of Systems Management*, September 1977, pp. 36–42.

Martin, James. *Principles of Data-Base Management.* Englewood Cliffs, N.J.: Prentice-Hall, Inc., 1976.

McFadden, Fred R., and James D. Suver. "Costs and Benefits of a Data Base System." *Harvard Business Review*, January-February 1978, pp. 131–139.

Ross, Ronald G. "Evaluating Data Base Management Systems." *Journal of Systems Management*, January 1976, pp. 30–35.

Schussel, George. "When Not to Use a Data Base." *Datamation*, November 1975, pp. 82ff.

Scott, George M. "Data Base for Your Company?" *California Management Review*, Fall 1976, pp. 68–78.

Yasaki, Edward K. "The Many Faces of the DBA." *Datamation*, May 1977, pp. 75–79.

Functional information systems

Appleton, Daniel S. "Strategy for Manufacturing Automation." *Datamation*, October 1977, pp. 64–68ff.

Brueningsen, A. F. "Kodak's Financial Information and Reporting System." *Management Accounting*, September 1975, pp. 21–24.

Cohen, Jerome B., and Sidney M. Robbins. *The Financial Manager.* New York: Harper & Row, Publishers, 1966.

Gershefski, George W. "Building a Corporate Financial Model." *Harvard Business Review*, July-August 1969, pp. 61–72.

Harris, B. J., and L. A. Rulis. "Materials Information System." *Journal of Systems Management*, June 1976, pp. 20–23.

Hopeman, Richard J. *Production: Concepts, Analysis, Control.* Columbus, Ohio: Charles E. Merrill Publishing Co., 1965.

King, William R. *Marketing Management Information Systems.* New York: Petrocelli/Charter, 1977.

Kotler, Philip. *Marketing Management: Analysis, Planning, and Control.* 3d ed. Englewood Cliffs, N.J.: Prentice-Hall, 1976, pp. 419–442.

Martin, R. Keith. "The Financial Executive and the Computer: The Continuing Struggle." *Financial Executive*, March 1977, pp. 26–32.

White, D. R. T. "Reporting Financial Information to Management." *Business Quarterly*, Spring 1977, pp. 73–78.

Quantitative decision-making techniques

Chambers, John C., Satinder K. Mullick, and Donald D. Smith. "How to Choose the Right Forecasting Technique." *Harvard Business Review*, July-August 1971, pp. 45–74.

Geoffrion, Arthur M. "Better Distribution Planning with Computer Models." *Harvard Business Review*, July-August 1976, pp. 92–99.

Hayes, Robert H., and Richard L. Nolan. "What Kind of Corporate Modeling Functions Best?" *Harvard Business Review*, May-June 1974, pp. 102–112.

Heenan, David A., and Robert Addleman. "Quantitative Techniques for Today's Decision Makers." *Harvard Business Review*, May-June 1976, pp. 32–62.

Konezal, Edward F. "Models Are for Managers, not Mathematicians." *Journal of Systems Management*, January 1975, pp. 12–15.

Tersine, Richard J., and Walter E. Riggs. "Models: Decision Tools for Management." *Journal of Systems Management*, October 1976, pp. 30–34.

Wheelwright, Steven C., and Darral G. Clark. "Corporate Forecasting: Promise and Reality." *Harvard Business Review*, November-December 1976, pp. 40–42ff.

MIS development

Axelson, Charles F. "How to Avoid the Pitfalls of Information Systems Development." *Financial Executive*, April 1976, pp. 25–31.

Boehm, George A. W. "Shaping Decisions with Systems Analysis." *Harvard Business Review*, September-October 1976, pp. 91–99.

Davis, K. Roscoe, and Bernard W. Taylor. "Systems Design through Gaming." *Journal of Systems Management*, September 1975, pp. 36–42.

Devine, D. J. "User Programming by Questionnaire." *Data Management*, January 1978, pp. 43–46.

King, William R., and David I. Cleland. "Design of Management Information Systems: An Information Analysis Approach." *Management Science*, November 1975, pp. 286–297.

Soden, V., and Charles C. Tucker. "Long-Range MIS Planning." *Journal of Systems Management*, July 1976, pp. 28–33.

Zachman, John A. "Control and Planning of Information Systems." *Journal of Systems Management*, July 1977, pp. 34–41.

MIS control

Allen, Brandt. "Embezzler's Guide to the Computer." *Harvard Business Review*, July-August 1975, pp. 79–89.

George, Frank F., and Frederick B. Palmer. "Systems Auditability and Control." *Internal Auditor*, April 1977, pp. 11–15.

Menkus, Belden. "Management's Responsibilities for Safeguarding Information." *Journal of Systems Management*, December 1976, pp. 32–38.

Methodios, Ioannis. "Internal Controls and Audit." *Journal of Systems Management*, June 1976, pp. 6–14.

Systems Auditability and Control Series. Altamonte Springs, Florida: The Institute of Internal Auditors, Inc., 1977.

Index